# Hume

Beginning with an overview of Hume's life and work, Don Garrett introduces the central aspects of Hume's thought in a clear and accessible style. These include: Hume's lifelong exploration of the human mind; his theories of inductive inference and causation; skepticism and personal identity; moral and political philosophy; aesthetics; and philosophy of religion.

The final chapter considers the influence and legacy of Hume's thought today. Throughout, Garrett draws on and explains many of Hume's central works, including his *A Treatise of Human Nature*, *An Enquiry concerning Human Understanding*, *An Enquiry concerning the Principles of Morals*, and *Dialogues concerning Natural Religion*.

*Hume* is essential reading not only for students of philosophy, but for anyone in the humanities and social sciences and beyond seeking an introduction to Hume's thought.

**Don Garrett** is Silver Professor of Philosophy, at New York University, USA. He is the author of *Cognition and Commitment in Hume's Philosophy* (1997) and the editor of *The Cambridge Companion to Spinoza* (1996). He has served as co-editor of *Hume Studies* and as North American editor of *Archiv für Geschichte der Philosophie*.

# Routledge Philosophers
*Edited by Brian Leiter*

University of Chicago

Routledge Philosophers is a major series of introductions to the great Western philosophers. Each book places a major philosopher or thinker in historical context, explains and assesses their key arguments, and considers their legacy. Additional features include a chronology of major dates and events, chapter summaries, annotated suggestions for further reading and a glossary of technical terms.

An ideal starting point for those new to philosophy, they are also essential reading for those interested in the subject at any level.

Available:

**Hobbes**
A P Martinich

**Leibniz**
Nicholas Jolley

**Locke**
E J Lowe

**Hegel**
Frederick Beiser

**Rousseau**
Nicholas Dent

**Schopenhauer**
Julian Young

**Freud**
Jonathan Lear

**Darwin**
Tim Lewens

**Rawls**
Samuel Freeman

**Spinoza**
Michael Della Rocca

**Merleau-Ponty**
Taylor Carman

**Russell**
Gregory Landini

**Wittgenstein**
William Child

**Heidegger**
John Richardson

**Adorno**
Brian O'Connor

**Husserl, second edition**
David Woodruff Smith

**Aristotle, second edition**
Christopher Shields

**Kant, second edition**
Paul Guyer

Forthcoming:

**Dewey**
Steven Fesmire

**Freud, second edition**
Jonathan Lear

**Mill**
Daniel Jacobson

**Plato**
Constance Meinwald

**Nietzsche**
Maudemarie Clark

**Einstein**
Thomas Ryckman and Arthur Fine

**Habermas**
Kenneth Baynes

**Berkeley**
Lisa Downing and David Hilbert

**Plotinus**
Eyjólfur Emilsson

**Levinas**
Michael Morgan

**Cassirer**
Samantha Matherne

**Kierkegaard**
Paul Muench

Don Garrett

# Hume

LONDON AND NEW YORK

First published 2015
by Routledge
2 Park Square, Milton Park, Abingdon, Oxon OX14 4RN

and by Routledge
711 Third Avenue, New York, NY 10017

*Routledge is an imprint of the Taylor & Francis Group, an informa business*

© 2015 Don Garrett

The right of Don Garrett to be identified as the author of this work has been asserted by him in accordance with sections 77 and 78 of the Copyright, Designs and Patents Act 1988.

All rights reserved. No part of this book may be reprinted or reproduced or utilized in any form or by any electronic, mechanical, or other means, now known or hereafter invented, including photocopying and recording, or in any information storage or retrieval system, without permission in writing from the publishers.

*Trademark notice*: Product or corporate names may be trademarks or registered trademarks, and are used only for identification and explanation without intent to infringe.

*British Library Cataloguing in Publication Data*
A catalogue record for this book is available from the British Library

*Library of Congress Cataloging-in-Publication Data*
Garrett, Don, author.
Hume / by Don Garrett.
pages cm. – (Routledge philosophers)
Includes bibliographical references and index.
1. Hume, David, 1711-1776. I. Title.
B1498.G37 2015
192–dc23
2014015332

ISBN: 978-0-415-28333-5 (hbk)
ISBN: 978-0-415-28334-2 (pbk)
ISBN: 978-0-203-11835-1 (ebk)

Typeset in Joanna MT and Din
by Cenveo Publisher Services

"The imagination, according to my own confession, [is] the ultimate judge of all systems of philosophy."
David Hume, *A Treatise of Human Nature* (THN 1.4.4.1/225)

"That there is a natural difference between merit and demerit, virtue and vice, wisdom and folly, no reasonable man will deny."
David Hume, "Of the Dignity or Meanness of Human Nature" (EMPL I.11: 81)

## Contents

| | |
|---|---|
| *Acknowledgements* | xi |
| *Abbreviations* | xiii |
| *Chronology* | xvii |
| *Preface: how to read this book* | xix |
| **Introduction** | 1 |
| **One** <br> **"A ruling passion"** | **9** |
| 1.1 Early life and education | 11 |
| 1.2 *A Treatise of Human Nature* | 14 |
| 1.3 *Essays, Moral and Political* and *Letter from a Gentleman* | 18 |
| 1.4 Two *Enquiries* and *Three Essays* | 20 |
| 1.5 *Political Discourses*, *History of England*, and *Four Dissertations* | 24 |
| 1.6 *A Concise Account* and *Dialogues concerning Natural Religion* | 28 |
| 1.7 Conclusion | 33 |
| Notes | 34 |
| Further reading | 35 |

## Two
## Perceptions and their principles — 36
2.1 Basic distinctions among perceptions — 38
2.2 Principles of perceptions — 43
2.3 Complex ideas — 50
2.4 Abstract ideas (concepts) — 52
2.5 Space and time — 60
2.6 Mental representation — 67
2.7 Conclusion — 77
Note — 79
Further reading — 79

## Three
## The mind and its faculties — 81
3.1 Mind and consciousness — 82
3.2 Imagination and memory — 86
3.3 Reason or the understanding — 88
3.4 Demonstrative reasoning and probable reasoning — 92
3.5 The senses — 97
3.6 The passions and taste — 105
3.7 The will — 109
3.8 Conclusion — 113
Further reading — 115

## Four
## Sense-based concepts — 117
4.1 The origins of BEAUTY and VIRTUE — 118
4.2 Features of BEAUTY and VIRTUE — 123
4.3 CAUSATION — 129
4.4 PROBABILITY — 137
4.5 Conclusion — 143
Further reading — 145

## Five
## Normative concepts — 146
5.1 Aesthetic and moral normativity — 147
5.2 The epistemic normativity of TRUTH — 152

5.3 The epistemic normativity of PROBABLE TRUTH 159
5.4 Features of sense-based normative concepts 164
5.5 Conclusion 168
Notes 170
Further reading 171

# Six
# Induction and causation 172

6.1 Causation and probable reasoning 174
6.2 The explanation and evaluation of probable reasoning 183
6.3 Necessary connection and definitions of 'cause' 187
6.4 Liberty and necessity 195
6.5 The relation of cause and effect 200
6.6 Conclusion 206
Notes 210
Further reading 210

# Seven
# Skepticism and probability 213

7.1 Kinds of skepticism 215
7.2 Skeptical considerations 218
7.3 Skeptical crisis and the Title Principle 227
7.4 The normativity of the Title Principle 231
7.5 The mitigation of skepticism 233
7.6 The labyrinth of personal identity 237
7.7 Conclusion 242
Notes 244
Further reading 245

# Eight
# Morality and virtue 247

8.1 Reason and moral distinctions 249
8.2 Natural virtues 257
8.3 Justice as an artificial virtue 262
8.4 Other artificial virtues 268
8.5 Moral diversity 274

|                                    |     |
|------------------------------------|-----|
| 8.6 Conclusion                     | 277 |
| Note                               | 281 |
| Further reading                    | 282 |

## Nine
## Religion and God — 283

|                                    |     |
|------------------------------------|-----|
| 9.1 Religious belief               | 284 |
| 9.2 The Design Argument            | 287 |
| 9.3 The Argument *A Priori*        | 292 |
| 9.4 Evil                           | 295 |
| 9.5 True religion                  | 297 |
| 9.6 Miracles                       | 302 |
| 9.7 Religion and morals            | 308 |
| 9.8 Conclusion                     | 312 |
| Notes                              | 313 |
| Further reading                    | 313 |

## Ten
## "Leaving it to posterity to add the rest" — 315

|                                               |     |
|-----------------------------------------------|-----|
| 10.1 Hume in the eighteenth century           | 318 |
| 10.2 Hume in the nineteenth century           | 324 |
| 10.3 Hume in the twentieth century            | 328 |
| 10.4 Conclusion: Hume for the twenty-first century | 334 |
| Notes                                         | 335 |
| Further reading                               | 335 |

***Glossary*** — 337

***Bibliography*** — 349

***Index*** — 355

# Acknowledgements

"Of all crimes that human creatures are capable of committing," Hume writes, "the most horrid and unnatural is ingratitude" (THN 3.1.1.24/466). My own first debt of gratitude is to the teachers who spurred my interest in Hume, and from whom I have learned more than I can express: Mendel Cohen, Barbara Lindsay, Michael Williams, and Robert Fogelin. My second debt of gratitude is to the many wise and congenial Hume scholars with whom I have discussed Hume's philosophy and who have shown me more facets to it than I could have guessed. These include Donald Ainslie, Peter Kail, Louis Loeb, Peter Millican, and Galen Strawson—all of whom provided invaluable comments on the manuscript—as well as Kate Abramson, Lilli Alanen, Henry Allison, Annette Baier, Helen Beebee, Jonathan Bennett, Donald Baxter, Simon Blackburn, John Bricke, Charlotte Brown, Rachel Cohon, Dorothy Coleman, Stephen Darwall, Lorne Falkenstein, Michael Gill, Livia Guimarães, James Harris, Tito Magri, Jane McIntyre, Kevin Meeker, William Edward Morris, David Owen, Lewis Powell, Elizabeth Radcliffe, Wade Robison, Stefanie Rocknak, Abraham Roth, Paul Russell, Geoffrey Sayre-McCord, Corliss Swain, Jacqueline Taylor, Saul Traiger, Wayne Waxman, Kenneth Winkler, John P. Wright and the members of the Hume Society collectively. I owe a special debt of gratitude to the students and former students who have tested and refined my understanding. These include Jonathan Cottrell, John Morrison, and Hsueh Qu—all of whom also provided invaluable comments on substantial parts of the manuscript—as well as Angela Coventry, Michelle Dyke, Tamra

Frei, Thomas Holden, Colin Marshall, John Russell Roberts, Karl Schafer, and Rico Vitz.

Special gratitude is due to the Institute for Advanced Studies in the Humanities at the University of Edinburgh for the support of a fellowship in the summer of 2011, and to Pauline Phemister, Anthea Taylor, Donald Ferguson, and the late Susan Manning, who together made it such a rewarding experience. My most immediate debt of gratitude is to Tony Bruce and Adam Johnson of Routledge for their patient encouragement and sound advice, and to an anonymous referee for the press for excellent comments and suggestions. My greatest debt of gratitude is to my wife Frances and to our sons Matthew and Christopher, from whom I have learned what is truly of value.

Portions of Chapter Two are based [2.1–4] on my "Hume's Theory of Ideas" (2008) and [2.6] on "Hume's Naturalistic Theory of Representation" (2006b). Portions of Chapter Four [4.3] and Chapter Six [6.5] are partly based on my "Hume" (2009). Portions of Chapters Three [3.3], Four [4.4], and Seven [7.3–5] are based partly on my "Reason, Normativity, and Hume's Title Principle" (2014). Portions of Chapter Seven [7.1–3] are also partly based on my "'A Small Tincture of Pyrrhonism': Skepticism and Naturalism in Hume's Science of Man" (2004) and "Hume's Conclusions in 'Conclusion of this book'" (2006a). Other portions of Chapter Seven [7.6] are based partly on my "Rethinking Hume's Second Thoughts About Personal Identity" (2011). Portions of Chapter Eight [8.3–4] are based in part on my "The First Motive to Justice: Hume's Circle Argument Squared" (2007b). Portions of of Chapter Nine [9.2, 9.6] are based partly on "What's True about Hume's 'True Religion'?" (2012).

# Abbreviations

## Abbreviations of works by David Hume

ATHN  *An Abstract of a Book lately Published; Entituled, A Treatise of Human Nature, &c. Wherein The Chief Argument of that Book is farther Illustrated and Explained*, included in *A Treatise of Human Nature*, ed. David F. Norton and Mary Norton (Oxford: Oxford University Press, 2007). Citations are by paragraph number.

DNR  *Dialogues concerning Natural Religion and Other Writings*, ed. Dorothy Coleman (Cambridge: Cambridge University Press, 2007). Citations are by part, paragraph number, and marginal page number. Marginal page numbers refer to *Dialogues concerning Natural Religion*, ed. Norman Kemp Smith (Indianapolis: Bobbs-Merrill, 1947).

DP  *A Dissertation on the Passions* (published with *The Natural History of Religion* as part of *The Clarendon Edition of the Works of David Hume*) ed. Tom L. Beauchamp (Oxford: Clarendon Press, 2007). Citations are by section and paragraph number.

EHU  *An Enquiry concerning Human Understanding*, ed. Tom L. Beauchamp (Oxford: Clarendon Press, 2000). Citations are by section and paragraph number, followed by page number in *Enquiries concerning Human Understanding and concerning the Principles of Morals*, ed. L. A. Selby-Bigge and revised by P. H. Nidditch (Oxford: Clarendon Press, 1975).

EMPL  *Essays Moral, Political, and Literary*, ed. Eugene F. Miller, Indianapolis: Liberty Fund, 1987. Citations are by part, essay number and/or title, and page number.

EPM  An Enquiry concerning the Principles of Morals, ed. Tom L. Beauchamp, Oxford: Clarendon Press, 1999. Citations are by section and paragraph number, followed by page number in Enquiries concerning Human Understanding and concerning the Principles of Morals, ed. L. A. Selby-Bigge and revised by P. H. Nidditch (Oxford: Clarendon Press, 1975).

HE  History of England, six volumes (Indianapolis: Liberty Fund, 1985). Citations are by volume, chapter, and page number.

LDH  Letters of David Hume, two volumes, ed. J. Y. T. Greig (Oxford: Oxford University Press, 1932). Citations are by letter number, followed by volume and page number.

LG  A Letter from a Gentleman to his Friend in Edinburgh, included in A Treatise of Human Nature, ed. David F. Norton and Mary Norton (Oxford: Oxford University Press 2007). Citations are by paragraph number.

NHR  The Natural History of Religion (published with A Dissertation on the Passions as part of The Clarendon Edition of the Works of David Hume) ed. Tom. L. Beauchamp (Oxford: Clarendon Press, 2007). Citations are by section and paragraph number.

NLDH  New Letters of David Hume, ed. Raymond Klibansky and Ernest C. Mossner (Oxford: Oxford University Press, 1954). Citations are by letter number followed by page number.

THN  A Treatise of Human Nature, ed. David F. Norton and Mary Norton (Oxford: Oxford University Press, 2007). Citations are by book, part, section, and paragraph number, followed by page numbers of A Treatise of Human Nature, ed. L. A. Selby-Bigge and revised by P. H. Nidditch (Oxford: Clarendon Press, 1978).

## Abbreviations of other primary works

EAPM  Reid, Thomas. Essays on the Active Powers of the Human Mind, ed. Knud Haakonssen and James Harris (University Park, PA: Pennsylvania State University Press, 2010). Citations are by essay and chapter, followed by page number.

EIPM  Reid, Thomas. Essays on the Intellectual Powers of Man, ed. Derek R. Brookes (University Park, PA: Pennsylvania State University Press, 2010). Citations are by essay and chapter, followed by page number.

ECHU  Locke, John. *An Essay concerning Human Understanding*, ed. P. H. Nidditch (Oxford: Clarendon Press, 1975). Citations are by book, chapter, and section number.

PAFM  Kant, Immanuel. *Prolegomena to Any Future Metaphysics*, ed. and trans. Gary Hatfield (Cambridge: Cambridge University Press, 2004). Citations are by page numbers of the Königliche Preussische Akademie der Wissenschaften edition, which are commonly used as marginal reference numbers across editions.

# Chronology

| | |
|---|---|
| **1711** | Born at Edinburgh, youngest of three children. |
| **1721–25** | Studies at the "Town's College" (now the University of Edinburgh) with older brother John. |
| **1725–34** | At Ninewells (family home in southern Scotland), reading law and philosophy. |
| **1734** | Attempts business career at Bristol. |
| **1734–37** | Lives in France (chiefly La Flèche) writing *A Treatise of Human Nature*. |
| **1737** | Moves to London to pursue publication. |
| **1739** | Publishes *A Treatise of Human Nature* Books 1 and 2; returns to Ninewells. |
| **1740** | Publishes *A Treatise of Human Nature* Book 3 and *An Abstract of a Treatise of Human Nature*. |
| **1741** | Publishes *Essays, Moral and Political* first volume. |
| **1742** | Publishes *Essays, Moral and Political* second volume. |
| **1745** | Publishes *A Letter from a Gentleman to his Friend in Edinburgh*; denied chair of "Pneumaticks and moral Philosophy" at Edinburgh. |
| **1745–46** | Serves as tutor to Marquess of Annandale. |
| **1746** | Serves as secretary to General St. Clair's expedition against l'Orient, France. |
| **1748** | Publishes *An Enquiry concerning Human Understanding* (originally under the title *Philosophical Essays concerning Human Understanding*) and *Three Essays Moral and Political*; serves as secretary to General St. Clair on diplomatic missions to Vienna and Turin. |

| | |
|---|---|
| 1751 | Publishes *An Enquiry concerning the Principles of Morals*; moves with sister Katherine to Edinburgh. |
| 1752 | Publishes *Political Discourses*; denied chair of Philosophy at University of Glasgow; appointed Librarian of Faculty of Advocates in Edinburgh. |
| 1753–56 | Publishes *Essays and Treatises on Several Subjects* (a collection of previous writings not including the *Treatise*). |
| 1754–62 | Publishes *History of England* in six volumes. |
| 1757 | Publishes *Four Dissertations*; resigns as Librarian. |
| 1763–65 | Serves in British Embassy in Paris. |
| 1765 | Returns to England with Rousseau. |
| 1767–69 | Serves as Undersecretary of State for the Northern Department. |
| 1769 | Returns to Edinburgh. |
| 1776 | Writes "My Own Life"; dies of colon cancer. |
| 1779 | *Dialogues concerning Natural Religion* published posthumously. |

# Preface
# How to read this book

As a comprehensive introduction to the philosophy of David Hume, this book aims to explain his most important ideas across the full range of philosophical topics he discussed and to do so within a manageable compass in a way that will be accessible to readers who have no specialized training in philosophy and little prior knowledge of Hume. At the same time, however, it strives to present those ideas and to reveal their relations in a distinctive way that will make the book of substantial interest to historians of philosophy and to other philosophers grappling with questions like those that animated Hume. One leading theme of the book that I hope will prove valuable to readers of all kinds is that the commonalities he explicitly and implicitly uncovers among such "sense"-based concepts as those of color, beauty, virtue, causation, and probability provide a key to understanding important and original aspects of his philosophy that would otherwise be obscure. A second and related theme, which again I hope will prove valuable to readers of all kinds, is that the commonalities he strongly suggests among such normative concepts as those of beauty, virtue, and truth and probable truth—concepts that serve for him to structure, respectively, the aesthetic, moral, and epistemic domains of value—provide a key to understanding the full significance of his philosophy.

Hume's thought is remarkably wide-ranging. It encompasses at least what would now be called philosophy of mind, epistemology, philosophy of science, metaphysics, ethics, aesthetics, political philosophy, and philosophy of religion. Within each of these fields, it is consistently rich and penetrating: he took pleasure in "taking the matter pretty deep" (to use his own repeated and memorable phrase) in ways that involve considerable complexity of analysis and argumentation. The constraint of manageability therefore requires that many important and fascinating details be passed over in the main text. Where the combined aims of comprehensiveness and philosophical significance have led me to enter nonetheless into some inherently complex matters that may at least initially be passed over by relative beginners, I have tried to indicate this explicitly—just as Hume himself sometimes did in his own later writings. These include the treatments of space and time (in Chapter Two), mental representation (also in Chapter Two), the psychological mechanisms of epistemic normativity (in Chapter Five), and the causes of Hume's later worries about personal identity (in Chapter Seven). References to some useful discussions of particular topics at greater length may be found in the annotated list of suggested further readings that follows each chapter.

Different readers across different generations have interpreted Hume's writings in many different ways. Some have seen him as an inspiring model or a prescient intellectual forebear, while others have seen him as a cautionary example or a wellspring of errors to be overcome. Even those who agree in their assessments of the value of his doctrines very often disagree quite fundamentally about their meaning. While the book endeavors to indicate where the most important interpretive disputes lie, manageability precludes devoting to most of them either the careful and exhaustive examination of texts, or the extensive engagement with secondary literature, that would be necessary to resolve them definitively. For this reason, the suggested further readings also offer a guide to fuller defenses both of interpretations that I adopt and of interpretations that I reject. If it is included among the suggestions for further reading and its bearing is clear from the annotations, I have generally not footnoted relevant secondary literature within the chapter itself, but in some cases I refer forward to a particular work of secondary literature by author and date.

Inevitably, a number of the defenses listed in the suggestions for further reading are my own. Of these, some appeared in my 1997 book *Cognition and Commitment in Hume's Philosophy*, a work that aimed to resolve a selected set of central interpretive puzzles; I have tried to limit references to this work to the most important. Others, however, have appeared in subsequent essays and articles published in a variety of disparate venues. In a few cases, the present book modifies an interpretation I have offered in the past; the most significant of these modifications are mentioned in the end-of-chapter annotations. In many more cases, however, the present book adds significant new elements, both large and small, beyond anything I have discussed before. In both respects, it is meant to function not only as an introduction to Hume's philosophy and to ongoing debates about its meaning and significance, but also, for anyone interested, as an organizing focus through which some of my own widely dispersed recent interventions in those debates can be organized and integrated within a new framework to form what I hope is a coherent and more comprehensive whole.

One of the most general interpretive controversies about Hume's philosophy is, in fact, whether that philosophy itself constitutes a coherent whole, or whether it can only be mined for stimulating but disconnected discussions of individual topics. I am firmly convinced of its overall consistency and coherence, and the organization of this book is intended to highlight those features. Hume saw his investigation of the human mind—which he called "the science of man"—as the foundation for the rest of his philosophy, and, indeed, for the rest of philosophy and the sciences generally. Accordingly, after an introduction and an initial chapter surveying his life and writings, the next four chapters of the book are devoted to aspects of that science that have implications, in one way or another, across multiple areas of philosophy. Only then does the book narrow its focus, in the subsequent four chapters, to particular areas of philosophical inquiry before concluding with a brief examination of Hume's reception, influence, and legacy. This way of proceeding makes it much easier, I believe, to see the coherence of Hume's approach and the consistency of his results than does the more obvious and common method of simply devoting successive chapters to coverage of individual topics or areas of philosophy.

It is a confirmation of Hume's own view about the foundational character of his science of man that it often proves necessary in later chapters to invoke concepts and doctrines introduced in the earlier chapters. In consequence, it will not always be easy for the reader to jump into a particular chapter or section on a topic of interest without having read the previous chapters. I hope that this inconvenience is at least mitigated by the prospect of a deeper and more integrated understanding resulting from the interrelation of chapters. Where a particular section of a previous or subsequent chapter is clearly essential to a topic at hand, however, I have employed a bracketed reference to it by chapter and section number; thus, for example, '[2.3]' indicates the relevance of Section 3 of Chapter Two.

As a further aid, a glossary at the end of the book provides definitions of technical or otherwise unfamiliar terms of whatever origin, including those that are employed in multiple chapters of the book. Where Hume provides his own philosophical terminology, as he very often does, I have tried to follow it consistently, resolving ambiguities by further specification when necessary. I have not hesitated, however, to employ applicable contemporary terminology where it is useful, nor to coin new terminology in the interests of clarity and convenience to express concepts and to designate doctrines that he discusses but does not specifically name. In order to mark the difference as easily as possible, Hume's own terms (and also those of his contemporaries, when context makes their particular source clear) are always introduced in double quotation marks, whereas contemporary technical terms and my own coinages are always introduced in italics. In addition, following relatively common disciplinary conventions, single quotation marks are used to designate linguistic items such as words or phrases, while small capital letters are used to designate concepts. (Thus, for example: 'causation' is a term that expresses the concept CAUSATION and names the relation of causation.) When useful, what Hume calls possible "matters of fact" (for example, *Rome exists* or *Sally is taller than John*) may be designated by a lower-case 'p'. Braces—'{ }'—will be used to create names for what Hume calls "ideas," so that '{p}' designates the idea of the possible matter of fact p. Ordinary quotation of the writings of others is indicated by standard double quotation marks (when the quotation is short) or indentation (when it is long). Outside of quotations, I consistently employ modern American spellings ('color', 'skeptic') even for terms Hume spelled otherwise. When quoting from the writings of Hume or others, however, I leave all orthography of the original unaltered—including any quotation marks, italics, capitalization, and spelling—without seeking to impose on their writings any of the conventions just mentioned.

The mixing of historical and contemporary terminology is emblematic of what I believe is a particularly fruitful approach to the philosophical history of philosophy. That is, we must begin by understanding a philosopher of the past in his or her own terms, but we should hope to end by understanding the philosopher in some of our own terms as well. Few intellectual experiences can match the excitement of encountering a great but very different mind from a very different time or place, and then discovering through study, reflection, and empathy that one can understand, appreciate, and appropriate for use in one's own thinking some of the thoughts of that other mind. I hope that this book will help readers, in one way or another, to have that experience with the mind and thought of David Hume.

# Introduction

A 1999 *Sunday Times* survey of British "opinion leaders" named David Hume the "Scot of the Millennium" then just ending. In earning this honor, Hume surpassed Robert Burns, Alexander Fleming, and his own friend Adam Smith. Given the dearth of recognized competitors from previous millennia, it seems safe to assume that this amounted to being recognized as the greatest Scot of all time.

Although Hume served at different times as a tutor, a librarian, and a diplomat, it is his writings that qualify him to be considered among the greatest of his countrymen. Among those writings, some of his essays made significant early contributions to economics and political science, and his judicious six-volume *History of England* was both popular and influential, but it is unquestionably his brilliant and wide-ranging philosophical writings that constitute his most distinctive and enduring legacy. Indeed, many academic philosophers consider him to be—with Plato, Aristotle, and Immanuel Kant—one of the four most important philosophers of all time. Because philosophy is the attempt to answer the most fundamental questions—those on which other important questions depend—every reflective person has reason to be interested in philosophy. Anyone with reason to be interested in philosophy, in turn, has many reasons to be interested in the philosophy of David Hume.

Some of the reasons lie in Hume's many *individual arguments* that are among the most groundbreaking and controversial, yet quite often also among the most misunderstood, in the history of philosophy. These include his arguments for the following conclusions:

- that all inference from what is observed to what is yet unobserved (the inferential process now called *induction*) depends ultimately not on reason but, rather, on habit;
- that the existence of a world of physical objects outside the mind cannot be established by reasoning;
- that the causal determination of human thoughts and actions is compatible with, and in fact required for, the only kind of free will worth having;
- that moral distinctions cannot be made by reason alone and depend essentially on human sentiments;
- that the obligations to respect property, keep promises, and obey one's government are not the result of natural rights but arise initially from self-interest, convention, and utility;
- that no testimony could ever establish the occurrence of a miracle in such a way as to provide adequate support for a revealed religion; and
- that there is unlikely to be a beneficent creator or ruler of the universe, but this does not undermine morality.

Other reasons lie in the number of distinctive, though contested, *approaches* to important philosophical topics that he pioneered and that are today denominated "Humean." These include:

- his treatment of constant conjunction (that is, regularities in nature) as essential to the relation of cause and effect;
- his conception of the self not as a single enduring substance, but as a system or "bundle" of causally related mental entities (which he calls "perceptions");
- his analysis of the passions as distinctive non-representational feelings that are associated with mental representations of persons or circumstances;
- his account of motivation to voluntary action as requiring passions (such as desire) as well as beliefs, with ultimate ends not subject to evaluation by reason;
- his explanation of moral evaluation as directed most fundamentally at features of character, rather than at the consequences of actions or the conformity of actions to principles of duty.

Yet further reasons lie in Hume's compelling development and elaboration of broad basic *philosophical orientations* that unify his treatments of particular topics. These include:

- *empiricism*—the endeavor to allow observation to dictate the content of theorizing, rather than allow antecedent theorizing to dictate the interpretations of observations (*methodological empiricism*), and to trace the meaning of all concepts to origins in experience (*concept empiricism*);
- *naturalism*—the pursuit of explanations without invoking entities (such as deities, universals, abstract entities), properties (such as explanatorily basic values or meanings), or events (such as miracles or uncaused acts of free will) that would be outside the scope of ordinary laws of nature or natural scientific investigation; and
- *skepticism*—doubt or diminution of belief; the recommendation of doubt or diminution of belief; or denying or minimizing the epistemic merit (that is, value derived from truth or the probability of truth) of belief.

Each of these basic orientations is a major influence in contemporary philosophy, and Hume remains among the most powerful exemplars of each. Yet it has seemed to many readers that his skepticism must ultimately undermine his naturalism and perhaps even his empiricism. This apparent conflict is perhaps the single most important source of the still-common judgment that his philosophy is inconsistent or incoherent taken as a whole, and the question of whether it can be resolved—and if so, how—is perhaps the single most important interpretive question concerning his philosophy as a whole. The investigation of this question has the power to illuminate some of the deepest issues in epistemology.

Hume's philosophical writing is unquestionably a pleasure to read; Immanuel Kant described it as a rare combination of "subtlety and grace." The aim of the present book is not to match its stylistic excellence—for that would be impossible—but rather to provide an aid to comprehending the subtlety of its parts and the sometimes elusive coherence of the whole in a way that will allow readers to assess its continuing value for themselves.

In order to understand Hume's philosophy in its parts and as a whole, however, it is essential to know something of the context—intellectual, social, political, and personal—in which the various works expressing it were written and the particular aims they were meant to serve. For this reason, Chapter One is devoted to an account of the events and circumstances of his life, together with brief descriptions of the writings that they helped to produce.

Hume was convinced from the very outset that a key to making progress in philosophy across a wide range of topics and issues lies in achieving a better understanding of: (i) the entities—which he calls "perceptions"—that constitute the elements of experience and thought; and (ii) the mental faculties that operate on them. Indeed, his philosophical project as a whole can be characterized as that of investigating the faculties of the human mind, by means of those very faculties, in order to determine which of their products human beings should accept and endorse. Accordingly, Chapter Two explains Hume's treatments of the various perceptions of the human mind and the basic principles that apply to them, while Chapter Three examines his account of the mind itself and of the various cognitive and conative faculties he distinguishes as operating within it. Chapter Two draws primarily but not exclusively on Hume's presentation in the early pages of his first book, *A Treatise of Human Nature*. Among the most important topics of those pages is his theory of what he calls "abstract ideas" and what we would call *concepts*. They provide his explanation of how ideas are able to represent with generality, and I try to reconstruct his overall theory of mental representation on their basis and on the basis of other more scattered texts. Chapter Three ranges more widely over the *Treatise* and other philosophical writings in order to provide a full map of the mental faculties he discusses—including the crucial faculty of reason, about which he makes so many innovative claims. Taken together, the various distinctions, principles, and doctrines considered in these two chapters, along with the arguments that support them, not only constitute central elements of his philosophy of mind and psychology but also undergird nearly all of his most important contributions to epistemology, philosophy of science, metaphysics, ethics, aesthetics, political philosophy, and philosophy of religion.

Although there are many different ways in which those varied contributions might be approached, it is notable that nearly all of the contributions themselves crucially involve one or more of a few key concepts: those that Hume calls the ideas of "causation" (or "cause and effect"), "probability," "truth" and "falshood," "virtue" and "vice," and "beauty" and "deformity." (We would now more likely use the term 'ugliness' rather than 'deformity', for the sense of the latter word has shifted and narrowed somewhat in the intervening centuries. So too, to a somewhat lesser extent, has the sense of the word 'vice'.) Importantly for our purposes, there are notable crucial commonalities and relations among these concepts. For example, Hume describes virtue and vice, beauty and deformity, as being discerned by a "moral sense" and a "sense of beauty," respectively, in conscious analogy with the ordinary senses of sight, hearing, smell, taste, and touch that provide sensory information about the world. And although he does not use the terms 'causal sense' and 'sense of probability', it is illuminating to see the extent to which his treatments of the origin, development, and use of the concepts of causation and probability parallel his treatments of the central concepts employed in morality and aesthetics. Indeed, I suggest that his conception of probability seems in many ways modeled ultimately on his conception of beauty. In any case, however, it is in the relations among these treatments of what I will call *sense-based concepts* that much of the full originality, coherence, and power of his philosophy emerge.

Just as importantly, however, the concepts of virtue and vice, and beauty and deformity, along with the concepts of truth, falsehood, probable truth, and probable falsehood, function for Hume as what we may call *normative concepts*. That is, their use expresses or implies approval or disapproval of persons or things as having particular kinds of value or disvalue—in these cases, moral, aesthetic, and epistemic value, respectively. Understanding what normativity is for Hume, and how concepts may acquire it, is a second crucial element in appreciating the originality, coherence, and power of his philosophy. Just as his conceptions of the aesthetic and moral senses shed light on his conceptions of causation and probability, so too his understanding of aesthetic and moral normativity sheds light on his understanding of epistemic normativity. Chapters Four and Five are therefore devoted to examining Hume's understanding of the development and employment of sense-based concepts and normative concepts, respectively, together with a consideration of some of the most important relations among those concepts and their consequences. These two chapters are yet more far-ranging, drawing on nearly all of his philosophical writings to assemble a structure of theoretical parallels that, in its detail at least, constitutes one of the main interpretive innovations of the book. I provide direct evidence of these parallels in the text, but their assembly requires by its nature some philosophical reconstruction of connections that Hume does not always make fully explicit. I hope that their attribution to Hume is justified also by their usefulness in explaining otherwise puzzling or unaccountable features of his texts as well as by their intrinsic philosophical interest and significance.

Following these four chapters that span the foundations of Hume's philosophy in relation to his philosophy of mind, Chapters Six, Seven, and Eight are each devoted to a set of philosophical issues connected more specifically with other particular areas of philosophy and with one of the "senses" discussed in Chapter Four. Chapter Six addresses issues in epistemology, philosophy of science, and metaphysics concerning induction and causation; these include the nature and epistemic status of inductive reasoning, our understanding of causation, the implications of that understanding for the dispute about freedom of the will, and the nature of the causal relation itself. Chapter Seven takes up further issues in epistemology concerning skepticism and probability; these include the varieties of skepticism, the nature of arguments leading to skepticism, the extent to which skepticism can and should be overcome, and the appropriate normative standards for belief. In doing so, it aims to resolve the crucial but vexed question of the relation between Hume's skepticism and his naturalism and empiricism. Chapter Eight examines issues in ethics and political theory concerning morality and virtue; these include the role of reason in motivation and morality, the roles of convention and self-interest in morality and political obligation, the extent to which virtue is in an agent's own interest, and the causes and significance of diversity in moral judgment.

Each of these issues was of great importance to Hume in its own right, and his treatment of each had a significant impact on his contemporaries and his successors. Yet perhaps no topic was of greater theoretical or practical importance to Hume throughout his philosophical career than religion and religious belief, and no feature of his philosophical outlook received broader attention—not to say notoriety—during his lifetime or after it than his so-called "infidelity" or irreligion. Drawing on his doctrines concerning causation, probability, and morals, Chapter Nine surveys Hume's treatments of philosophical issues bearing directly on the philosophy of religion and what he calls "a sense of religion." These include the origin of religion in human nature, the standing of arguments for the existence of God, the problem of evil, the nature and prospects of a philosophical religion, the credibility of testimony for miracles, and the relation between religion and morality.

Hume was a significant influence, in one way or another, on many of the most important movements and developments in philosophy over the last two hundred and fifty years, including Scottish common-sense philosophy, German idealism, psychological associationism, ethical utilitarianism, and logical positivism. The nature and significance of his contributions to philosophy have been variously interpreted in various eras. Yet his ideas continue to exert power in most areas of contemporary philosophy, including philosophy of mind, epistemology, philosophy of science, metaphysics, and ethics. Chapter Ten concludes the book with a brief summary of his role in philosophy's past and his continuing impact on philosophy's present and future.

# One
## "A ruling passion"

In April 1776, four months before his death and in full knowledge that his illness was fatal, David Hume wrote a remarkable autobiographical essay of a few thousand words that he called "My Own Life." Near the outset of the essay, he recalled that he had been "seized very early with a passion for literature, which has been the ruling passion of my life, and the great source of my enjoyments." At its conclusion, he offered this sketch of his own character:

> I am, or rather was (for that is the style, I must now use in speaking of myself; which emboldens me the more to speak my sentiments); I was, I say, a man of mild dispositions, of command of temper, of an open, social, and cheerful humour, capable of attachment, but little susceptible of enmity, and of great moderation in all my passions. Even my love of literary fame, my ruling passion, never soured my temper, notwithstanding my frequent disappointments … . I cannot say there is no vanity in making this funeral oration of myself, but I hope it is not a misplaced one; and this is a matter of fact which is easily cleared and ascertained.
> (EMPL "My Own Life": xl–xli; LDH: I.7)

There appears to be a subtle discrepancy between the opening and closing declarations: was it a pure "passion for literature" itself or merely a "love of literary fame" that was his true ruling passion? Or did the latter come at some point to displace the former?

In fact, Hume's ruling passion was a complex affair. His essays on writing ("Of Simplicity and Refinement in Writing," "Of Essay-Writing"), his own meticulous care in constructing the elegant rhythms of his prose, and his patronage in later life of poets and dramatists all provide powerful evidence that he appreciated good writing for its own sake. From an early age, however, his love of books was above all a powerful spur to curiosity. In a long letter written to a physician at the age of twenty-three, setting out what he then called "a kind of History of my Life," he noted that, left to his own devices, his reading had at first inclined "almost equally to Books of Reasoning & Philosophy, & to Poetry & the Polite Authors." Yet what had struck him most about these readings, the young David reported, was that there was nothing yet established, but only "endless Disputes," in both philosophy and literary criticism. Accordingly, he wrote,

> Upon Examination of these, I found a certain Boldness of Temper, growing in me, which was not inclin'd to submit to any Authority in these Subjects, but led me to seek out some new Medium, by which Truth might be establisht.
>
> (LDH 3: I.13)

The hope of success in this endeavor, in turn, led him to "think of no other way of pushing my Fortune in the World but that of Scholar & Philosopher." Yet, as his own philosophical investigations into the nature of the passions would soon lead him to remark, curiosity and the ambition to make a name for oneself through the establishment of valuable truths are interdependent sentiments: it is difficult to be satisfied with philosophical or scholarly fame unless one thinks it is warranted by the worth and accuracy of one's discoveries (THN 2.1.11.9–13/320–22), and it is difficult to remain confident that one has established the truth without the agreement and approbation of others whose judgment one respects (THN 1.4.7.2/264). Love of literature, curiosity, and ambition for literary fame were for Hume—as they surely are for many authors—inextricably entwined. He was both perceptive enough to observe the fact and candid enough to admit it.

Hume developed and cherished many close friendships within and without the learned world, and by nearly all accounts he was, just as he declared near the end, sociable and cheerful even through the various disappointments of his literary life. Those who visited him in his final months confirmed that he remained so even in the face of death and despite his firm denial of personal immortality. One important factor in his ability to retain his equanimity and good spirits was no doubt something that he declared "very requisite to happiness": namely, the ability to make "a satisfactory review of [one's] own conduct" (EPM 12.23/283). In particular, he felt a due degree of pride for the discoveries he had made, the works he had written, and the warranted fame that he had finally achieved in the republic of letters.

## 1.1 Early life and education

The youngest of three children, David Hume was born as "David Home"—he later changed the spelling to aid its proper pronunciation—in Edinburgh on April 26, 1711, just four years after the Act of Union that created Great Britain from England and Scotland. His family—"good [but] not rich," he later pronounced—split its time between Edinburgh, where his father Joseph practiced law, and the family estate of Ninewells, just south of Chirnside in the county of Berwickshire near the border with England. Joseph died, however, when David was barely two years old. His mother Katherine, daughter of an eminent jurist, never remarried, instead choosing to raise her family and, until David's elder brother John came of age, administer Ninewells on her own. David was clearly very close to her, even though she had a religious devotion as a Presbyterian that he did not share. In an oft-repeated story—though one without any first-hand verification—she is said to have declared at some point in his youth, "Our Davie's a fine good-natured crater [creature], but uncommon wake-minded." This has in later years been interpreted, especially by his critics, as an indication that his own mother thought him especially weak-minded or stupid. According to the most comprehensive dictionary of eighteenth-century Scottish dialect, however, 'wake' (derived from the Latin verb '*vacare*') meant "vacant" or "unoccupied" rather than "weak."[1] Hence, if his mother made the remark at all, she is more likely to have meant that he was often dreamy or lost in his own thoughts. Certainly Hume took himself to be a good student, for fellow Scot James Boswell (1740–95, best known as the biographer of Samuel Johnson) reported of their final meeting:

> He said ... he used to read *The Whole Duty of Man* [an Anglican compendium of morals]; that he made an abstract from the catalogue of vices at the end of it, and examined himself by them, leaving out murder and theft and such vices as he had no chance of committing, having no inclination to commit them. This, he said, was strange work; for instance, to try if, notwithstanding his excelling his schoolfellows, he had no pride or vanity.
> ("An Account of my Last Interview with David Hume, Esq."[2])

At the age of ten, David entered the University of Edinburgh—the "Town's College" then in many ways more like an advanced high school—at the same time as his brother John, then age twelve. He attended for four years, leaving without taking a degree, as was common. All students studied Latin and Greek, as well as logic, metaphysics, and natural philosophy (that is, what would now be called natural science); they also had the opportunity to study mathematics and ethics. He left the university just before Colin Maclaurin—a prominent early proponent and popularizer of Isaac Newton's experimentally grounded mathematical physics—joined the faculty in 1725, but he would likely have become familiar with the writings of Newton's friend John Locke (1632–1703), the author of *An Essay concerning Human Understanding*, *Two Treatises of Government*, and *A Letter concerning Toleration*; of Anthony Ashley Cooper, third Earl of Shaftesbury (1671–1713), the moral philosopher whose education had been supervised by Locke; and of Newton's ally Samuel Clarke (1675–1729), the metaphysician, moralist, and philosophical theologian. Locke's thorough and empirically minded account of human cognition and knowledge, his theory of civil society as legitimated by a social contract that served to protect natural rights, and his defense of religious toleration (not including atheists and Roman Catholics) were all highly influential. Shaftesbury's idea that morality is discerned by a "moral sense" led to one prominent strand in eighteenth-century British moral thought, while Clarke's conception of morality as consisting in eternal relations that, like those of mathematics, are discerned by reason led to another. Young David might also have been exposed at this early date to works of George Berkeley (1685–1753), whose "immaterialism," rejecting the existence of material substances in favor of a universe consisting only of minds and ideas, was much discussed.

After leaving the University and returning at least part-time to Ninewells, David began reading law as preparation for a legal career—an obvious choice for the younger son of Joseph and Katherine Home, especially given his intellectual talents. Soon enough, however, his own preferred kinds of literature came to dominate his attention. As recounted in "My Own Life," he "found an insurmountable aversion to everything but the pursuits of philosophy and general learning; and while they fancied that I was reading Voet and Vinnius, Cicero and Vergil were the authors I was secretly devouring." The spring of 1729 saw an apparent breakthrough in the search for the "new Medium" for establishing truth:

> At last, when I was about 18 Years of Age, there seem'd to open up to me a new Scene of Thought, which transported me beyond measure, & made me, with an Ardor natural to young men, throw up every other Pleasure or Business to apply entirely to it.
>
> (LDH 3: I.13)

The nature of this breakthrough has, quite naturally, been a matter of considerable speculation. In his landmark 1941 book *The Philosophy of David Hume*, Norman Kemp Smith proposed that it was a realization prompted by reflection on the sentiment-based moral theory of Francis Hutcheson (1694–1746)[3]—specifically, that a similar feeling-based approach could be "carried over to the theoretical domain" of belief.[4]

As we will see in some detail in Chapter Four, parallels between these two domains are indeed crucial to Hume's philosophy. Whatever the precise character of the "new Scene of Thought" was, however, his enthusiasm for it at first brought not success but unexpected illness. Within six months, he was complaining of difficulty in concentrating and a chronic lowness of spirits, as well as of physical symptoms. He followed a course of treatment, prescribed by his local physician, that included "Anti-hysteric Pills," wine, and exercise. He subsequently found that he was becoming able to work, although not with the intensity that he wished. During this period, he also studied French and Italian. Finally, in 1734, although still intent on being a philosopher, he moved to Bristol to become a clerk to a merchant, with the aim of improving his health through a "more active Scene of Life." Within a few months, the experiment with commerce was over, and he sailed for France to write the book he had been projecting.

## 1.2 *A Treatise of Human Nature*

After a short time in Paris, where he had letters of introduction, Hume moved to Rheims, which was much less expensive. Finding after a year that he could not hold his expenses down to his modest patrimonial annual income of £50 even in Rheims, he moved a second time, to La Flèche in Anjou. La Flèche was home to the Jesuit college where the philosopher and mathematician René Descartes (1596–1650) had been educated more than a hundred years before; more directly to Hume's purposes, the college possessed a very substantial library, to which he was granted access. In addition to Descartes, he also read such important French philosophers as Nicolas Malebranche (1638–1715), who denied the existence of any real necessary causal connections among finite things in favor of attributing all genuine causality to God. Although he would later tell Boswell that he "never had entertained any belief in Religion since he began to read Locke and Clarke," he maintained friendly relations with the Jesuits of the college. It was in La Flèche that Hume composed, over the next two years, most of what is by many accounts the greatest work of philosophy ever written in English, *A Treatise of Human Nature: being an Attempt to introduce the experimental Method into Moral Subjects*.

By 'Moral Subjects', Hume means not only morality or ethics but all subjects centering on human life. In fact, as the Introduction to the work explains, he proposes to develop a "science of man" that would provide a "compleat system of the sciences, built on a foundation almost entirely new, and the only one upon which they can stand with any security" (THN Introduction 6/xv). This is because many sciences, such as "Logic [the science of thought and reasoning], Morals [morality or ethics proper], Criticism [aesthetics, especially of literature], and Politics [political science]," are intimately connected with human nature, while even such sciences as "Mathematics, Natural Philosophy [natural science], and Natural Religion [religion available to reason without special revelation]" are judged by human mental faculties and hence may be improved by a better understanding of those faculties. By 'the experimental Method', Hume means a method of relying on revealing experiences to support appropriate generalizations. As he tells the history of human enquiry, the inauguration of natural philosophy by the ancient cosmologist Thales (c. 624 BCE–c. 546 BCE) preceded Socrates's (c. 469 BCE–399 BCE) inauguration of moral philosophy by something more than a century; and similarly, Francis Bacon's (1562–1626) introduction of the experimental method into natural philosophy was followed after a similar period by "some late philosophers in *England*"—Locke, Shaftesbury, Bernard Mandeville (1670–1733), Hutcheson, and Joseph Butler (1692–1752) are named in a footnote—who began to put the science of man on a comparable footing. Unstated but clearly enough implied by this comparison is that, just as Newton reached new heights in natural philosophy after Bacon, so too Hume hopes to reach new heights in moral philosophy after Locke and others.

One might expect the application of the experimental method to human nature to be largely introspective, but Hume warns that premeditation and reflection may disturb or distort the phenomena observed; instead, therefore, enquirers must "glean up … experiments" from "a cautious observation of human life, and take them as they appear in the common course of the world" (THN Introduction 10/xix). While the result is intended to be the establishment of a science "not … inferior in certainty … and much superior in utility to any other of human comprehension," the methodological dependence on experience places strict limits on what can be known. Because we cannot penetrate into the "essence" of either mind or matter, we can judge the powers or faculties of each only by observing what they produce; and while we may explain some causal principles as instances of others more general, there is no prospect of explaining in turn the ultimate and most general principles through such an assimilation, regardless of how few or many of them there may be. They must remain, to us at least, inexplicable brute facts.

The *Treatise* consists of three "Books," which are divided into "parts" that are in turn subdivided into "sections." Book 1, "Of the Understanding," contains four parts: "Of ideas; their origin, composition, abstraction, connexion, &c."; "Of the ideas of space and time"; "Of knowledge and probability"; and "Of the skeptical and other systems of philosophy." Book 2, "Of the Passions," consists of three parts: "Of pride and humility"; "Of love and hatred"; and "Of the will and direct passions." Book 3, "Of Morals," also consists of three parts: "Of virtue and vice in general"; "Of justice and injustice"; and "Of the other virtues and vices." The eighty sections of the *Treatise* range over such topics as the nature of thought, including thought possessing generality; the nature and basis of knowledge, probability, and reasoning; the nature and behavior of belief itself; the relation between causes and effects; the nature of sense perception and the source of beliefs about an external world of bodies (that is, physical objects); the alleged immateriality of the soul; the nature of the self and the conditions for its persistence through time; the limitations, infirmities, and "contradictions" inherent in human cognition; the nature and complex operations of the various passions; the sources of human voluntary action; freedom of the will; the nature and source of moral distinctions and evaluations; the origin and nature of property and promises; the origin of government, and the nature and extent of the obligation to obey it; and the best kind of person to be. Irreligious consequences, although mostly tacit, are frequently made apparent. Taken together, these elements were intended to produce a philosophical revolution. Filled with anticipation, Hume sailed for London in the fall of 1737 to arrange for the book's publication.

Hume's friend Henry Home (later Lord Kames), a jurist and a philosopher in his own right, had met Joseph Butler—one of the "late philosophers of *England*" mentioned in the Introduction to the *Treatise*—in London the previous year. Butler was already famous as the author of *Fifteen Sermons Preached in the Rolls Chapel* (an important contribution to moral philosophy) and of *The Analogy of Religion* (concerning the natural evidence for God's existence), and had been recently installed as chaplain to Queen Caroline. Accordingly, Hume hoped to meet Butler and win his approbation for the *Treatise*. Although he obtained a letter of introduction from Home, Butler subsequently proved to be away from London, and they did not meet. In reviewing his manuscript prior to its intended presentation to Butler, however, Hume decided to remove a discussion of miracles—containing an argument that, he reported, had first occurred to him in a discussion with a Jesuit in La Flèche—as likely to offend the clergyman. Hume reached an agreement with the publisher John Noon to publish an edition of one thousand copies of the first two Books of the *Treatise*, and the two volumes appeared anonymously (which was not then uncommon, especially for new authors) in January of 1739. They included an "Advertisement" promising that, if this portion of the *Treatise* met with success, it would be completed by "*the examination of* Morals, Politics, and Criticism." The discussion of miracles remained excised from Book 1. Hume, after correcting the proofs, had already returned to Ninewells to await the reviews.

Such reviews as the first two Books of the *Treatise* received in the learned journals of England, France, and Germany—a few of them quite lengthy—were almost entirely uncomprehending and almost entirely negative. Hume responded to the lack of sympathetic reviews by writing *An Abstract of a Book lately Published; Entituled, A Treatise of Human Nature, &c. Wherein The Chief Argument of that Book is farther Illustrated and Explained*. The "chief argument" to which the majority of the *Abstract* is devoted is the deeply original line of thought concerning reasoning from experience and the relation of cause and effect that has as its main conclusions: (i) "we are determined by custom alone to suppose the future conformable to the past"; (ii) "belief consists merely in a peculiar feeling or sentiment"; and (iii) "we have no idea at all of force and energy, and these words are altogether insignificant, or they can mean nothing but that determination of the thought, acquired by habit, to pass from the cause to its usual effect." Originally intended to serve as a review or basis for reviews—the work refers to the officially anonymous author of the *Treatise* in the third person—the *Abstract* was published as an anonymous pamphlet in early 1740.

Also in 1740, Hume returned to London to arrange the publication of Book 3 of the *Treatise* which he had in the meantime been revising and about which he had solicited the advice of Hutcheson, another of the "late philosophers of *England*." The Glasgow professor recommended his own London publisher, Thomas Longman, who brought out the volume in November 1740. This third volume contained no examination of criticism, but it did include an "Appendix" that made a number of additions and corrections to Book 1, some of which were proposed insertions into the main text and some of which were freestanding. (A second edition of the first two volumes was out of the question; under his contract with Noon, Hume was obliged to buy up any unsold copies of the first edition before a second could be issued.) Remarkably, nearly half of the paragraphs of the freestanding portion of the Appendix are devoted to a newfound problem about the section "Of personal identity" (THN 1.4.6) without specifying exactly what that problem is [7.6]. The final volume did no better in garnering sales or approbation than had the first two. Hume memorably reflected years later in "My Own Life" about the reception of the *Treatise*: "It fell *dead-born from the Press*; without reaching such distinction as even to excite a Murmur among the Zealots."

## 1.3 Essays, Moral and Political and Letter from a Gentleman

With his *Treatise* behind him, Hume set about mastering a different literary genre that was becoming increasingly popular and influential: the essay. In 1741, he brought out a volume of *Essays, Moral and Political*, addressing topics in social and personal ethics (with some relation to aesthetics), politics, and political history; in the following year, a second volume of essays under the same title appeared. Among the best-known philosophical essays of the two-volume work—befitting his interest in the psychology of philosophizing—are a set of four "characters," each exemplifying a different approach to happiness that he relates loosely to a different sect of philosophers: "The Epicurean," "The Stoic," "The Platonist," and "The Sceptic." Other notable essays include "that Politicks may be reduc'd to a Science," "Of Superstition and Enthusiasm" (concerning the sources of popular religion in fear and hope, respectively) and "Of the Delicacy of Taste and Passion." Their success, though not extravagant, was nearly immediate; by the middle of 1742, a second edition of the first volume was needed.

In 1744, it appeared somewhat likely that Hume would be appointed to the chair of "Pneumaticks and moral Philosophy" at the University of Edinburgh. ('Pneumaticks' in this context referred not to air, but rather to the mental or spiritual). He had the support of the Lord Provost of Edinburgh and of many friends in the city. The incumbent holder of the chair, Dr. John Pringle, had joined the British army in Flanders in the lucrative post of physician-general and seemed unlikely to return soon. Yet the absent professor resisted resignation and, while negotiations about possible extensions of his leave bogged down, opposition to Hume's candidacy grew. In 1745, an unsigned pamphlet was circulated entitled "A Specimen of the Principles concerning RELIGION and MORALITY, said to be maintain'd in a Book lately publish'd, intituled, *A Treatise of Human Nature*." Its concluding "Sum of the Charge" accused Hume of "Universal Scepticism," "Principles leading to downright Atheism," "Errors concerning the very Being and Existence of a God," "Errors concerning God's being a first Cause, and prime Mover of the Universe," "Denying the Immateriality of the Soul," and "Sapping the Foundations of Morality."

Hume replied to each charge in turn in *A Letter from a Gentleman to his Friend in Edinburgh*. (The "friend" in question was the Lord Provost, but the letter was published as a pamphlet by Henry Home.) He asserted that his skepticism was intended only to produce "Modesty and Humility, with regard to the Operations of our natural Faculties, ... not an universal Doubt"; he denied that the *Treatise* affirmed atheism or errors about God; he insisted that he had not positively denied the immateriality of the soul but only rejected the intelligibility of the question of whether the soul is an immaterial substance, as a consequence of finding that we lack a suitable idea of "substance"; and he rejected the suggestion that his account of the virtues did anything to sap their foundations.

Hume's candidacy was submitted to an advisory vote of the Edinburgh clergy; their negative verdict ended the effort. In the meantime, however, he had accepted an offer to serve in England as tutor to the twenty-five-year-old Marquess (or Marquis) of Annandale, who proved to be an erratic and emotionally troubled young man whose affairs were overseen by a rather mercenary and unpleasant older cousin.

## 1.4 Two Enquiries and Three Essays

The tutorship of the Marquess lasted for slightly more than one difficult year, although a dispute about a final quarter-year salary dragged on for much longer. Just when Hume was at loose ends in London and planning to return to Scotland without employment, he met a distant relative, General James St. Clair, who offered him a position as his secretary on an imminent military expedition to drive the French—then at war with Britain as part of the War of the Austrian Succession—from Canada. Hume accepted the offer immediately. Because of his knowledge of law, he was soon also appointed as the expedition's Judge Advocate, charged with administering military justice. Due to unfavorable winds and varying orders, the expedition was unable to sail for Canada in time to permit a campaign, and it was decided instead to attack France itself somewhere along the coast of Brittany, with the hope of drawing French troops away from Flanders, the main site of battle. At the last moment, the city of l'Orient was selected. The mission proved something of a disaster due to inadequate materials, incompetent military engineers for the artillery, and an almost complete lack of advance intelligence about the local roads and defenses. Although St. Clair's troops laid siege to the city, they were quickly disadvantaged by French reinforcements, and they abandoned the effort, returning to their ships. They did so, as it turned out, just as the municipal leaders were deciding to surrender as demanded; somewhat comically, the surrender found no takers. Years later, the French philosopher and author Voltaire (1694–1778) ridiculed the conduct of the expedition, and Hume composed a defense of his kinsman's conduct.

The end of the ill-fated expedition saw Hume again in London, but when it was decided not to renew the attack against French Canada for the following year, he returned home to Ninewells. He wrote several essays ("Of National Characters," "Of the Original Contract," and "Of Passive Obedience") that were to appear together under the title *Three Essays, Moral and Political*; he also wrote

"Of the Protestant Succession," which was originally intended for the same volume. Even more important, he was at work on the book that first appeared in print as *Philosophical Essays concerning Human Understanding*. In later editions of his collected writings, he changed the title to that by which it is now universally known: *An Enquiry concerning Human Understanding*.

In "My Own Life," Hume described this first *Enquiry* as a "recasting" of the material of Book 1 of the unfortunate *Treatise*, resulting from his realization that the problem with the earlier work had been "more in the manner than in the matter," and that he had made the common mistake of authors of "going too early to the press." Whereas the *Treatise* had ranged as widely as Hume's energetic young intellect, with an often intense and sometimes provocative tone to match, the new work consisted of just twelve sections, all of them urbane and restrained in tenor, and with something of the style of free-standing essays despite their frequently direct dependence on preceding sections. Whereas the *Treatise* had called for a revolutionary new "science of man" and offered many ingenious proposals of mental mechanisms as contributions to it, the *Enquiry* characterizes its starting point as a more modest-sounding "mental geography" that seeks only to distinguish and delineate the different powers and faculties of the human mind; and while it also proposes to uncover at least some of the "hidden springs" of mental operations, it usually presents its psychological theories in strikingly less detail. Its first section begins with a distinction between the "easy and obvious philosophy" that merely paints virtue "in its most amiable colours," on the one hand, and the "accurate and abstruse philosophy" on the other. It then offers an apology for the need to enter, this once, into the difficult and abstruse philosophy, and it promises to make the enterprise as pleasant and untaxing as possible by "care and art, and the avoiding of all unnecessary detail" (EHU 1.17/16). This book, Hume was determined, would have a greater impact than its unfortunate philosophical predecessor.

Accordingly, where the *Treatise* was self-assertive—"abounding throughout with egotisms," one reviewer had written, alluding to the frequent use of the first person—the *Enquiry* is at least superficially restrained and conciliatory. On the topic of free will, for example, what in the *Treatise* had been a rousing defense of the "doctrine of necessity" against the "doctrine of liberty" becomes a "reconciling project" to show that everyone had really always accepted both doctrines, in fact if not in name—a result that Hume achieves chiefly by the simple expedient of re-defining the term 'doctrine of liberty' so as to make it designate a view with which he agrees. While the tone is distinctly more conciliatory, however, the content is more explicitly subversive of established religion. The need to pursue the "difficult and abstruse philosophy," he explains, results from the need to chase "superstition" from its lair—that is, to show that philosophy properly understood does not support the doctrinal tenets of organized religion that it has been recruited to defend.

It should be noted that when Hume criticizes particular Christian beliefs or practices as "superstition," his examples are almost always specifically Catholic. This is, of course, more acceptable to many of his British readers than criticizing Anglicanism or Protestantism would be, and he does hold that Catholicism is more superstitious, as depending on fear, than is Protestantism, which has a greater share of "enthusiasm" derived from hope. He is quite clear, however, that all popular religions involve some mixture of superstition and enthusiasm.

In accordance with Hume's aim of rescuing philosophy from superstition, his implicit principle for the inclusion of topics in the *Enquiry* is stringent: he includes just enough about the mind's operations generally and the nature of causal reasoning in particular to support irreligious conclusions about such topics as free will, the continuity between human reason and animal reason, rewards and punishments in a future state, and the desirability of abandoning both zealotry in general and all claims about the "origin of worlds" in particular. The topic of miracles, cautiously removed from the *Treatise*, receives a prominent place in the *Enquiry*. Published in the spring of 1748 with the author listed as "David Hume, Esq.," the work cemented Hume's reputation as an "infidel." *Three Essays, Moral and Political*, designed to be combinable with a new third edition of *Essays, Moral and Political*, followed it within a few months.

By the time these works appeared, however, Hume was already on the continent, serving once again as secretary to General St. Clair, this time on a military embassy to Vienna and Turin for the purpose of ensuring that troops proposed for the war effort would be provided. A peace treaty late in the year brought the embassy to an end and Hume back to Ninewells. There he worked on a "recasting" of the material of Book 3 of the *Treatise*, which was published in 1751 as *An Enquiry concerning the Principles of Morals*. In this second *Enquiry*, he sets himself two explanatory aims at the outset: (i) to analyze the various traits constitutive of virtue or "personal merit," so as to discover what is common to them all; and, upon that basis, (ii) to "find those universal principles, from which all censure or approbation is ultimately derived" (EPM 1.10/174). The first goal is achieved by the discovery that virtues are mental characteristics that are either useful or immediately agreeable to their possessors or others. The second is achieved by two further discoveries: (a) "principles of sympathy and humanity," whereby human beings are pleased by one another's pleasures and pained by their pains; and (b) the causal consequence that human beings feel distinctive sentiments of moral approbation when considering character traits that are useful or agreeable to their possessors or others, and distinctive sentiments of moral disapprobation when considering character traits that have the opposite features.

While the second *Enquiry* differs from Book 3 of the *Treatise* both in its ordering of topics and in the varying amounts of attention (greater or lesser) they receive, the central discoveries just noted had already featured prominently in Book 3 of the *Treatise*, where Hume had argued in the two sections of its first part that moral distinctions are "not deriv'd from reason" alone but are instead "deriv'd from a moral sense" consisting in the capacity for moral sentiments. In keeping with the newly conciliatory tenor of the *Enquiries*, however, Hume now presents what is largely the same account of moral epistemology by emphasizing the important but distinct and complementary roles of both sentiment and reason in making moral judgments. Furthermore, in keeping with the endeavor of the *Enquiries* to ensure accessibility by "avoiding all unnecessary detail," he defers the close examination of this relation between sentiment and reason to an appendix, where he argues that reason provides information about the consequences of traits, after which sentiment responds favorably or unfavorably to traits on the basis of this information. In keeping with the same endeavor, the *Treatise*'s detailed explanation of the psychological mechanism of sympathy [3.6] is omitted.

Arguably, however, Hume's second Enquiry is at least as irreligious as the first. It locates the source of moral distinctions entirely within human nature, without any mention of duties to, or derived from, God. It criticizes the tendency of religious zealots to favor the unworkable proposal that property should be allocated according to religious merit, rather than in accordance with conventions that are socially useful as a general scheme (EPM 3.23–24/192–193). Most famously, it criticizes the "monkish virtues" of "celibacy, fasting, penance, mortification, self-denial, humility, silence, and solitude" as neither useful nor agreeable to the possessor or others; it is a merit of his account of virtue, he thinks, that we can transfer them to the category of vices (EPM 9.3/270). The final sentence of the entire work refers to the morally distorting effects of "the illusions of religious superstition" (EPM "A Dialogue" 57/343).

In "My Own Life," Hume describes *An Enquiry concerning the Principles of Morals* as "of all my writings, historical, philosophical, or literary, incomparably the best." Unfortunately, he did not give his reasons for this verdict. He may have been judging partly on the basis of its embodiment of his "experiment method": its many historical and literary references, both classical and modern, constitute a particularly clear case of "gleaning up experiments" from the "observation of human life." He may also have been judging partly on the basis of the work's polished and mature literary style. Perhaps the most important element in his evaluation, however, was a judgment of its practical value. Hutcheson had complained about a draft of the *Treatise* that it "wants a certain Warmth in the Cause of Virtue" (LDH 13: I.32), a lack that Hume then sought both to justify and ameliorate in a revised final section of the *Treatise*. Aimed at a broad readership, the recast second Enquiry seeks to explain human morality at the expense of religion; but it also undertakes in its final section to argue in greater detail why morality, far from being an onerous imposition, is instead not only essential to the wellbeing of society as a whole, but also to the greatest happiness of the virtuous individual [8.4].

## 1.5 Political Discourses, History of England, and Four Dissertations

A letter written to his friend Gilbert Elliot in March of 1751 (LDH 72: I.153–57), the same year in which the second Enquiry appeared, shows that Hume was already at work composing a set of dialogues addressing what is now often called "the Design Argument"—that is, the attempt to use the order and seeming adaptation of means to ends in nature to establish the existence of an intelligent deity as the designer of the universe [9.2]. This topic had already been broached, rather obliquely, in the final paragraph of Section 11 of *An Enquiry concerning Human Understanding* ("Of a Particular Providence and of a Future State"). Cautiously, however, and with the advice of friends, he did not publish what became his *Dialogues concerning Natural Religion* during his lifetime.

Later in that year, Hume's brother John married. In order to give the newlyweds sole occupancy of Ninewells, David and his sister Katherine moved to Edinburgh, where they found a flat—though called a "house"—to share. Within a year of his move, he was a candidate for an academic appointment again, this time at the University of Glasgow. The Professor of Moral Philosophy had died, and the twenty-eight-year old Adam Smith, whom Hume had befriended, had been chosen to replace him, leaving Smith's own previous chair of Logic open. While Smith personally preferred Hume as his successor, he was also cautious about the possibility of public opposition to his now somewhat notorious friend. Ecclesiastical resistance indeed developed, and for the second time in Hume's career an academic appointment went to a less qualified candidate. As before, a different position offered itself, but in this case one much preferable to the tutorship of the unfortunate Marquess; through the efforts of his friends, Hume was appointed in 1752 as Keeper of the Faculty of Advocates Library in Edinburgh. The position carried a small salary, but it also carried responsibility for—and hence access to—a substantial library. At about the same time, Hume published his final set of new essays on broadly political topics, *Political Discourses*, which he declared in "My Own Life" to be "the only work of mine that was successful on the first publication ... well received abroad and at home." Of its twelve essays, more than half concern topics—such as money, interest, public credit, taxes, and the balance of trade—that would now be classified as economics or political economy.

Hume had been thinking of trying his hand at history, and the new library appointment provided the perfect opportunity. History was, for him, a rich and instructive source of experiments in the science of man. His *History of England*, while designed as an impartial and fair-minded narrative, nevertheless afforded him ample opportunity to draw instructive lessons from historical events—among them, the value of both liberty and political stability, and the dangers of religious superstition and enthusiasm in politics. The first volume, covering the reign of the first two Stuart kings, was published in Scotland in 1754. He nearly resigned his post as Keeper in the following year in a dispute over three French books he had ordered that were rejected as "indecent." He needed the position for his research, however, and so, to preserve his honor, he arranged for his salary to be given henceforth to the blind Scottish poet Thomas Blacklock, whose work he admired. Sales of the first volume of the *History* had been disappointing, but the second volume, continuing through the subsequent two Stuart monarchs and the Revolution of 1688 that supplanted the second of them, fared considerably better when it was published in London in 1757.

Hume did finally resign his position in that same year, allowing his friend Adam Ferguson (1723–1816)—later to be professor of moral philosophy at the University of Edinburgh and sometimes called "the father of modern sociology"—to take up the post. Ferguson, in turn, granted him continued access to the Library. Later volumes of the *History* took up the Tudor reigns before the accession of the Stuarts and then proceeded through earlier periods back to the first Roman invasion; in all, there were six volumes, the last appearing in 1762. For the remainder of his life, Hume's literary fame, and also his fortune, owed at least as much to this increasingly popular—and ultimately long-lived—work as to any of his more strictly philosophical writings.

Time-consuming as it was, however, the *History* was far from being Hume's only literary endeavor in this period. Beginning in 1753, he brought out, over several years, *Essays and Treatises on Several Subjects*, a four-volume collection of his non-historical writings that omitted the *Treatise* but included his essays and the two *Enquiries*. The work underwent many subsequent editions, with further corrections and additions by the author. In 1755, he endeavored to publish a set of four "dissertations" that he had composed over the previous few years.

The first of these dissertations was "A Natural History of Religion," a work that explicitly foregoes the philosophical question of the "foundation of religion in reason" (the question taken up in the then-unpublished *Dialogues concerning Natural Religion*) to address instead that of the "foundation of religion in human nature." In it, Hume locates the psychological origins of religion—that is, belief in "invisible intelligent power"—in the passions of hope and especially fear, and he argues that the original form of religion is a polytheistic one with very little moral elevation of its deities. Monotheism (which he calls simply "theism") is, on this account, a natural later development arising from the human need to magnify the degree of praise of a deity. Yet because such a supreme being is difficult to imagine and engage with, monotheistic religions tend naturally to lapse back toward polytheistic conceptions of divinity (as for example, he suggests, in the role of Mary and the saints in Roman Catholicism) in what he dubs "the flux and reflux of polytheism and theism." Hume then compares monotheism and polytheism in a number of different dimensions and includes a penultimate section on the "Bad Influence of Popular Religions on Morality."

The second dissertation, "Of the Passions," is a compact "recasting" of Book 2 of the *Treatise*. The third dissertation, "Of Tragedy," addresses the puzzle of how the artist's production of sympathetic grief, fear, and other unpleasant passions in an audience can enhance their aesthetic pleasure; Hume argues, on the basis of many analogous phenomena, that aesthetic pleasure at the artistry of the piece can swallow up and "convert" to itself the emotional force of these passions. The final dissertation was originally to be a work that is described in correspondence variously as "some Considerations previous to Geometry & Natural Philosophy" and "on the Metaphysical Principles of Geometry." A conversation with a mathematician friend convinced him to withdraw the work, however, and no copy has ever been found.

Because his publisher judged the remaining three dissertations too short to make up a volume, Hume offered to include two additional essays, "Of Suicide" and "Of the Immortality of the Soul," that he had not previously intended to publish. The former argues that suicide can often be "free of imputation of guilt and blame," as violating no duty to God, to others, or to oneself. The latter considers metaphysical, moral, and physical arguments bearing on the immortality of the soul and finds the arguments against more persuasive than those in favor. Copies of *Five Dissertations* were duly printed in 1756 and a few advance copies circulated. At the last moment, however, Hume and his publisher decided not to go forward with the volume as then constituted. He wrote later only that he had decided to suppress its two last-minute additions "from my abundant Prudence," but other contemporary correspondence refers to a possible threat of prosecution by the Lord Chancellor.

Lacking, once again, enough dissertations to make a book, Hume wrote an entirely new essay, "Of the Standard of Taste." His deep interest in literary and artistic criticism had been more than manifest from his earliest correspondence, his advertisement to the *Treatise*, his essays, and "Of Tragedy"—not to mention his frequent claims, from the *Treatise* onward, that virtue is a kind of moral beauty, and that both virtue and beauty are discerned by distinctive sentiments of taste. This extended essay, however, constitutes his most sustained and foundational contribution to what is now called aesthetics. It locates the proper "standard" for applying terms of aesthetic evaluation in the responses of "true critics": those who possess "strong sense, united to delicate sentiment, improved by practice, perfected by comparison, and cleared of all prejudice" (EMPL I.23: 241). In most cases of disagreement about matters of aesthetic taste, he affirms, one verdict is superior to the other; but there is nevertheless considerable room for blameless disagreement in relative valuation where the differences result simply from differences of individual temperament among true critics. *Four Dissertations*, containing "Of the Standard of Taste," finally appeared in 1757. An unauthorized French translation of the two suppressed essays "Of Suicide" and "Of the Immortality of the Soul"—derived from one of the advance copies of the earlier suppressed version of *Five Dissertations*—appeared in 1770, but no English version appeared until after Hume's death.

## 1.6 *A Concise Account* and *Dialogues concerning Natural Religion*

Hume spent a considerable amount of time in London in 1758–59 and again in 1761–62, doing historical research and overseeing publications, particularly the later volumes of the History of England. In 1763, however, with the History complete and the Seven Years War with France recently concluded, he received an invitation to attend the newly installed British Ambassador to France, Lord Hertford, with the prospect of being formally appointed Secretary of the Embassy upon the resignation of the unsatisfactory but well-connected incumbent Secretary. He accepted the invitation and upon his arrival in Paris was immediately greeted with gratifying popular acclaim. Whereas the irreligious character of his philosophical writings had always made his situation in Edinburgh somewhat uncomfortable—during the late 1750s there had been efforts to have him formally excommunicated from the Church of Scotland, which would have been socially and politically discomfiting—he found his writings and ideas much in favor in free-thinking France, where he was regarded by many as the greatest British man of letters of the day. (Indeed, it seems likely that his literary popularity in France was part of the rationale for appointing him to the Embassy in the first place, at a time when Britain was seeking to renew good relations.) Hume soon found himself personally beloved for his wit, honesty, benevolence, and amiability as well. He became friends with the leading intellectuals collectively called the "*philosophes*"—including Jean le Rond d'Alembert (1717–1783), Denis Diderot (1713–1784), and Paul-Henri Thiry, Baron d'Holbach (1723–1789)—and was enormously popular in Parisian *salon* society, in which he was known as "*le bon David.*" He formed a particularly close personal relationship with the Comtesse de Boufflers—the organizer and hostess of a particularly important intellectual salon—that endured for the rest of his life. After twenty months, Lord Hertford was appointed Viceroy of Ireland, and Hume, who had only recently attained the promised formal title of Secretary of the Embassy, became its *chargé d'affaires* as well, effectively managing British diplomacy in France for four months until the arrival of the new Ambassador.

Just when Hume was preparing to leave France, the celebrated author and political philosopher Jean-Jacques Rousseau (1712–1778) found himself again in political trouble over his writings. Although they had never met, they had many mutual friends, and Hume offered to take steps to ensure his wellbeing. Accordingly, Hume and Rousseau sailed together for England, where Hume set up his new acquaintance in a country house and helped to arrange for a pension from King George III. Rousseau was initially delighted by Hume's friendship. Sensitive, impetuous, and deeply suspicious by nature, however, he soon decided, quite without justification—in part as the result of the publication in the English press of critical pieces in which Hume had played no real part—that his philosophical protector was in fact part of a great conspiracy with d'Alembert to damage his reputation. Rousseau made wild accusations in letters to Hume and others, and Hume felt compelled to send a complete narrative including the text of the relevant correspondence to d'Alembert, giving him permission to publish it if he thought necessary. D'Alembert did so at once, and an English version, *A Concise and Genuine Account of the Dispute between Mr. Hume and Mr. Rousseau*, appeared in the following month. Although Hume consistently followed his rule of never replying to attacks on his writings, he felt he could not let Rousseau's assault on his character remain unanswered. He declared Rousseau to be blamelessly mad, but the two never reconciled.

Although Hume returned to Edinburgh in 1766, public service called again the following year, when he was invited to serve as Undersecretary of State for the Northern Department by Lord Hertford's brother, General Seymour Conway. Hume judged that he could not properly refuse, and so he returned to London. His duties were important but not arduous, and he typically worked from ten in the morning until three in the afternoon. The domain of the Northern Department included not only foreign affairs but also the home affairs of Scotland. Ironically, he was now in a position to further the interests of the moderate wing of the clergy in Edinburgh, among whom he counted a number of friends, and he composed the annual "King's Letter" to the General Assembly of the Church of Scotland—the same body that less than a decade earlier had been considering his excommunication. He held the position for a year, until General Conway resigned, but he remained in London for another year-and-a-half, retiring once more to Edinburgh only in 1769, now "opulent," as he put it, from the sale of his books combined with his earnings and pensions from government service. A new section of the city was being erected, and he built a house for himself in the "New Town" on St. David Street (a name that popular lore later came to treat as a reference—ironic or affectionate—to him).

In his final years, Hume was surrounded by his many friends in Edinburgh and occupied himself with revising and polishing his *History of England* and *Essays and Treatises on Several Subjects* for new editions. James Beattie (1735–1803)—a professor at Aberdeen and a proponent of the "Common Sense" school of philosophy originated by Thomas Reid (1710–96)—published *An Essay on the Nature and Immutability of Truth; in Opposition to Sophistry and Scepticism*, which was largely an attack on Hume's philosophy, quoting extensive portions of *A Treatise of Human Nature*. Hume had amicable relations with Reid despite Reid's sharp philosophical criticism, but Beattie's attack was personal and his tone abusive. In response, Hume added an "Author's Advertisement" to the second volume of *Essays and Treatises*—the volume containing the two *Enquiries*—asking that the later work alone be taken to represent his philosophy:

> Most of the principles, and reasonings, contained in this volume, were published in a work in three volumes, called *A Treatise of Human Nature*: A work which the Author had projected before he left College, and which he wrote and published not long after. But not finding it successful, he was sensible of his error in going to the press too early, and he cast the whole anew in the following pieces, where some negligences in his former reasoning and more in the expression, are, he hopes, corrected. Yet several writers who have honored the Author's Philosophy with answers, have taken care to direct all their batteries against that juvenile work, which the author never acknowledged, and have affected to triumph in any advantages, which, they imagined, they had obtained over it: A practice very contrary to all rules of candour and fair-dealing, and a strong instance of those polemical artifices which a bigotted zeal thinks itself authorised to employ. Henceforth, the Author desires, that the following Pieces may alone be regarded as containing his philosophical sentiments and principles.[5]

This, he declared to his publisher, was "a compleat Answer to Dr. Reid and to that bigotted silly Fellow, Beattie" (LDH 509: II.301). It was "compleat" not because it was comprehensive in detail, but because it was general and the only answer he intended to give. Its comparison of the *Treatise* with the *Enquiries* is compatible with his remark in "My Own Life" that the lack of success of the former "proceeded more from the manner than the matter." Because he did not quantify the "negligences in his former reasoning," however, or describe how misleading those "of the expression" might be, it remains a disputed question whether the *Treatise* or the *Enquiries* should be taken to be the better representation of his philosophical views—and whether the omission from the latter of many claims and arguments contained in the former should be interpreted as indicating any dissatisfaction with them.

A particularly important object of revision in the final years of Hume's life was his *Dialogues concerning Natural Religion*; his final revisions were made shortly before his death. He had asked the reluctant Adam Smith to oversee their posthumous publication, but in a codicil to his will he left the manuscript to their mutual publisher, William Strahan, with a request that it be published within two years of his death. Publication of the two previously suppressed essays, "Of Suicide" and "Of the Immortality of the Soul" was left to Strahan's discretion. Hume also instructed, however, that his nephew and namesake (John's son, later a professor of Scots law at Edinburgh) should bring out the *Dialogues* if it had not already appeared within two-and-half years of his death. In the published *Dialogues*, a young man reports in a letter on discussions he has heard among Demea (a religious rationalist, whose views are broadly comparable to Clarke's), Cleanthes (a religious empiricist, whose views are broadly comparable to Butler's), and Philo (an empiricist skeptic, closest to Hume). The existence of a Deity, understood minimally as a first cause or causes of order in the universe, is formally granted by all parties to the *Dialogues*; the questions at issue among them concern the nature of that cause—particularly its supposed intelligence and moral goodness.

Hume's health began to decline in 1772. By 1775, he was losing weight rapidly from what he called "a disorder in my bowels"—evidently intestinal cancer. In April of 1776, he wrote "My Own Life" and then undertook a trip to Bath to take the waters. In London, he visited, for diagnostic purposes, the same Dr. John Pringle whose professorship at Edinburgh had once been the object of his ambition.

The trip provided no useful treatment, although it did become apparent that he now had a tumor on his liver as well. Back in Edinburgh, he died on August 25. The leading light of what came to be called "the Scottish Enlightenment," he was buried on Calton Hill, beneath a monument for which he left money in his will. The *Dialogues* were published under the direction of his nephew David in 1779.

## 1.7 Conclusion

Because of Hume's known irreligion, there was considerable popular curiosity about how he would face his death. Soon afterwards, Adam Smith—whose recently published *Wealth of Nations* Hume had read and praised to Boswell—published a letter, addressed to William Strahan, in which he recounted the philosopher's final days. He wrote, in part:

> It is with a real, though a very melancholy pleasure, that I sit down to give some account of the behavior of our late excellent friend, Mr. Hume, during his last illness … .
>
> Mr. Hume's magnanimity and firmness were such, that his most affectionate friends knew that they hazarded nothing in talking or writing to him as to a dying man, and that so far from being hurt by this frankness, he was rather pleased and flattered by it … . But, though Mr. Hume always talked of his approaching dissolution with great cheerfulness, he never affected to make any parade of his magnanimity. He never mentioned the subject but when the conversation naturally led to it, and never dwelt longer upon it than the course of the conversation happened to require: it was a subject, indeed, which occurred pretty frequently, in consequence of the inquiries which his friends, who came to see him, naturally made concerning the state of his health.

He concluded by offering his own summary sketch of Hume's character:

> Thus died our most excellent and never to be forgotten friend; concerning whose philosophical opinions men will, no doubt, judge variously, every one approving or condemning them,

according as they happen to coincide or disagree with his own; but concerning whose character and conduct there can scarce be a difference of opinion. His temper, indeed, seemed to be more happily balanced, if I may be allowed such an expression, than that perhaps of any other man I have ever known. Even in the lowest state of his fortune, his great and necessary frugality never hindered him from exercising, upon proper occasions, acts both of charity and generosity. It was a frugality founded, not upon avarice, but upon the love of independency. The extreme gentleness of his nature never weakened either the firmness of his mind or the steadiness of his resolutions. His constant pleasantry was the genuine effusion of good nature and good humour, tempered with delicacy and modesty, and without even the slightest tincture of malignity, so frequently the disagreeable source of what is called wit in other men. It never was the meaning of his raillery to mortify; and, therefore, far from offending, it seldom failed to please and delight, even those who were the objects of it. To his friends, who were frequently the objects of it, there was not perhaps any one of all his great and amiable qualities, which contributed more to endear his conversation. And that gaiety of temper, so agreeable in society, but which is so often accompanied with frivolous and superficial qualities, was in him certainly attended with the most severe application, the most extensive learning, the greatest depth of thought, and a capacity in every respect the most comprehensive. Upon the whole, I have always considered him, both in his lifetime and since his death, as approaching as nearly to the idea of a perfectly wise and virtuous man, as perhaps the nature of human frailty will permit.
(EMPL "Letter from Adam Smith": xliii–xlix; LDH: I "Appendix L")

Hume's philosophy was an expression not only of his beliefs but also of his passions and of his character.

## Notes

1 John Jamieson (1895) *Jamieson's Dictionary of the Scottish Language*, abridged by John Johnstone, revised and enlarged by John Longmuir, Edinburgh: W. P. Nimmo, Hay, and Mitchell: 596.

2 James Boswell (1931) *The Private Papers of James Boswell*, twelve volumes, edited by Geoffrey Scott and Frederick A. Pottle. Oxford: Oxford University Press: XII.227–32.
3 Hutcheson had published his *Inquiry into the Original of our Ideas of Beauty and Virtue* in 1725; he became Professor of Moral Philosophy at the University of Glasgow in 1729.
4 Norman Kemp Smith (1941) *The Philosophy of David Hume*. Houndmills and New York: Palgrave I.1: 12–13.
5 The advertisement is reproduced at the beginning of many editions of the first Enquiry, including EHU.

# Further reading

Emerson, Roger (2009) *Essays on Hume, Medical Men, and the Scottish Enlightenment: Industry, Knowledge and Humanity*, Aldershot: Ashgate. (See especially the essay "Hume's Intellectual Development Part II," which very usefully supplements the essay of M. A. Stewart cited below.)

Guimarães, Livia (2008) "Skeptical Tranquility and Hume's Manner of Death," *Journal of Scottish Philosophy* 6: 115–34. (An illuminating account of Hume's death in relation to his irreligious philosophy and the reactions of his contemporaries.)

Kemp Smith, Norman (2005) *The Philosophy of David Hume*, introduction by Don Garrett, Houndmills and New York: Palgrave Macmillan, first edition published 1941. (A classic comprehensive commentary on Hume's philosophy.)

Mossner, Earnest Campbell (1980) *The Life of David Hume*, second edition, Oxford: Oxford University Press. (The standard biography, somewhat dated but thorough and enjoyable; the present chapter owes a great deal to it.)

Norton, David Fate and Mary Norton (2007) *A Treatise of Human Nature*, Volume 2: *History of the Treatise*, Oxford: Clarendon Press. (An authoritative account of the composition, publication, and reception of the *Treatise*, by the editors of the standard scholarly edition.)

Russell, Paul (2008) *The Riddle of Hume's Treatise: Skepticism, Naturalism, and Irreligion*, New York: Oxford University Press. (Contains a rich and detailed account of the religious context and irreligious content of Hume's writings, with particular emphasis on the influence of Thomas Hobbes and on the failed appointment at the University of Edinburgh.)

Stewart, M. A. (2005) "Hume's Early Intellectual Development, 1711–1752," in *Impression of Hume*, edited by Marina Frasca-Spada and P. J. E. Kail, Oxford: Oxford University Press. (An essential contribution to the understanding of Hume's development as an author and thinker.)

# Two
## Perceptions and their principles

Put in the most general terms, Hume's philosophical project is to investigate the operations of the human mind—employing, inevitably, many of those very operations—so as to shed light on an extraordinarily wide range of important philosophical questions, both in the philosophy of mind and far beyond. In conducting such an investigation, it is essential to understand the entities on which those operations take place and the faculties or powers of the mind by which they take place. The latter are the topic of Chapter Three, while the former constitute the topic of the present chapter.

Like many of his predecessors, including Descartes and Locke, Hume holds: (i) that conscious mental life requires the immediate presence to the mind of certain entities on which mental operations are performed; and (ii) that experience or thought of things that are not immediately present to the mind is accomplished through the capacity of at least some of these entities to *represent* those other things or to be in some other way *of* or *about* them. Whereas his predecessors typically use 'idea' as their most general term for these entities, however, Hume employs instead the term 'perception' for this purpose, limiting 'idea' to a subset of them.

At the outset of his investigation in the *Treatise*, and again in Section 2 of the first *Enquiry*, Hume distinguishes perceptions into "impressions" and (what *he* calls) "ideas." He also distinguishes all perceptions—both impressions and ideas—into "simple" and "complex," and he further distinguishes impressions into "impressions of sensation" and "impressions of reflection." As he proceeds, he propounds four general principles governing perceptions, each of which he later invokes in important philosophical arguments. Hume's four principles of perceptions also facilitate his explanations of several different kinds of ideas. These kinds of ideas include the complex ideas of "substances," "modes," and "relations." They also include "abstract ideas"—that is, *concepts*—which allow thought to achieve generality so that the mind can think of kinds of qualities and things. He sees his explanation of abstract ideas, inspired in part by Berkeley, as a fundamental contribution to the science of man, and he refers back to it quite often. It is very helpful to keep it in mind when seeking to understand his explanations of mental—and especially conceptual—phenomena.

In the dense and neglected but nevertheless important second part of *Treatise* Book 1, Hume explains space and time as "manners" in which some perceptions, and the things represented by them, are arranged or (in his terminology) "disposed." A fundamental question for seventeenth- and eighteenth-century natural philosophers concerned the metaphysics of space and time: Are space and time merely relations among real things, or are they real things in their own right standing in relations of *co-location* (that is, being in the same place) with other things? A further question was whether finite portions of space and time are infinitely divisibility, a question to which an affirmative answer seemed to many—notably Pierre Bayle (1647–1706)—both mandated by mathematics and yet absurd. Hume's treatment of space and time is intended to answer both questions and to show in the process how his science of man can provide a new foundation to "all the sciences," even "Mathematics and Natural Philosophy" [1.2].

Although the *Treatise* and first *Enquiry* discuss perceptions as mental representations at considerable length, neither work addresses in full generality the question of how some—but not all—perceptions are able to represent things at all. Yet Hume's doctrine, shared with Berkeley, that many perceptions of sight and touch are literally spatially extended provides an important clue, and he says enough in the course of his discussions of various kinds of ideas and impressions to enable us to extract his implicit answer to this crucial question about them.

The precise character of Hume's main distinctions among perceptions, the evidential support of his basic principles about them, the consistency and coherence of his account of their spatial and temporal arrangement, and the content of his views about their representational capacities are all matters of great importance in understanding his philosophy. As is often the case with Hume, however, all have also been matters of some interpretive disagreement. Philosophical novices may wish to survey the discussions of space, time, and mental representation briefly and return to the details later.

## 2.1 Basic distinctions among perceptions

Impressions, for Hume, include "all our sensations, passions, and emotions, as they make their first appearance in the soul," whereas ideas are "the faint images of these in thinking and reasoning" (THN 1.1.1.1/1; see also EHU 2.1–3/17–18). For example, he remarks, "all of the perceptions excited by the present [printed] discourse" are ideas except for those arising immediately from sight and touch, plus any "immediate pleasure or uneasiness" the discourse may produce. This difference between "feeling" (with impressions) and "thinking" (with ideas), he claims, consists essentially in different degrees of what he variously calls "liveliness," "force," "vivacity," "solidity," "firmness," and "steadiness."

Some of the many terms that Hume employs interchangeably for this defining difference between impressions and ideas—for example, 'liveliness' and 'vivacity'—may seem descriptive of an immediately experienced feature or character of perceptions, without any obvious causal implications. Others—such as 'force' and 'steadiness'—seem to many readers more suggestive of causal powers. Hume is very clear, however, that the mind never directly perceives causal power or efficacy as a feature in the causes themselves [4.3, 6.3]; instead, powers can only be recognized through the repeated experience of causes being followed by their effects. Moreover, he seems to take for granted that we can typically discern merely by immediate consciousness or memory whether a perception is an impression or an idea, without the need for any inferences about causal consequences. It seems evident, therefore, that by his ready interchange of a variety of terms he means to capture, in the first instance, a particular immediately experienced feature of perceptions, but one that, as one can soon discover from repeated experience, also gives those perceptions possessing it greater causal weight and influence in the mind. The mind experiences a somewhat similar feeling, but one having much less causal force and steadiness, in "poetical enthusiasms" (THN 1.3.10.10–12/630–31).

In calling his defining difference "vivacity," Hume sometimes suggests an analogy with visual brightness, but the analogy will seriously mislead if it is mistaken for an identity. In fact, the analogy can mislead in two different ways. First, brightness is a feature only of visual perceptions, whereas all kinds of perceptions are susceptible to differences in mental vivacity on his view. Second, two visual perceptions can exhibit the very same degree of brightness of color while still differing very markedly in their mental vivacity—as, indeed, an impression and an idea of the same bright shade of blue, for example, are bound to do. The point of his analogy is simply that, just as two colors can differ in brightness while still having the same hue (and, as color theorists would say, the same saturation), two perceptions can differ in vivacity while still having all of their other immediately experienced features in common. In order to avoid these sources of confusion and for the sake of both consistency and convenience, I will use Hume's equally common 'liveliness' as the primary term for this immediately experienced feature of some perceptions.

When introducing the distinction between impressions and ideas in the *Treatise*, Hume remarks that, although these two kinds of perceptions are in general "easily distinguished, it is not impossible in particular instances they may very nearly approach each other." In sleep, fever, or madness, for example, ideas may "approach to" impressions, whereas some impressions are so "faint and low that we cannot distinguish them from ideas" (THN 1.1.1.1/2; see also EHU 2.1/17, which omits the instance of sleep and the claim that some impressions are faint and low). If Hume grants that some impressions are genuinely *equal* to some ideas in degree of liveliness, that would of course undermine his previous claim that the difference between the two kinds of perceptions consists in a difference of that very feature. That, in turn, would leave us to look for the basis of the distinction in some other difference, such as a difference of causal origin, accompaniments, or causal consequences.

Upon closer inspection, it may be observed that Hume does not explicitly grant the equality. Ideas could "approach" impressions without ever quite equaling them, after all, and it may be beyond one's capacity to "distinguish" in a clear way small differences between fleeting perceptions even if such differences do actually exist. The first *Enquiry* states that the inability to distinguish impressions from ideas is a result of a mind's becoming "disordered," which may suggests an inability to keep track of genuine differences.

Nevertheless, as Hume's initial reference to a "first appearance in the soul" suggests, impressions and ideas do typically differ in their types of causal *origin*, in his view. Furthermore, in order to explain how there can be "ideas of ideas," he remarks, "In thinking of our past thoughts we not only delineate out the objects, of which we were thinking, but also conceive the action of the mind in the meditation, that certain *je-ne-scai-quoi*, of which 'tis impossible to give any definition or description, but which every one sufficiently understands" (THN 1.3.8.16/106). If this "*je-ne-scai-quoi*" is unique to ideas ("thinking"), its presence may serve as an indication of the presence of an idea, as contrasted with an impression. Again, impressions and ideas do also differ to some extent in their causal *consequences*, in his view, and he is clearly interested in the ways in which the causes and effects of similar perceptions tend to differ with degrees of liveliness, even if there turn out to be a few explicable exceptions to these correlations. Because it is at least difficult to see how Hume could be completely confident that fever and madness *always* involve differences of liveliness too small to be clearly distinguished, it may be reasonable to suggest that he is at least willing to use similarities and differences of causal origin, of accompanying feelings, or of causal consequences to help draw the distinction between impressions and ideas in the relatively rare cases of borderline degrees of felt liveliness.

Turning now to a second crucial distinction, Hume declares that simple perceptions "are such as admit of no distinction nor separation," while "the complex are the contrary to these, and may be distinguished into parts" (THN 1.1.1.2/2). Locke describes his own distinction between simple and complex ideas in similar terms, and many readers have taken Hume simply to be adopting Locke's distinction without modification. In fact, however, Hume applies his own simple/complex distinction to perceptions in a quite different way that often yields quite different results. He offers as an example the complex perception of an apple, which has perceptions of its "colour, taste, and smell" as parts, just as Locke might, but it later emerges that the perception of the color of the *whole* apple must itself be composed of individual perceptions of the color of spatial parts of the apple [2.4, 2.5]. Similarly, whereas Locke declares the idea of "extension" (that is, spatial extent) to be simple, Hume treats it as complex ("compound") because it must consist of spatial parts (THN 1.2.3.12–15/38 and THN 1.4.4.8/228; see THN 1.1.6.2/16 for evidence of the equivalence of 'complex' and 'compound'). Furthermore, Locke treats some ideas—such as those of existence and unity—as simple and yet inseparable from others, whereas Hume denies that any simple perceptions are inseparable (THN 1.1.7.3/18) and emphasizes that one simple idea can have multiple aspects of resemblance with others and thereby represent many different classes of resembling things (THN 1.1.7.17–18/24–25). The simple/complex distinction plays an especially important role in Hume's treatments of the *Separability Principle* [2.2], "distinctions of reason" [2.4], space and time [2.5], and causal "necessary connexions" [6.3]. (See also the discussion of complex abstract ideas and *semantic simplicity* [4.2–4].)

In contrast with the distinctions drawn thus far, the further distinction that Hume draws between impressions of sensation and impressions of reflection is an entirely causal one. Impressions of sensation "arise from unknown causes," whereas impressions of reflection "are deriv'd in a great measure from our ideas" (THN 1.1.2.1/7–8). That is, impressions of reflection, unlike impressions of sensation, are feelings that typically arise as reactions to previous ideas, although Hume does not rule out the possibility that on some occasions they may be produced as immediate reactions to other impressions. Impressions of reflection include the various passions—such as love, hatred, pride, humility, joy, grief, hope, fear, desire, and aversion—as well as such other responsive or reactive feelings as "volition" (that is, the feeling of willing), aesthetic pleasure and unease, sentiments of moral approbation and disapprobation, and, in addition, the "impression of necessary connexion" to which he assigns a prominent place in the processes of causal inference and causal judgment.

Hume's reference to impressions of sensation as having "unknown causes" should not be read as a casual endorsement of radical skepticism about the very existence of an external physical world. From the very beginning of both the *Treatise* and the first *Enquiry*, he presupposes that physical objects ("bodies" in a general sense) are typically the external causes of sensations through their effects on human sense organs, and he confirms at the beginning of Book 2 of the *Treatise* that impressions of sensation "arise in the soul, from the constitution of the [human] body, from the animal spirits, or from the applications of objects to the external organs" (THN 2.1.1.1/275 and EHU 4.1/25; [3.5]). He can nevertheless characterize the causes of sensations as "unknown" for two reasons. First, he sets an extremely high standard for "knowledge" in his strict technical sense. It must depend solely upon unchangeable "relations of ideas" themselves, so that the denial of what is known is absurd and inconceivable. Knowledge in this sense cannot extend to "matters of fact and real existence"—whose denials are always conceivable—and non-trivial instances of it are largely confined to mathematics (THN 1.3.1.1–5/69–71; [3.3]). In practice, he does not always restrict himself to this usage; throughout his writings, he often uses 'know' and 'knowledge' in a looser and more colloquial way. Nevertheless, because causal questions always concern "matters of fact and real existence," he holds that we cannot "know" in the strict technical sense that our sensations are not produced in us directly by divine volition or some other non-physical cause. (Indeed, we could not know in this sense even that they really had causes.) Second, the specific mechanical and physiological causes of sensations are complex, difficult to penetrate, and belong "more to anatomists and natural philosophers than to moral" philosophers such as himself (THN 1.1.2.1/8); in this respect, they are "unknown" even in the looser and more colloquial sense.

Hume appeals to differences of liveliness not only to draw the distinction between impressions and ideas, but also to help draw two crucial distinctions within the realm of ideas. First, while they lack the very high degree of liveliness possessed by impressions, "ideas of memory" nevertheless typically have more liveliness than do mere "ideas of the imagination" [3.2]. In addition, ideas of memory are more constrained in the temporal and spatial arrangement of their elements: parts of ideas can be varied only by the imagination, with a resulting loss of liveliness (THN 1.1.3.1–4/ 8–10). (In THN 1.3.4–5, he uses the surprising phrase 'impressions of memory', but he means by this that memory ideas have enough liveliness to serve in place of present impressions in the belief-supporting respect there under discussion.) Second, while typically lacking the quite high degree of liveliness possessed by memories, "beliefs" are ideas that nevertheless have significant degrees of liveliness, something that ideas merely entertained without any belief lack (THN 1.3.7 and EHU 5). That memories and beliefs are perceptions having a feature in *some* degree that impressions have in a *greater* degree is one of Hume's most distinctive doctrines. It helps him to explain both how believing something is psychologically similar to seeing or otherwise perceiving it and how belief has its ultimate source in impressions. It also helps to explain why belief is not always responsive to reasoning in the ways we expect [7.3].

As his definitions suggest, Hume regards memories and beliefs as being, in the first instance, lively ideas that occur in the mind consciously at particular times. However, he also recognizes that the mind has standing dispositions to have certain memories and beliefs recurrently when prompted. In this sense, one may be said to always believe or remember even things that are not always present in thought.

## 2.2 Principles of perceptions

After distinguishing first between impressions and ideas, and then between simple and complex perceptions, Hume propounds what he calls "the first principle I establish in the science of human nature" and what is now often called his *Copy Principle*:

> [Copy Principle:] That all our simple ideas in their first appearance, are derived from simple impressions, which are correspondent to them, and which they exactly represent.
> (THN 1.1.1.7/4)

Because all complex ideas are themselves composed of simple ideas, this principle requires that all ideas whatever, whether simple or complex, are either derived from corresponding impressions or are composed of simpler ideas that are each so derived. This includes, he notes, ideas of ideas, which are derived from ideas that are themselves derived from impressions.

In Hume's account of the mind, all mental representations are perceptions, and "experience" (in a sense that is contrasted with mere thought) consists in the having of impressions. The Copy Principle therefore undergirds one aspect of Hume's empiricism described in the Introduction to this book: namely, concep empiricism, or the endeavor to trace all mental representations to origins in experience. An earlier expression of this same aspect of empiricism is Locke's repeated denial in *An Enquiry concerning Human Understanding* that there are any "innate ideas." Hume characterizes the Copy Principle as a clearer and more comprehensible version of this denial (EHU 2.9n/22), and he endorses the general outline of Locke's account of the idea of God as arising from the combination and augmentation in degree of ideas we acquire from experience of our own minds (EHU 2.6/19). Hume's confidence in concept empiricism stands in direct opposition to the views of many important seventeenth-century philosophers, including Descartes, Malebranche, Benedict [Baruch] de Spinoza (1632–1677), and Gottfried Wilhelm Leibniz (1646–1716), according to whom there are many powerful ideas pertaining to "the intellect" that are not derived from experience, and which can often represent things and qualities that ideas derived merely from experience cannot.

The Copy Principle features prominently in many important Humean arguments—including arguments concerning abstract ideas [2.4], space and time [2.5], causation [4.3, 6.3], substance [3.1, 3.5], and the self [3.1, 7.6]. Hume also uses it to support a methodological directive to trace ideas or purported ideas to impressions from which they are or would be derived. In some cases, the purpose of the tracing is clarificatory: we should trace the ideas with which we reason to the impressions from which they are derived, because the "clarity" of the impression will bestow a like clarity on both the idea and the reasoning (THN 1.2.3.1/33; THN 1.3.2.4/74–75; and EHU 7.4/62). For Hume, an idea that is not "clear" is instead "obscure," with the result that the mind is unable to "tell exactly [its] nature and composition" (THN 1.2.3.1/33).

Presumably, then, rendering ideas and reasonings clearer will allow the mind to form more accurate ideas of them and hence to think more accurately about them. In other cases, the purpose of the attempted tracing is confirmatory: if we suspect that a word is being used without signifying any idea, and hence without any meaning, we should seek for an impression from which the supposed idea could be derived; the failure to find one may then serve to "confirm our suspicion" that there is no such idea (EHU 2.9/22).

Hume offers two complementary arguments for the Copy Principle, both drawn from empirical observation. The first is that whenever someone has a given simple idea, it will be found upon investigation that the individual has first had the corresponding simple impression. The second is that whenever someone lacks a given simple impression—whether because of a defect in the relevant sense organs or simply because of lack of opportunity—the individual will also lack the corresponding simple idea.

Having proposed and defended the Copy Principle, Hume immediately goes on, in both the Treatise and the first Enquiry, to concede a possible exception to it: the famous "missing shade of blue." He imagines that someone has experienced every shade of blue but one, and that the experienced shades are all arranged in order from darkest to lightest. In such a circumstance, he readily allows, the individual would be aware that there is a shade missing from the array and would be able to imagine it—that is, form an idea of it—without having had the precisely corresponding impression. He concludes his discussion of the example by remarking that "the instance is so particular and singular, that 'tis scarce worth our observing, and does not merit that for it alone we should alter our general maxim" (THN 1.1.1.10/6 and EHU 2.8/21).

This seemingly rather insouciant treatment of the proposed counter-example—made all the more so by his ignoring the prospect of parallel examples concerning audible pitch and other scalable qualities associated with other sense modalities—has unsettled many readers and has prompted considerable critical commentary. Hume's lack of alarm is understandable, however. The Copy Principle is, for him, an empirical generalization (in accordance with one common meaning of his term 'maxim') in the science of human nature about the causal relations among perceptions of different degrees of liveliness, some of which are the basis of thought; it is not, as has sometimes been proposed, a strict *a priori* constraint on the possibility of meaningful thought itself [10.3].[1] Modest deviations from it are therefore not out of the question, and this one is readily explained by the mind's observed but quite limited capacity to vary even simple ideas in a specific discernible qualitative dimension of similarity (such as darker to lighter) when assisted by many surrounding examples arrayed in that dimension. Moreover, his many philosophical uses of the Copy Principle prove upon examination to require at most: (i) that simple ideas always be derived from impressions that correspond to them by resembling them either exactly or *almost* exactly; and (ii) that there be possible impressions corresponding exactly to those ideas. The missing shade of blue—like the parallel modest exceptions that should presumably be granted for other sense modalities—do not seriously threaten the satisfaction of these requirements. What would threaten his philosophical uses of the Copy Principle would be the existence of purely "intellectual" ideas—for example, purely intellectual ideas of God, power, substance, or "vacuum" (that is, empty space)—that do not resemble, and whose elements do not resemble, any impressions at all.

If the Copy Principle is Hume's first principle in the science of human nature, then what is now often called his *Separability Principle* has a strong claim to be the second. This is so even though it appears explicitly only in the *Treatise*, where its earliest formulation reads:

> [Separability Principle:] Whatever objects are different are distinguishable, and whatever objects are distinguishable are separable by the thought and imagination.
> (THN 1.1.7.3/18)

Hume does not follow this statement of the principle with any defense of it; instead, he describes it as something that has already been "observ'd" earlier in the *Treatise*. This description is evidently an allusion to his brief discussion a few sections earlier of a closely related "principle of the liberty of the imagination to transpose and change its ideas" (THN 1.1.3.4/10). While he makes several remarks in support of this principle of imaginative liberty with respect to the separation and recombination of ideas, the most important is that it is "an evident consequence of the division of ideas into simple and complex." Taking this as a clue, we may observe that on four plausible—though perhaps not inevitable—assumptions, the full Separability Principle itself follows from his definitions of 'simple' and 'complex' [2.1] if these are taken as generalized beyond their original application to perceptions. (Thus, the simple is whatever will "admit of no distinction nor separation," while "the complex are the contrary to these, and may be distinguished into parts.") The four assumptions are: (i) that the two definitions are indeed, as he says, "contrary" (that is mutually exclusive); (ii) that things that are "different" from each other can always be considered as parts of some whole; (iii) that something can in principle "be distinguished into parts" if and only if it *has* those parts as parts; and (iv) whatever is separable and distinguishable at all is, at least in principle, separable and distinguishable in thought.

On some topics, Hume uses the Separability Principle to argue from inseparability in thought to an absence of different parts—for example, in connection with composition in space and time [2.5]. On other topics, he uses it to argue from difference of parts to separability in thought—for example, in connection with the supposed inherence of qualities in a substantial substratum [3.1, 3.4, 7.6] and the relation between causes and effects [6.1–3]. Hume sometimes drops the qualification "by the thought and imagination" from statements of the Separability Principle, and he also accepts the converse of the resulting unqualified version of the principle—namely, that "whatever is separable is distinguishable, and whatever is distinguishable is different" (THN 1.1.7.3/18). He treats this converse as an uncontroversial statement of the preconditions for separability and distinguishability, respectively. One reason why he is able to drop the qualification concerning "thought and imagination" from the Separability Principle—thereby taking difference as requiring distinguishability and separability *simpliciter*—is that the unqualified version already follows from the broadened definitions of 'simple' and 'complex' plus the first three assumptions alone. More generally, however, inferences from possibility in thought to possibility *tout court* are licensed by a third Humean principle sometimes called the *Conceivability Principle*.

Hume offers at least two somewhat different formulations of his Conceivability Principle:

> [Conceivability Principle, Version 1:] Nothing of which we can form a clear and distinct idea is absurd and impossible.
> (THN 1.1.7.6/19–20)

> [Conceivability Principle, Version 2:] Whatever we conceive is possible, at least in a metaphysical sense.
> (ATHN 11/650)

Two of the differences are merely verbal. Although Version 1 refers to "forming an idea" of something while Version 2 refers to "conceiving" it, these notions are equivalent in Hume's usage. Similarly, Version 1 states a sufficient condition for being not impossible while Version 2 states a sufficient condition for being possible, but these are equivalent as well.

Two other differences, however, are more substantial. Version 1 goes beyond Version 2 by requiring that the idea in question be "clear and distinct." 'Clear' and 'distinct', as applied to ideas, are technical terms that play central roles for Descartes, Locke, and many other early modern philosophers. Unlike many others, Hume does not try to define them, and so it remains somewhat uncertain exactly what he means by them. We have seen, however, that he treats the clarity of ideas as facilitating the formation of accurate ideas of them. For both Descartes and Locke, moreover, the distinctness of an idea involves its insusceptibility to being confused with others. It is plausible, therefore, that the restriction to clear and distinct ideas in Version 1 is intended to ensure that the correct principle stated in Version 2 is not misapplied through inaccuracy, confusion, or lack of specificity about what exactly is being conceived. Like Locke, Hume recognizes the existence of "relative ideas," by means of which the mind seeks to conceive something without forming ideas of some or all of its particular qualities, using in their place the idea of a relation and the idea of something supposed to stand in that relation to the thing [2.3]. Merely relative ideas are especially dangerous for use with the Conceivability Principle, we may suspect, for Hume regards such ideas as "imperfect" in a sense close to that of the term's original meaning of "incomplete" (THN 1.4.3.8/222; EHU 12.16/155). Their lack of specificity about one of the related items may therefore obscure an impossibility that would become apparent upon considering more fully the seemingly open alternatives.

Version 2 goes beyond Version 1, on the other hand, by indicating that the possibility in question is that of a "metaphysical sense" of the term. Hume distinguishes (i) metaphysical possibility, which requires only internal consistency and freedom from contradiction, from (ii) causal possibility, which requires, in addition, compatibility with the actual causal laws of nature—laws that he thinks are not themselves metaphysically necessary and the denial of which would not be inconsistent or contradictory [6.3]. Version 2 thereby resolves an ambiguity inherent in Version 1.

Hume does not argue for the Conceivability Principle at all. His thought seems to be that whatever object or circumstance can be fully and accurately conceived with internal consistency and freedom from contradiction of its representation must satisfy the minimal constraint on existence itself that consists in internal consistency and freedom from contradiction in the nature of the thing. It is important to note that the Conceivability Principle does not entail that whatever a given individual *cannot* conceive is *impossible* (or, equivalently, that an individual can conceive whatever is possible), since an incapacity for conception may result simply from the individual's own personal lack of the requisite ideas, rather than any incompatibility in the nature of either the ideas or the things themselves. It is only when the inconceivability results from a contradiction in the attempted thought itself (see THN 1.2.2.8/32 for an example) that we can be assured of metaphysical impossibility.

Finally, Hume propounds a *Principle of the Association of Ideas*:

> [Principle of the Association of Ideas:] RESEMBLANCE, CONTIGUITY in time or place, and CAUSE and EFFECT ... produce an association among ideas, and upon the appearance of one idea naturally introduce another.
>
> (THN 1.1.4.2/11)

Locke appeals to the mind's tendency to associate certain ideas under certain circumstances in order to explain cognitive errors and instances of irrationality (ECHU 2.33, "Of the Association of Ideas"); in some cases, this requires only that the ideas often have been elicited together. For Hume, however, the relations that give rise to association are relations holding or naturally taken to hold among the *objects* of the associated ideas: for example, it is the experienced or inferred resemblance, contiguity, or causation between a father and son that leads to association between the ideas of them—not any experienced or inferred resemblance, contiguity, or causation between the ideas themselves. Furthermore, Hume appeals to association in the course of explaining many more features of the mind's operations, including the formation of complex ideas at single times; the formation of natural sequences of ideas (temporally complex "trains of thought," as one might say) over time; and even personal identity [3.1, 7.6]. Indeed, he writes at the conclusion of his *Abstract* of the *Treatise* that "if any thing can entitle the author to so glorious a name as that of an *inventor*, 'tis the use he makes of the principle of the association of ideas, which enters into most of his philosophy" (ATHN 35/661–62). This power of attraction, as it were, among related ideas is one of the features of Hume's psychology that most naturally invites comparison with Newton's physics [1.2, 10.2].

## 2.3 Complex ideas

One of Hume's uses of the Principle of the Association of Ideas is to explain why certain simple ideas are naturally combined into complex ideas. Some of these ideas allow the mind to think about complex qualities, while others allow the mind to think about things having such qualities. Following Locke, the former he calls ideas of "modes" whereas the latter are ideas of "substances."

Locke maintains that ideas of modes (such as "dancing") and ideas of substances (such as "dancer") alike include ideas of individual qualities as parts. The difference between them he locates in a further component that, he holds, only ideas of substances possess, as their "first and chief" element. He calls this further component the idea of "substance-in-general," which he also characterizes as a "confused," "obscure," and "relative" idea of a "something-I-know-not-what" in which qualities, unable to exist alone, "inhere" for their metaphysical support (ECHU 2.12, "Of Complex Ideas"). While Locke struggles to explain the origin in experience of this idea, he nevertheless feels obliged to recognize it in order to honor the basic intuitions that: (i) there is a difference between things and their qualities, captured by the thought that qualities cannot exist without being the qualities of some thing; and (ii) that there is a consequent difference between merely thinking about qualities of things and thinking about things themselves.

Locke notes that the qualities represented in complex ideas of both modes and substances occur together with one another, but Hume goes beyond Locke in proposing that simpler ideas are combined into complex ideas of modes or substances specifically as a result of the associative relations of causation and contiguity found among the qualities they represent. He concedes to Locke that the mind "commonly refers" qualities to an unknown substratum that supposedly supports them, although he also states that this "fiction" need not always "take place" (THN 1.1.6.2/16). His Copy Principle and Separability Principle lead him to deny, however, that there is any idea either of such a substratum or of a relation of inherence (Hume says "inhesion") in which qualities might stand to it. Even without such an attempt, however, the associative forces linking the composing ideas in the mind are sufficiently strong, in Hume's view, that a new idea can come to be added to the complex idea without inducing the mind to change the word it employs to signify that complex idea. Thus, for example, one may continue to use the same word 'gold' even after coming to add ideas of newly attributed sensible or chemical qualities to one's previous complex idea of that metal. In the case of ideas of modes, in contrast, any addition to the complex idea brings with it the application of a different term. This difference in functional role alone is sufficient, on Hume's account, to distinguish the two kinds of ideas.

In addition to ideas of modes and substances, Hume also recognizes complex ideas of "relations" (THN 1.1.5). In a narrow sense of the term, only represented features of pairs or larger multiplicities of things that lead to mental association among their ideas qualify as relations; these are what he calls "natural relations," which he limits to resemblance, contiguity, and causation.

In a broader sense of the term, however, any respect in which two or more things may be compared at all is a relation between them, and Hume classifies these "philosophical relations" under seven general headings: resemblance, identity, relations of space and time, quantity or number, degrees of a quality, contrariety, and causation. Of these kinds of relations, only four—resemblance, contrariety, quantity or number, and degrees of a quality—are "unalterable," given only the intrinsic nature of the ideas of the related things, in the way needed to underwrite knowledge in Hume's strict sense [2.1].

The existence of ideas of relations allows, in turn, the formation of the "relative ideas" mentioned in the previous section. By using ideas of sisterhood and being younger than, for example, one may form the idea of Sally's youngest sister. To take a philosophically more significant case, one may use the idea of causation to form the idea of *the causes of our impressions of sensation* (THN 1.2.6.9/68). Although Hume does not belabor the notion of relative ideas, he does explicitly employ it, as in the latter example. Furthermore, the ordinariness of examples like the former suggests that relative ideas should be, in his view, very common in human thought. In many cases, however, as with the attempted idea of "the substratum supporting qualities," it is at least dubious whether there is even any possible relation of support or inherence that is applicable to qualities and has the characteristics that philosophers *suppose* it to have, and the suspicion-confirming use of the methodological principle derived from the Copy Principle then comes into play [2.2]. To "suppose" something, in Hume's usage, is to act in at least many respects as though one believed something, but without necessarily forming a lively idea of it. This also occurs, for example, when human beings and even animals suppose the uniformity of nature without formulating it as a belief. (See also [6.5] on relative ideas of causal necessitation.)

## 2.4 Abstract ideas (concepts)

Relative ideas require the mind to conceive a given relation with generality—that is, as applicable to many different things at once, without conceiving each of those things individually. Hume devotes the final section of *Treatise* 1.1 to the crucial topic of how the mind is able to think with generality. Like Locke, he calls the representations that make this possible "abstract or general ideas"; he also calls them "abstract notions" or, sometimes, simply "notions." In a more contemporary idiom, we would call them *concepts*. While adopting Locke's terminology, however, Hume regards himself as parting ways with Locke on the fundamental question of whether these ideas "*be general or particular in the mind's conception of them*" (THN 1.1.7.1/17).

Rightly or wrongly—his interpretation is sometimes disputed—Hume reads Locke as a proponent of the first alternative. So understood, Locke holds that the mind forms an abstract idea by separating out some part or parts of a particular complex idea given in experience, leaving an idea that is intrinsically indeterminate in some way. Thus, for example, beginning from the fully determinate experience of a particular human being, the mind might form an abstract idea of "man" by removing the ideas of such individualizing features as size, color, and amount of hair to produce an idea that was indeterminate in these respects (ECHU 2.9.9–11; ECHU 3.3, especially 3.3.7–9).

Rejecting this view, Hume pronounces Berkeley's elaboration of the other alternative "one of the greatest and most valuable discoveries that has been made of late years in the republic of letters" (THN 1.1.7.1/17) and proclaims that "'tis utterly impossible to conceive a quality or quantity, without forming a precise notion of its degrees" (THN 1.1.7.2/18). Hume offers three arguments for this conclusion, each of which makes reference to one or another of his first three basic principles concerning perceptions. First, the Copy Principle requires that if there were to be indeterminate ideas, then, absurdly, there would equally be indeterminate impressions from which they could be copied; indeed, such impressions would differ from indeterminate ideas only by a difference in their liveliness. (The quite considerable indeterminacy of peripheral vision, which Hume does not mention, suggests that this is not as absurd as he indicates.) Second, an object and its particular degrees of quantity and quality (for example, a line and its length) are not different or distinguishable; hence, by the converse of the Separability Principle, their ideas are not separable, either—as would be required for an idea of a line of indeterminate length. Third, the existence of real objects that are indeterminate in quantity or quality is obviously impossible and absurd; but if there were indeterminate ideas, they could be used to conceive indeterminate objects, which, by the Conceivability Principle, would then be possible after all.

Hume's negative conclusion leaves him with the positive task of explaining how ideas that are entirely determinate and "particular" in their own nature can nevertheless be general in what and how they represent. Berkeley was content to claim that the mind can "attend" selectively to just some particular features of fully determinate ideas and thereby employ those ideas to represent all things having those selected features in reasoning. Hume seeks to explain this process more fully, without a primitive mental activity of "attending." He does so by appealing to: (i) the mental operation of "habit" (which he also calls "custom"), whereby "the repetition of any particular act or operation produces a propensity to renew the same act or operation, without being impelled by any process of the understanding" (EHU 5.5/43; see also THN 1.3.8.10/102); and (ii) the associative character of the relation of resemblance, in accordance with the Principle of the Association of Ideas.

More specifically, Hume declares that when a number of different but resembling objects or qualities are perceived over a period of time, they and their resembling ideas tend to elicit a common verbal response, with which they become habitually conjoined. (Critics have often objected that Hume's explanation is circular, on the grounds that recognizing two things as *resembling* requires that the mind already have a concept or abstract idea of the kind to which they belong. This objection misses the mark, inasmuch as the mere capacity of similar things to elicit a similar response does not in general depend on the occurrence of any thought *about* their similarity.) New occurrences of the verbal response then tend to elicit one particularly common or salient determinate idea while also "reviving the custom" or habit of forming the other resembling ideas as well. As a result, a large number of ideas are potentially, although not actually, present to the mind, and, moreover, the mind is typically able to "revive" any one of the ideas themselves as needed in reasoning or discourse. For example, the false assertion "*all triangles are equilateral*" can immediately bring to mind an idea of a particular non-equilateral triangle, even if the idea originally elicited happened to be of an equilateral triangle. The occasional failure to revive a needed idea is, he notes, a cause of "false reasoning and sophistry" (THN 1.1.7.8/21). Nevertheless, by means of its causal relation to other resembling ideas as mediated through a general term, a particular idea comes to serve as an "abstract or general idea" and is able to represent "in this imperfect manner" (THN 1.1.7.7/290) an entire class of resembling objects.

For terminological ease, let us call this larger set of ideas disposed to be revived the *revival set* of an abstract idea, and let us call the particular idea that is initially elicited by the general term the *exemplar*. Further, let us consider the exemplar idea to be, trivially, also a member of the revival set. Different members of the revival set, so defined, may serve as the exemplar in the minds of different users of the term, or even (especially when the habit is new) in the mind of the same user at different times. As Hume notes, two different occurrences of what is qualitatively the same idea may serve as exemplars for two different revival sets, and hence as two different abstract ideas, if they are elicited by different general terms with different associated revival sets. For example, the determinate idea of Fido may serve as the abstract idea of dogs when elicited by the term 'dog' (associated with a revival set consisting of ideas of dogs) and as the abstract idea of animals when elicited by the term 'animal' (associated with a revival set consisting of ideas of animals).

If Hume's theory of abstract ideas is to explain the full range of cases he intends it to cover, at least four fairly obvious elaborations must be made beyond those that he explicitly offers. First, it seems evident that an abstract idea of a relation, in contrast to an abstract idea of a quality, would require an exemplar idea of a pair or larger multiplicity of things, associated with a general term for the relation and disposing the mind to revive as needed any member of a revival set of ideas of other multiplicities whose objects may be compared in a similar way. It is a further question whether or how relations that are direct converses of each other—such as *taller than* and *shorter than*—should be distinguished or assimilated; perhaps different general terms become associated with taking the individual members of the multiplicities in different orders.

Second, there should be abstract ideas not only of qualities and kinds, but also of *individuals* in order to explain how the name of an individual thing can be associated with ideas of multiple different parts (spatial, temporal, or other) each serving to represent the entire individual from a particular perspective. In these cases, a name will elicit an exemplar idea and a readiness to revive other ideas that are of the same individual—for example, an idea of a monument as seen from the front and another of it as seen from the back, or an idea of a person as a child and another of her as an adult, or one of the music of a theatrical performance and another of its choreography.

Third, a distinction must be made between an *ordinary* revival set, limited to ideas of things believed to exist, from an *expanded* revival set that includes also ideas of suitably resembling possible things that are merely conceived without being believed to exist. Ordinary judgments about what actually exists, such as "*all dogs have fur,*" will draw assent or dissent based on an ordinary revival set. Judgments involving possibility or necessity, however—for example, "*it is possible that an elephant could fly*" or "*there cannot be round squares*"—will require the use of an expanded revival set. Indeed, different expanded revival sets will often be needed to distinguish between metaphysical and causal possibilities and necessities: it is metaphysically possible but (arguably) not causally possible (given the actual laws of nature) that an elephant should fly.

Finally, and most important, a distinction must be made between: (i) the *actual* revival set (either ordinary or expanded) that is associated with a general term in a given person's mind at a particular time; and (ii) the *idealized* revival set that would result from an indefinite extension of veridical experience concerning the existence and character of objects, together with greater reflection on resemblances and greater exposure to the classificatory tendencies of others who employ the same term. Such an idealized revival set may include ideas not included in the actual revival set (for example, of resembling objects whose existence or relevant features are unknown to the individual mind at the time), and it may omit ideas of objects that are included in the actual revival set (for example, of objects whose existence or relevant features have been misperceived by the individual mind). Without such a distinction, it is not possible to explain the full range of possible *truths* and *errors* in judgment using abstract ideas.

Important as the revival sets of an abstract idea are to its meaning, however, Hume quickly adds:

> In talking of *government, church, negotiations, conquest,* we seldom spread out in our minds all the simple ideas of which these are compos'd. 'Tis however observable, that notwithstanding this imperfection we may avoid talking nonsense on these subjects, and may perceive any repugnance among the ideas, as well as if we had a full comprehension of them. Thus if instead of saying, *that in war the weaker have always recourse to negotiation,* we should say, *that they have always recourse to conquest,* the custom, which we have acquir'd of attributing certain relations to ideas, still follows the words, and makes us immediately perceive the absurdity of that proposition.
> (THN 1.1.7.14/23)

Explaining the full meaning of an abstract idea or concept therefore involves, in principle, several elements for Hume. The explanation must begin from the idea's actual and idealized ordinary and expanded revival sets. As we shall see later, we may further distinguish an aspect of meaning that lies in the particular operations by which a revival set is typically elicited [4.2–4]. The explanation will still not be complete, however, unless it also specifies the "relations" that have, as a result of custom or habit, come to be "attributed" to the concept: for example, that if the concept STRONGER IN WAR applies to something, then so does the concept HAS RECOURSE TO CONQUEST. This element or aspect may be called the concept's *inferential role*: the various inferences involving the concept that have come by habit to be accepted even without specifically invoking its relevant revival set. More broadly still, we may distinguish a concept's *conceptual role*, consisting in its inferential role plus the various other mental transitions (for example, to sentiments, passions, and volitions) involving the concept that have come by habit to be accepted in a similar way. Philosophical error can arise, for Hume, through a concept's acquisition of an inferential role that is ill matched to its actual or idealized revival set, as occurs with concepts of identity [3.1, 3.5], while the normativity of concepts may be explained partly by appeal to their broader conceptual role [5.1–3; 8.1].

Because Hume's theory of abstract ideas is his theory of what we would call concepts, later chapters will treat the terms 'abstract idea' and 'concept' as equivalent in application to his philosophy and will continue the convention (noted in the Preface and employed in the previous paragraph) of designating concepts with small capital letters in discussing Humean abstract ideas. Hume refers or makes essential appeal to his theory of abstract ideas a number of times throughout the course of the *Treatise* and also in the first *Enquiry*. In particular, he does so in connection with the ideas of space and time (THN 1.2.3.5–6/34–35; see also THN 1.2.4.12/43); the error of mathematicians and philosophers in supposing the need for "intellectual" ideas to explain the generality of mathematical thought (THN 1.3.1.7/72); the idea of causal power (THN 1.3.14.13/161); the idea of the causal relation itself (THN 1.3.6.15/93 and THN 2.3.1.16/405, passages that make literal sense only if understood in terms of the theory); the lesser impact of abstract ideas on the imagination and thereby on the passions (THN 2.3.6.2/424–25); the "correction" of our "abstract notions" (that is, abstract ideas) derived from the moral sense and of similar notions derived from "all the senses" (THN 3.3.1.16/582 and THN 3.3.1.21/585); the idea of existence in relation to belief (THN Appendix 2/623); ideas of "primary" and "secondary" qualities of bodies (EHU 12.15/154–55); and the solution to paradoxes of infinite divisibility (EHU 12.20n34/158).

More generally, Hume's tendency to use 'abstract reasoning' as an alternate term for what he officially calls "demonstrative reasoning" (THN 1.3.1.1/69, THN 1.3.9.19/177, EHU 12.18/156) seems to presuppose that such reasoning makes essential use of abstract ideas. Furthermore, demonstrative reasoning produces knowledge, in his view, and it is hard to see how the four relations of ideas (resemblance, contrariety, degrees in quality, and proportions in quantity or number) that he specifies as sufficient to underwrite all knowledge in the strict sense [2.1] could suffice for that purpose without the relations of resemblance that are offered by abstract ideas sharing elements of their revival sets [3.4]. In addition, his frequent uses of the term 'notion'—aside from a very small number that refer to doctrines—seem to treat that term as equivalent to 'abstract idea' (see especially EPM 5.42/229). Hume's first application of the theory, however, occurs even before he leaves the section on abstract ideas itself, where he uses it to explain "that *distinction of reason*, which is so much talk'd of, and so little understood, in the schools" (that is, in the neo-Aristotelian philosophical tradition of *scholasticism*). If he does not explicitly invoke his basic theory of abstract ideas in connection with every kind of general thought he mentions, it is nonetheless reasonable to assume that he intends such thought to be explained and understood in terms of it.

A "distinction of reason" involves one thing conceived in two different ways or under two different aspects or forms. Hume's Separability Principle, however, renders such "distinctions" problematic, for it requires that if there are not two different things, then there is also no distinguishability or distinction. His primary example of a distinction of reason is that between the color and the "figure" (i.e., shape) of a white marble globe. Unlike the top and the bottom of the globe, and perhaps unlike some other pairs of its sensible qualities, its present color and its present figure are not really two different things for Hume: the whole globe's figure simply is its arrangement of colored points, and the whole globe's color simply is that same arrangement of colored points.

Hume's solution to his problem has two parts. First, the globe is only one (complex) "object" that is both white and round; and as required by the Separability Principle, this object is neither different, nor distinguishable, nor separable from itself. Second, the white globe can nevertheless belong to two different classes of resembling things—namely, the class of globes (of various colors) and the class of white things (of various figures)—and it can do so without the color and the figure being two different parts of it in the way that its top and bottom are. In support of this latter point, he notes in the Appendix (THN 1.1.7.7n5/637) that two simple things must resemble each other in being simple, and yet, by hypothesis, they cannot have parts in common. Rather than perceiving the color and the figure of the globe as different parts of the globe, then, the mind simply has two different—but of course also distinguishable and separable—associated abstract ideas of white and round (namely, WHITE and ROUND), each with a revival set that is different, distinguishable, and separable from that of the other. The terms 'white' (or 'whiteness') and 'round' (or 'roundness') do not signify "objects" at all, but only different manners in which objects can resemble one another; and because these manners are not objects, they do not fall within the scope of the Separability Principle.

It might be supposed that Hume should feel obliged to explain further *how* individual white or round things are able to resemble each other—for example, by postulating their standing in a relation of *shared participation* to *universals* of whiteness and roundness as objects or things in their own right. He does not accept this explanatory demand, however, agreeing instead with Locke that there are no "universal" beings or existences. Indeed, it is arguable that all explanation for Hume must ultimately be causal explanation, so that postulated explanatory relations such as *shared participation in a universal* could not be genuinely explanatory in any case. Because a single object can resemble others in multiple ways, and without sharing parts in common with them, the same perception can also qualify as being "a perception of"—that is, as exemplifying, representing, or otherwise being about—more than one quality or attribute, and can do so without distinct perceptions of those qualities or attributes being different parts of it.

## 2.5 Space and time

Among the seven kinds of philosophical relations that Hume distinguishes, he devotes particular attention to those of space and time, which are important both to the understanding of mind and to the understanding of the material world. These occupy nearly all of *Treatise* 1.2 ("Of the ideas of space and time").

Just as whiteness and roundness are not things in their own right for Hume, neither are space and time. Instead, whereas whiteness and roundness are merely "manners" in which white and round perceptions and objects can resemble one another, space and time are two "manners" in which perceptions and other objects can be "disposed" (that is, ordered or arranged) relative to one another. While the temporal manner of disposition applies to perceptions and things generally, the spatial manner of disposition applies strictly only to visual and tactile perceptions and—at least so far as human beings can discern—visual and tactile qualities.

What Hume calls his "system" concerning space and time involves two main theses (THN 1.2.4.1–2/39–40). The first thesis may be called Minimism:

[Minimism:] Any finite spatial extension or finite temporal duration is not infinitely divisible but is composed of only a finite number of simple and indivisible parts (minima).

The second thesis, which presupposes the first, may be called Qualitivism:

[Qualitivism:] The simple and indivisible parts of any finite spatial extension or finite temporal duration are conceivable only as having some real quality that distinguishes them as existents.

From Qualitivism, he concludes that it is impossible to conceive either "vacuum" (that is, empty space) or "duration without a succession" (that is, time without change).

In asserting Minimism, Hume is consciously setting himself against the geometrical orthodoxy that finite extension is infinitely divisibility and against a parallel orthodoxy about temporal duration. His strategy involves establishing two lemmas, which may be called *Idea* Minimism and Conformity:

[Idea Minimism:] Our *ideas* of space and time are only finitely divisible and consist of only a finite number of simple indivisible parts.

[Conformity:] What our ideas of space and time *represent* must be "conformable" to our ideas of them with respect to composition by simple and indivisible parts.

To establish Idea Minimism, in turn, Hume offers an argument from the mind's finite capacity (THN 1.2.1.2/26–27), a limitation that he claims is both universally allowed and obvious from observation:

{1} The capacity of the mind is limited, and can never attain a full and adequate conception of infinity.
{2} Whatever is capable of being divided *ad infinitum* must consist of an infinite number of parts.

{3} It is impossible to set any bounds to the number of parts, without setting at the same time bounds to the division. (from {2})

{4} The idea which we form of any finite quality, is not infinitely divisible, but that by proper distinctions and separations we may run up this idea to inferior ones, which will be perfectly simple and indivisible. (from {1}&{3})

Hume's use of Step {1} assumes that a "full and adequate conception of infinity" requires an idea with infinitely many parts. This could certainly be disputed—especially by proponents of purely intellectual ideas—but it is consistent with his own views about "adequate" conception as requiring an isomorphism between an idea and what is conceived through it. Step {2} assumes that something cannot be divided into parts unless it already consists of those parts. This is an assumption that Aristotle would reject, although—as Thomas Holden (2004) has shown—it is one that most early modern philosophers would accept. The same assumption also finds expression in Hume's previously noted acceptance of the converse of the Separability Principle [2.2], which requires that whatever is separable consists of different parts.

Although Hume's argument is framed specifically in terms of conception and ideas, the consideration of the mind's limited capacity applies to perceptions more generally. Given the close relation between ideas and impressions—which differ chiefly in liveliness [2.1]—it is not surprising that Hume holds that the division of spatially or temporally complex impressions, too, must terminate in simple and indivisible minima. He gives as an example the minimal impression of an ink spot on a receding piece of paper just before the spot completely disappears, and he reinforces the claim that its simplicity (that is, lack of parts) entails its indivisibility (that is, its inseparability) by appeal to a formulation of his Separability Principle: "What consists of parts is distinguishable into them, and what is distinguishable is separable" (THN 1.2.1.3/27).

It is precisely because Hume holds that some of our visual and tactile ideas and impressions have this minimal—that is, simple and indivisible—character that he remarks, "nothing can be more minute, than some ideas, which we form in the fancy; and images, which appear to the senses" (THN 1.2.2.5/28). In order to be simple and indivisible, these minimal parts must, as he conceives them, lack any left or right, any top or bottom, or indeed any shape at all. Instead, they must be literally unextended—spatially arrangeable but themselves lacking any spatial extent. Extension results, he proposes, from the combination of such minima into a complex of two or more that are contiguous to one another; two such adjacent minima would thus constitute the shortest possible line. In this way, he intends his minima to serve as a kind of golden mean between: (i) "physical points" if understood as extended and shaped, and hence still metaphysically divisible into smaller parts (even if no causal process can actually separate them); and (ii) "mathematical points," if understood not only as unextended themselves, but also as incapable of giving rise to extension by their finite conjunction or combination. In the *Treatise*, he describes his own third option as offering an improved version of "mathematical points," while in the first *Enquiry* he describes it as offering a better version of "physical points."

Hume next proceeds in the *Treatise* to offer four arguments for Conformity. The first he formulates only for space, but he claims that a similar argument applies to time. As formulated, it appeals to his previous claim that "nothing can be more minute"—that is, smaller—than our indivisible and individually unextended, yet spatially arrangeable, ideas. Because nothing at all can be smaller than such ideas, they must be "adequate," in respect of smallness, to represent properly the size of the very smallest possible parts of any extension. Yet the idea of an infinite number of even such smallest possible parts—each of which must make some (equal and positive) contribution to the extent of the whole—is, he claims, the idea of an infinite, not a finite, extension. Because there cannot therefore be a finite extension with infinitely many parts, finite extensions cannot be infinitely divisible and their division must instead terminate in simple and indivisible minima. As this argument illustrates, the infinite divisibility of extension would require that there be no minimum size for parts—and hence, that there be something more minute than any given idea.

The second argument for Conformity appeals to a principle that any plurality of things can exist only in virtue of the existence of the units that compose it. Because extension is admitted to be a kind of plurality, however, it follows that if it were infinitely divisible, without terminating in simple and indivisible units to provide a grounding existence, no extension could exist at all. Hume calls this a "very strong and beautiful argument" of "Mons. Malezieu" (THN 1.2.2.3n/30) referring to Nicolas de Malezieu (1674–1748), although the argument is better known from the first article of Leibniz's *Monadology*. For this argument, too, he claims, there is a temporal analogue.

The third argument, in contrast, applies only to time. Unlike the nature of space, the distinctive nature of time is, Hume asserts, to be composed of parts succeeding and being succeeded by others, parts that do not co-exist and are entirely distinct. Yet if the division of a finite time did not terminate in indivisible moments, he continues, there would have to be "an infinite number of different yet co-existent moments, or parts of time," which is an "arrant contradiction" (THN 1.2.2.4/32). His reason for this claim is not entirely obvious, for an infinite division of time need not yield moments that entirely co-exist with one another for their entire duration; it requires only that every part of time partially overlap with shorter parts of time. Yet some parts of time evidently do partially overlap with others: the year 1737 and the summer of 1737, for example. Presumably, he is thinking: (i) that such overlaps of parts of time are compatible with the nature of time *only* if they are always the consequence of composition by smaller parts of time that are themselves entirely distinct and not even partially co-existing; and (ii) that without temporally simple and indivisible temporal minima, this compositional burden would continue to arise anew at every level of division without ever being adequately discharged.

The fourth argument appeals to this result about time in order to draw a parallel conclusion for space. Given that motion occurs as the successive occupation of contiguous places through time, Hume argues, the infinite divisibility of space plus the reality of motion would require the infinite divisibility of time; hence, the finite divisibility of time plus the reality of motion requires the finite divisibility of space.

Hume ultimately devotes two entire sections of the *Treatise* to answering likely objections to his "system" (THN 1.2.4–5, "Objections answer'd" and "The same subject continu'd"). He declares in advance, however, that the contrary of Minimism cannot be genuinely demonstrated—that is, made an object of knowledge, in his strict sense, by inference [2.1, 3.3–4]. "He bases this confidence on two considerations. First, he claims to have just fully demonstrated the truth of Minimism as the first main thesis of his system; but two contraries cannot both be demonstrated, because whatever is contrary to a genuine demonstration is impossible. Second, he claims, Minimism is at least conceivable, and the Conceivability Principle therefore allows us to infer its metaphysical possibility; but whatever is metaphysically possible cannot be demonstrated to be false. Against purported geometrical demonstrations of the infinite divisibility of finite extension—and in mitigation of Minimism's many consequences incompatible with standard Euclidean geometry—he boldly asserts in the *Treatise* (though not in extant later writings [1.5]) that Euclidean geometry is only approximately true. For example, because "straight" is an indefinable property recognizable only by its general appearance, it remains open: (i) that there may be more than one straight line between two given points; and (ii) that two straight lines, if approaching one another only very gradually, may intersect in a common segment rather than a single point.

Hume's defense of Qualitivism, the second element of his system, begins by lauding the Copy Principle and emphasizing the utility of the methodological directive derived from that principle: to examine the impressions from which our ideas are derived (THN 1.2.3.1/33) [2.2]. The result of tracing the ideas of space and time to their sources in impressions, he argues, is a recognition (i) that there are no impressions of space or time that are "separate or distinct" from the impressions of things spatially or temporally arrayed, and (ii) that the idea of space and the idea of time are both abstract ideas (THN 1.2.3.5–7/34–35) [2.4].

Despite the fact that Hume begins this defense by citing the Copy Principle, critics sometimes object that Hume's denial of separate or distinct impressions of space and time constitutes a violation of it. This is simply a mistake, however. In his view, *every* complex impression composed of spatially or temporally arranged impressions is thereby also *an* impression of space or time, respectively; as the case of distinctions of reason [2.4] shows, a perception can serve as a perception of more than one thing, quality, or relation at the same time. As abstract ideas, the idea of space and the idea of time each consist of an exemplar idea that is, respectively, spatially or temporally complex, associated with a general term, and thereby associated with revival sets including other spatially or temporally complex ideas. The exemplar idea and the other ideas in the revival sets are all either copied directly from resembling complex impressions or composed of simpler ideas that are so copied, in accordance with the Copy Principle.

On Hume's account, an absence of spatially ordered perceptions is simply no perception of space at all and hence cannot be a perception of vacuum or empty space; similarly, an absence of successively changing perceptions is simply no perception of time at all, and hence cannot be a perception of changeless time. Newtonians affirmed the existence of "absolute space" and "absolute time" as metaphysically real entities in their own right, capable of containing objects but also capable of existing in their absence. Locke more cautiously declared that he did not know whether space should be regarded as a substance (ECHU 2.13.17). Hume, in contrast, denies that we can even conceive of absolute space and time as things in their own right capable of existing without things in spatial or temporal array.

At the same time, however, it is important not to overstate the intended metaphysical consequences of this conclusion. Hume freely grants, in the Appendix to the *Treatise*, that there may be circumstances in which bodies (that is, physical objects) neither touch each other nor have any body between them, and are yet capable of having something subsequently "placed" between them without either one moving; such a situation is one of what he calls "fictitious distance." Moreover, he asserts, "if the *Newtonian* philosophy be rightly understood, it will be found to mean no more" (THN 1.2.5.26n/639). He is not denying, of course, that Newtonians often tried to say more, but he is also emphatically refusing to endorse, against the Newtonians, the Cartesian doctrine that the universe must necessarily be a *plenum*, in which any non-contiguous portions of matter must have other matter between them, leaving not even what Hume defines as a fictitious distance. His conclusions are not meant to resolve the question of whether the universe in point of fact comprises such a plenum, but rather to clarify the ontological status of space and time themselves as we conceive them. These conclusions require only that, metaphysically speaking, there be: (i) no such conceivable *thing* or *object* as a vacuum or "empty space" between non-contiguous objects; and (ii) no such thing or object as "time without succession" in which no change occurs.

Hume draws a highly unusual consequence from his conclusion that there is no real duration without change: namely, that a single unchanging object—which he calls a "steadfast" object (THN 1.2.3.17/37)—itself undergoes no real duration and hence has no real temporal parts. Strikingly, it lacks such parts on his view even when other objects co-existing with it do undergo change and so do have temporal parts. Indeed, a steadfast object lacks real temporal parts of its own even when a complex object consisting of the steadfast object *plus* one or more other objects (i) undergoes change via a change in or in relation to one or more of those other objects and thereby (ii) does have temporal parts. Each thing, whether simple or complex, thus has its own real temporal structure for Hume, in such a way that a steadfast object can be temporally simple (literally lacking in any duration or temporal complexity of its own) and yet co-exist with each of two successive objects. This may, of course, appear to violate his stated principle that different parts of time cannot be co-existent (THN 1.2.2.4/31). Presumably it does not do so because the steadfast object and the changing objects each have their own duration and hence their own temporal structure, each obeying the stated principle—as, too, does the further, complex object composed of them. The maximally complex thing constituting the entire universe, we may infer, undergoes change whenever anything in the universe changes, and it thereby has a more fine-grained temporal structure than any of its proper parts.

## 2.6 Mental representation

Locke's willingness to regard the ideas of extension and figure as simple—that is, as lacking parts—suggests that he did not regard these ideas as literally extended or shaped. More strongly, it is hard to see how he could have regarded any ideas as extended or shaped, given that he regarded ideas as mere "modes" of thinking substances and regarded thinking substances themselves as very probably immaterial and entirely unextended. Yet, after distinguishing (i) "primary qualities" of bodies such as extension, figure, motion, and size from (ii) "secondary qualities" such as colors, sounds, tastes, smells, and heat and cold, he declares that our ideas of primary qualities differ from our ideas of secondary qualities by "resembling" the qualities themselves (ECHU 2.8.15–23). Secondary qualities, in contrast, he treats as powers, grounded in the primary qualities of the insensibly small parts of bodies to produce ideas in us that do not resemble the sensations produced. He takes this distinction to be required by the likely truth of the *mechanistic* conception of physics, according to which bodies interact through communication of motion that is determined only by the size, shape, and motion of the interacting bodies.

In order to understand how Locke could maintain his stance about the resemblance between primary qualities and the ideas of them, it is useful to consider briefly Descartes's theory of how ideas are of or about things or qualities—a feature of the mental now called *intentionality*. In Descartes's view, derived from his scholastic predecessors, an idea is about something by "containing" it in a certain way. This containment is possible, he thought, because there are two kinds of being or existence, rather than just one. The first is "formal" being, which is a thing's existence outside of ideas; hence, it is what we would ordinarily think of as its existence *simpliciter*. The second is "objective" being, which is a thing's genuine—but of course not formal—presence "in" an idea that is (thereby) of or about it. It is a distinctive feature of ideas, for Descartes, that they are inherently capable of containing the objective reality of other things in this way. Although Locke does not employ Descartes's technical terminology, he does sometimes contrast "real existence" with "existence in the mind" to the same effect (e.g., ECHU 2.8.18 and ECHU 2.11.9). Moreover, he seems to hold, like Descartes, that at least some ideas are of particular qualities not by exemplifying them but rather by containing them in a different, and inherently intentional, way. An idea of largeness or squareness is not itself large or square, for example but rather contains these qualities in a different way. The resemblance between primary qualities in bodies and the ideas of those qualities is grounded for Locke in the resemblance between: (i) a quality as it exists outside the mind in what exemplifies but does not contain it; and (ii) that very quality as it is contained in an idea that does not exemplify it.

Although it is tempting to read Hume as implicitly following in this tradition of the inherent intentionality of ideas, there is overwhelming textual evidence that he, unlike Descartes and Locke but like Berkeley, grants a very literal exemplification of size and shape to some perceptions—namely, those that are visual or tactile. As we have just seen, he regards such perceptions as complex precisely because they are composed of perceptions of spatial parts [2.5]. Furthermore, he directly compares ideas in respect of size both to other perceptions and to external bodies when he asserts that nothing can be "more minute, than some ideas, which we form in the fancy," and he describes spatially complex ideas as "swelling up to a considerable bulk" (THN 1.2.2.2/29). Similarly, he refers to "the impressions of touch" as "simple impressions, except when consider'd with regard to *their* extension" (THN 1.4.4.14/230; emphasis added). He later claims that "the vulgar" (that is, as he says, everyone at least most of the time) do not distinguish between their impressions of sensation and extended bodies (THN 1.4.2.14/193 and THN 1.4.2.43/210)—a conflation that seems very difficult to make unless some sense impressions are themselves literally extended. Moreover, as we shall see [3.1, 3.5], he argues that the vulgar would be *right* to regard their impressions of sensation as real bodies if only those impressions were at some times causally unrelated to other perceptions constituting a mind—a state of affairs that he regards as metaphysically entirely possible, if not actual. Relatedly, he grants that we usually conceive of bodies simply by attributing different causal "relations, durations, and connexions" to perceptions themselves (THN 1.2.6.9/68).

Perhaps most tellingly of all, however, in his discussion of the alleged immateriality of the soul Hume states forcefully:

> What is extended must have a particular figure, as square, round, triangular; none of which will agree to a desire, or indeed to any impression or idea, *except of those two senses [sight and touch] above-mention'd* ... . An object may be said to be no where, when its parts are not so situated with respect to each other, as

to form any figure or [extended] quantity; nor the whole with respect to other bodies so as to answer to our notions of contiguity or distance. Now this is evidently the case with all our perceptions and objects, *except those of the sight and feeling.*
(THN 1.4.5.9–10/235–36; emphasis added)

And again:

The most vulgar philosophy informs us, that no external object can make itself known to the mind immediately, and without the interposition of an image or perception. That table, which just now appears to me, *is only a perception, and all its qualities are qualities of a perception. Now the most obvious of all its qualities is extension. The perception consists of parts. These parts are so situated, as to afford us the notion of distance and contiguity; of length, breadth, and thickness* ... . *And to cut short all disputes, the very idea of extension is copy'd from nothing but an impression, and consequently must perfectly agree to it. To say the idea of extension agrees to any thing, is to say it is extended.*
(THN 1.4.5.15/239–40; emphasis added)

To say that a visual or tactile impression or idea is itself extended and has spatial relations to other perceptions is not, however, to say that it must be spatially located relative to those in other minds or to bodies in the material world—for example, located at some particular place in the brain. In fact, not only is there no requirement that perceptions of the mind stand in any spatial relation to those in others minds or to bodies in the external world, there is not even a requirement that all visual and tactile perceptions stand in spatial relations to all other such perceptions in the same mind. For all that Hume says, visual or tactile impressions may not always be spatially disposed relative to visual or tactile ideas (as when imagining an object without imagining it in any spatial relation to a viewed scene), and tactile perceptions may not always be spatially disposed relative to visual perceptions.

Hume shares with Berkeley the doctrine that complex visual and tactile perceptions (visual and tactile "ideas," in Berkeley's terminology) are themselves literally spatially extended and composed of minima—although Berkeley goes on to deny that anything exists outside of minds that such entities might resemble. This doctrine of extended perceptions allows Hume to jettison completely the Cartesian distinction between formal and objective being, with its corresponding doctrine that ideas have inherent intentionality by containing objective being. He is free to hold instead that perceptions possess qualities in only one way—namely, by literally exemplifying them. This is part of what he means when he insists that there is only one kind of existence (THN 1.2.6.1–8/66–68), and it is why he can write, as he does in explaining his theory of abstract ideas, that "the reference of the idea to an object [is] an extraneous denomination, of which in itself it bears no mark or character" (THN 1.1.7.6/20). This way of thinking about perceptions, in turn, explains his confidence in a central tenet of his treatment of abstract ideas already emphasized: that perceptions cannot be indeterminate with respect to quantity or quality. Whereas Descartes or Locke might suppose an idea to contain a general quality objectively without containing a full determination of its degree or specific character, for Hume there is no such containment relation. Instead, Humean ideas could be indeterminate only by being indeterminate in their own formally exemplified qualities—a prospect that he finds absurd [2.4].

The implicit but clear rejection of the Cartesian theory that an idea has an inherent reference to what it is about by containing it means that Humean perceptions cannot have intentionality in consequence of qualities contained by them but only in consequence of qualities exemplified by them and the relations to which those qualities give rise. Yet every idea does *have* "a reference to" an object that it is of or about, on Hume's view. Some, but not all, impressions do so as well. Notably, impressions of sensation typically represent external bodies [3.5], as he states explicitly when discussing representations of size or extension (THN 1.2.1.5/28, THN 1.2.3 15/38) and again in the first *Enquiry* (EHU 12.9/152). In contrast, those impressions of reflection that are passions do not themselves represent anything (THN 2.3.3.5/215), he thinks, although they typically occur together with ideas that represent something to which the passion is directed [3.6]. Hence the question urgently arises of how some—but not all—Humean perceptions manage to have intentionality at all, especially when the primary distinction between impressions and ideas is chiefly or exclusively one of mere liveliness, and the distinction between impressions of sensation and impressions of reflection is only one of causal origin.

The language of the Copy Principle, according to which ideas are derived from impressions "which are correspondent to them, and which they exactly represent," has naturally suggested to many readers that, for Hume, the intentionality of an idea consists in its *representing* something else simply in virtue of being a copy of it—that is, in virtue of resembling it through being causally derived from it. This cannot be the whole story, however. First, many things are copies of other things without representing them, as Hume would be among the first to observe. Second, he recognizes both representation without exact resemblance and representation without causal derivation. False ideas can be false—an idea of the planet Mars that includes canals, for example—largely because they fail to resemble completely what they represent, while ideas that represent future events cannot literally be caused by them. Furthermore, two ideas that have both the same resemblance relations and the same source in impressions can be made to represent different things under different circumstances. As already noted, for example, two qualitatively identical complex ideas can represent either a substance or a mode, depending on the idea's relation to the use of words [2.3]. As also noted, two qualitatively identical ideas can serve as the exemplars for different abstract ideas, thereby representing different classes or collections of things, depending on what general term it is associated with and what revival set of other ideas it is poised to elicit [2.4]. Moreover, qualitatively identical ideas can represent either an external body, an impression caused by that body, or even (when serving as an "idea of an idea") an idea caused by that impression [2.1, 3.5].

All of these examples suggest that perceptions represent as they do, for Hume, at least partly in virtue of the kinds of causal or functional roles they come to play within the mind. This suggestion is strengthened by the various examples of non-mental representations that Hume sprinkles throughout his writings: words can represent "facts or objects" (THN 1.3.9.12/113) and "impressions" (THN 2.1.2.1/277); a child can represent a parent's family in eliciting passions from others (THN 2.1.9.13/309); money can represent the beautiful and agreeable objects that it affords the power of obtaining (THN 2.2.5.6/359); the giving of "stone and earth" can represent the conveyance of a manor in property law (THN 3.2.4.2/515); and a "taper, habit, or grimace" may represent a religious mystery (THN 3.2.4.2/515–16). In each of these cases, Hume uses the term 'representation' because the representing item or event is taking on a significant part of a causal or functional role of what is said to be represented, doing so through its tendency to produce specific mental effects such as ideas, beliefs, sentiments, passions, and volitions.

In some of the cases just mentioned, a representation reliably indicates the presence of what it represents, and thereby serves reliably as a causal intermediary for it in the production of mental effects that are responsive to it. This occurs, for example, when a word is used to indicate the presence of the thing named, and it also occurs when impressions of sensation indicate the presence of a body or its sensible qualities. We might call this representation by *indication*. In other cases, the representation replicates part of the functional role of the represented object, quality, or event by producing effects in the mind that resemble or parallel effects that are or would be produced by the represented object itself. This occurs, for example, when objects and events play a role in stimulating passions and actions during religious ceremonies that is parallel to the role played by religious doctrines in the course of devotional life. It also occurs when an impression or lively idea (for example, of a rolling billiard ball) produces additional lively ideas in the mind (for example, of motions of other billiard balls) that themselves resemble the effects that would be produced in the external world by the presence of something resembling the original impression or idea. We might call this representation through *modeling*. Both kinds of representation may be combined in a single case. For example sensations of impressions may indicate to a hunter the qualities of an environment and the location of prey, thereby causing specific volitions for pursuit of the prey, while at the same time producing beliefs in the predator's mind that anticipate and parallel the behavior of the prey in that environment, thereby modeling them and also guiding behavior toward them.

In some cases, Hume explains how certain functional roles allow certain ideas to represent—ultimately, we may suppose, through indication, modeling or both—as they do. For example, he explains how linguistic usage allows complex ideas to represent either substances or modes, and how abstract ideas allow particular exemplars to model many things at once. Further explanations of different representational capacities could be developed within Hume's psychology—for example, of how the presence or absence of particular tendencies to associations, inferences, passions, and volitions might allow an idea to represent only an impression, or also represent an external body, or also represent instead another idea. It should be emphasized, however, both: (i) that Hume does not undertake the task of developing an explicit and general theory of mental representation; and (ii) that the task of developing an adequate general theory of mental representation remains a daunting one to the present day, with many obstacles not considered here.

Nevertheless, if this is indeed at least roughly how Hume thinks about mental representation, then it is readily understandable how he could suppose: (i) that some impressions represent while others do not; (ii) that qualitatively identical perceptions with different causal and function roles could represent differently; (iii) that mental representation is potentially a matter of degree, and something that can be done better or worse; (iv) that the same perception can represent more than one thing or quality, at least to some extent; and (v) that resemblance and causal derivation are each conducive to mental representation, without either being essential to it. It is even understandable why he should remark that ideas—whatever else they might also represent—"always represent the impressions or objects from which they are derived" (THN 1.3.3.11/37). Because ideas share all or nearly all of their features other than liveliness with the impressions from which they are derived, they are particularly suitable for indicating and modeling within a mind—and hence mentally representing—those impressions.

The most basic form of belief, for Hume, is a particular, non-abstract idea serving as a mental model and having sufficient liveliness to influence behavior in much the same way—if not with quite the same degree of power—that the corresponding impression would [2.1]. This kind of *unconceptualized* belief does not require abstract ideas and is common in animals just as it is in humans. Insofar as Hume does not regard animals as using general terms, however, he cannot regard them as having abstract ideas or conceptualized beliefs [2.4]. Accordingly, while animals might believe in the existence of a particular circle having a particular shade of red by having a lively idea exemplifying that shape and that shade of red, they cannot think of it as explicitly "a geometrical figure" or as "something red" more generally.

Abstract ideas allow human beings to form conceptual judgments—that is, judgments in which one or more things is classified as belonging to a general kind, having a general quality, or as standing in a general relation. Hume does not specify exactly how such conceptualized beliefs work, but he does refer to propositions that "contain a subject and a predicate" (THN 1.4.2.26/200), and we can infer what the nature of such beliefs must be. Because he holds that all belief consists in an idea's having liveliness, it seems that conceptual judgments must consist in the occurrence of a lively idea within the revival set of the appropriate occurring abstract idea elicited by a general term. Although he does not mention the possibility, there is no bar in principle to an abstract idea (such as DOG) itself occurring within the revival set of another abstract idea (such as MAMMAL). In such a case, the liveliness of the idea DOG would consist in the liveliness of its exemplar idea when functioning as the exemplar.

Whereas Hume describes liveliness as a feeling of positive belief, he does not propose the existence of any opposing or contrasting feeling of denial or rejection. Yet the simple absence of belief-constituting liveliness would not be denial, but rather mere absence of assent—doxastic indifference (that is, indifference with respect to belief). Accordingly, he is obliged to explain the mental denial of a proposition in terms of a positive belief in its contrary, and this in turn raises the question of how he understands contrariety within his theory of ideas. Although he says little about negative judgments as such, he does include "contrariety" as one of the seven philosophical relations [2.3], and he makes this initially puzzling statement about it:

> The relation of *contrariety* may at first sight be regarded as an exception to the rule, *that no relation of any kind can subsist without*

*some degree of resemblance*. But let us consider, that no two ideas are in themselves contrary, except those of existence and non-existence, which are plainly resembling, as implying both of them an idea of the object; tho' the latter excludes the object from all times and places, in which it is suppos'd not to exist.
(THN 1.1.5.8/15)

To understand this remark fully, we must distinguish between a conceptualized and a non-conceptualized way of representing the non-existence of something.

Non-conceptually—that is, without employing abstract ideas—the mind may in effect, at least to some extent, represent the non-existence of a particular object, quality, or event in a particular place at a particular time simply by:

(i) representing the place at that time;
(ii) *not* representing the object, quality, or event in it; and
(iii) being mentally *resistant* to including a representation of the object, quality, or event in it.

Perhaps the simplest manner of resistance would be to represent the place as completely filled with other objects and hence as spatially excluding the object in question. As Jonathan Cottrell (unpublished) has pointed out, however, the more general characterization is needed for two reasons. First, many objects—including sounds, smells, and passions—are neither spatially disposed nor well represented as spatially disposed for Hume, and so can neither be spatially excluded nor spatially represented as excluded by other things. Second, given his views about space, Hume must allow that the mind can represent an object as not existing in a place even as it represents that there are two other objects with nothing else between them in that place [2.5]. A more general mode of resistance to inclusion would consist in a tendency not to include, perhaps even when inclusion might be suggested by other psychological forces.

Representations of non-existence of this non-conceptualized kind may be highly non-specific, inasmuch as it is not necessary to form an idea of the excluded object in order to be resistant to including it. Accordingly, a single perception, whether simple or complex, may function through such resistance equally and simultaneously as an implicit representation of the non-existence of very many different things. Indeed, one could represent a room in this way as not containing an elephant—and also not a giraffe or a zebra—without one's ever having had an idea of an elephant, or a giraffe, or a zebra.

Forming a conceptualized representation (that is, an abstract idea) of the-non-existence-of-an-elephant, in contrast, would require use of a general term, an exemplar, and an appropriate further revival set of ideas of situations without elephants. In order to form a revival set whose members resemble each other precisely in their exclusion of elephants, however, it would presumably be necessary to employ an explicit idea of an elephant for purposes of contrast. Hence, when it comes to abstract ideas, at least, the idea of the existence of a thing and the idea of its non-existence are, as Hume remarks, "plainly resembling, as implying [i.e., requiring] both of them an idea of the object."

## 2.7 Conclusion

Hume aims to make progress in philosophy through an empirical investigation of the mind's contents and operations—what would now be called psychological and cognitive science. He finds conscious mental life itself to consist in a succession of perceptions, which he distinguishes into kinds by their degrees of intrinsic liveliness, by their composition, and by their causal and functional roles. One of his most distinctive theses of his psychology is that sensing and feeling, believing, and thinking without believing differ not in the qualitative character of the perceptions involved, but in their degree of liveliness—a feature of perceptions that also explains their ability to influence on voluntary action.

Hume can maintain this doctrine partly because he claims to discover that the perceptions involved in thinking are similar to, and derived from, the perceptions, a discovery expressed in his Copy Principle. His methodological empiricism thus supports his concept empiricism. The Copy Principle is one of four main principles concerning perceptions to which he frequently appeals in a wide range of contexts. His Separability Principle underwrites a kind of mental atomism whereby perceptions are composed of parts capable of distinction and full separation, at least in thought. His

Conceivability Principle brings this atomism directly to metaphysics, allowing a very broad scope to metaphysical possibility and imposing relatively few metaphysical necessities. His Principle of the Association of Ideas facilitates the explanation of many features of the behavior and interaction of ideas by appealing not to logical relations among them, but rather to the resemblance, contiguity, or causal relations of their objects. Hume offers positive empirical support for both the Copy Principle and the Principle of the Association of Ideas, while the Separability Principle relies primarily on Hume's application of the simple/complex distinction, and the Conceivability Principle seems to express his conception of possibility itself.

Whereas less empiricist predecessors such as Descartes, Malebranche, Spinoza, and Leibniz recognized intellectual ideas with rich innate semantic content not derivable from experience, Hume's theory of perceptions requires him to explain all mental operations in terms of ideas derived from impressions. In order to do so, he focuses on the differing causal and functional roles they can take on within the mind. Among the most important elements of his cognitive psychology is his theory of abstract ideas, or concepts. He invokes it frequently and uses it to explain the generality of thought without appeal to fundamental intrinsic intentionality, to indeterminate representations, or to universals as objects in which particulars participate. Like some contemporary philosophers of mind, he conceives of concepts not simply as dispositional abilities, but as real mental particulars that are causally active in thought. Although his treatment of abstract ideas is in many ways not fully developed, his recognition of an essential role for general terms, revival sets of ideas (representing the range of things falling under the concept), and a separate inferential or conceptual role nonetheless provide him with many resources for explaining mental phenomena not available to his predecessors.

Hume's empiricist account of the origins in experience of the concepts of space and time leads him to reject Newtonian conceptions of absolute space and time as things in their own right in favor of a conception of them as consisting in, and depending on, relations among things. His radical rejection of the infinite divisibility of space and time requires that he accept the conceivability and the reality of unextended points that compose extension by their conjunction, and it requires him to reject elements of Euclidean geometry. He was by no means the first philosopher in history to deny the infinite divisibility of space and time, and his finitistic Minimism has not been widely endorsed, but his fearlessness in questioning Euclidean geometry in the *Treatise* may be considered a salutary development, even if it is not a direct ancestor of subsequent non-Euclidean geometries.

Hume's acceptance of the literal extension of visual and tactile perceptions and his rejection of the containment model of intentionality lead him in the direction of a naturalistic conception of intentionality. On this conception, not all perceptions have intentionality, but those that do serve as mental representations because the qualities they exemplify allow them to take up a considerable share of the causal or functional role of other things—by indication, modeling, or both—in the production of effects within the mind. In that respect, as in so many others, he is a precursor of contemporary naturalists.

## Note

1 Hume himself emphasizes in a letter to Thomas Reid that the Copy Principle is not a mere pronouncement because he has offered two empirical arguments for it. See P. B. Wood (1986) "David Hume on Thomas Reid's *An Inquiry into the Human Mind, On the Principles of Common Sense*: A New Letter to Hugh Blair from July 1762," Mind 95(380): 411–16.

## Further reading

Ainslie, Donald C. (2010) "Adequate Ideas and Modest Scepticism in Hume's Metaphysics of Space," *Archiv für Geschichte der Philosophie* 92.1: 39–67. (An interpretation of Hume's treatment of space and time, with interesting relations to Kant.)

Boehm, Miren (2013) "Hume's Foundational Project in the *Treatise*," *European Journal of Philosophy* 21.3. (A valuable account of Hume's attempt to use his "science of man" to provide foundations for logic, mathematics, and natural philosophy.)

Baxter, Donald L. M. (2008) *Hume's Difficulty: Time and Identity in the Treatise*, London: Routledge. (Contains an excellent account of Hume's theory of time and "steadfast objects," as well as provocative arguments that Hume cannot recognize complex objects. See also the symposium devoted to this book in *Philosophical Studies* [2009]: 146.3.)

Bennett, Jonathan (2001) *Learning from Six Philosophers*, two volumes, Oxford: Clarendon Press. (Chapters 32 and 33 contain sustained reflections on Hume's theory of ideas, including an interpretation of Hume's Copy Principle according to which it is best understood as an *a priori* constraint on meaning.)

Cottrell, Jonathan (forthcoming) "A Puzzle about Fictions in the *Treatise*," *Journal of the History of Philosophy*. (Poses the question of how Hume can regard some fictions of the imagination, such as that of an unchanging object enduring through time, as "improper.")

Fodor, J. A. (2003) *Hume Variations*, Oxford: Clarendon Press. (A short, lively, and intentionally ahistorical defense, by a leading contemporary philosopher of mind, of the thesis that Hume was largely right in treating concepts as mental particulars.)

Frasca-Spada, Marina (1998) *Space and the Self in Hume's Treatise*, Cambridge: Cambridge University Press. (The richest and most detailed account of Hume's treatment of space.)

Garrett, Don (1997) *Cognition and Commitment in Hume's Philosophy*, New York: Oxford University Press. (Chapters 2 and 3 discuss in some detail Hume's support for, and applications of, the Copy Principle and the Separability Principle, as well as the topics of abstract ideas and distinctions of reason.)

Garrett, Don (2006) "Hume's Naturalistic Theory of Representation," *Synthese* 152.3: 301–319. (A fuller defense and application of the interpretation of Hume's theory of representation presented in [2.6].)

Holden, Thomas (2004) *The Architecture of Matter: Galileo to Kant*, Oxford: Clarendon Press. (Traces the history of the dispute over whether infinite divisibility requires an infinity of actual parts or only an infinity of potential parts, and discusses the way in which Hume's acceptance of the former view influences his view of space and time.)

Landy, David (2006) "Hume's Impression/Idea Distinction," *Hume Studies* 32.1 (April): 119–139. (A sophisticated treatment of the issues involved in interpreting the idea/impression distinction, arguing that Hume must supplement the criterion of liveliness.)

Shafer, Karl (2013) "Hume's Unified Theory of Mental Representation," *European Journal of Philosophy* 21.2. (An interpretation of Hume's theory of mental representation on which copying explain the representation of intrinsic properties and causal/functional role explains the representative of relational properties.)

# Three
## The mind and its faculties

Hume criticizes earlier philosophers for their abuse of the term 'faculty': "They need only say, that any phaenomenon, which puzzles them, arises from a faculty or an occult quality, and there is an end of all dispute and enquiry upon the matter" (THN 1.4.3.10/ 224). In such cases, he thinks, philosophers have had no specific idea of what it is that causes the phenomenon in question but at most a relative one [2.3], and so they have really given no effective causal explanation of it at all. This criticism does not prevent him from frequently employing the term 'faculty' himself in his account of the mind. On the contrary, he never hesitates to infer from the fact that the mind regularly does something of a particular recognizable kind that it has a power to do it and a faculty by which it does it.

Hume does not rest content with such superficial inferences, however. Instead, he aims to conduct "an accurate scrutiny into the powers and faculties of human nature" (EHU 1.13/13). This scrutiny involves two stages or levels. First, it requires what he calls "mental geography": the classification of faculties of the mind in accordance with clear and perspicuous distinctions. The faculties he seeks to distinguish in this way include "the imagination," "memory," "reason" (both "demonstrative" and "probable") or "the understanding," "the senses," "the passions," "taste," and "the will." The boundaries he draws among them and the relations he proposes between them are often original. Second, it requires, to the extent possible, well-supported causal explanations of the nature, origin, and characteristic manners of operation of the faculties so distinguished—that is, explanations of what he calls "their secret springs and principles," which often involve multiple sub-processes and are often subject to multiple influences. These explanations, too, are often highly original. Ultimately, he subjects the deliverances of these faculties to normative evaluations in light of those classifications and explanations. In order to understand his conception of the mental faculties, however, it is useful to understand his conceptions of mind and consciousness themselves.

### 3.1 Mind and consciousness

Many early modern philosophers, including Descartes and Locke, held that qualities and ideas—the latter what Hume calls "perceptions" [2.1]—cannot exist independently and must instead "inhere" in a substance: sensible qualities must inhere in material substances (that is, bodies), and what they call ideas must inhere in thinking substances (that is, minds). They thereby claim to conceive of substance as a metaphysically necessary underlying support, or substratum, for qualities or ideas that also serves to unify them as being the qualities or ideas of a single thing [2.3]. Hume claims, however, that individual qualities and perceptions are all different and hence, by the Separability Principle, separately conceivable. The Conceivability Principle then entails the possibility of their separate existence without the need for any such relation of metaphysical support. As previously observed, he finds no impression either of this relation or of a substantial substratum to which qualities or perceptions might bear it, and the Copy Principle thus serves to confirm that there are no such Humean ideas (THN 1.4.5.1–2/232). In the particular case case of the mind, he reports in a well-known passage:

> For my part, when I enter most intimately into what I call *myself*, I always stumble on some particular perception or other, of heat or cold, light or shade, love or hatred, pain or pleasure. I never can catch *myself* at any time without a perception, and never can observe any thing but the perception ... . If any one, upon serious and unprejudic'd reflection, thinks he has a different notion of *himself*, I must confess I can reason no longer with him. All I can allow him is, that he may be in the right as

well as I, and that we are essentially different in this particular. He may, perhaps, perceive something simple and continu'd, which he calls *himself*; tho' I am certain there is no such principle in me.

(THN 1.4.6.3/252)

Instead of treating the "mind," "person," or "self" as something different in kind from its perceptions, therefore, Hume characterizes it simply as "a bundle or collection of different perceptions, which succeed each other with an inconceivable rapidity, and are in a perpetual flux and movement" (THN 14.6.4/252). Some perceptions in the bundle—namely, those of sight and touch—are spatially disposed and hence capable of what he calls "local conjunction" (that is, being conjoined with respect to place) while the others are not [2.5–6]. Accordingly, and in the absence of any kind of substantial substratum, he rejects as unintelligible the very question of "the materiality or immateriality of the soul" (THN 1.4.5.6/234).

More specifically, Hume compares the mind to "a republic or commonwealth, in which the several members are united by the reciprocal ties of government and subordination" and give rise in their turn to other members who "propagate the same republic in the incessant changes of its parts" (THN 1.4.6.19/261). This comparison also serves to clarify the relation by which the perceptions are bundled together: all of "the several parts are still connected by causation." When "the mind" acts, it does so largely in virtue of the causal activity of the very perceptions that compose it.

Hume endorses what we may call *Universal Determinism*: "*that like objects, plac'd in like circumstances, will always produce like effects*" (THN 1.3.8.14/105). As he understands this principle, it requires that all events, whether physical or mental, occur in accordance with fully deterministic laws of nature—that is, laws that, in conjunction with any previous state of the universe, are sufficient to determine every aspect of any later state of the universe. He affirms this doctrine not because its denial would be metaphysically impossible; on the contrary, the falsehood of the doctrine is readily conceivable and so, by the Conceivability Principle, metaphysically possible. Rather, he affirms it because it seems to him that the history of increasingly successful searches for ever more precise causal explanations provides empirical support for its truth. The human mind, he argues, is in principle no less predictable than other aspects of nature in this regard, and the causal necessity involved is of precisely the same kind in both cases [6.4].

Yet causal generalizations concerning perceptions that Hume offers in his own science of man do not come close to being fully deterministic laws. He remarks, for example, that the Principle of the Association of Ideas provides only a "gentle force, that commonly prevails" (THN 1.1.4.1/10); while it makes one thought more probable than another, it cannot provide for any given thought a prediction with deterministic certainty of what the next thought will be. Moreover, he requires that complete causes must precede their effects immediately (THN 1.3.2.7/76), yet he holds that repeated experiences often produce permanent habitual associations between kinds of perceptions that are then manifested only intermittently over lengthy periods of time. Past experience likewise produce capacities for memory that are manifested, in many cases, only years later. Hume recognizes that persons can acquire standing dispositions to believe, ready to be elicited when their topic arises [2.1], and he emphasizes the importance of differences among persons in their enduring character traits—including virtues and vices—that involve dispositions to be motivated by different passions. He also recognizes differences in mental capacities among persons. Yet if Universal Determinism is true, there must be some enduring differences beyond the flux of fleeting perceptions that explain these differences in dispositions, traits, and capacities. For all of these reasons, Hume is therefore committed to the existence of what might be called enduring *background structures* pertaining to the mind, in addition to the perceptions themselves. These background structures must at least sometimes be produced or influenced by particular perceptions, and they must in turn serve to influence and facilitate mental operations. Hence, there must also be *background events* involving these structures.

Such structures and events are presumably, if not necessarily, located in the brain. He suggests as much in the course of explaining the tendency to conflate resembling objects:

> I shall therefore observe, that as the mind is endow'd with a power of exciting any idea it pleases; whenever it dispatches the

spirits into that region of the brain, in which the idea is plac'd; these spirits always excite the idea, when they run precisely into the proper traces, and rummage that cell, which belongs to the idea. But as their motion is seldom direct, and naturally turns a little to the one side or the other; for this reason the animal spirits, falling into the contiguous traces, present other related ideas in lieu of that, which the mind desir'd at first to survey. This change we are not always sensible of; but continuing still the same train of thought, make use of the related idea, which is presented to us, and employ it in our reasoning, as if it were the same with what we demanded. This is the cause of many mistakes and sophisms in philosophy; as will naturally be imagin'd, and as it wou'd be easy to show, if there was occasion.
(THN 1.2.5.20/61)

Just as a commonwealth may be composed of its citizens but nevertheless requires territory and many material goods in order to exist, so too a mind, for Hume, is composed of its perceptions but nevertheless requires a great deal of background structure in order to exist.

Because Hume holds that the mind itself is a system or bundle of causally related perceptions, without a postulated substantial substratum, he cannot and does not construe the mind's "consciousness" of its perceptions as a kind of mental inspection of perceptions by a mental substance or soul in which they inhere. Rather, the mind's consciousness of its perceptions consists simply in their inclusion within the causally related bundle itself; and degrees of consciousness pertaining to individual perceptions may plausibly correspond to degrees of causal power or activity of those perceptions within the bundle. This conception of consciousness explains his several remarks about the infallibility of the mind's consciousness of its own perceptions (THN 1.4.2.7/190; EHU 7.13/66): there is no possibility of misrepresentation in consciousness, and hence no possibility of falsehood either, for the simple reason that the consciousness of a perception does not itself require forming any purported representation of it with which the perception might fail to correspond. "Reflection," on the other hand, does involve forming an idea of a perception, and this process can involve obscurity or misrepresentation due to the difficulty of remembering or reconstructing perceptions that are often fleeting, fluctuating, and of little liveliness (EHU 1.13/13; EHU 7.1/60). At one point in the Appendix to the *Treatise*, Hume refers to "consciousness" as a kind of "reflected thought or perception," of the kind that might occur in memory (THN App 20/635); however, this characterization occurs within the scope of a report of what "most philosophers"—notably Locke—"seem inclin'd to think," and so employs the usage of those philosophers, not his own.

In the same portion of the Appendix, Hume famously reports finding a "contradiction" in his previous treatment of the identity of persons in the main body of the *Treatise*. Notoriously, he does not succeed in conveying clearly what precisely this contradiction is. Because he finds in it a further cause of skepticism, the nature of this apparent contradiction will be discussed in Chapter Seven [7.6].

## 3.2 Imagination and memory

Hume rejects the common seventeenth-century distinction—emphasized, for example, by Descartes, Malebranche, Spinoza, and Leibniz—between the intellect and the imagination as two different faculties of mental representation [2.2], each producing its own distinctive kind of idea. Ideas of the imagination were typically taken to derive from prior experiences and to resemble them in character, as implied by their assignment to a faculty of "images." For Hume, however, all ideas have this origin and character. The intellect, when contrasted with the imagination, is for him a merely supposed faculty for having "refin'd and spiritual ideas" that is posited in the first instance by mathematicians to explain their remarkable successes, but which is then readily endorsed by philosophers who seek to "cover many of their absurdities" by appeal to a special and higher source of knowledge (THN 1.3.1.7/72). According to Hume, the successes of mathematicians are in fact to be attributed not to their possession of any specially refined intellectual ideas, however, but rather to the operation of abstract ideas as he has explained them [2.4]. In rejecting the postulation of an intellect as a separate representational faculty, he is thus already cutting off a resource by which many of his predecessors had sought to make high-level theoretical considerations dictate the interpretation of empirical observation, thereby clearing the field for his own avowed methodology of allowing plain empirical observation to dictate theory—that is, methodological empiricism.

Making no room for a separate intellect, Hume draws a different distinction between two faculties for generating ideas (THN 1.3.3). The first is the imagination: the faculty of having ideas—copied at least in their simple parts from impressions [2.2]—that generally possess something less than the highest degree of liveliness possible for ideas. The second is memory: the faculty for having ideas capable of this highest level of liveliness that are also fixed and invariable with respect to order. A particular memory thus always involves, for him, a succession of ideas whereby it represents an object or event as being in the past. In addition, however, the order of their succession, fixed by the order of the impressions that they copy, cannot be altered without losing the liveliness that characterizes it. The liveliness of memory ideas can diminish somewhat over time, but if the ideas entirely lose their liveliness, it will typically be because they have been reproduced and reordered by the imagination instead [2.1].

In this broad sense of the term 'imagination', in which it denotes a faculty of having any ideas that are naturally less lively or "fainter" than memories, all of the operations that determine the ways in which the mind generates or modifies non-memory ideas qualify as operations of the imagination. This includes what he calls "reason." Hume also uses the term 'imagination' in a narrower sense, however, differing from the broader sense only in its exclusion of reason from its scope. He explains the difference between these two senses of the term in an important footnote:

> In general we may observe, that as our assent to all probable reasonings is founded on the liveliness of ideas, it resembles many of those whimsies and prejudices which are rejected under the opprobrious character of being the offspring of the imagination. By this expression it appears that the word, *imagination*, is commonly us'd in two different senses; and tho' nothing be more contrary to true philosophy, than this inaccuracy, yet in the following reasonings I have often been oblig'd to fall into it. When I oppose the imagination to the memory, I mean the faculty, by which we form our fainter ideas. When I oppose it to

reason, I mean the same faculty, excluding only our demonstrative and probable reasonings. When I oppose it to neither, 'tis indifferent whether it be taken in the larger or more limited sense, or at least the context will sufficiently explain the meaning.
(THN 1.3.9.19n/117)

For convenience and clarity, we may express this distinction as one between *inclusive imagination* and *unreasoning imagination*.

## 3.3 Reason or the understanding

Like Locke and many others, Hume often uses the pluralizable word 'reason' to mean roughly "an approved or proper consideration for belief or action," and the term 'reasonable' to describe beliefs or actions for which there is a balance of reasons. Also like Locke and others, however, he often uses the term 'reason' in an unpluralizable way as the name for what he also calls "our reasoning faculty" (THN Introduction 5/xv; THN 1.3.15.12/176; ATHN 3/646). Finally, again with Locke and others, he recognizes two kinds of reasoning identified in the footnote just quoted: demonstrative and probable. For Hume, demonstrative reasoning always yields knowledge in the strict sense [2.1] and concerns what he calls "relations of ideas"; probable reasoning yields belief and concerns what he calls "matters of fact" [2.1, 2.3]. The distinction between relations of ideas and matters of fact is often called *Hume's Fork*.

The version of the manuscript of the *Treatise* that Hume sent to his printer contained, in Book 2, a similar short footnote, but he subsequently arranged for its removal and replacement by the lengthier Book 1 version. The shorter original footnote is nearly identical to the final sentences of its replacement, except that it has 'the understanding' in place of 'reason':

> To prevent all ambiguity, I must observe, that where I oppose the imagination to the memory, I mean in general the faculty that presents our fainter ideas. In all other places, and particularly when it is opposed to the understanding, I understand the same faculty, excluding only our demonstrative and probable reasonings.
> (originally placed as a note to THN 2.2.7.6/371)

As Peter Millican (Garrett and Millican 2011) has rightly observed, Hume seems to use the terms 'reason' and 'the understanding' interchangeably in many passages for the sake of mere verbal variation. Yet this is puzzling, since the latter term, at least, is usually taken to have a broader scope than merely "our demonstrative and probable reasonings."

One notable example of this broader scope is found in Locke himself, whose entire *magnum opus* is devoted to "Human Understanding" while containing a single chapter (ECHU 4.17, "Of Reason") devoted to the reasoning faculty. According to him,

> The Power of Perception is that which we call the *Understanding*. Perception, which we make the act of the Understanding, is of three sorts: 1. The Perception of *Ideas* in our Minds. 2. The Perception of the signification of signs. 3. The Perception of the Connexion or Repugnancy, Agreement or Disagreement, that there is between any of our *Ideas*. All these are attributed to the *Understanding*, or Perceptive Power, though it be the two latter only that use allows us to say we understand.
>
> (ECHU 2.21.5)

Although Locke uses the term 'understanding' for the power of perception generally, he limits the term 'reason' to the specific power to engage in reasoning. He explains reasoning as the discovery and ordering of "intermediate" ideas so as to enable the mind to come to perceive the "Connexion or Repugnancy, Agreement or Disagreement" of ideas constituting the truth of a conclusion; reason is thus specifically the faculty or power of "*Illation or Inference*" (ECHU 4.17.2). This inference-based perception can be either demonstrative or probable, for Locke, but in either case it is to be contrasted with immediate and non-inferential "intuition" of the agreement or disagreement between ideas.

Hume's typical narrower use of 'the understanding', as at least roughly equivalent to 'reason', seems to result from two respects in which his account of the mind differs from Locke's. First, he does not recognize "perception" as a specific act or operation that the mind performs on its contents at all. Instead, as we have seen, Hume conceives of the mind as a system or "bundle" of perceptions, and the mind's conscious awareness of these perceptions consists simply in the holding of the distinctive causal relations among them in virtue of which they together compose that mind [3.1]. He does allow that the mind sometimes forms further reflective ideas of its perceptions, but this is not essential to their being perceptions in the mind. Moreover, even Locke allows that the perception of "*Ideas*" in the mind is not generally expressed by saying "we understand," thereby implicitly licensing a narrower sense. Second, although Hume discusses the perception of the signification of (verbal) signs—and incidentally acknowledges in his phrasing of the original version of the footnote that he "understands" the signification of the word 'understanding' in two different ways—he treats it as a species of association that is itself implicated in probable reasoning concerning intended meanings (THN 1.3.6.14–15/93), so that it need not be considered as an operation of the understanding distinct from reasoning.

The third and remaining element on Locke's list, however—namely, perception of the agreement or disagreement of ideas—is precisely the kind of perception that Locke regards as always the result of either intuition or reasoning. Accordingly, Hume can easily arrive, from a Lockean starting point, at a sense of 'the understanding' that makes it nearly co-extensive with 'reason'. It differs at most only in that intuition—which is immediate and non-inferential—is an exercise of understanding, but not strictly speaking of reasoning. This seemingly does not prevent his ready interchange of the two terms in the many contexts in which he is concerned with what "reason" can accomplish, however, inasmuch as what may be known by immediate intuition may generally be known or confirmed by reasoning as well.

Hume arguably uses the term 'understanding' with a broader scope closer to Locke's in his titling of *Treatise* Book 1, "Of the Understanding," and perhaps also in the title of *An Enquiry concerning Human Understanding*. Both titles seem intended partly to remind the reader of the relation of Hume's writings to Locke's, and Hume can employ a suitably broader sense of 'understanding' for this purpose by: (i) treating the understanding as including the "perceiving of" impressions and ideas (as per Locke's first "act of the Understanding"); and then (ii) treating the "perceiving of" impressions and ideas simply as their inclusion in a mind. In contrast, Hume's use of the term in a section title of the first *Enquiry*—"Sceptical Doubts concerning the

Operations of the Understanding" (EHU 4)—readily lends itself to the narrower reading that is equivalent to "the reasoning faculty."

Another broader use of the term may be found in an important footnote in the *Treatise* describing "a very remarkable error" inculcated by "the schools" and consisting in a "vulgar division of the actions of the understanding into *conception, judgment, and reasoning*" together with the definitions given of them (THN 1.3.7.5n20/96–97). This use of 'the understanding', however, is clearly meant to be that of scholastic philosophers, rather than Hume himself. The definitions to which he objects treat conception as the mere survey of ideas, judgment as their separating or uniting, and reasoning as judgment through the interposition of other ideas. He objects to them on three grounds. First, judgment need not always involve multiple ideas; instead, something can be believed to exist simply by having a lively idea of it [2.1, 2.6]. Second, probable reasoning need not involve the interposition of other ideas; instead, in a suitably prepared mind, it can proceed immediately from cause to effect or vice versa [3.4]. Third, all judgment and reasoning can be regarded as particular ways of coming to have ideas and hence both can be reduced to conception. Although many might classify judgment as a function of the understanding distinct from reason, evidently for Hume judgment is simply the faculty of having knowledge or belief as a result of reasoning or intuition, and hence its exercises always arise from the understanding in the narrow sense. In consequence of his claims, conception, judgment, and reasoning can all be regarded as exercises of the inclusive imagination—but that is a distinctive Humean doctrine that would lend itself to misunderstanding if first proposed in a title.

Early in *Treatise* Book 3, Hume characterizes reason as "the discovery of truth or falshood" (THN 3.1.1.9/458), and this remark, with its definite article, suggests to some readers that he employs the term 'reason' in a broader way as well, encompassing within its scope other cognitive faculties such as intuition, memory, and the senses. Such a usage was quite common in eighteenth-century British philosophy—as Millican has documented. Elsewhere, however, he writes of reason more specifically as the "judgment" of truth and falsehood (THN 2.3.3.8/417; DP 5.1). In context, it is not obvious that he means anything more than that reason is *a* kind of discovery (uncovering, revealing) of truth and falsehood—which is all that his argument in *Treatise* Book 3 requires. In any case, he continues throughout his writings to contrast both "reason" and "the understanding," on the one hand, with the senses and memory, on the other, and to argue that various mental operations cannot be produced "by reason" solely on the grounds that they can be produced neither by demonstrative reasoning, nor by probable reasoning (THN 1.3.6 [3.4]; THN 2.3.3 [3.7]; THN 3.1.1 [8.1]).

## 3.4 Demonstrative reasoning and probable reasoning

Like Locke, Hume regards demonstrative reasoning as requiring a series of intuitions, each of which is or depends on the awareness of a relation among ideas. Although Locke declares that sensation of external objects "passes under the name of Knowledge" (ECHU 4.2.14) along with intuition and demonstration, Hume regards intuition and demonstration as the only sources of knowledge in the strict sense. For him, only four invariable kinds of relations are capable of underwriting strict knowledge: resemblance, contrariety, degrees in quality, and proportions in quantity and number [2.3]. Furthermore, it is commonly only proportions in quantity and number that require demonstration, he holds, since relations of the other three kinds are usually intuitively evident at first appearance.

For Hume, with his rejection of a separate perceiving substance of the kind envisioned by Locke, the most rudimentary consciousness or awareness of one of these "relations of ideas" presumably lies merely in the relevant ideas existing together in a mind in such a way as to be capable of affecting, through their relation, that mind's future perceptions (usually ideas). Yet it is notable that he never describes animals—which must lack full-fledged abstract ideas, if they lack the use of general terms—as engaging in demonstrative reasoning. Furthermore, he sometimes uses the term 'abstract reasoning' interchangeably with 'demonstrative reasoning' [2.4]. Both of these facts strongly suggest, although he does not say as much, that he thinks successful demonstrative reasoning typically involves recognizing relations among abstract ideas by way of successful or unsuccessful efforts at operations of inclusion, exclusion, combination, and intersection of their revival sets. This, in turn, would help to explain—what would otherwise be mysterious—how knowledge of such truths as {all dogs are mammals} could be accommodated within the constraints of the four knowledge-underwriting kinds of relations. For the abstract idea DOG *resembles* the abstract idea MAMMAL in having all of the members of its revival set included in the revival set of the latter idea, and this allows the class of dogs to be represented as resembling the class of mammals in this inclusionary respect.

Hume agrees with Locke that probable reasoning provides belief rather than knowledge, but he diverges dramatically from Locke in his account of such reasoning; indeed, it is here that perhaps the greatest originality in Hume's entire account of human cognitive faculties lies. Locke models his treatment of probable reasoning on his treatment of demonstrative reasoning: in both cases, "intermediate" ideas serve to allow the mind to perceive relations that it otherwise would not, but in the case of probable reasoning the relations perceived are themselves only "probable" or "for the most part." Locke distinguishes two "grounds of probability": testimony and conformity to past experience (ECHU 4.15.4). Presumably, he thinks that ideas either of perceived testimony or of past events in similar circumstances are the intermediate ideas that somehow allow the mind to perceive the probable connection. For Hume, in contrast, probable reasoning depends only on conformity to past experience: testimony is not a separate ground of probability at all but instead functions simply as a species of it, in virtue of (and only to the extent that one has) experience of the past veracity of particular kinds of testimony [9.6]. Moreover, instead of regarding memories of experienced past occurrences as intermediaries present at the time of probable inference, Hume treats those past experiences as setting up an habitual association in the mind, so that there is no need for any present recall of past instances at the time of inference.

More specifically, according to Hume, all probable inference requires past perception of the "constant conjunction" of two types of events or objects, experiences in which an event or object of one type (call it a C) is always immediately followed by an event or object of a second (call this an E). After a series of such experiences has established an association, the occurrence in the mind of a perception of something of either type (call this perception, whether of a C or of an E, the *initiating perception*) will immediately lead the mind to form an idea of something of the other type. In doing so, the mind in effect treats an event or object of the first type in the constant conjunction (the C) as a cause and the event or object of the second type in the constant conjunction (the E) as its effect. Furthermore, when this initiating perception has a high degree of liveliness—whether because it is an impression, or a memory, or even just a belief produced by a previous instance of probable reasoning—the idea that follows it by association will also acquire some liveliness from it, sufficient to render that idea a belief. This explains how belief-generating inferences can be made either from cause to effect or from effect to cause. For Hume, all probable reasoning is ultimately "causal" in this way.

When, in contrast, the initiating perception is a "mere" (that is, unlively) idea rather than an impression, memory, or belief, the associated idea that follows it will be a mere idea as well, and the conclusion will be merely hypothetical rather than a belief. In either case, however, the inferential operation is an instance of the more general psychological principle that he calls "custom or habit" [2.3]—that is, the mental mechanism by which the past repetition of a performance of some kind leads naturally to a new performance in similar circumstances "without any new reasoning or conclusion" (THN 1.3.8.10/102; see also EHU 5.5/43).

In Hume's view, then, a crucial component of probable reasoning—which, he emphasizes, is itself the basis of nearly all human judgment about the world beyond memory or present perception, including most judgments in the sciences outside mathematics—is closely akin to the mental operation by which animals are trained and by which human beings come to perform regular rituals of grooming. His famous argument that this crucial component is *not* due to "reasoning, or any operation of the understanding," but instead to the (unreasoning) imagination, will be analyzed in Chapter Six [6.1], and his treatment of its potentially skeptical implications will be further examined in Chapter Seven [7.2–3].

Much as Hume uses 'imagination' in broader and narrower senses [3.2], he also uses the term 'probability' in broader and narrower senses. In the inclusive sense just discussed and employed—which corresponds to Locke's only sense of the term—probability is contrasted with demonstration or knowledge and includes all inferences from experience, regardless of the particular degree of confidence they engender. This we may call *inclusive probability*. Hume goes on, however, to divide this inclusive probability into "proof" and "probability" in a narrower sense—a sense that, he emphasizes, corresponds more closely to the common use of the term (THN 1.3.11.2/124; see also EHU 6, "Of Probability"). Proof, in Hume's sense, while not demonstration, provides a high level of psychological certainty resulting from the experience of completely uniform and pervasive constant conjunction. In contrast, probability in the narrow sense—*sub-proof probability* we may call it—encompasses only conclusions of somewhat lesser psychological certainty and is always a matter of degree. He further divides the various mental operations that produce degrees of belief that are below the level of proof into "philosophical" and "unphilosophical" probabilities. A species of probability is philosophical if it is reflectively approved by philosophical enquirers, and it is unphilosophical if it "has not had the good fortune to obtain the same sanction" (THN 1.3.13.1/143).

One species of philosophical probability is "the probability of chances" (THN 1.3.11; EHU 6). In every instance of the probability of chances, one aspect of an outcome is rendered psychologically certain by the completely uniform past experience that constitutes a proof—for example, that a rolled die will land with one of its faces turned up, rather than on point or on one edge (or disappearing in a puff of smoke). Past experience may suggest nothing, however, about which one of multiple possible *versions* of this certain outcome will occur—for example, about what will be marked on the face that turns up. Accordingly, the mind will form one idea of each face of the die, and each idea will have an equal similar share of the total liveliness that is derived from the initiating perception and possessed by the belief in the certain but more general ("face up") outcome. If any of these equal "chances" are similar to one another—for example, if multiple faces of the die have the same marking—then their images will coalesce and combine their liveliness, resulting in a single idea having a greater proportion of the total liveliness than is possessed by any single "chance." This will provide the mind with a proportionately higher degree of belief in the outcome represented by this united image. In offering this account, Hume implies, he is also explaining how what was historically a non-quantitative notion of "chance" as a mere "absence of causes" has become a quantifiable notion of "the chances"—a notion that can then be extended to the psychologically quite similar case of what he calls "the probability of causes" as well.

In the fully developed form of "the probability of causes," (THN 1.3.12; EHU 6), there is a less-than-exceptionless constancy in previous experience: of twenty ships sent out, to take Hume's example, nineteen return safely. In such cases, each past experience functions as an "experiment" that generates, upon a new instance of an initiating perception, a "view" of an outcome with a certain limited degree of liveliness. Much like chances, the views of the numerically predominant type (of ships returning, to continue the example) coalesce with one another, pooling their liveliness in the process; but the incompatible views of the numerically lesser type (a ship not returning) also have some lesser (though still pooled, if more than one) liveliness and serve to diminish the liveliness of the stronger idea. The result is a degree of liveliness—and hence, belief—for the predominant united idea that corresponds to the proportion of "positive" experiments in the total number of experiments.

Although it does not lend itself so readily to mathematical treatment, Hume considers "analogy" to be a third kind of philosophical probability (THN 1.3.13.25/142; EHU 10.36/128). In analogy, a series of past experiences may itself be entirely uniform, but the degree of resemblance between the experienced cases and a new kind of case (provided by the initiating perception) to which it is applied is less than perfect, resulting in a transfer of a lesser degree of liveliness. The probability of analogy plays a crucial role in the Design Argument for the existence of God [9.3]; it can also play a role, at least in principle, in deciding between conflicting proofs, as in the case of miracles [9.6].

In addition to these three species of philosophical probability, Hume describes four species of unphilosophical probability (THN 1.3.13, "Of unphilosophical probability"), each of which involves a feature of the inclusive imagination by which liveliness is enhanced or diminished. The first applies to inferences in which the initiating perception is a memory: in such cases, there is a tendency for the initiating memory to generate livelier (and hence stronger) belief when it is fresh, but to generate less lively (and hence weaker) belief as the liveliness of the memory itself begins to fade. The second derives from the tendency of the most recent experiments (which need not be remembered) to produce greater degrees of belief than earlier experiments simply because the relative freshness of their associative link to the initiating perception allows them to convey a greater share of liveliness from it to the "views" derived from them. The third derives from the tendency of long arguments with disparate steps to generate less belief merely because some liveliness is lost at each step of the fatiguing and attention-weakening chain of different ideas. The fourth derives from the tendency to "*general rules*, which we rashly form to ourselves" and typically maintain even in the face of "observation and experience" to the contrary. Ethnic and national prejudices—errors to which "perhaps this nation as much as any other" is subject, the Scottish Hume writes to his predominantly English original audience—are notable examples of such unphilosophical rules.

Philosophers disapprove the influence of these four species of probability, Hume holds, primarily because each can be seen upon reflection to promote inconstancy and inconsistency in belief without any corresponding change or difference in the experience itself. That is, they cause conclusions derived from the very same sets of experience to differ in their liveliness in a single person at different times and among different persons even at the same time.

## 3.5 The senses

Hume uses the term 'sense' not only for the external senses of sight, hearing, taste, smell, and touch, but also for capacities to have characteristic sentiments of humor, beauty and deformity, and virtue and vice [3.6, 4.1–2]. He calls the latter "senses" on analogy with the former, and he treats other important capacities of the mind on analogy with these [4.3–4]. Following common usage, however, he uses the unqualified plural term 'the senses' to apply only to the five external senses. "The senses," therefore, is the faculty of having impressions of sensation by means of the stimulation of sense organs. Because such impressions typically represent, and facilitate belief in the existence of, external bodies and their qualities, however, he writes of these functions as included within the scope of the senses as well. (At THN 1.2.5.26/46, for example, the senses discover "external properties"; at THN 1.3.6.2/87, the conjunction of external causes and effects is "perceiv'd by the senses"; at THN 1.4.2.38/207, the mind is said to "see and feel" things that at other times are no longer present to the mind; at EHU 12.6/151, perceptual illusions concerning bodies constitute an "argument against the senses.") Because no perceptions are inherently representational, however, he must explain how impressions of sensation are taken to provide information about external bodies [2.6].

Hume provides the details of his explanation—the "secret springs and principles"—only in the *Treatise* (THN 1.4.2, "Of scepticism with regard to the senses"), where he begins by remarking:

> We may well ask, *What causes induce us to believe in the existence of body?* but 'tis in vain to ask, *Whether there be body or not?* That is a point, which we must take for granted in all our reasonings.
> (THN 1.4.2.1/187)

His intricate explanation begins from an analysis of what exactly we believe when we believe in the existence of bodies. Whereas Locke appealed to an unanalyzed idea of "real" or "external existence" and Berkeley denied that bodies could be conceived at all as anything other than collections of ideas in minds, Hume holds that the belief in bodies is the belief in the existence of things having "continu'd and distinct existence." By this he means: (i) existence that continues even when not perceived by the mind; and (ii) existence that is distinct from the mind in being both (a) "external" to (that is, not "in") it, and (b) causally "independent" of it with respect to both "existence" and "operation." He distinguishes two versions of the belief in bodies. The "vulgar" view, which arises at an early stage of development of every human mind, does not draw a distinction between impressions of sensation and bodies; rather, it attributes continued and distinct existence to some of the very impressions of which it is immediately conscious. It does so, he proposes, because of an error or confusion about "identity."

A thing has "strict" or "perfect" identity, as Hume understands it, if and only if it undergoes no change or interruption itself but co-exists with multiple distinct elements of a temporal succession

[2.6] in such a way as to be treated by the mind as "participating" in that succession. Crucially, however, the feeling of mentally reviewing some changing or interrupted successions of closely related things is very similar in its smooth "facility" and ease to the feeling of mentally reviewing an instance of perfect identity. In consequence, the mind readily mistakes such successions—which he later calls "imperfect" or "fictitious" identities—for instances of perfect identity. Presumably, this involves misremembering instances of imperfect identities as though they were perfect identities and/or at least sometimes including instances of imperfect identities in the revival set of the abstract idea of identity while nevertheless retaining an inferential or conceptual role [2.4] more appropriate only to perfect identity. The identity (in Hume's sense) of the mind itself ([3.1]; THN 1.4.2.39/207; THN 1.4.6) is also an imperfect or fictitious one, in consequence of the many relations of causation and also resemblance (the latter chiefly as a result of memory) present within the bundle of perceptions that constitutes the mind.

The source of the error about identity that contributes to the vulgar belief in bodies lies in two general features of the mind's impressions of sensation: their "constancy" and their "coherence." Constancy, as Hume explains it, is the tendency for sense impressions to be followed by qualitatively identical impressions after interruptions (such as typically occur upon closing one's eyes or turning one's head, for example). This constancy leads the mind to misattribute a perfect identity to the in-fact-interrupted succession of many of its impressions. Subsequently noticing that the objects of its immediate perception are in fact interrupted at least in its consciousness of them, but still unable to resist for long the attribution of perfect identity to them, the mind avoids incipient conflict by conceiving of these objects as continuing to exist even when they are not perceived; the liveliness required to render this conception a belief is provided by the impressions before and after the interruption. Finally, because the mind now treats these immediate objects of perception as having continued existence, it is obliged to treat them as having existence that is distinct from the mind as well.

Coherence, as Hume explains it, is the tendency of sense impressions to exemplify, even with some interruptions, portions of commonly recurring successions of closely related events. For example, one might often perceive the sequence of sense impressions characteristic of a log burning to ash in the fireplace; but if one begins perceiving such a sequence and then is interrupted, perceiving other things while missing its intermediate elements, one will often nevertheless find the final parts of the characteristic sequence occurring after the interruption. The attribution of continued and distinct existence to (what are in fact) impressions of sensation is strengthened by their coherence, because this allows the mind to retain a sense of the uniformity of previously observed constant conjunctions [3.4] that would otherwise by contradicted by the failure to perceive *both* elements of the conjunction in a new case. Because the belief in bodies enables the mind to interpret the world as continuing to exemplify previously observed constant conjunctions, Hume characterizes the belief as being due in part to a kind of probable reasoning; it is irregular and "oblique" reasoning, however, because, unlike regular probable reasoning, it leads the mind not just to attribute observed degrees of regularity to unobserved cases but to attribute much higher degrees of regularity to the world than it strictly observes there (THN 1.4.2.21/ 197–98; see also THN 1.4.5.20/242).

While the coherence of sense perceptions makes a contribution to the attribution of continued and distinct existence, it is the mistake about identity facilitated by their constancy that plays the primary role, in Hume's view. This is not only because that operation is more powerful than the one by which the mind tends to attribute a greater degree of regularity than it finds—he compares the latter to the operation by which a galley once set in motion by its oars continues further in the same direction without any new impulse—but also, one may suppose, because the very regularities in question are much more easily discerned once the mind is already thinking of a world of continued and distinct bodies. Accordingly, despite the role of a kind of irregular reasoning, he ascribes to the unreasoning imagination that sub-operation of the senses that results in the belief in continued and distinct existence (THN 1.4.2.2–14/187–93).

Hume emphasizes that there is no contradiction at all in the vulgar belief that the very entities of which we are immediately conscious in sense perception—namely, impressions of sensation— often exist unperceived. This is because the mind itself can be conceived, and indeed rightly is conceived, simply as a bundle or collection of causally related perceptions; hence, the same thing can be "in" (and so perceived by) the mind at some times and "out" of (and so unperceived by) the mind at other times, simply by temporarily acquiring or losing those causal relations. It is easy enough to see why it should be of great importance to him that the belief he attributes to the vulgar not be simply contradictory: his Conceivability Principle requires that what is metaphysically impossible is also inconceivable, and his theory that belief is a lively idea entails that what is inconceivable (that is, cannot be represented by an idea) also cannot be believed.

Yet while the vulgar view of bodies is by no means contradictory, it can, Hume argues, readily be shown to be false by simple experiments concerning the operations of sense perception. By pressing one's eyeball, for example, one can double the number of impressions of sensation one has of a given object; by varying the distance to the object one can vary the size of the impression; and other impressions vary with the health or disorder of the sense organs. Given this great potential variety of incompatible numbers, sizes, and qualities of impressions, it seems that sense organs should not be understood as allowing immediate consciousness of objects that are external to and independent of the mind, but instead of entities that are internal to and dependent on the mind. If, however, these entities are not causally independent of or external to the mind—that is, are not distinct existences in Hume's sense—then they cannot have continued existence, either.

One obvious response to this discovery of the falsehood of the vulgar view would be to deny that there really are any bodies at all. In fact, however, the mind is too firmly committed to the existence of continued and distinct existences—primarily through the original mistaken attribution of identity—for this proposal to acquire or maintain any significant degree of belief. Instead, Hume reports, philosophers postulate a separate set of continued and distinct existences that they take to resemble and cause the sense impressions of which the mind is immediately conscious. These further existences are typically taken to bear a close resemblance to sense impressions simply because that is psychologically the easiest and most natural way to conceive of them. Indeed, because philosophers do not usually conceive of bodies as "specifically different"—that is, having different qualitative features (THN 1.2.6.8–9/67–68; THN 1.4.5.19/241)—from sense impressions, Hume at one point calls these postulated bodies "a new set of perceptions" (THN 1.4.2.56/218). It can be tempting to interpret this rhetorical maneuver as a commitment on Hume's part at least temporarily to *idealism* or *immaterialism*, the doctrine that everything is or exists in some mind, or at least to the doctrine that alternatives to idealism are inconceivable. Against this interpretation, however, it should be borne in mind that he has already declared that perceptions themselves, as he uses the term, can be extended and can in principle exist outside of any mind. Hence, to call things a "second set of perceptions" in this ironic fashion is not to deny that they would *also* be bodies.

Hume argues that this "philosophical" view of "double existence" (that is, of the existence of both sense impressions on the one hand and bodies on the other) has "no primary recommendation either to reason or the [unreasoning] imagination" (THN 1.4.2.47/212). It has no primary recommendation to reason because: (i) the topic, as concerned with matters of fact, is not suitable for demonstrative reasoning; and yet (ii) probable reasoning requires immediate experience of a constant conjunction between cause and effect—something that is impossible in this case because the mind is immediately aware only of its perceptions, and not *also*, immediately preceding them in experience, of the distinct bodies that are supposed to cause them. The philosophical opinion of double existence also has no primary recommendation to the unreasoning imagination, because that faculty naturally gives rise not to the philosophical view but rather to the vulgar view, through the process based on constancy and coherence just described. The liveliness required for any belief in bodies derives entirely from the somewhat confused psychological operations giving rise to the vulgar view; the philosophical view merely re-channels that liveliness, by reflection and reasoning on the empirical facts of sense perception, into a somewhat new direction.

Because it is not the natural outcome of either the unreasoning imagination or reflective reasoning operating alone, Hume calls the philosophical view the "monstrous offspring" of these "two principles." In calling it "monstrous," he need not be expressing epistemic disapproval of the view, but merely describing it as falling outside the species boundaries of each of its parents. Nevertheless, in reflecting on the newly discovered origins of the belief in bodies, in both its vulgar and philosophical versions, he experiences a momentary wave of intense doubt, which he expresses thus:

> I cannot forbear giving vent to a certain sentiment, which arises upon reviewing those systems. I begun this subject with premising that we ought to have an implicit faith in our senses, and that this wou'd be the conclusion, I should draw from the whole of my reasoning. But to be ingenuous, I feel myself *at present* of a quite contrary sentiment, and am more inclin'd to repose no faith at all in my senses, or rather imagination, than to place in it such an implicit confidence. I cannot conceive how such trivial qualities of the fancy, conducted by such false suppositions, can ever lead to any solid and rational system. They are the coherence and constancy of our perceptions, which produce the opinion of their continu'd existence; tho' these qualities of perceptions have no perceivable connexion with such an existence. The constancy of our perceptions has the most considerable effect, and yet is attended with the greatest difficulties. 'Tis a gross illusion to suppose, that our resembling perceptions are numerically the same; and 'tis this illusion, which leads us into the opinion, that these perceptions are uninterrupted, and are still existent, even when they are not present to the senses. This is the case with our popular system. And as to our philosophical one, 'tis liable to the same difficulties; and is over-and-above loaded with this absurdity, that it at once denies and establishes the vulgar supposition ... . What then can we look for from this confusion of groundless and extraordinary opinions, but error and falshood? And how can we justify to ourselves any belief we repose in them?
> (THN 1.4.2.56/217–18)

The philosophical view is "liable to the same difficulties" as the vulgar view inasmuch as its etiology depends on the same "trivial qualities of the fancy"—that is, of the unreasoning imagination—as the vulgar view. Through its essential dependence for its doxastic force on the vulgar view that it rejects, it at once "denies and establishes" that view. There is nevertheless one difficulty of the vulgar view to which the philosophical view is, of course, not subject on Hume's account: unlike its predecessor, it cannot be shown to be false by a few experiments. Furthermore, it is hard to avoid the conclusion that his own considered opinion is an instance of the philosophical view that there *are* continued and distinct existences that cause our sense impressions "from the applications of objects to the external organs" (THN 2.1.1.1/275; see [2.1]). This much is so even though he remains diffident, for reasons considered in a later section of the *Treatise* (THN 1.4.4, "Of the modern philosophy"; [7.2]), about the *extent* of their resemblance to impressions of sensation, and even though he acknowledges that he, like other philosophers, will readily slip back into the vulgar way of thinking in ordinary life. For he readily acknowledges the vulgar view to be positively false, while denial or suspense of judgment about continued and distinct existences is no viable option at all, despite our admitted permanent susceptibility to temporary bouts of doubt:

> This sceptical doubt ... with respect to ... the senses, is a malady which can never be radically cur'd, but must return upon us every moment, however we may chase it away, and sometimes may seem entirely free from it. It is impossible upon any system to defend ... [our] senses; and we but expose them further when we endeavour to justify them in that manner. As the sceptical doubt arises naturally from a profound and intense reflection on those subjects, it always encreases, the farther we carry our reflections, whether in opposition or conformity to it. Carelessness and in-attention alone can afford us any remedy. For this reason I rely entirely upon them; and take it for granted, whatever may be the reader's opinion at this present moment, that an hour hence he will be perswaded there is both an external and internal world.
> (THN 1.4.2.57/218; see also EHU 12.15n32/155)

Throughout the *Treatise* and throughout his other works, Hume makes innumerable claims that require the existence of bodies for their truth, and many of these require as well a "philosophical" distinction between bodies and impressions of sensation that are caused by them. How—or whether—the admittedly inevitable acceptance of a double-existence view can be a philosophically satisfactory state of affairs, however, is a topic not entirely settled until the final sections of Treatise Book 1 and the first Enquiry. These sections, and their bearing on belief in the existence of bodies, will be considered in Chapter Seven.

## 3.6 The passions and taste

Hume divides impressions of reflection into two general kinds, which he calls the "calm" and the "violent" (THN 2.1.1.3/276). The violent kind he calls "passions," and the faculty of having them is, collectively, "the passions." In distinguishing the passions from other impressions of reflection on the basis of their relative violence, however, he is careful to emphasize that the application of this criterion is to the *typical* level of violence for each type of impression of reflection; particular instances of a given passion may nevertheless be quite calm, and particular instances of other impressions of reflection can occasionally rise to a level of considerable violence. Within the domain of the passions themselves, he draws a separate distinction between "violent passions" and "calm passions" (THN 2.3.3.8–9/417–18); this is a distinction that applies not to whole types of passions but rather to individual instances of passions. Hence, a "calm passion" is a calm instance of a type of impression of reflection that is often violent.

Evidently, calmness and violence are not intrinsic features, or not simply intrinsic features, of individual perceptions in the way that liveliness is an intrinsic feature of individual impressions, memories, and beliefs. Rather, calmness and violence are a matter of the degree of accompanying "emotion," which Hume describes as a separate but closely associated "sensation" of agitation or turbulence (THN 2.2.8.4/373). Although he writes that calm passions "produce little emotion in the mind, and are more known by their effects than by their immediate feeling or sensation" (THN 2.3.3.8/417), he does not assert that they have *no* immediate feeling or are strictly unconscious (which would seemingly leave them outside the mind altogether); rather, we may suppose, their relative lack of accompanying emotion often simply renders them relatively unremarkable and makes it more difficult to form and retain memories of them. Their occurrence may therefore often be merely inferred rather than recalled.

Because individual passions are simple impressions [2.1], they are represented by simple ideas. Hence, the names of passions cannot be defined by means of decomposition of a complex idea into simpler ideas. Hume allows that it is possible, however, to describe and distinguish them by characterizing their different origins, causal roles, and resemblances; for even simple impressions are susceptible of multiple aspects of resemblance ([2.3–4]; THN 1.1.7.7n/637). One of his most important distinctions based on differences of these kinds is that between "direct" and "indirect" passions. The direct passions "arise immediately from pleasure or pain" and include desire, aversion, joy, grief, hope, and fear. What these passions are passions *for* or *about* is represented not by the simple impression that is the passion itself, but rather by a closely associated idea. Although the indirect passions also arise from pleasure or pain, they do so not immediately but "by the conjunction of other qualities" (THN 2.1.1.4/276).

Among the indirect passions, four—pride, humility, love, and hatred—are generated through a mental process that Hume calls (with evident pride of his own) "the double relation of impressions and ideas." This process involves four elements. The first is an initial impression of pleasure or pain. The second is an idea of a "cause" of that pleasure or pain, a cause consisting of a "quality" placed in some "subject" that may be either a person or a thing. The third is an impression of pride, love, humility, or hatred that resembles—either in pleasurable or painful feeling or in motivational tendencies—the initial impression of pleasure or pain. The fourth is an idea of a person who either is or is closely related to the "subject"; this person is the "object" of the passion—by which Hume means, at least in part, that the passion consistently fixes the mind on the idea of that person. An idea of the person's own body may be considered a part of this idea, he seems to suggest (THN 2.1.8.1/298; THN 2.1.9.1/303), and this may be practically essential in conceiving specifically of most other persons. In relation to the purely mental "person" or "self" first described in connection with personal identity in *Treatise* Book 1 [3.1], however, the body would only qualify—like a person's possessions, friends, and relatives—as a closely related "subject."

As the process unfolds, the resemblance between the two impressions, aided by the close association between the two ideas, produces a transition from (i) a conjunction of the initial impression of pleasure or pain with the idea of the cause, to (ii) a conjunction of one of the indirect passions with the idea of its object. Pride and love resemble each other in being pleasurable, while humility and hatred resemble each other in being painful. Pride and humility resemble each other, however, in having the self as object, while love and hatred resemble each other in having other persons as their objects. Accordingly, an initial pleasure with a cause related to self will produce pride, while an initial pain with a cause related to self will produce humility. An initial pleasure with a cause related to another person will produce love of that person, while an initial pain with a cause related to another person will produce hatred of that person.

Other indirect passions, such as pity and ambition, arise through the operation that Hume calls "sympathy" (though we would now more likely call it *empathy*). In this operation as described in the *Treatise* (the second *Enquiry* is much less specific and may no longer endorse the details) a belief about another person's feelings is further enlivened by the "idea, or rather impression of ourselves"— presumably some one or more impressions in the bundle of perceptions that is the self. This enlivening occurs in virtue of the associative resemblance between oneself and the other person, to the point where the liveliness of one's idea of the other's feeling is raised to the level of an impression in its own right. In this way, the belief that an individual like oneself feels pleasure or pain produces a pleasure or pain of a similar kind in oneself. In the case of pity, sympathy for the pain or sorrow of another then leads to concern for the other and a benevolent desire for the alleviation of his or her suffering. In ambition, recurring sympathy with the passions of others towards oneself leads to a desire to be loved by them (THN 2.1.11, "Of the love of fame").

Malice and envy, in Hume's account, arise from the process of "comparison," which is in many ways the opposite of sympathy. Because the human mind tends to judge and to feel by comparing one thing with another, human beings tend to be more satisfied with their own state and circumstances when these appear to be superior to those of others, and less satisfied when their own state and circumstances appear inferior. As a result, belief in the pain of others can also cause pleasure, and belief in the pleasure of others can also cause pain. Accordingly, one can maliciously desire the pain or unhappiness of others and feel envious distress and hatred at their success. Comparison helps to explain why love is often mixed with humility, and hatred with pride (THN 2.2.8, "Of malice and envy"). Whether sympathy or comparison will predominate on a particular occasion depends on many factors, including the degrees of perceived similarity to, and distance from, the other person, as well as one's own particular temperament.

For many of those impressions of reflection that are of types generally calmer than the passions, Hume uses the term 'sentiment', and he calls the faculty of having such sentiments "taste." Hence Hume's essay "Of the Delicacy of Taste and Passion," which contrasts sensitivity of feeling and discernment as it applies to taste and to the passions; he recommends developing delicacy of taste, but not of passion (EMPL I.1). Among the products of taste are the sentiments of wit and humor, but also among them are pleasing "sentiments of beauty" and displeasing "sentiments of deformity," which may be produced by many kinds of objects, natural or artificial, ranging from human bodies to houses to musical or theatrical performances to literary compositions. In many cases—as, for example, with architecture—these sentiments arise partly from sympathy with those who are imagined to employ the object in question (THN 2.1.8, "Of beauty and deformity").

Most importantly, the "disinterested" consideration of human character traits—that is, their consideration without special regard to their effect on one's own personal interests—often produces a distinctive kind of sentiment of "moral beauty or deformity." Hume calls these sentiments of beauty or deformity of character "moral approbation" and "moral disapprobation," respectively. Most typically, these moral sentiments arise from sympathy with those who are imagined to be affected either pleasurably or painfully by the person whose character is being considered. Just as the sentiments of beauty and deformity in objects are the ultimate source of aesthetic distinctions, so the sentiments of moral approbation and disapprobation are the ultimate source of moral distinctions. The kind of taste that consists in the capacity to feel sentiments of beauty and deformity Hume calls "the sense of beauty"; we would also call it the *aesthetic sense*. Similarly, the kind of taste that consists in the capacity to feel sentiments of moral approbation and disapprobation Hume calls "the sense of virtue" or "the moral sense." The qualities of beauty or deformity of a person's body or possessions, as detected by the aesthetic sense, are among the causes of the indirect passions of love, pride, hatred, and humility; but even more important are the qualities of virtue and vice in a person's character, as detected by the moral sense (THN 2.1.7; THN 3.1.2). The abstract ideas—that is, concepts—derived from these senses will be examined in Chapter Four and their normative character in Chapter Five.

## 3.7 The will

Another very important kind of calmer impression of reflection, neither passion nor sentiment in Hume's classificatory scheme, is that of "willing" or "volition," which occurs whenever "we knowingly give rise to any new motion of our body, or new perception of our mind" (THN 2.3.1.2/399). Although volitions are themselves impressions, they are accompanied with associated ideas of the intended objects of volition. 'The will' is his term for the faculty of producing bodily movements or perceptions by means of such volitions. Each volition is, in turn, caused by one or more passions in conjunction with other perceptions (generally including beliefs), traits of character, and additional mental background structures or events [3.1]. While violent instances of passions tend, more often than not, to motivate more powerfully than calmer ones, this is not a strict correlation: "strength of mind" consists precisely in a motivational predominance of calm over violent passions. Despite the complexity of their causes, many of which are unknown in particular circumstances, all human volitions and actions are fully causally determined (and so also causally necessitated) by the causal factors that precede them, in accordance with Hume's Universal Determinism [3.1; 6.4].

Hume sharply criticizes the common doctrine that reason and the passions can conflict in the determination of the will. Instead, he maintains, reason is by itself ("alone") motivationally inert; its direct and immediate role in motivation is simply to provide beliefs about the means to achieve ends that are themselves set by the passions, including desire and aversion. As he famously puts it: "Reason is, and ought only to be, the slave of the passions, and can never pretend to any other office than to serve and obey them" (THN 2.3.3.4/414). He admits that this opinion "may appear somewhat extraordinary," but he defends it by means of two arguments. His primary argument has two lemmas:

> [Lemma 1:] Reason alone can never be a motive to any action of the will.
> [Lemma 2:] Reason can never oppose any passion in the direction of the will.

Hume's defense of the first lemma begins from the claim [3.3–4] that all reasoning is either demonstrative or probable. Demonstrative reasoning, however, operates in the wrong domain to motivate action in its own right: because such reasoning concerns relations of ideas, rather than matters of fact and real existence, it affects action at all only insofar as it gives guidance—as, for example, in the use of arithmetic in commerce—in thinking about causes and effects the existence of which has already been established in another way. This brings him to the realm of probable reasoning. Yet all probable reasoning, as he has previously explained [3.4], serves only to "discover causal connexions"; and such discoveries cannot make any contribution to motivation, he asserts, unless they reveal the causal connection of an action to "some prospect of pleasure or pain that touches our passions," a prospect in which we thereby take some "concern." Thus it is evident, he claims, that "the [motivational] impulse arises not from reason, but is only directed by it." The mere discovery of a causal connection would in itself always leave us indifferent; and "as [probable] reason is nothing but the discovery of this connexion, it cannot be by its means that the objects are able to affect us" (THN 2.3.3.3/414).

Having thus established his first lemma, Hume argues for the second—that reason can never oppose passion in the direction of the will—on the grounds that, in order for reason to oppose passion in this respect, it would have to produce a motivating impulse in the opposite direction; and such an impulse would, in the absence of the opposing passion, itself be a motive to action, contrary to the first lemma. We may call the whole of this primary argument by which he first reaches his famous conclusion about the slavery of reason to the passions the *Impulse Argument*.

Hume then offers a further argument, sometimes called the *Representation Argument*, to "confirm" this conclusion:

{1} A passion is an original existence, and has no representative quality.
{2} A contradiction to truth and reason consists in the disagreement of ideas with what they represent.
{3} Hence, passions cannot be opposed by or contradictory to truth and reason. (from {1} and {2}) (THN 2.3.3.5/415)

Central to this argument is Hume's conception of reason as the faculty of reasoning or inference to beliefs; as such, it is a faculty for producing entities that can be evaluated for truth or falsehood. Such entities are allowed by reason if they would be judged true and opposed by reason if they would be judged false; indeed, it is psychologically almost impossible, given Hume's conceptions of belief and truth [5.2], to hold a belief while denying that it is true. Because passions are not representations at all, however [2.6], they cannot be assessed for truth or falsehood, and hence they cannot be contrary to (nor in any particular conformity with) reason.

Passions are nevertheless typically accompanied by ideas and beliefs, and Hume recognizes two respects in which a passion may "improperly" be said to be contrary to reason: first, when the passion itself arises from a belief in the existence of objects that do not really exist; and second, when acting on a passion employs means that are insufficient, because of a mistaken judgment about causes and effects, to achieve the object or aim of the passion. It is improper to describe the passion itself as "contrary to reason" in these cases, however, for the contrariety applies rather to the associated belief. As Hume famously elaborates:

> 'Tis not contrary to reason to prefer the destruction of the whole world to the scratching of my finger. 'Tis not contrary to

reason for me to chuse my total ruin, to prevent the least uneasiness to an *Indian* or person wholly unknown to me. 'Tis as little contrary to reason to prefer even my own acknowledg'd lesser good to my greater, and have a more ardent affection for the former than the latter.

(THN 2.3.3.6/416)

The prevalence of the opinion that reason and the passions can conflict in the motivation of action arises, he explains, because calm passions (that is, calm instances of passions) often conflict with more violent ones, and calm passions are often conflated with reasoning because of a similar lack of violence in their feeling. Although passions, volitions, and actions cannot properly be said to be true or false, and hence cannot for Hume be "conformable or contrary to reason," they are nevertheless subject to normative evaluations of other kinds—including evaluations of conduciveness to wellbeing and also moral evaluation [5.1] insofar as they reveal traits of character. To say that an action is not conformable or contrary to reason is compatible with saying that is it "reasonable" or "unreasonable" in Hume's more usual sense of that term, in which a belief or action is reasonable if there is a balance of approvable considerations in its favor and unreasonable if there is a balance of approvable considerations against it.

In claiming that "reason alone" cannot motivate, it should again be emphasized, Hume does not mean that reason plays no role at all in motivation. On the contrary, he emphasizes that reasoning about the means to desired ends contributes to the production of new desires for those means and thereby serves to motivate action towards them. In this way, "reason and judgment may, indeed, be the mediate cause of an action, by prompting, or by directing a passion" (THN 3.1.1.16/462), and he devotes an entire section of Book 1 (THN 1.3.10) to "the influence of belief" in motivating action, especially by causing beliefs about the sources of pleasure or pain. Rather, as the Impulse Argument suggests, his point is that the faculty of reason is alone insufficient for motivation to voluntary action and instead requires input from a separate faculty: the passions. This will often take the form of causal cooperation between a new belief and a desire, aversion, or other passion that is already being felt; but in other cases, the belief may itself initiate the occurrence of a passion to which the mind already has a standing tendency or disposition in virtue of its background structure [3.1]. He treats his doctrine that reason alone cannot move the will as a substantive claim about the causal origins of volitions. As such, he must regard that doctrine not as a relation of ideas, in his technical sense, but as a matter of fact, well supported by observations of the effects of having or lacking passions as "concerns" in the presence of reasoning. In adding that reason not only "is" but also "ought" only to be the slave of the passions, he presumably intends to express the thought that human psychology functions well as it is.

## 3.8 Conclusion

In proposing that the mind or self is a bundle of related perceptions, Hume provides an especially prominent naturalistic alternative to views of the self as a simple immaterial substance underlying its perceptions or acting as a further mental spectator of them. He treats the mind as conscious of its own perceptions, and, although he allows that the mind sometimes forms reflective ideas of its own perceptions, he treats consciousness itself naturalistically as a part/whole relation—namely, as the inclusion of perceptions within the causally integrated bundle of perceptions that constitutes a mind or self. Yet it seems that individual perceptions are not inherently conscious for Hume apart from these relations, since bodies can be conceived simply by attributing different causal relations to them. Nor does it seem that causal relations among things *generally* bestow consciousness on causally related elements or the wholes they constitute in his view, since unconscious bodies stand in many causal relations to each other and often have causally related parts. Although all perceptions in the mind have some degree of liveliness or other, it is not clear that perceptions existing outside any mind would—nor, if so, what degree of liveliness that would be.

Hume's analyses of the mind's specific faculties constitute an important contribution to philosophy in many respects. By rejecting a separate faculty of "intellect" and subsuming its functions within the inclusive imagination, he places metaphysical theorizing under substantial empiricist constraints and at the same time facilitates a naturalistic explanation of the mind's many cognitive operations. By treating reason as a faculty of inference or reasoning, rather than as a broader and more amorphous faculty of discerning or responding to "good reasons," he makes it much easier not only to treat inference naturalistically and to assess it normatively, but also to separate out empirically the contributions to motivation and morals of such distinct mental operations as sympathy and moral sentiment. One of his most striking theses is that the unreasoning imagination is not merely a source of whimsy and error but also plays an essential role, through its involvement in custom and habit, in the operation of probable reason and, through its involvement in attributions of identity, in the operations of the senses as well. He also provides an original account of the content of the belief in an external world of bodies in terms of continued and distinct existence, and he is among the first to treat that belief as the result of a natural developmental process occurring in infancy. In the course of his investigation of the springs and principles of human cognitive operations, he makes a number of discoveries that he considers epistemically disturbing. The final evaluation of the skeptical import of these discoveries he leaves, however, for the final section of *Treatise* Book 1 and the final section of the first *Enquiry*.

Hume offers a naturalistic account of human action as the causal production of bodily movements or perceptions by impressions of volition that are themselves caused by passions. Although he distinguishes taste—as the source of aesthetic, moral, and other sentiments—from the passions, taste is able to influence the passions because its sentiments are themselves pleasures and pains. While pleasure and pain play central roles in motivation, Hume is no egoist: the operation of sympathy guarantees that human beings are concerned for the pleasures and pains of others as well as their own, and he recognizes other basic instinctual desires and aversions besides the desire for pleasure and aversion to pain. The conception of motivation as essentially requiring both a desire (or other passion) and a belief concerning the conditions for its satisfaction is often called the *Humean Theory of Motivation*.

Because passions are required to set ultimate ends in Hume's view, he is often interpreted as an *instrumentalist*: that is, as one who holds that the only function of *practical*, as opposed to *theoretical*, reason is to derive desires for means from (i) existing desires for ends, plus (ii) beliefs about the means to those ends. In fact, however, reason itself for Hume is always inferential and theoretical, rather than practical: it is concerned only with the production of belief or knowledge. If someone with a desire for an end and belief about the means to it nevertheless fails to have any desire for the means, that is a failure of prudence, in Hume's view, but not itself a failure of the faculty of reason.

## Further reading

Árdal, Páll S. (1966) *Passion and Value in Hume's Treatise*, Edinburgh: Edinburgh University Press. (The classic study of Hume's treatment of the passions, set in relation to his moral theory.)

Baier, Annette (1991) *A Progress of Sentiments: Reflections on Hume's Treatise*, Cambridge MA: Harvard University Press. (A landmark contribution to the understanding of Hume's philosophy, emphasizing the role of the social, the passions, and reflection; it offers an account of "reason" contrary to that offered here, one according to which the term is ambiguous for Hume and increases its scope by degrees throughout the *Treatise*.)

Garrett, Don (2013) "Hume on Reason, Normativity, and the Title Principle," in *The Oxford Companion to Hume*, edited by Paul Russell, Oxford: Oxford University Press. (Contains a fuller analysis of the relation between "reason" and "the understanding.")

Garrett, Don and Peter Millican (2011) "Reason, Induction, and Causation," *Occasional Papers of the Institute for Advanced Studies in the Humanities*, Edinburgh: University of Edinburgh Institute for Advanced Studies in the Humanities. (A debate in large part about Hume's map of the cognitive faculties, especially reason.)

Millgram, Elijah (1995) "Was Hume a Humean?" *Hume Studies* 21.1: 75–93. (Argues convincingly that Hume is not an instrumentalist about practical reason because he does not treat the production of a new desire or volition as an exercise of reason.)

Owen, David (1999) *Hume's Reason*, New York: Oxford University Press. (An important analysis of Hume's conception of reason as applied to such central topics as induction, belief in bodies, and skepticism, in the context of non-formalist early modern theories of reasoning and Locke's own conception of reasoning as requiring intermediate ideas; essential reading.)

Smith, Michael (1987) "The Humean Theory of Motivation," *Mind* 96: 36–61. (Formulates and discusses the model of motivation, ascribed to Hume, that requires the conjunction of a belief with a desire for voluntary action.)

Stroud, Barry (1977) *Hume*, London: Routledge & Kegan Paul. (Still one of the best and philosophically most astute comprehensive commentaries on Hume's philosophy, with important chapters on the belief in bodies and the relation between reason and action, among others topics.)

Waxman, Wayne (1994) *Hume's Theory of Consciousness*, Cambridge: Cambridge University Press. (A comprehensive interpretation of Hume's epistemology and metaphysics as highly skeptical, grounded in a distinctive interpretation of his philosophy of mind as allowing feelings immanent to consciousness that are neither impressions nor ideas.)

# Four
Sense-based concepts

Central to Hume's metaphysics and epistemology are his examinations of causation and probability. Central to his ethics are his examinations of virtue and vice. At the core of these examinations, in turn, lie his accounts of the origin and application of the corresponding concepts—that is, the abstract or general ideas—of causation, probability, virtue, and vice. Taken together, his accounts of these concepts are intended to explain a great deal about why human beings think and feel about the world and other people as they do.

As we have seen in Chapter One, Hume's earliest correspondence reveals that his twin ambitions were to contribute to aesthetic criticism (particularly criticism of literature) and to philosophy. As also noted there, Norman Kemp Smith proposed that the "new scene of thought" that so inspired the young Hume lay in his realization that aspects of Hutcheson's moral sense theory could be carried over to the realm of belief [1.1]. These two facts are not as unrelated as they might seem. First, Hume follows Hutcheson in seeing important parallels between aesthetics and morals, going so far as to describe virtue as "moral beauty" and to propose that beauty and virtue are each discerned by their own distinctive "sense." Second, Hume's treatments of both causation and probability appear, upon examination, analogous in many crucial respects to his treatments of both beauty and virtue.

Kemp Smith also suggested that Hume actually composed Books 2 and 3 of the *Treatise* ("Of the Passions" and "Of Morals") before Book 1 ("Of the Understanding"); in this, Kemp Smith certainly went far beyond what any textual evidence warrants. In describing

Hume as rejecting "evidence" in the theoretical domain in favor of feeling, he substantially misrepresented the nature of the parallels that exist. Nevertheless, given the earlier development in Hutcheson of conceptions of beauty and virtue as discerned by "senses," it is not unreasonable to suppose that the parallels with causation and probability result at least in part from Hume's extension, however conscious or unconscious, of the former to the latter. Without endorsing Kemp Smith's thesis about the order of composition of the Books of the *Treatise*, therefore, it will be useful to consider the cases of beauty and virtue before those of causation and probability—and to consider the origins and shared features of the concepts themselves before turning in subsequent chapters to their distinctive applications. The full elaboration of their origins and shared features will require some extrapolation from his accounts of individual cases.

## 4.1 The origins of BEAUTY and VIRTUE

It is uncontroversial that some ideas are derived from specific senses. The visual, auditory, olfactory, gustatory, and tactile senses provide impressions of sensation by which the mind distinguishes the colors, sounds, smells, tastes, and heat or cold of bodies. According to what Hume calls "the modern philosophy" (THN 1.4.4)—that is, the mechanistic conception of bodies identified with Galileo, Descartes, and Locke, among others—such sensory experiences result from features of the size, shape, arrangement, and motion of the insensibly small parts of bodies, and not, as might be vulgarly supposed, from qualities of bodies that in some way resemble those experiences. It is because of this doctrine that Locke classifies the qualities of bodies that actually produce these experiences as secondary qualities; this is in contrast with such primary qualities of bodies as extension, size, shape, motion, and solidity, which he claims do resemble their mental representations [2.6] and so represent them as they are in their own nature.

Hume follows Hutcheson in recognizing, in addition to the external senses, a "sense of beauty" as the source of aesthetic distinctions, and a "moral sense" as the source of moral distinctions. Hutcheson also discusses, in effect, the sense of "humor" (in the modern sense of the term that was then of recent development), and Hume follows him in writing of "wit" (also in the modern and then recently developed sense captured in their shared phrase 'wit and humour') as discerned by "a certain sense" (THN 3.3.4.11/ 612). Although they disagree about many features of the objects and operations of these senses, both emphasize the analogy between beauty and virtue (THN 3.3.1.9–10/577–78; EPM 1.3/170), and between both of these and such secondary qualities of bodies as color, sound, smell, taste, and heat and cold, as these latter qualities are understood "by the modern philosophy" (THN 3.1.1.26/469). In each case, the mind distinguishes among things on the basis of feelings that do not or need not resemble any feature in the things themselves. In treating virtue and vice as qualities perceived by a sense, on analogy with external sense perception, Hume sets himself in opposition to such moralists as Clarke [1.1], who regard morality as a determination of reason much more on analogy with mathematics.

Because of Hume's willingness to use the term 'sense' in this way, we may call the class of abstract ideas that he regards as resulting from primitive capacities to have specific kinds of felt mental response *sense-based concepts*. Moreover, we may distinguish four elements—best thought of as overlapping stages—in the full development of a Humean sense-based concept.

The first element is *repeated activation*: the repeated production, as a result of characteristic stimuli, of a characteristic mental response. In the case of the external senses, this activation typically requires the causal influence of bodies on functioning sense organs and yields impressions of sensation. In the case of the sense of beauty, it requires that appropriate objects or events be perceived by the senses or considered in the imagination, and it yields what Hume calls "sentiments of beauty" and "sentiments of deformity." In the case of the moral sense, it requires a consideration of an enduring mental trait of a person and yields "sentiments of moral approbation" and "sentiments of moral disapprobation," typically mediated by sympathy [3.6]. In the case of the sense of humor—to which he gives much less theoretical attention—it requires the perception or thought of events (often remarks or stories) and yields feelings of "mirth," or amusement of the kind expressed in laughter.

The second element is *initial generalization*: the natural formation, facilitated by the similarity of the multiple instances of that characteristic response, of an abstract idea with an actual revival set [2.4] encompassing ideas of things that elicit that response.

The third element is *natural correction*. Hume describes the origins of this process most systemically in the case of the moral sense, where he calls it "correcting [our] sentiments ... to regulate our abstract notions" (that is, abstract ideas) but he also emphasizes that "such corrections are common with regard to all the senses" (THN 3.3.1.16/582). Although similarities of response tend naturally toward the production of an abstract idea, differences either in the conditions of observation or in the state of respondents will often elicit different responses to the same stimulus, both among different persons and from the same person at different times. Such differences of response are often naturally disturbing to the individuals who observe or experience them, thereby inclining them toward some way of reaching and maintaining intrapersonal and interpersonal agreement in their reactions. This outcome is achieved primarily by the gradual adoption and refinement, through a tacit convention [8.3], of what Hume calls a "standard" by which to judge. He mentions the existence of *standards of judgment* in many different contexts.

In its general form, it seems clear from Hume's examples, a standard of judgment for a sense-based concept always consists of an idealized situation or "point of view" from which to be responsive, plus idealized endowments or "qualities" of a perceiver with which to be responsive. (Other concepts, such as that of equality in number, are said to have "standards" of other kinds; see, for example, THN 1.3.1.5/71, sometimes called *Hume's Principle*.) In the case of colors, for example, the two-part standard is "objects in day-light, to the eye of a man in health" ("Of the Standard of Taste," EMPL I.23: 234). For beauty and deformity in the arts, it is a situation "cleared of all prejudice" by taking up the point of view of the artist's intended audience, combined with the partly natural and partly developed qualities constitutive of the "true critic": "a strong sense, united to delicate sentiment, improved by practice, and perfected by comparison" ("Of the Standard of Taste,"

EMPL I.23: 241). For visual beauty and deformity in particular, he adds, the idealized point of view also includes a distance adequate for viewing the whole with minimal loss of detail (THN 3.3.1.15/582). He explicitly compares this idealized point of view with that of what he calls "the standard of virtue and morality," which lies in what he calls the "steady and general points of view" or "common point of view" of those who are affected by the individual judged—namely, that individual himself together with those who "have a connexion with him" (THN 3.3.1.15/581; THN 3.3.1.30/591). This point of view corrects for differences in spatial, temporal, and social distance that may affect the strength of sympathetic pleasures and pains and hence also the strength of the resulting moral sentiments [3.6]. The idealized qualities of the respondent include sympathy, strong but delicate moral sentiments, and comprehensive understanding of causes and effects in human life.

In each of these cases, human beings come to regard as the correct or proper revival set of the concept the idealized one that would result from classifications made in accordance with the standard [2.4]. It is important to emphasize, however, that Hume does not treat them as striving to adopt a particular standard because it is somehow antecedently the correct or "ideal" one at which to aim, from a semantic or linguistic point of view. Rather, it becomes the operative standard of correctness, thereby helping to determine the nature of the concept, because it is the one on which human beings naturally converge—though they often do so, of course, at least in part for good and understandable practical reasons.

The socially agreed-upon idealized point of view and respondent qualities that constitute a standard of judgment can nevertheless be difficult to attain completely, even if only imaginatively, in particular cases. Partly for this reason, human beings often also develop, as a second mode of correction, "rules by which to judge" the application of a sense-based concept. These rules are typically derived from experience with past applications of the abstract idea that have subsequently proven, upon approaching closer to the standard, to be satisfactory or unsatisfactory. Perhaps because the standards for judging colors, sounds, tastes, and smells are often so easily achieved, Hume does not mention any special rules for judging them—although he does note (in a passage added to the Appendix) that "general rules" of spatial perspective can be used for judging primary qualities such as size (THN 1.3.10.12/632). For beauty and deformity, however, he recognizes many "rules of art" or criticism, such as principles of literary composition or dramatic plotting, that can be used to anticipate and also to explain the responses of idealized true critics, as well to guide artists in creating works that would be approved in accordance with the standard.

The final element is *relational attribution*. The process of natural correction operates to shape and regulate the proper revival sets of a sense-based concept and hence to determine the meaning of its associated general term. As previously remarked, however, Hume also makes allowance for a further dimension of meaning consisting in an inferential or conceptual role that results from what he calls "the custom ... of attributing certain relations to ideas" (THN 1.1.7.14/ 23) [2.4]. This process of relational attribution is by no means unique to sense-based concepts in Hume—as his chosen examples of GOVERNMENT and WAR attest—but it does apply to them as well.

As this four-element account suggests, Hume treats each sense as giving rise to one or more concepts that serve as the original or *directly* sense-based concept or concepts for that sense. These are the concepts—such as BLUE, SWEET, HUMOR, BEAUTY, DEFORMITY, VIRTUE, and VICE—that arise most directly from the sense through the processes of repeated activation, initial generalization, natural correction, and relational attribution. Such further concepts as BLUE POINT, HUMOROUS STORY, BEAUTIFUL HOUSE, and JUSTICE (that is, VIRTUOUS RESPECT FOR PROPERTY), all of which Hume employs in his writings, may be considered as *indirectly* sense-based concepts, inasmuch as they are constituted by the application of a directly sense-based concept to a particular limited kind of case. Other concepts may be considered as indirectly sense-based inasmuch as they are constituted by the application of a directly sense-based concept in some relation to something else— as, for example, ARTIST is the concept of a person who produces beauty, and VIRTUOUS ACTION is for Hume the concept of an action indicating the presence of a virtue. The activation of many senses— such as those of humor, beauty, and virtue, as well as the external senses—also leads to indirectly sense-based concepts of particular *degrees* of the quality in question; Hume mentions, for example, ENORMITY for great vices and FAULT for small ones. These, we may assume, will typically be generalized in response to different degrees of intensity of the repeatedly activated characteristic mental response, and then (at least in many cases) corrected in relation to a standard and rules, and attributed specific relations constituting their own inferential or conceptual roles.

## 4.2 Features of BEAUTY and VIRTUE

All of the immediate sense-based concepts just mentioned appear to share the same four Humean elements of development. For this reason, they also share five distinctive features when fully established.

First, the concepts resemble one another in having a particular kind of simplicity. In Locke's philosophy, it is perhaps not always clear when ideas are functioning as concepts, but the question of a concept's parts is itself a straightforward one: a concept is always a single idea that either is, or is not, composed of simpler ideas. In Hume's philosophy, in contrast, it is always clear which ideas are concepts—namely, those that are abstract ideas—but the question of a concept's parts becomes more complicated. Considered in one way, a "part" of an abstract idea would simply be an idea that is a member of its revival set—as, for example, the idea of a particular female fox is a member of the revival set of VIXEN. In another mode of composition, a part of an abstract idea is either: (i) an idea that is a simpler part of the exemplar idea; or, more extensively, (ii) an idea that is also a simpler part of every idea in the revival set—as, for example, an idea of a head having a distinctive pointy shape is presumably a part of the exemplar and also of each other member of the revival set of VIXEN. In a third mode of composition, however, the parts of an abstract idea may be considered to be the other abstract ideas, if any, on which combinatorial operations must typically be performed in order to obtain the revival set of the abstract idea in question. The concept VIXEN, for example, is typically both acquired and deployed by taking the intersection of the revival sets (including exemplars) of the concepts FOX and FEMALE.

The question of whether a concept is simple in this third respect—which we may call *semantic simplicity*—is entirely distinct from the question of whether some or all of the individual members of the revival set are themselves simple ideas. BLUE POINT, for example, has a simple exemplar and all of the other members of its revival set are simple as well [2.1, 2.5], but the concept is nevertheless semantically complex. The revival set of BLUE, on the other hand, has some members that are simple (namely, those that are minimal points) and others that are complex (namely, those that are extended and composed of such points), but the concept itself is semantically simple. Presumably all of the ideas in the revival sets of BEAUTY and DEFORMITY, VIRTUE and VICE are complex, but the concepts themselves are once again semantically simple. This is so even though practical mastery of the standard of judgment and the rules of judgment for these concepts may of course require the use of other concepts—just as long as these other concepts are not employed as semantic parts in the sense specified, to generate the appropriate revival set through operations such as union, intersection, and exclusion.

There is perhaps a rough-grained way of individuating Humean concepts according to which any two abstract ideas with the same revival set would qualify as "the same concept," no matter how that revival set is actually generated; and to concepts so individuated, the distinction between semantic simplicity and semantic complexity would not apply except pragmatically. On a narrow-grained and arguably more useful way of individuating concepts, however, the identity of a concept may be determined at least partly by the manner in which its revival set is actually determined. (It may also be determined partly by associated inferential or conceptual roles, which may differ even when revival sets do not.) When taking concepts as individuated in this fine-grained way, no term signifying a semantically simple concept can be strictly synonymous with (that is, express the same concept as) any term signifying a semantically complex concept.

Although no term signifying a semantically simple concept can be defined by way of providing a synonymous word or phrase that purports to provide a semantic analysis of it in terms of operations with other concepts, a term signifying a semantically simple concept can nonetheless often be defined in Hume's own sense of the term 'definition'. This is because a "definition" is for him simply any specification, using other ideas, of the idea for which a term stands. Concepts are definable in this sense if it is possible to give a usable characterization of the membership of its revival set by employing terms signifying other ideas. (Thus, specifying the membership of a revival set by specifying ideas that constitute the parts of each idea in the revival set may, in some cases, be one particular way of defining a term.) In this sense, there will always be in principle, if not in practice, not just one but at least two approaches to defining any term signifying a sense-based concept: either by specifying the feature or features things have in virtue of which they are typically able to evoke a response characteristic of the sense, without specifying what that response is; or by specifying what that evoked response is, without specifying what feature or features of things typically evoke it.

This in-principle susceptibility to dual Humean definitions is the second shared feature of sense-based concepts. We may call these two kinds of definitions *productive* and *responsive*, respectively. A rough responsive definition of 'warmth', as the term applies to bodies, would be: "that which produces the sensation-of-warmth in spectators." Insofar as he sympathizes with "the modern philosophy" [3.5], Hume would likely accept as a rough productive definition "that which has a relatively high degree of motion among its very small corpuscular parts." He would not presume to know a specific productive definition of 'blue' as it applies to bodies, but he would grant that, if the modern philosophy is correct, it must involve in some way the size, shape, arrangement, and motion of small parts.

Similarly, a rough responsive definition of 'beauty' would be: "whatever produces the sentiment of beauty in an observer." Others have tried to specify what all beautiful objects have in common: Hutcheson, for example, proposes "uniformity amidst variety." Hume himself argues that utility or disutility often plays a great role, through sympathy, in producing aesthetic sentiments toward objects, but he does not venture a general productive definition of 'beauty'. In both the *Treatise* and the second *Enquiry*, however, he does offer both productive and responsive definitions of 'virtue' or (a term that he treats as generally equivalent) 'personal merit': "every quality of the mind, which is *useful* or *agreeable*, to the *person himself* or to *others*" (EPM 9.12/277) and "*whatever mental action or quality gives to a spectator the pleasing sentiment of approbation*" (EPM App 1.10/289). The former definition is productive, the latter responsive.

Third—as just hinted in connection with the definitions of 'warmth' and 'blue'—sense-based concepts are susceptible in principle to a systematic ambiguity in which the same term is used to denote either: (i) the characteristic mental response that results from the activation of the sense; or (ii) the quality of things, picked out by the sense-based concept, that the sense ultimately serves to detect. In the original case of sensible secondary qualities, Locke uses color, sound, taste, smell, and heat-or-cold terms in both ways, which he disambiguates (when necessary) by writing of colors or warmth (i) as they "are Ideas," and (ii) as they "are in the Bodies" which we "denominate from" those ideas (ECHU 2.8.8, 2.8.14–16, 2.8.21, and 2.32.14). Following a similar pattern, which he perhaps regards as licensed by Lockean usage, Hume writes of virtue and beauty both as sentiments "in the mind" (or "in the breast") of spectators and as "qualities in" a virtuous or beautiful "subject" that may serve as the causes of such sentiments (and thereby also of indirect passions) in spectators (THN 2.1.7 and 2.1.8) [3.6].

Fourth, sense-based concepts are susceptible at least in principle to a particular kind of disagreement in application that results from their essential relation to a standard of judgment. To be sure, even non-sense-based concepts of various kinds may be susceptible to vagueness or indeterminacy in practice for Hume, simply because resemblance often comes in finely varying degrees. In consequence of this variation in degrees of resemblance, a general term that is associated with an exemplar idea might revive different members of a potential revival set with varying degrees of reliability and strength, and those ideas might then be employed in discourse and reasoning with varying degrees of regularity and confidence, both by a single individual over time and by a group of individuals at the same time. The result would be that the application of a term (and hence the associated concept) to a range of borderline cases becomes or remains a matter of hesitancy or even indifference.

Humean sense-based concepts are distinctive, however, in their reliance on a two-part standard of judgment consisting of a respondent point of view and a set of respondent qualities. While convergence on such a standard serves to reduce intrapersonal and interpersonal disagreement in the application of a term, it is unlikely that the process of convergence would ever produce agreement about the inclusion or exclusion of every possible aspect of an idealized point of view or idealized set of qualities that might in some circumstances generate a difference in constitutive response. Accordingly, different responses to the same stimulus may be elicited in the same individual at different times or among different individuals at the same time without that difference in response being subject to adjudication by appeal to the standard. This kind of disagreement may often affect the application of the direct sense-based concepts themselves, and it may even more often affect the application of concepts of their degrees.

Color concepts provide one example of this kind of disagreement. The standard's idealized point of view, according to Hume, is "daylight"; but the quality of such light can differ significantly in different meteorological conditions and times of day, with a resulting possibility for unresolved differences in the application of particular color terms and concepts. Hume notes in "Of the Standard of Taste" that different works of art have greater or lesser appeal to persons of different ages and temperaments, without the differences preventing a respondent from being regarded as a true critic. He calls this "blameless diversity" and writes of it, "such preferences are innocent and unavoidable, and can never reasonably be the object of dispute, because there is no standard, by which they can be decided" (EMPL I.23: 244). Similarly, he emphasizes in the appendix to the second *Enquiry* entitled simply "A Dialogue," judges from different eras or nations sometimes prefer different combinations of traits and set somewhat different boundaries to approved dispositions and motives without the sensibility of one era or nation being more authoritative than the other. As it happens, it seems clear that aesthetic concepts have the greatest range of such blameless diversity in application, while moral concepts have somewhat less, and concepts of secondary qualities relatively little.

Finally, and despite their susceptibility to blameless diversity due to the openness of their standard of judgment, sense-based concepts also exhibit a certain general *resistance to global error*. For example, Hume writes concerning morals:

> For it must be observ'd, that the opinions of men, in this case, carry with them a peculiar authority, and are, in a great measure, infallible. The distinction of moral good and evil is founded on the pleasure or pain, which results from the view

of any sentiment, or character; and as that pleasure or pain cannot be unknown to the person who feels it, it follows, that there is just so much vice or virtue in any character, as every one places in it, and that 'tis impossible in this particular we can ever be mistaken.

(THN 3.2.8.8/546–47)

Similarly, in the first *Enquiry*, when he rejects the proposal that human actions could not be morally blamable if they were consequences of the design of a beneficent Deity, he does so specifically on the grounds that such theoretical considerations are too distant to affect the morally authoritative moral sense (EHU 8.33–35/100–3).

Nevertheless, Hume is careful to characterize the "peculiar authority" of the corrected and refined moral sense as "infallible" only "in a great measure." Sense-based concepts are only resistant, not immune, to global error. Not only can standards of judgment prove extremely difficult to apply properly in any particular case, but the process of developing a sense-based concept, investigating its applications, and reflecting on the results may ultimately undermine the application of that very concept. On one prominent view—though not on Hume's—this actually occurs in the case of color judgments derived from the sense of color, so that enquiry convinces us that no qualities corresponding to the requirements of color concepts can actually exist. Furthermore, Hume seems to treat "moral sceptics" as holding a similar view about moral concepts, for he describes them as "denying the reality of moral distinctions." The rejoinder he proposes is equally apt for the proposed wholesale rejection of the applicability of any sense-based concept:

Let a man's insensibility be ever so great, he must often be touched with the images of RIGHT and WRONG; and let his prejudices be ever so obstinate, he must observe, that others are susceptible of like impressions. The only way, therefore, of converting an antagonist of this kind, is to leave him to himself. For, finding that no body keeps up the controversy with him, it is probable he will, at last, of himself, from mere weariness, come over to the side of common sense and reason.

(EPM 1.2/169–70)

## 4.3 Causation

Hume does not use the terms 'sense of causation' or 'causal sense'. Upon examination, however, it can be seen that CAUSATION, too, functions as a sense-based concept in his philosophy. It arises in consequence of the repeated activation of a two-part mental response to a distinctive kind of two-part stimulus. The stimulus consists of a new initiating perception against a background of previously experienced constant conjunction [3.4]. One part of the characteristic mental response is a probable inference that produces an idea with the feeling of liveliness derived from the initiating perception; the second part of the response is an impression of reflection that he calls "the impression of necessary connexion." This impression arises in the course of the mental transition from the initiating perception to the lively idea—that is, to the belief— that constitutes the conclusion of the probable inference. Because it reliably indicates the mind's determination to make the inference, this impression can be properly said to be the impression "of" that determination [2.6]. The capacity for having this two-part response constitutes what we may call *the causal sense*.

In its generation of a two-part rather than a simple response, the causal sense differs from the sense of beauty and the moral sense, as well as from the external senses. This difference is not as stark as it may appear, however, for Hume emphasizes that: (i) the sentiments of moral approbation and disapprobation are typically preceded by distinct sympathetic pleasures or pains; and (ii) aesthetic and moral sentiments alike often give rise to passions of pride or humility, love or hatred, and benevolence or anger in their train [3.6]. There is a second notable difference from the senses of beauty and morals as well. These latter senses are each capable of producing, on different occasions and depending on the stimulus, either of two contrasting responses, one pleasurable and one painful: a sentiment of beauty or of deformity, or a sentiment of moral approbation or disapprobation, respectively. But while the response characteristic of the activation of the causal sense has two parts, that response is itself always the same in kind, without contrasting pleasurable and painful alternatives. The absence of such contrasting alternatives is by no means unique to the causal sense, however. The various impressions of the external senses are most often not pleasures or pains at all, and most often admit of only less sharp contrasts. The sense of humor does not give rise to such contrasting alternatives either, for the sole characteristic response of the sense of humor is evidently always pleasurable, without a painful opposite. Finally, the external, aesthetic, moral, and risible (humorous) senses give rise to concepts of qualities, whereas the causal sense gives rise to the concept of a relation. Yet the generation of the concept of the relation of causation ("the relation of cause and effect") from the Humean causal sense is strikingly similar, in its four-stage structure, to the generation of concepts from other Humean senses.

In making a probable inference, as Hume explains it, the mind in effect represents two objects or events as causally related (EHU 4.4/26–27), with the earlier represented as the cause of the later. Humans and animals alike share the capacity for such inferences, and hence too the capacity for such representation. The development of an abstract idea of the causal relation, in contrast—like the development of practically any other abstract idea, for Hume—is an accomplishment only of human beings, requiring the use of a general term. Presumably like all abstract ideas of relations between two things, this abstract idea will have as its revival set ideas of (perhaps ordered) pairs of things that are taken as resembling other pairs of things whose ideas are also included in the revival set [2.4]. In the case of CAUSATION, pairs of ideas initially enter the revival set in virtue of representing pairs of contiguous and successive things belonging to kinds whose members have been experienced as constantly conjoined. Hume expresses this point when he writes, "We must not here be content with saying, that the idea of cause and effect arises from objects constantly united; but must affirm, that 'tis the very same with the idea of these objects" (THN 2.3.1.16/405).

Because different individuals are exposed to different courses of experience, however, the specific constituents of their actual revival sets [2.4] for the concept CAUSATION will naturally differ. The standard of judgment for causation, we may surmise, lies in the qualities of a normal human faculty of reason and a normal human appreciation of degrees of similarity, exercised from a point of view that includes a range of experience of representative samples sufficiently broad that no additional observations of other actual instances would alter the respondent's judgments. Thus, Hume writes that we make "experience...the standard of our future judgments" (ATHN 25/656). No actual human being can fully attain this point of view about everything, of course, and for that reason no one is an infallible universal judge of causal relations; but presumably we nevertheless agree that the correct causal judgment is the one that would be made with those qualities from that point of view.

Fortunately, even without fully achieving the point of view of the idealized causal judge, both the quality of human causal judgments and the ability of individuals to achieve consensus about them can be significantly improved by two factors, in Hume's account. First, as the mind acquires experience of the reliability or unreliability of various kinds of testimony of other persons—that is, experience of how reliably what others assert conforms to reality under various circumstances—their testimony becomes an indirect source of "experience" about the object of testimony for the recipient of the testimony (EHU 9–10). Second, we may discover and employ a set of rules of judging, comparable to the "rules of art" in the aesthetic case. These are the "Rules by which to judge of causes and effects," described in the *Treatise* section of the same name (THN 1.3.15). These rules, he reports, are "form'd on the nature of our understanding, and on our experience of its operations in the judgments we form concerning objects" (THN 1.3.13.11/149)—that is, they are derived from past experience of satisfactory and unsatisfactory inferential predictions. Particularly important among these rules is his fourth, Universal Determinism [3.1]. As he interprets it, this rule requires that there be only one causally possible total outcome from any complete set of circumstances. It thereby serves as "the source of most of our philosophical reasonings," for it allows us to infer that wherever a change in a single circumstance is followed by a different outcome, the new circumstance is at least a partial cause of that difference in outcome.

Hume begins his discussion of causation in the *Treatise* (THN 1.3.2, "Of probability; and of the idea of cause and effect") by identifying three aspects of causal relations: (i) the temporal priority of the cause to the effect; (ii) the spatial contiguity of the cause and effect (a condition later waived for objects not spatially disposed [2.5, 7.6]); and (iii) an as-yet-unexplained "necessary connexion" between cause and effect. It is often assumed that ideas of these three aspects of the causal relation are intended as literal parts of a complex idea of that relation. Because of its generality, the idea of causation is clearly an abstract idea, however, and it is implausible to suppose that these are its three semantic parts—that is, it is implausible to suppose that one must first acquire the concepts of temporal priority, contiguity, and necessary connection and then perform operations on them in order to deploy the basic concept CAUSATION [4.2]. Moreover, the temporal priority of causes and their contiguity with their effects are the first two of Hume's "rules by which to judge of causes and effects"; and as just noted, he regards such rules as learned from experience, rather than imposed as a matter of conceptual composition. It is more plausible, therefore, to treat CAUSATION as an immediate sense-based concept and hence as semantically simple. We may certainly suppose—invoking the second notion of parthood for abstract ideas distinguished previously [4.2]—that each pair of ideas in the revival set can represent the object of its first element as prior to, contiguous with, and necessarily connected with the object of its second—but the crucial question that will remain is *how* these objects are represented as necessarily connected.

Were causal necessary connection itself well understood, the three aspects just distinguished could easily serve for at least a Humean productive definition of 'cause'. Because Hume thinks it is not well understood, however, the methodological directive derived from the Copy Principle [2.2] requires him to search for the impression from which the idea of necessary connection is derived; and this search provides the overall structure and rationale for the discussion of causation and probable reasoning that occupies all of sections 3–14 of *Treatise* 1.3 ("Of knowledge and probability"). The section of the *Treatise* entitled "Of the idea of necessary connexion" (THN 1.3.14) and the corresponding section of the same name in the first *Enquiry* (EHU 7) present his account of the origin and nature of that impression—the impression that constitutes the second part of the characteristic response of the causal sense.

Prior to experience of particular kinds of objects or events occurring in succession, Hume argues, the mind never attributes any necessity to them at all, nor does it originally do so after a single experience of such a succession. Unless assisted, in the way just noted, by a belief in Universal Determinism (a belief itself resulting from repeated experience), the mind attributes a necessary connection only after repeated experience of an object or event of one kind being followed by an object or event of another—that is, of constant conjunction. Yet experiencing a repetition of the same sequence of perceptions is not itself the having of any new simple impression. Hence, he concludes, the impression of necessary connection must be an internal impression—that is, an impression of reflection [2.1]. Specifically, it is an impression of the determination of the mind to make a mental transition constituting inference from one object or event to another, a determination that arises only after experienced constant conjunction has established a custom or habit [3.4]. The mind then typically *projects* this impression onto the cause and effect themselves—that is, it treats it in representation as a quality of the cause and effect pair itself, rather than of the state of mind productive of the inference. Whereas we typically suppose that we make an inference because we perceive a necessary connection, he remarks, we in fact perceive a necessary connection because we make an inference (THN 1.3.6.3/88). The idea of necessary connection is simply the idea copied from this impression.

Having given this explanation of the idea of necessary connection, Hume declares that he is now in a position to define the term 'cause'. Not surprisingly, given the sense-based character of the concept, he provides two definitions, one productive and one responsive:

> We may define a CAUSE to be "An object precedent and contiguous to another, and where all the objects resembling the former are plac'd in like relations of precedency and contiguity to those objects, that resemble the latter."

and

> "A CAUSE is an object precedent and contiguous to another, and so united with it, that the idea of the one determines the mind to form the idea of the other, and the impression of the one to form a more lively idea of the other."
>
> (T 1.3.14.31/170)

These two definitions, he remarks, "are only different by their presenting a different view of the same object, and making us consider it either as a *philosophical* or a *natural* relation." That is, in accordance with his distinction between two senses of the term 'relation' [2.3], each definition provides a characterization of the revival set of the concept CAUSATION: the first leads us to consider how a cause and its effect can be compared by the mind directly, while the second calls attention to the fact that causation between objects is a relation that renders the ideas of the cause and the effect associated in the mind.

These two definitions are of course not strictly synonymous with each other, and neither of them is synonymous with the term 'cause'. Instead, the two definitions provide two different semantically complex ways of roughly specifying the contents of the revival set of the abstract idea of causation—each by deploying other concepts (including PRECEDENCY, CONTIGUITY, and RESEMBLANCE, in the first case, and PRECEDENCY, CONTIGUITY, IDEA, IMPRESSION, and DETERMINATION in the other). The term 'cause', in contrast, is deployed not through combinatorial operations on any other concepts; rather, it is deployed through the development of the causal sense that responds to constant conjunction with association, inference, and the impression of necessary connection, thereby rendering pairs of things that exemplify constant conjunction saliently similar to one another. As we should expect of a directly sense-based concept, it is semantically simple.

Many readers have judged these two definitions to be not only different from one another, but also inconsistent with one another, as picking out different classes of pairs of things as causes and effects. It seems, for example, that instances of a never-observed constant conjunction would satisfy the first definition, but not the second, while pairs that mistakenly appear on the basis of an unrepresentative sample to be instances of a constant conjunction would seemingly satisfy the second definition, but not the first. It should be recognized, however, that Hume employs, in effect, both an *absolute* sense of 'cause' and a *spectator-relative* sense. In the absolute sense, which is primary, things are related as cause and effect if and only if they are instances of a genuine constant conjunction that would give rise to inference and association in an idealized respondent from the idealized point of view. In the secondary sense, things are related as cause and effect *for a particular spectator* if and only if they are instances of a constant conjunction within the experience of that person and give rise to association and inference in that individual. The former sense is that required for discussing the genuine causal relations among objects and events themselves, whereas the latter is required for discussing which represented objects and events function as though causally related in the psychological organization of an individual mind for purposes of the Principle of the Association of Ideas [2.2].

Although Hume does not explicitly draw this distinction between absolute and spectator-relative senses, it applies equally to his two parallel definitions of 'virtue' [4.2], for which it is virtue in the spectator-relative sense that is the cause of love and pride [3.6]. Moreover, as we shall see, he avails himself of a similar distinction concerning miracles [9.6]. The wording of his first definition of 'cause' more readily suggests the absolute sense, while the wording of his second definition more readily suggests the spectator-relative. In fact, however, both definitions are systematically ambiguous between the two senses—the first because it does not specify whether the constant conjunction is universal or restricted to the experience of a spectator, the second because it does not specify whether "the mind" in question is idealized or individual—and he utilizes both definitions in both ways at different times. Whenever the pair of definitions are both understood in the same way, however—either both in the absolute sense or both in a spectator-relative sense—they pick out the same pairs as cause and effect.

This ambiguity in Hume's definitions of 'cause' is to be sharply distinguished from an ambiguity in his use of the terms 'necessary connexion' and 'power' themselves. As already noted in the cases of such sense-based concepts as those of secondary qualities, beauty, and virtue, he often allows systematic ambiguity in the use of the same terms for (i) impressions in the mind, and (ii) the qualities in a subject that produce those impressions. Since one of the two elements of the characteristic mental response that is crucial to the causal sense is an impression, it is not surprising that Hume writes in many places of "necessary connexion" or "power" as an impression that exists only in the mind, while in other places he writes of "necessary connexion" as a relation or "power" as a quality properly attributable to the causally related objects and events that the sciences investigate.

Like all Humean sense-based concepts, CAUSATION is in principle susceptible to disagreement of the kind that results when convergence on a standard of judgment leaves open some aspects of the standard that would sometimes make an effective difference to the characteristic response to a stimulus. Because he accepts Universal Determinism as a rule for judging causes and effects, however, he is committed to the view that there is one actual set of causal regularities—laws—that is sufficient to provide for the causal determination of every later state of the universe from any earlier state of the universe. Had the degree of regularity in the universe been in some respects very much less than Universal Determinism requires—something that is perfectly conceivable and hence, by the Conceivability Principle [2.2], metaphysically possible for Hume—then the distinction between representative and unrepresentative samples could be, even in principle, difficult to draw. In that case, blameless diversity in the application of CAUSATION resulting from the openness in its standard of judgment might well have been as common as blameless aesthetic diversity. With Universal Determinism, however, all actual disagreement about causal relations must be attributed not to the openness of the idealized standard of judgment, but solely to the difficulty of having sufficient experience, combined with the appropriate respondent qualities, to approximate to it.

Indeed, given the resistance to global error exhibited by sense-based concepts generally [4.3], mistakes about causal relations will be difficult to conceive as resulting from anything other than such failures of sufficient experience or shared qualities. In particular, two hypotheses seem ruled out by his understanding of CAUSATION: (i) that some relations fail to be genuinely causal even though they instantiate constant conjunctions that would be judged causal from the standard of judgment for CAUSATION (THN 1.3.14.32/171; [6.3]); and (ii) that some relations among individual objects or events are genuinely causal even though they fail to exemplify a constant conjunction that would be judged causal through the application of that standard of judgment (EHU 11.30/148).

## 4.4 Probability

Hume writes:

> Thus all probable reasoning is nothing but a species of sensation. 'Tis not solely in poetry and music, we must follow our taste and sentiment, but likewise in philosophy.
> (THN 1.3.8.12/103)

It is not difficult to see what the primitive sensibility constituting a Humean sense of probability would be: it is the capacity to feel liveliness, in varying degrees, in having ideas of how things might be, or—as we may say, following Hume—conceiving possible matters of fact [2.1, 3.3]. This is why he continues in the passage just quoted:

> When I am convinc'd of any principle, 'tis only an idea, which strikes more strongly upon me. When I give the preference to one set of arguments above another, I do nothing but decide from my feeling concerning the superiority of their influence.
> (THN 1.3.8.12/103)

This very feeling, in Hume's view, constitutes the mind's basic belief in what the idea represents [2.1], and even though it is not an impression of reflection, he intentionally assimilates it to aesthetic and moral sentiments by referring to it frequently as "the sentiment of belief." Indeed, he famously asserts that "*belief is more properly an act of the sensitive, than of the cogitative part of our natures*" (THN 1.4.1.8/183), further reinforcing the notion that the capacity to feel the liveliness constitutive of belief is suitable to serve as a sense. The primary sources of this sentiment are: (i) the (external) senses, which deliver, in addition to impressions of sensation, beliefs about the continued and distinct existence of bodies [3.5]; (ii) memory, which delivers non-inferential beliefs about the past [3.2]; and (iii) probable reasoning, which delivers beliefs about matters of fact that are themselves neither provided by the senses not directly remembered [3.4].

In treating the capacity to feel liveliness in conceiving possible matters of fact as a *sense of probability*, we must understand the term 'probability' in an inclusive Locke-inspired sense that encompasses within its scope not only sub-proof probability, but also proof as well—excluding only knowledge in the strict technical sense [2.1, 3.4]. For Locke himself, knowledge in the strict sense requires the perception of relations of agreement or disagreement among ideas, and it admits of three "degrees": intuition, demonstration, and "sensation." Locke classifies sensation as a degree of knowledge because he regards it as involving the perception of an agreement between a present idea of sensation and an idea of "real existence" (ECHU 4.2; [2.6]). He also seems to allow memory to qualify as knowledge, at least when it is understood to consist in the retention of previous knowledge, including sensory knowledge. Hume retains Locke's doctrine that knowledge in a strict sense depends only on awareness of relations of ideas, which he contrasts with matters of fact [3.4]; but because he does not treat the senses or memory as involving perceived "agreement" with an idea of "real existence," he does not include either of them within the scope of knowledge in this sense. Instead, the senses and memory provide a high degree of liveliness to ideas, in his view [2.1]—a degree at least as high as that founded on proof. We may therefore consider the senses and memory, like proof, as within the scope of the Humean sense of probability in this most inclusive sense.

In the development of the Humean concept of probability, we can again readily discern the same four elements that characterize the development of other sense-based concepts. First, the repeated activation of the capacity to feel degrees of liveliness—that is, degrees of the sentiment of belief—occurs in conceiving possible matters of fact through the senses, memory, or probable reasoning. Second, although such sentiments themselves occur in animals as well as in humans, resemblances among the instances of this characteristic response lead human minds to generalize, forming an abstract idea of probability as a quality of the possible matters of fact that are represented by the lively ideas. As in the case of many other Humean senses, the human mind also forms abstract ideas of particular degrees of the quality in question—including, in this case, both proof and sub-proof probabilities—in response to different degrees of the characteristic mental response.

Third, divergent sentiments of probability concerning the same possible matter of fact are naturally corrected and refined through convergence on a standard of judgment and the development of rules of judgment. The idealized respondent qualities encompassed in the standard of judgment for probability are those of "a wise man," who "proportions his belief to the evidence" (EHU 10.4/ 110). In doing so, the wise person bestows greater degrees of belief in response to greater numbers of experiments and greater uniformity among them. The wise person also avoids the belief-enhancing effects of surprise, wonder, and hope; of sympathy with the belief of testifiers, which gives rise to "credulity"; and of the unapproved liveliness-altering mechanisms that Hume calls "unphilosophical probability" [3.4]. Concerning the idealized point of view partly constitutive of the standard, however, Hume writes only that the "true standard" of judgment for the probability of matters of fact lies in "experience" (THN 1.3.9.12/113). Although extensive experience also plays a crucial role in the standard of judgment for CAUSATION, the precise role of experience as part of the standard of judgment for PROBABILITY proves to be somewhat different.

While the qualities of the idealized respondent for probability judgments are reasonably well articulated, it is somewhat more challenging to specify further the idealized point of view consisting of "experience." Where one set of experiences is a subset of another, we may naturally defer to the more comprehensive. Yet the seemingly natural extension of this deference into an idealized point of view—such as (i) *everything experienced by human beings to date*, (ii) *everything that ever will be experienced*, or (iii) *everything that could be experienced*—would often be of relatively little value, it seems, at least outside of particular well-defined sequences with well-defined relative frequencies. Furthermore, if Universal Determinism is correct, then the third alternative would threaten to collapse the degrees of probability into just two: the certainty (proof) of a conceived matter of fact and the certainty (proof) of its denial. Accordingly, Hume seems open to *relativizing* many judgments of probability to a relevant non-ideal individual or shared body of evidence, allowing that something may be highly probable relative to one body of evidence, possessed at a time by one individual or group, and less probable relative to another. He evidently allows a certain amount of similar relativization in connection with morals: a trait that is a virtue in one set of broad cultural or even physical circumstances (traits such as military skill or respect for property) can genuinely be (and not just as a matter of blameless diversity [4.2]) less of a virtue, or not a virtue at all, in different cultural or even physical circumstances [8.5].

As in the case of the rules by which to judge of causes and effects [4.3], the value of rules of judgment is often proportional to the difficulty of achieving the fully idealized qualities and point of view embodied in a standard of judgment. Hume notes that there are rules for judging the probability of matters of fact that discount the seeming liveliness of "poetical enthusiasms" [2.1], and he notes other rules to "keep ... from augmenting ... belief upon every [momentary] increase of the force and vivacity [i.e., liveliness] of our ideas." At the same time, another rule requires attributing "full conviction" to opinions that "admit of no doubt or opposite probability," even if these opinions are not always felt with the highest liveliness (THN 1.3.10.11–12/631–32). He explicitly compares these rules to those for correcting the sensory appearances of the distances of bodies. These two sets of rules can only be understood as regulating the revival sets of abstract ideas—of degrees of probability and of degrees of distance, respectively—so as to maintain intrapersonal and interpersonal agreement. In addition, of course, Hume's treatments of the probability of chances and the probability of causes recognize more specifically mathematical rules for the weighing and balancing of degrees of probability based on the number of experiments, "subtracting" the force of a lesser number of experiments from the force of a greater number of them [3.4]. These mathematical rules also facilitate the elaboration of the inferential roles attributable to probability concepts, including concepts of particular degrees.

If PROBABILITY is indeed a directly sense-based concept for Hume, then we may expect that it will be both semantically simple and subject in principle to dual non-synonymous definitions. Although he does not explicitly provide such definitions, the responsive definition of 'probability'—if broad enough to include sensation, memory, and probable reasoning—should be at least roughly *such as to be conceived with liveliness by a spectator*. For the productive definition, *conformity to experience* would serve, as long as the continued and distinct existence of bodies corresponding to constant and coherent impressions of sensation [3.5] is regarded as a species of conformity to experience. For the cases of memory and probable reasoning, however, the conformity may be indicated more specifically as *conformity to past experience*—which is the very term that Locke uses to designate one of his own two "grounds of probability" (along with testimony), and the only one that Hume allows as basic [3.4].

As previously remarked, Hume uses not only secondary quality terms but also the terms 'beauty', 'virtue', and 'power' in a way that is systematically ambiguous between a feeling on the one hand, and a quality productive of that feeling, on the other. It is not surprising, therefore, that he also uses the term 'evidence' as signifying, on the one hand, the liveliness of an idea (e.g., THN 1.3.13.3/144 and THN 1.4.1.6/183) and, on the other, as signifying the feature of objects of experience to which the wise person proportions his or her belief (EHU 10.4/110). This is one reason why Kemp Smith was mistaken to characterize Hume as "rejecting evidence" in favor of feeling.

As with beauty and virtue, one should expect room for some blameless diversity in the application of concepts of degrees of probability as a result of openness in the determination of its standard of judgment. Although the relativization of probability to a specified or assumed body of experience limits the openness of the specification of the idealized point of view, a considerable domain of blameless disagreement may remain as a result of openness in the specification of an idealized set of respondent qualities. Such qualities include the salience and power of different resemblances and uniformities under different psychological circumstances. Disagreements about degrees of probability may arise especially when the probability of a given possible matter of fact is subject to multiple distinct and incommensurable bodies of evidence. If, for example, 90 of 100 mammals (none of them dogs) found in the wild have been aggressive, while 35 of 50 dogs (none of them found in the wild) have been friendly, the probability that a given wild dog is aggressive, relative to the combined body of experience, will in principle require: (i) balancing the weight of wildness and canininity as relevant aspects of resemblance, and (ii) balancing these weights in relation to different degrees of uniformity. This balancing will be further complicated if, for example, dogs are also analogous, in different respects, to foxes and cats, each of which exhibit yet a different experienced proportion of aggressiveness to friendliness. Because degrees of analogy are less susceptible to mathematical treatment than other species of philosophical probability, we may expect greater scope for blameless diversity in connection with it—as proves to be the case for Hume with the hypothesis of an intelligent designer of the universe [9.2].

Finally, just as Hume holds that the ultimate arbiter of morality is the ideally corrected and refined moral sense of all humankind, so the ultimate judge of the probability of truth is the ideally corrected and refined sense of probability. Thus, for example, he dismisses the question of whether a possible matter of fact for which there is "a superior number of equal chances" is therefore *really more probable to occur*, on the grounds that it is a question about an "identical proposition" (THN 1.3.11.8/127), to which the answer is trivially affirmative. For although it is a (modest) empirical discovery that probability, as detected by the sense of probability, lies in a conformity to experience, he has just delineated the probability of chances as that particular *species* of conformity, and hence of probability, that lies in "a superior number of equal chances" [3.4]. To ask, therefore, whether a possible future matter of fact having this feature is *really more probable to occur* is to suggest a prospect of error where none is readily available. In just the same way that it is difficult to conceive how all humankind could always be wrong about what colors things are, or what things are witty or beautiful, or what characters are virtuous, or which pervasive regularities are really causal, so it will be difficult to conceive, on Hume's view, how all humankind could always be wrong about what is probable relative to a given body of experience.

Nevertheless, just as one can entertain the thought of rejecting *all* conceptualized color distinctions or moral distinctions [4.2], one can entertain the thought of rejecting all distinctions of degrees of probability. In fact, Hume himself does so quite seriously, in response to a series of skeptical reflections concerning human reason, near the end of *Treatise* Book 1:

> The *intense* view of these manifold contradictions and imperfections in human reason has so wrought upon me, and heated my brain, that I am ready to reject all belief and reasoning, and can

look upon no opinion even as more probable or likely than another.

(THN 1.4.7.8/268)

Fortunately, however, this is a report of a transitory episode, and it is explicitly labeled as such both in the remainder of the section and in *A Letter from a Gentleman*. Through a process to be considered in detail in Chapter Seven, the force of probability distinctions—like the force of moral distinctions—properly returns.

## 4.5 Conclusion

It is widely recognized that Hume sees aesthetic and moral ideas as being the result of their own distinctive "senses," and that he sees both as being analogous to ideas of secondary qualities of bodies discerned by the external senses. It has not been fully appreciated, however, how detailed and sophisticated an account of the origin and nature of such sense-based concepts—as involving a four-stage developmental process of repeated activation of a distinctive sensibility, initial generalization, natural correction via standards and rules, and relational attribution—can be elicited from his remarks about them. Also not fully appreciated, therefore, is the extent to which he treats the ideas of causation and of probability—partly explicitly and partly implicitly—as sense-based concepts following this developmental schema.

The Copy Principle does not require that all concepts arise through the four-stage development process by which sense-based concepts arise, but the process is one that is fully in accordance with the principle. Accordingly, Hume's accounts of the origin and nature of the concepts BEAUTY and DEFORMITY, VIRTUE and VICE, CAUSATION, and PROBABILITY are all central instances of his concept empiricism. Because these concepts are natural psychological entities, evolving through time and possessing intentionality as a consequence of their causal and functional roles, his accounts of their origin and nature are equally central instances of his naturalism—a naturalism, moreover, that allows that all of these qualities and relations are fully real. At the same time, the resistance to global error that follows from his accounts of the origin and nature of these concepts provides resources for limiting the scope of the kind of skepticism that would deny the reality of the distinctions drawn by means of them.

Finally, because the parallels among BEAUTY and DEFORMITY, VIRTUE and VICE, CAUSATION, and PROBABILITY in Hume have not been fully appreciated, it has also not been fully appreciated that all exhibit the characteristic features of Humean sense-based concepts: (i) conceptual simplicity; (ii) in-principle susceptibility to dual productive and responsive definitions; (iii) systematic terminological ambiguity between feeling and quality; (iv) susceptibility to blameless disagreement through openness of the standard of judgment; and (v) general resistance to global error. As the remaining chapters indicate, each of these features proves important both for resolving textual puzzles about Hume's meaning and for appreciating the continuing significance of his philosophy.

The proposal that there is a distinctive and important class of *response-dependent concepts*—that is, concepts in which a characteristic mental response plays a special conceptual and epistemological role—has attracted considerable attention in recent and contemporary philosophy. For at least some of its proponents, the analogy developed by Hume and others between concepts of secondary qualities and moral qualities was part of the initial inspiration for the proposal. Because contemporary treatments of response-dependence have developed along several different tracks, with several different definitions and criteria, I have chosen to employ the more strictly etiological and slightly more Hutchesonian and Humean term 'sense-based concept'. In particular, although the concepts in question pick out qualities that, as things stand, do produce a characteristic response in (idealized) respondents under (idealized) circumstances, Hume should not be interpreted as claiming that these concepts must pick out mere so-called *relational properties*—that is, properties that consist simply in *being so related to (idealized) respondents as to produce the characteristic response in them (in idealized circumstances)*. Rather, standing in such a relation is, in principle, just one feature of the quality itself. With this proviso understood, however, one way of expressing a main idea of this chapter would be to say that for Hume, the response-dependent concepts include not only those of secondary qualities, BEAUTY and DEFORMITY, and VIRTUE and VICE, but also, surprisingly enough, CAUSATION and PROBABILITY.

## Further reading

Beck, Lewis White (1974) "'Was-Must Be' and 'Is-Ought' in Hume," *Philosophical Studies* 26.3/4: 219–28. (A useful comparison of Hume's treatment of causation and his treatment of morality.)

Corvino, John (2008) "Hume and the Secondary Quality Analogy," *Journal of Scottish Philosophy* 6.2: 157–73. (A recent examination and defense of the importance for Hume of the analogy between secondary qualities and moral qualities.)

Coventry, Angela (2006) *Hume's Theory of Causation: A Quasi-Realist Interpretation*, New York: Continuum. (Contains an important discussion of the role of standards of judgment.)

Garrett, Don (2009) "Hume" in *The Oxford Handbook of Causation*, edited by Helen Beebee, Christopher Hitchcock, and Peter Menzies, Oxford: Oxford University Press: 73–91. (Contains an extensive discussion of the causal sense in Hume, including discussion of the two definitions.)

Robinson, J. A. (1962) Hume's Two Definitions of 'Cause'," *The Philosophical Quarterly* 12.2: 162–71. (The original stimulus to a great deal of subsequent literature about the two definitions of 'cause'.)

Sayre-McCord, Geoffrey (1994) "On Why Hume's General Point of View Isn't Ideal—and Shouldn't Be," *Social Philosophy and Policy* 11.1: 200–228. (A good discussion of convergence on the respondent qualities and point of view of a standard of judgment for virtue.)

Wedgwood, Ralph (1997) "The Essence of Response-Dependence," *European Review of Philosophy* 3: 31–54. (A useful recent discussion of conceptions of response-dependence.)

# Five

Normative concepts

A *normative* concept is one the application of which implies some prescription or proscription (typically expressible by 'ought' or 'ought not') or some evaluation (typically expressible by 'good' or 'bad' or 'right' or 'wrong'). Some sense-based concepts, such as LOUD, BLUE, and CAUSATION, are clearly not normative concepts at all for Hume.[1] Others, however, are applied as positive or negative evaluations to at least some degree. The concept HUMOR seems at least mildly normative, insofar as to call something "humorous"—in the modern sense (relatively new in Hume's time) responsively definable as "such as to inspire mirth, amusement, or laughter"—is at least usually to express a kind of approval of it. The concepts BEAUTY and DEFORMITY are more clearly normative, it is fair to say: almost anything would be understood to be better for being beautiful than not, other things being equal. The concepts VIRTUE and VICE are even more normative—or, one might better say, even more seriously normative.

Each of these concepts, however, involves its own distinctive kind of value or corresponding disvalue—risible, aesthetic, or moral, respectively. In each case, moreover, we may distinguish the concepts that Hume treats as *fundamentally normative* from those that he treats as *derivatively normative*. The former are those—such as HUMOR for remarks or other events, BEAUTY and DEFORMITY for objects or events, and VIRTUE and VICE for traits of character or other mental attributes—that he regards as expressing primary values or disvalues that structure an entire normative domain. The latter are those that imply a prescription, proscription, or evaluation that is dependent on a fundamental value or disvalue in some particular way. For example, such concepts as MAN OF

WIT, SKILLFUL ARTIST, or GENEROUS ACTION, all of which he employs, are quite clearly derivatively normative in this manner for him, at least with respect to risible, aesthetic, and moral value, respectively. (While some might regard GENEROUS ACTION as fundamentally normative in the moral domain, Hume holds that actions have moral value only because they are signs of a virtue of character. Because MAN OF WIT and SKILLFUL ARTIST involve mental characteristics of persons, they also have some derivative moral normativity, for Hume.) It is notable that the fundamentally normative concepts in the risible, aesthetic, and moral domains are, for him at least, also directly sense-based.

Yet although some normative concepts have their normativity in a way that is not derived from that of other concepts, part of Hume's naturalism lies in his general unwillingness to accept any normativity as explanatorily basic *tout court*: if some things have value of a specific kind, it should be explicable how there is such a kind of value and how things come to be valued in relation it. As it happens, careful attention to his texts suggests, again, four overlapping developmental stages.

Commentators have frequently interpreted Hume's avowed skepticism as requiring that he reject the attribution of any positive *epistemic*—that is, theoretical truth- or knowledge-related—value to beliefs. If that were so, however, it would call into question not only the propriety of his own praise for scientific discoveries as contrasted with his condemnation of the beliefs of the superstitious, but also the value of his own philosophical enterprise as a contribution to the science of man. If, on the other hand, Hume's theory of the sense-based character of aesthetic and moral concepts can serve to shed light on his conception of probability, we may also hope that his approach to aesthetic and moral normativity will shed light on his understanding of epistemic normativity.

## 5.1 Aesthetic and moral normativity

Hume recognizes that many kinds of things can produce aesthetic sentiments and so become objects of aesthetic evaluation: human and animal bodies, inanimate natural objects and scenes, artifacts, and performances. What makes the description of something as beautiful not only an attribution, but also an evaluation?

It is highly relevant to this question that the sentiment of beauty is a pleasure and the sentiment of deformity is a pain. Emphasizing that senses are not inferential, Hume writes that "in our judgments concerning all kinds of beauty, and tastes, and sensations ... [o]ur approbation is imply'd in the immediate pleasure" (THN 3.1.2.3/ 471). Yet he does not propose that every species of pleasure or pain underlies a robustly normative evaluation. For while many things are causally related, in his view, it is conceivable and hence (by the Conceivability Principle) metaphysically possible for any object to exist without any other that is distinct from it—and this includes all simple impressions. Accordingly, he must grant that the very feelings that are the sentiments of beauty and deformity might, in some other metaphysically possible psychology, have had quite different causes and quite different effects from those they actually have. They might, for example, have been produced only by mosquito bites and have led only to compulsive and self-destructive scratching. In such circumstances, the same feelings would likely not have been the source of a concept of an important domain of value. In order to understand the normative character of BEAUTY and DEFORMITY in Hume, therefore, we must understand the role that he thinks these concepts—and the qualities they signify—play in human life. We may distinguish four main elements of this role.

First, in addition to personal pleasure, there must be a *shared appreciation or deprecation* of a quality signified by the concept, as that quality occurs in relation to oneself and to others. This shared appreciation or deprecation of certain qualities is often greatly strengthened by the operation of sympathy, whereby sentiments believed to be felt by others are also felt or augmented in oneself [3.6]. Sympathy of this kind is especially effective in the case of beauty and deformity, in which many persons can in principle experience the same object or event pleasurably together. Beauty and deformity are also powerful causes of many of the most powerfully pleasurable and painful passions. Beauty of face, for example, is a quality in a subject that produces a pleasurable sentiment; hence, by the double relation of impressions and ideas [3.6], it is also a cause of love and pride, whereas its opposite is a cause of hatred and humility by the same operation. These passions are readily produced in multiple observers, and they are, in turn, themselves greatly strengthened within a social group by the mechanism of sympathy. The same double relation of impressions and ideas, strengthened by sympathy, causes human beings to love both those who produce beautiful objects and those who acquire them. Indeed, love of those who possess beautiful objects results, for Hume—like love of the rich more generally (THN 2.2.5, "Of our esteem for the rich and powerful")—primarily from sympathy with the pleasures of the possessors. The additional sympathy of those possessors with the sympathetic pleasures of those who love the possessors for their possessions then further increases the pleasure of the possessors; and this greater pleasure of the possessors becomes, in turn, the basis for additional sympathy-based love on the part of others. Thus, Hume remarks, "the minds of men are mirrors to one another" (THN 2.2.5.21/365); and this "reverberation" can only increase the significance of beautiful objects or events in shared felt appreciation.

Second, however, the shared appreciation or deprecation must generate positive or negative *interpersonal consequences* by means of the passions. The pleasing sentiments of beauty, for example, produce the desire to experience the objects or events that cause them, while the displeasing sentiments of deformity produce aversion to the objects that cause them; and because these pleasures and pains are readily shareable, they readily give rise to joint plans and cooperative enterprises. Even more importantly, love of a person, according to Hume's psychology, naturally produces "benevolence" toward that person—that is, the desire for the person's happiness and an aversion to the person's misery—whereas hatred produces "anger," which is a desire for the person's misery and an aversion to the person's happiness (THN 2.2.6, "Of benevolence and anger"). In this way, beauty and deformity serve to determine whom human beings are more likely to seek to benefit (do "good offices" for, as he puts it) and whom they are more likely to seek to harm.

Third, in addition to shared appreciation and significant interpersonal consequences effected through the passions, full normativity typically involves users of a concept in recognizing and accepting a *personal engagement* to favor, uphold, and further the quality valued through it, or to disfavor, reject, and impede the quality disvalued through it, at least should the opportunity arise. Thus, for example, one comes to see oneself as a willing friend or proponent of beauty or the arts.

Finally, as a result of shared appreciation, interpersonal consequences, and personal engagement, the general terms associated with the concepts, such as 'beauty' and 'deformity', come to be understood as expressing or "implying" praise or condemnation as an element of their very meaning. As Hume puts it in a phrase that he employs in comparing moral and aesthetic terminology, certain terms "come to be taken in a good [or bad] sense" (EMPL I.23: 227). That the term acquires this element of meaning shows that the shared appreciation or deprecation, interpersonal consequences, and personal commitment associated with the concept are themselves mutually recognized and accepted by users. We might well think of this as a particular kind of conceptual role, consisting of attributed relations [4.1]. In this case, however, the relations are not narrowly inferential ones solely to beliefs, but are rather accepted transitions from the application of the concept to favorable or unfavorable sentiments, passions, and volitions.

Like the sentiments of beauty and deformity, the sentiments of moral approbation and disapprobation are pleasures and pains that are shared and augmented by sympathy, and they too cause love and hatred (toward others), or pride and humility (toward oneself), respectively, by the double relation of impressions and ideas. Indeed, exemplifying his distinctive philosophical emphasis on the importance of passions and their consequences, Hume remarks that the production of love, hatred, pride, and humility "is, perhaps, the most considerable effect that virtue and vice have upon the human mind" (THN 3.1.2.5/473). Because his conceptions of virtue and vice are broad enough to include any mental characteristics of a person that produce approbation or disapprobation [4.2], he goes so far as to write:

> These two particulars are to be consider'd as equivalent, with regard to our mental qualities, *virtue* and the power of producing love or pride, *vice* and the power of producing humility or hatred. In every case, therefore, we must judge of the one by the other; and may pronounce any quality of the mind virtuous,

which causes love or pride; and any one vicious, which causes hatred or humility.

(THN 3.3.1.3/575)

Furthermore, although the moral sentiments themselves are often "delicate," they frequently produce these passions in a much higher degree than do beauty and deformity, and with even more serious favorable or unfavorable interpersonal consequences. This is, in part, because a person's own mental characteristics are the qualities most intimately related to the person—even more intimately related than are bodily characteristics or possessions.

Human beings thus desire to associate with the virtuous and to avoid the vicious. Moreover, the benevolence and anger resulting from virtue and vice, respectively, may be expected to be much stronger than the same passions resulting from aesthetic qualities. In the case of the moral qualities, these natural responses constitute desires to reward the virtuous and punish the vicious; and these desires are strengthened by the evident social utility of creating and encouraging incentives to acts manifesting virtue and disincentives to acts manifesting vice.

The degree of personal engagement with virtue and vice may be supposed to be typically greater than the personal engagement with beauty and deformity as well. As Hume writes, "What is honourable, what is fair, what is becoming, what is noble, what is generous, takes possession of the heart, and animates us to embrace and maintain it" (EPM 1.7/172), so that we come to "form, in a manner, the *party* of human kind against vice or disorder, its common enemy" (EPM 9.9/275).

Finally, as a result of shared appreciation or deprecation, practical interpersonal consequences, and personal engagement, the terms 'virtue' and 'vice' come to be taken "in a good or bad sense," respectively, and the general terms for particular character or other mental traits that are recognized as virtues or vices come to be taken in a good or bad sense as well. One of the primary aims of Hume's second *Enquiry* is to determine what all virtues have in common, an aim that is ultimately satisfied by discovering the productive and responsive definitions of 'virtue' [4.2]. Revealingly, the first methodological step he proposes is to identify which traits are virtues and which are vices; and this, he asserts, requires only ordinary linguistic competence, precisely because there are certain terms that, "in all languages," are always or almost always taken in a good sense. As in the aesthetic case, this linguistic feature may be understood as the result of a kind of attributed relation constituting part of the conceptual role of the concept for which these terms stand. One thus violates a kind of conceptual implication if one pronounces a person or trait virtuous but does not participate in valuing the person or trait:

> [A]s every tongue possesses one set of words which are taken in a good sense, and another in the opposite, the least acquaintance with the idiom suffices, without any reasoning, to direct us in collecting and arranging the estimable or blameable qualities of men.
> (EPM 1.10/173)

He expresses the same thought about what he calls this further "part" of the full meaning or "idiom" of the fundamentally normative moral terms in "Of the Standard of Taste":

> The word *virtue*, with its equivalent in every tongue, implies praise; as that of *vice* does blame: And no one, without the most obvious and grossest impropriety, could affix reproach to a term, which in general acceptation is understood in a good sense; or bestow applause, where the idiom requires disapprobation.
> (EMPL I.23: 228; see also EMPL I.11: 81, concerning terms "denoting...approbation or blame")

## 5.2 The epistemic normativity of TRUTH

At the outset of the first *Enquiry*, Hume describes it as a central task of philosophy to "[fix] the foundation of morals, reasoning, and criticism" and to "determine the source" of the distinctions between "truth and falsehood, vice and virtue, beauty and deformity" (EHU 1.2/6). He characterizes "opinions" as subject not only to "assent" but also to "approbation" (for example, THN 1.4.7.2/264–65 and THN 3.3.2.2/592) when they are regarded as true. Determining what the fundamental normative concepts of the epistemic, moral, and aesthetic domains are—or even whether there are any—is of course a matter of considerable controversy among philosophers. These facts about Hume's texts suggest that for him, however, the concepts of TRUTH and FALSEHOOD (applied to beliefs) are at least among the fundamentally normative concepts in the epistemic domain of value, in much the way that BEAUTY and DEFORMITY (applied to objects and events) and VIRTUE and VICE (applied to human mental traits) are for him the fundamentally normative aesthetic and moral concepts, respectively.

Unlike these latter normative concepts, however, TRUTH and FALSEHOOD are *not* themselves sense-based for Hume; instead, as he remarks at the outset of *Treatise* Book 3, "truth...is discern'd merely by ideas, and by their juxtaposition and comparison" (THN 3.1.1.4/ 456–57). Leaving aside the limited special case of the intuitable and demonstrable "relations of ideas" that, as in mathematics, are subjects of knowledge in the strict Lockean sense, Hume defines 'truth' for "matters of fact" in terms of *correspondence*, as "[agreement] of ideas, consider'd as copies, with those objects, which they represent" (THN 2.3.3.5/415) and as "the conformity of our ideas of objects to their real existence" (THN 2.3.10.2/448). Falsehood, in contrast, is the failure of this conformity or agreement. It is thus ideas themselves that are the primary bearers of truth and falsehood for Hume. From these definitions, plus his account of belief as "a lively idea" [2.1], several important consequences follow. To express these consequences, let 'p' designate a possible matter of fact, and braces— '{}'—be used to create names for ideas, so that '{p}' designates an idea of the possible matter of fact, p [see Preface].

The original and most basic form of belief for Hume is non-conceptual. Such beliefs lack separate ideas of subject and predicate. They consist instead simply in a lively idea functioning, or capable of functioning, as a kind of action-guiding mental map. In a conceptual judgment, in contrast, a lively idea must occur as an element in an occurring lively abstract idea [2.6]. Among the kinds of ideas Hume recognizes are ideas of—that is, ideas that represent—other ideas [2.1]. For any **belief-that-p**, therefore, whether itself conceptual or non-conceptual, there may in principle be further beliefs—again either conceptual or non-conceptual—*about* that belief. By Hume's account of 'belief', **belief-that-p** consists in an idea, {p}, that is lively; and by his definition of 'truth' for matters of fact as correspondence between an idea and what it represents, the non-conceptual form of **belief-that-{p}-is-true** consists simply of a lively idea of the conjunction of the idea of p with p itself: that is, {{p} & p}. On the reasonable assumption that lively complex ideas are composed of lively parts, the non-conceptual **belief-that-{p}-is-true** will then literally contain, as a part, a **belief-that-p**. Conversely, because reflecting on one's own **belief-that-p** involves retaining the belief while also coming to have a lively idea of that belief [2.1], reflecting on one's own **belief-that-p** leads naturally to a non-conceptual **belief-that-{p}-is-true**. Accordingly, there will be easy transitions in both directions between **belief-that-p** and non-conceptual **belief-that-{p}-is-true**, while it will be very difficult to have one of these beliefs and yet be resistant to the other. Parallel consequences follow for conceptual beliefs about truth, since to have a conceptual belief that an idea is true must be to include a lively idea of that idea in the actual ordinary revival set [2.4] of the abstract idea TRUTH. This is a revival set in which *all* of the members are, at least in principle, ideas of ideas for which the mind also has, paired with them, lively ideas of their objects.

Because falsehood is simply the absence of truth for ideas, it will presumably be attributed to ideas either non-conceptually or conceptually by means of the general psychological operation for contrariety. This operation requires not merely failing to attribute truth to an idea—an omission that does not require attributing falsehood—but actual resistance to attributing truth to it [2.6].

How do TRUTH and FALSEHOOD, so understood, come to be normative concepts for belief, implying prescription or evaluation? It is a merit of Hume's philosophy that it induces us to ask this question. He does not pose the question in quite those terms himself, but he does go on to emphasize and explain the shared human appreciation of true belief in the section of the *Treatise* entitled "Of curiosity, or the love of truth." He gives this section the important role of concluding *Treatise* Book 2 ("Of the Passions"), thereby putting it on a par with the crucial concluding sections of Book 1 ("Of the Understanding") and Book 3 ("Of Morals"). This structural pride of place is entirely appropriate, for, as we shall see in Chapter Seven, curiosity is one of the two passions, along with ambition, that make possible a return to philosophizing in the concluding section of Book 1, a return that itself makes the rest of the *Treatise* possible.

Hume begins "Of curiosity, or the love of truth" by writing:

> But methinks we have been not a little inattentive to run over so many different parts of the human mind, and examine so many passions, without taking once into the consideration that love of truth, which was the first source of all our enquiries.
> (THN 2.3.10.1/448)

In fact, he discusses in this section two quite different sources of pleasure related to truth. The first is the pleasure that results from "exertion of genius" on an object of enquiry for which the truth is taken to be of some practical importance. He compares this kind of pleasure to the pleasure taken in hunting and gaming. The second is the satisfaction of having settled belief on a question that is of interest to the mind. The feeling of liveliness, he holds, is always somewhat pleasant, especially in contrast to the unpleasant torpor of uncertainty or the painful vacillation of doubt about topics that are related to us in a way sufficient to attract and maintain the mind's attention to them. As a nice example of such a topic—and one that illustrates how degree of interest can vary among persons at the same time and change for the same person over time—Hume mentions the history of a town in which one has recently come to reside. For Hume himself, of course, that would be La Flèche [1.2].

Given these two features of the human mind, we can readily see how human beings can come to take significant pleasure in the thought that their own beliefs about topics of practical value or personal interest are true. First, there is the experienced practical utility of many of the beliefs that one judges to be true, in comparison to many of the possible beliefs that one judges to be false. Second, there is the further immediately pleasurable exertion involved in acquiring such (self-judged) truths. Third, there are also immediately pleasurable enlivening and stabilizing "easy transitions" from the **belief-that-p** to the **belief-that-{p}-is-true** and vice versa. We may call these two directions of transition *semantic ascent* and *semantic descent*, respectively.[2] Indeed, both the stabilizing enlivenments and the transitions themselves may be pleasurable—the latter through what Hume calls "the pleasure of facility" (THN 2.3.5.2–3/423). There are, in contrast, unpleasant losses of liveliness and painful vacillations of doubt in the attempted combination of **belief-that-p** with **belief-that-{p}-is-false**.

Moreover, we can also readily see how human beings could come to take pleasure in the thought that the beliefs of *other* persons are true. First, one finds that one has, more often than not, an enhanced capacity to cooperate usefully with those whose beliefs one deems to be true, in comparison with those whose beliefs one deems to be false. Second, the operation of sympathy serves to communicate not only passions but also sentiments of belief, according to Hume. Hence, when the beliefs one acquires through sympathy with others are beliefs that one already deems to be true, the new sympathetic belief enhances the pleasurably enlivening and stabilizing easy mental transitions between one's own first-order beliefs and one's beliefs that those beliefs are true. In contrast, when the beliefs that one often cannot help but acquire to some degree through sympathy are beliefs one already deems to be false, the result is an unpleasant loss of liveliness and a painful vacillation of doubt through the attempted combination of a new **belief-that-p** with one's previous and persisting **belief-that-not-p** and **belief-that-{p}-is-false**:

> So close and intimate is the correspondence of human souls, that no sooner any person approaches me, than he diffuses on me all his opinions, and draws along my judgment in a greater or lesser degree. And tho', on many occasions, my sympathy with him goes not so far as entirely to change my sentiments, and way of thinking; yet it seldom is so weak as not to disturb the easy course of my thought, and give an authority to that opinion, which is recommended to me by his assent and approbation. Nor is it any way material on what subject he and I employ our thoughts.
> (THN 3.3.2.2/592)

By this operation of sympathy, at least, the attribution of true beliefs to others is pleasurable regardless of topic. Indeed, the enhancement of similarity by shared belief will also make it much easier to share sympathetically as well in the separate pleasures that others derive from their own beliefs and from their beliefs that those beliefs are true [3.6].

Given these original connections between (attributed) truth and pleasure, beliefs in the truth of one's own or others' beliefs will naturally lead by the double relation of impressions and ideas to the further pleasures of pride or love, respectively. Given the original connections between (attributed) falsehood and pain, beliefs suggesting the falsehood of one's own or others' beliefs will naturally lead, by the same double relation of impressions and ideas, to the further pains of humility or hatred, respectively. As Hume writes in the final paragraph of the *Treatise*, knowledge gives "a new lustre in the eyes of mankind, and [is] universally attended with esteem [a form of love with some admixture of humility] and approbation" (THN 3.3.6.6/620). However, because he also holds that the causes of these four indirect passions must typically be at least relatively enduring and at least relatively distinctive, these passions will typically be strongest in response to those stable standing beliefs taken to be true that are unusual either in their number or in their content—just as these passions are typically strongest in response to mental traits that are rare either in degree or kind, and in response to possessions that are either unusual in number or kind. As remarked at the outset of Chapter One, however, the attribution of truth to one's discoveries is also conducive to the pleasurable satisfaction of two further passions of crucial importance to Hume: curiosity and ambition.

Truth thus comes to be socially appreciated and falsehood deprecated, as normativity requires. Furthermore, our love of those who believe (what we judge to be) truths and our hatred of those who believe (what we judge to be) falsehoods bring with them benevolence and anger, respectively, and, along with other passions, a wealth of positive or negative interpersonal consequences—as does the difference in possibilities of cooperation with those whose beliefs one regards as true or false.

In addition, Hume expresses a reflective personal engagement with truth. Contrary to the suggestion of Samuel Johnson—who famously remarked of him, "truth is a cow which will yield such people no more milk, and so they are gone to milk the bull"[3]— Hume declares his commitment to favoring, upholding, and furthering, or "embracing and maintaining," truth. Thus he writes in the Introduction to the *Treatise* that "where experiments of this kind are judiciously collected and compar'd, we may hope to establish on them a science ... " (THN Introduction 10/xix), and again near the conclusion of Book 1 he writes, "For my part, my only hope is, that I may contribute a little to the advancement of knowledge" (THN 1.4.7.14/272).

Finally, it is reasonable to suppose that 'true', like 'virtue', serves for Hume as a term of approbation, signifying a practical conceptual role by an idiomatic requirement of being "taken in a good sense." Hume notes that 'learned' is a term of "praise" (HE V.52: 222–23), and he often employs terms for other concepts related to TRUTH in a way meant to express approbation and approval as well.

It may naturally be objected to this Humean explanation of the normativity of truth that it locates the source of approbation not in truth *itself*, but rather in the acquisition and possession of ideas that *seem* true; hence, it seems, the quality we should find ourselves valuing is not truth but instead merely the appearance of truth, or the ability to appear as true. Hume can properly reject this objection, however, for at least two reasons. First, as human beings reflect on their own past beliefs and the past beliefs of others, it is the ones that they retrospectively judge *were* true rather than the ones they judge to have then seemed true, even though they were false, that they generally deem to have been most useful. Indeed, seeming true while actually being false is, experience itself suggests, a particularly dangerous quality for a belief to have.

Second, and more generally, however, truth is quite parallel in this respect to other qualities that human beings appreciate, such as the virtues, beauty, or physical talents that often inspire pride in or love of their possessors. *Seeming* to have virtue of course plays an essential role in the proximate causation of our love of others for their virtue: we cannot actually love persons for their virtue unless they also seem virtuous to us, and we will continue to love persons for their supposed virtue in that case even if we are mistaken about their actual virtue. It is nevertheless the virtue itself and not (or at least not primarily) the ability to seem virtuous that is valued, just as it is beauty or physical talents for *which*, on Hume's account, the possessors of those traits are (at least primarily) loved. It is true that a certain kind of individual might take a particular pride precisely in *seeming* virtuous to neighbors, but this would likely be almost entirely because it would allow for a more unrestrained pursuit of the individual's own vicious pleasures. Indeed, the mere thought that someone seems virtuous, but might secretly be vicious—like the thought that a belief seems true, but might secretly be false—tends to undermine the primary approbation in question. In the case of truth, the thought does so precisely by compromising the belief's thoroughgoing ability to seem true, just as the parallel suspicion about virtue compromises the individual's thoroughgoing ability to seem virtuous.

## 5.3 The epistemic normativity of PROBABLE TRUTH

Whereas the Humean concept TRUTH, as we have been considering it, is not itself sense-based, the Humean concept PROBABILITY, as we have been considering it, is not itself normative. To say that a possible matter of fact is probable is in no way to praise or condemn it; to say that afternoon rain tomorrow is probable, for example, says nothing about whether afternoon rain tomorrow would be good or bad. One application of PROBABILITY does have an epistemically normative status, however—namely, the mediately sense-based concept PROBABLE TRUTH as applied to beliefs. This concept is mediately sense-based because it results from the application of PROBABILITY to that subset of possible matters of fact that consist in *a belief's being true*. Hume himself simply uses the unrestricted term 'probability'— writing, for example, of "the general term of probability" as distinguished from "knowledge" (THN 1.3.11.2/124)—in contexts in which its scope is clearly understood to be the truth of beliefs. Nevertheless, in order to avoid confusion with the broader immediately sense-based concept PROBABILITY already considered, we will continue to use the term 'PROBABLE TRUTH'. There are, presumably, corresponding negative normative concepts—differing, perhaps, in their manner of utilizing the relation of contrariety, but equivalent in their practical application to ideas—of PROBABLE FALSEHOOD and IMPROBABILITY OF TRUTH.

Like many other qualities conceived at least partly through sense-based concepts, probability of truth admits of degrees, and hence of corresponding mediately sense-based concepts of particular degrees. As with many qualities conceived at least partly through sense-based normative concepts, greater degrees correspond to greater degrees of value within their normative domain. In the case of probable truth—where the idea of a possible matter of fact and the idea of its denial may readily involve inversely varying degrees of the "sentiment of belief"—a low degree of probable truth will carry not merely a lower degree of value, but rather a degree of disvalue. In general, positive value will require a degree of probable truth that is greater than the degree of probable truth of its denial. When PROBABLE TRUTH is characterized as a positive normative concept in what follows, it should be understood as the concept of probability of truth that is of at least this degree.

What could explain the normativity of PROBABLE TRUTH, so understood? It might naturally be suggested that the concept simply derives its normativity from the more fundamental normativity of TRUTH itself, by way of an epistemically approvable inference from **{p}-is-probably-true** to the already normatively positive **{p}-is-true**. By itself, however, this cannot provide the needed explanation. As already observed, probability is not a quality that is broadly valued in application to matters of fact—for example, afternoon rain—that do not consist in the truth of beliefs. Why then should the proposed inference be epistemically approvable, given that it is not guaranteed to preserve truth? From the premise that **{p}-is-probably-true** it follows strictly not that **{p}-is-true** but only that **it-is-probably true-that-{p}-is-true**; and concerning this latter claim, the question immediately recurs about the source of normativity for the mere *probable truth* of **{p}-is-true**. Instead, therefore, it seems that the Humean concept PROBABLE TRUTH must acquire its normativity not derivatively but fundamentally, not from that of TRUTH but rather in *parallel* with it. In fact, it should acquire normativity for very much the same reasons that TRUTH itself does. In consequence, epistemic normativity for Hume will simply be the kind of normativity that is structured by the two positive values of truth and probable truth for beliefs, and the two disvalues of their opposites.

If what we have said thus far is correct, then the non-conceptual form of **belief-that-it-is-probable-that-p** should consist for Hume simply of an idea {p} that is lively to a sufficient degree. (This will be the same thing as **belief-to-a-sufficient-degree-that-p**. As before, the **belief-that-p** itself may in principle be either conceptual or non-conceptual.) The non-conceptual form of **belief-that-{p}-is-probably-true** should consist simply of the idea {{p} & p} that is lively to a sufficient degree. On the reasonable assumption that complex ideas lively to a certain degree are composed of parts that are lively to at least that degree, the non-conceptual **belief-that-{p}-is-probably true** will literally contain the **belief-that-it-is-probable-that-p** as a part. Conversely, because reflecting on one's own **belief-that-it-is-probable-that-p** involves retaining that belief while also coming to have a lively idea of it, reflecting on one's own **belief-that-it-is-probable-that-p** leads naturally to a non-conceptual **belief-that-{p}-is-probably-true**. Accordingly, there will again be easy transitions in both directions—transitions that we may again call *semantic ascent* and *semantic descent*—between the two beliefs, while it will be very difficult to have one of the beliefs while being resistant to the other.

Parallel considerations apply to conceptual beliefs about probable truth—that is, beliefs that employ the concept PROBABLE TRUTH. Because concepts can represent with generality, however, we may now allow a "degree" of probability to be either a precise degree or a range of degrees. To have a conceptual **belief-that-{p}-is-probably-true** will be to locate an idea, {idea of p}, that is lively to a sufficient degree, in the actual ordinary revival set of PROBABLE TRUTH [2.4, 2.6]. Each member of this revival set will be an idea of an idea of a possible matter of fact, paired with an idea, lively to a sufficient degree, of that matter of fact. Thus, on the one hand, conceptual **belief-that-{p}-is-probably-true** requires at least a disposition of readiness to **belief-that-it-is-probable-that-p**. Conversely, reflection on one's own **belief-that-it-is-probable-that-p** leads naturally, for those who have concepts of degrees of probable truth, to a conceptual **belief-that-{p}-is-probably-true**. Accordingly, there will be easy transitions in both directions between **belief-that-it-is-probable-that-p** and conceptual **belief-that-{p}-is-probably-true**, while it will be very difficult to combine one of these with resistance to the other.

Because the dynamics of the relations between belief and the concept PROBABLE TRUTH parallel in this way those between belief and TRUTH, the same features of the mind that give rise to love of truth will also give rise to love of probable truth. In addition to the pleasurable exertion of its faculties in inquiry through probable reasoning about useful topics, the mind will experience the practical utility of beliefs judged to be probably true, relative to those judged to be probably false—and the more so the greater the degree of probability. Furthermore, the mind will also experience pleasurably enlivening and stabilizing easy transitions between **belief-that-it-is-probable-that-p** and **belief-that-{p}-is-probably-true**, while it experiences an unpleasant lack of liveliness and painful vacillation of doubt in the attempt to combine **belief-that-it-is-probable-that-p** with **belief-that-{p}-is-probably-false**. These feelings lead to pride in holding beliefs that are probably true and humility for holding beliefs that are judged probably false. These effects, too, vary in strength with the degree of probability.

Similarly, the mind comes naturally to value probable truth in the beliefs of others as well. On the one hand, one finds that, more often than not, one has an enhanced capacity to cooperate usefully with those whose beliefs one deems to be probably true, compared with those whose beliefs one deems to be probably false. When the beliefs acquired through sympathy with others are beliefs that one has already deemed to be probably true, they enhance the pleasurably enlivening and stabilizing transitions between one's own first-order beliefs and one's own beliefs that those beliefs are probably true. In contrast, when the beliefs that one often cannot help but acquire through sympathy are beliefs deemed to be probably false, the result undermines one's belief and introduces an unpleasant loss of liveliness and painful vacillation in the attempt to combine a newly and sympathetically acquired **belief-that-it-is-probable-that-p** with a previous and persisting **belief-that-{p}-is-probably-false**. In addition, the similarity of shared belief about what is probable will enhance sympathetic participation in the separate pleasures of those who deem their own (similar) beliefs to be probably true. The result is a degree of love for those whose beliefs are judged probably true and a degree of hatred for those whose beliefs are judged probably false. All of these effects, too, vary in strength as the probability itself varies in degree.

We may now summarize the full development of the Humean concept PROBABLE TRUTH. It begins with the repeated activation—through memory, the senses, and probable reasoning—of a primitive sensibility consisting in the capacity to feel liveliness in an idea of a possible matter of fact. The similarity among instances of this characteristic response serve through initial generalization to produce an abstract idea of PROBABILITY, along with concepts of particular degrees and ranges of degree. These concepts are then naturally corrected and refined through shared convergence on a standard of judgment consisting of (i) a point of view of extensive experience (often relativized to a given body of experimental evidence), and (ii) the qualities of the wise man who proportions belief to the evidence. The application of the standard is aided, and the standard qualities further specified, by the adoption of rules of probability. These rules may also be incorporated, along with other features, into an inferential role for each concept of probability [4.4].

Although these concepts of probability apply to possible matters of fact across the board, they can also be applied specifically to the probability that a given belief corresponds to how the world is—that is, for Hume, to the probability of the belief's being true. Human beings acquire a shared appreciation of the probability of truth in their own beliefs and in the beliefs of others, for reasons parallel to those for which they share an appreciation of truth itself. Through its effects on the passions, this shared appreciation gives rise to practical interpersonal consequences. In addition, human beings adopt and recognize a personal engagement on behalf of probable truth as conceived through those concepts, aiming to embrace and maintain it. Accordingly, like attributions of truth, attributions of probable truth come to be "taken in a good sense," thereby developing for PROBABLE TRUTH a conceptual role that implies not merely assent, but also approbation.

Hume's own personal commitment to probable truth is expressed perhaps most powerfully in the concluding section of *Treatise* Book 1. Despite the acknowledged fact that "two thousand years with such long interruptions, and under such mighty discouragements are a small space of time to give any tolerable perfection to the sciences," he writes:

> [W]e might hope to establish a system or set of opinions, which if not true (for that, perhaps, is too much to be hop'd for), might at least be satisfactory to the human mind, and might stand the test of the most critical examination.
> (THN 1.4.7.14/272)

This passage suggests that he—and we—can uphold an ongoing commitment to probable truth relative to present experience, even when truth itself may seem too grand an achievement to claim in the present early state of enquiry. It is for this reason that he refers in the *Abstract* to "probabilities, ... on which life and action intirely depend, *and which are our guides even in most of our philosophical speculations*" (ATHN 4/647; emphasis added).

PROBABLE TRUTH is thus able to function as a mediately sense-based fundamentally normative concept for Hume, one that constitutes, along with TRUTH, one of the two positive fundamentally normative concepts of epistemic value, and one that is suitable for judging epistemically even systems of philosophy, including his own. Hume memorably declares "that the imagination, according to my own confession, [is] the ultimate judge of all systems of philosophy" (THN 1.4.4.1/225). We can now understand how it does so: through its capacity to feel liveliness and to generate concepts of probable truth that are able to acquire normative force, the inclusive imagination [3.2] judges systems of philosophy precisely by judging the probability of their being true.

## 5.4 Features of sense-based normative concepts

The Humean aesthetic, moral, and epistemic domains of value are structured at least in part by fundamentally normative concepts that are also immediately or mediately sense-based. For this reason, the three domains exhibit, in Hume's treatment of them, two distinctive features.

The first feature is this: many or all of the substantive principles governing the application of the normative concepts that structure these domains are *a posteriori* rather than *a priori* in the modern senses to which these terms were already evolving in Hume's time. That is to say, such principles are knowable (in a broad sense) only from evidence provided by experience, rather than knowable prior to, or independent of, such evidence. In "Of the Standard of Taste" for example, Hume explicitly remarks, "none of the rules of composition are fixed by reasonings *a priori*" (EMPL I.23: 231). Because certain terms, both in aesthetics and in morals, come to be "taken in a good sense," it requires only knowledge of "the language" to know that "elegance" and "simplicity" are to be praised in writing, or "justice" and "humanity" in character (EMPL I.23: 226–29); and, accordingly, "whoever recommends any moral virtues, really does no more than is implied in the terms themselves." But while knowledge that beauties or virtues are to be praised may be considered *a priori* in consequence of the conceptual roles of the concepts involved, Hume emphasizes that the proper boundaries of the beauties or virtues themselves are determined by aesthetic and moral experience, respectively, and may be the subjects of considerable disagreement hidden beneath the verbal agreement that beauties and virtues are to be praised. Indeed, there is, within his theory of the mind, no way in which such substantive aesthetic or moral normative principles *could* be known *a priori*. Instead, he begins with moral and aesthetic senses or sensibilities, which are then corrected and refined to yield final moral and aesthetic verdicts [4.1–2]. While he does of course endorse morally and aesthetically normative principles, these principles are themselves verdicts that depend on the empirical deliverances of the aesthetic and moral senses.

Because TRUTH is not a sense-based concept, principles governing its application may more readily be *a priori*; presumably, principles governing mathematical and other demonstrative reasoning would qualify as *a priori* for Hume. Like Locke and many other early modern philosophers, however, he disparages the practical value of Aristotle's logic of demonstration. Instead, he writes somewhat defiantly that his eight "rules by which to judge of causes and effects"—"form'd [from experience] on the nature of our understanding" (THN 1.3.13.11/149)—constitute "all the LOGIC I think proper to employ in my reasoning" (THN 1.3.15.11/175).

Probable reasoning, of course, depends in Hume's view on the empirical "discovery" of causal relations [3.4], while PROBABLE TRUTH, precisely because it is sense-based, more closely resembles VIRTUE and BEAUTY in the dependence of its principles on experience. There is, once again, no way within his theory of the mind in which substantive normative principles governing probable truth could be known *a priori*. Instead, he begins with a sense of probability, which is then corrected and refined to yield final verdicts [4.4]. While he does of course endorse epistemically normative principles concerning probability, these principles are themselves verdicts that depend on the empirical deliverances of the sense of probability. Even though the probability of chances and of causes can be treated mathematically, their suitability for mathematical treatment can be discovered only by experience, much as the suitability of physics to mathematical treatment can be discovered only by experience (EHU 4.13/31–32).

It is therefore a mistake to suppose that Hume implicitly combines *a priori* normative epistemic premises with his empirical findings in the science of man in order to reach skeptical conclusions. In particular, he does *not* combine his discovery that certain cognitive outcomes cannot be produced by reasoning [6.1, 7.2] with an *a priori* normative epistemic principle to the effect that only beliefs produced in that way can be probably true on the available evidence or have epistemic value. Rather, his skepticism begins from empirical discoveries about the various "infirmities" of human cognitive faculties that call into question the probable truth of the beliefs they produce; and the amount of belief-diminishing force that these discoveries properly have is to be determined precisely by their considered impact on the corrected and refined sense of probability itself. At the same time, it is not ruled out in advance that the corrected and refined sense of probability should ultimately disapprove of a form of otherwise quite regular probable reasoning that fails to have its expected effect on liveliness—as in fact occurs in the final section of *Treatise* Book 1 [7.3].

The second distinctive feature of these domains is this: the senses underlying them can, in principle, be used to evaluate both themselves and other senses through the application of the normative sense-based concepts to which they give rise. In the final section of *Treatise* Book 3, for example, Hume famously argues that the moral sense approves morally of itself and its own operations:

> [T]his sense [of morals] must certainly acquire new force, when reflecting on itself, it approves of those principles, from whence it is deriv'd, and finds nothing but what is great and good in its rise and origin ... . According to [our] system, not only virtue must be approv'd of, but also the sense of virtue: And not only that sense, but also the principles, from whence it is deriv'd. So that nothing is presented on any side but what is laudable and good.
> (THN 3.3.6.3/619)

This fact constitutes what he calls, in a revealing phrase, the "dignity of virtue." Generally unnoticed, however, is the fact that the results of the corrected moral sense also seem to win *epistemically* normative approval in the very last sentence of the *Treatise*, where Hume, for the first time since the promissory note of the Introduction, pronounces morality to be a "science" whose precepts are "correct":

> And thus the most abstract speculations concerning human nature, however cold and unentertaining, become subservient to *practical morality*: and may render this latter science more correct in its precepts, and more persuasive in its exhortations.
> (THN 3.3.6.6/621)

As we shall see in Chapter Seven, the corrected and refined sense of probability does ultimately achieve epistemically normative approval in the final section of *Treatise* Book 1, although only with much turmoil and with a diminished degree of probable truth for its results. In *Treatise* Book 3, the corrected and refined sense of probability also achieves morally normative approval from the corrected and refined moral sense. Thus Hume writes in his survey of the virtues, "wisdom and good-sense are valu'd [as virtues] because they are *useful* to the person possess'd of them" (THN 3.3.4.8/611).

Because Hume's confrontation with doubt-inducing considerations is so fraught, many readers have concluded that his ultimate epistemically normative judgment on all belief must be entirely negative, and that he can approve of the tendency to believe only from a moral or even a self-interestedly practical point of view, as something that is useful and/or agreeable to its possessor and/or others, or as satisfying his own personal passions of curiosity and ambition. Yet nearly all stable moral approval depends essentially for Hume on stable beliefs about the causal consequences of actions and characters, and even merely self-interested endorsement typically requires stable beliefs about the probability of achieving one's self-interested ends by the approved means. Epistemic disapproval of the corrected and refined sense of probability, by suggesting that our beliefs are not probably true, would not only undermine the stability of beliefs about the causal consequences of actions and characters, it would also prevent the satisfaction of Hume's own saving passions of curiosity and ambition—both of which require for their satisfaction that he achieve results that (he regards as) genuinely true or at least probably true [7.4]. Accordingly, sustainable moral or self-interested approval of the corrected and refined sense of probability depends at least to some extent on a prior epistemic approval of the sense of probability—as judged, of course, by the imagination's sense of probability itself.

## 5.5 Conclusion

Although it is characteristic of Hume's approach to normativity to treat each discrete domain of value as structured by a small number of fundamentally normative concepts, some might regard this approach as misguided for at least some normative domains. It might be objected, for example, that his emphasis on BEAUTY and DEFORMITY oversimplifies aesthetics by ignoring a large number of equally fundamental aesthetically normative concepts.[4] Others might grant that a given normative domain is structured by a small number of fundamentally normative concepts but differ from Hume about which concepts those are, and even what they serve primarily to evaluate. For example, many would insist that RIGHT and WRONG are the fundamental morally normative concepts, serving primarily to evaluate actions, while evaluations of character are derivative from them. Others would hold that the fundamental morally normative concepts are GOOD and BAD, serving primarily to evaluate states of affairs or outcomes of actions, with evaluations of character and of actions both derivative from these. Similarly, some might propose that the fundamental epistemically normative concepts are WISE and FOOLISH, serving primarily to evaluate cognitive traits, or RELIABLE and UNRELIABLE, serving primarily to evaluate cognitive processes. Others would agree with Hume that beliefs are the primary objects of epistemic evaluation, but insist that KNOWN and JUSTIFIED are the fundamental epistemically normative concepts employed for that purpose. Such disputes may be difficult to adjudicate, and they may themselves turn partly on empirical questions of psychology and semantics and partly on normative questions about what would be best for human beings in the arts, ethics, and scientific inquiry.

Hume's confidence in his own treatment of the structure of the aesthetic, moral, and epistemic normative domains is in part the result of his confidence in his account of the senses that underlie or (as in the epistemic case) partly underlie them. For example, his confidence that BEAUTY and DEFORMITY are the only fundamental aesthetically normative concepts is partly the result of his judgment that there are two basic kinds of aesthetic sentiments—one pleasurable and one painful—even though the precise character of these sentiments may well differ somewhat from case to case. Similarly, his confidence that VIRTUE and VICE are the fundamental morally normative concepts is partly the result of his judgment that there are two basic kinds of moral sentiments—one pleasurable and one painful—even though the precise character of these sentiments may, again, differ somewhat from trait to trait (THN 3.3.4.2/607; EPM App 4.6/316–17). His confidence that it is these traits, rather than actions or their consequences, that are the primary objects of moral evaluation is due in part to his confidence in his account of the role of the causes and consequences of these sentiments: while the pleasurable or painful outcomes of actions themselves affect the moral sense, they are only instrumental in helping to determine the reactions of that sense to the traits that produce them, and actions themselves are evaluated morally only as expressions of mental traits that have already been morally approved (THN 3.1.1.2–4/477–78). At the same time, however, his preference for grounding morality in virtue and vice may reflect his own sympathy with ancient moral philosophy in contrast with what he takes to be more law-based Christian approaches.

Similarly, Hume's willingness to treat PROBABLE TRUTH and PROBABLE FALSEHOOD as fundamental epistemically normative concepts, serving primarily to evaluate beliefs, results in part from his confidence in his account of liveliness as the sentiment of probability. Cognitive traits (including wisdom or foolishness) are, as we have seen [5.4], also objects of the moral sense for him, but there is no further explanation in his philosophy of how they could earn specifically epistemic approval independent of the value of truth and probable truth. Distinctively epistemic evaluations are therefore directed in the first instance at beliefs, for him, not at the mental traits of believing individuals—just as aesthetic evaluations are directed in the first instance not at mental traits of artists but at individual objects and events that they (and nature) produce. Probable truth relative to present experience might be understood simply to be Hume's version of the justification of beliefs, but he employs the term 'justified' only for persons, never for beliefs, and he applies the term 'just' only to reasonings and the drawing of conclusions. Accordingly, it seems that 'just' signifies for him a derivatively normative concept, applied to reasonings in virtue of their producing beliefs that are true or at least probably true relative to the available evidence, while 'justified' designates a derivatively normative concept applied to persons in virtue of their holding beliefs that are at least probably true. His treatment of truth and probable truth as more fundamentally normative than knowledge reflects his lively sense of pervasive human fallibility and also what he hints (in the *Dialogues concerning Natural Religion*) [194] is a personally skeptical temperament [9.2, 9.5].

Hume's naturalism and empiricism together require that there be a naturalistic explanation of how sense-based concepts develop from experience. His naturalism also requires, however, that there be a naturalistic causal explanation of how normative concepts, whether sense-based or not, acquire normative status. Part of his confidence in his treatments of at least some fundamental normative concepts in the aesthetic, moral, and epistemic domains as sense-based plausibly lies in the possibility of applying the elements of his implied four-stage account of the acquisition of normative status to them. In his implementation of this requirement, he is an important precursor of contemporary naturalistic approaches to normativity more generally.

## Notes

1 Specific applications of these concepts on particular occasions may, of course, be evaluated by means of linguistically normative concepts (such as LINGUISTIC CORRECTNESS) or epistemically normative concepts (of the kind soon to be considered). But to call a thing blue, loud, or a cause is not itself to attribute value or disvalue to it.
2 I owe the helpful suggestion of these terms to Louis Loeb.
3 James Boswell (2003) *The Life of Samuel Johnson*. Tokyo: Synapse Edition, I.444.
4 Frank Sibley (1959) "Aesthetic Concepts," *Philosophical Review* 68.4: 421–50 is a classic article that mentions many normative aesthetic concepts without suggesting that any small number of them are more fundamental, in the present sense, than the others.

## Further reading

Baier, Annette (1991) *A Progress of Sentiments: Reflections on Hume's Treatise*, Cambridge MA: Harvard University Press. (Includes an influential interpretation of Humean normativity as "successful reflexivity.")

Broughton, Janet (2003) "Hume's Naturalism about Cognitive Norms," *Philosophical Topics* 31.2: 1–19. (Defends an interpretation of Hume's project as beginning with pre-established "cognitive norms" governing enquiry, norms that the science of man then shows cannot be met by human beings, resulting in radical theoretical skepticism.)

Garrett, Don (2007) "Reasons to Act and Reasons to Believe: Naturalism and Rational Justification in Hume's Philosophical Project," *Philosophical Studies* 132.1 (January): 1–16. (Aims to develop a Humean account of normativity, reasons, and justification for both belief and action; includes a preliminary and less developed account of the value of truth than that presented here.)

Korsgaard, Christine (1996) *The Sources of Normativity*, Cambridge: Cambridge University Press. (An important series of lectures on normativity, with application to Hume as a proponent of a "reflective endorsement" account; includes comments by other prominent philosophers.)

Loeb, Louis (2002) *Stability and Justification in Hume's Treatise*, Oxford: Oxford University Press. (An important and sustained argument for an interpretation of justification as the fundamental epistemic value in the *Treatise*, one that consists in having been produced by a mental mechanism the outputs of which are typically stable.)

Schafer, Karl (2013) "Curious Virtues in Hume's Epistemology," *Philosophers' Imprint* 1.1: 1–20. (A "virtue epistemology" interpretation that treats character traits as the fundamental objects of Humean epistemic evaluation, with central roles for the passions of curiosity and ambition.)

Schmitt, Frederick F. (2014) *Hume's Epistemology in the Treatise: A Veritistic Interpretation*, Oxford: Oxford University Press. (A detailed reading of Hume that locates truth as the primary merit of beliefs and treats the epistemic justification of a belief as the reliability of the cognitive operations that produce it.)

Townsend, Dabney (2000) *Hume's Aesthetic Theory: Sentiment and Taste in the History of Aesthetics*, London: Routledge. (A useful guide to Hume's aesthetics.)

# Six
Induction and causation

Of all the many relations that Hume discusses, none is more important, or more important to him, than causation. Everyday understanding of the world, he recognizes, is primarily an understanding of the causes operative in it, and the sciences (mathematics aside) consist largely of a more systematic and sophisticated search for causes; arguably, at least, he regards all explanation as ultimately causal explanation. Even the production of passions and the motivation of actions depend largely on determining the causes of pleasures and pains, and so does human morality. If, as it seems, all mental representation is for Hume a matter of perceptions playing a share of the causal and/or functional role of something thereby represented [2.6], then it follows that thought itself would be impossible for him without causal relations. His own science of man is an investigation of the causes of mental phenomena—including, prominently, the causes of human beings thinking about causes as they do. He draws a number of important philosophical consequences from his results, including, notably, a proposed solution to the problem of free will, which he calls "the long dispute question concerning liberty and necessity" (EHU 8.2/81).

Of the many operations of the mind that Hume discusses, none is more important, or more important to him, than what he calls "probable reasoning" or "probable inference"—with the term 'probable' employed in its inclusive sense [3.4]. Because of its source, he also calls it "reasoning from experience"; because of its character, he calls it "reasoning from cause and effect"; and because of its pervasiveness in the conduct of human life, as well as its contrast with the certainty that is characteristic of demonstration, he calls it (in the first *Enquiry*) "moral reasoning" in a broad eighteenth-century sense of 'moral' that is now uncommon. Because it involves a belief-generating extrapolation from experience of observed instances to unobserved instances of a generalization—although for Hume these past experiences need not be remembered or employed as premises—it is now often called "inductive reasoning" or "induction." By whatever name it is called, however, it is for him not only essential to the operation of the causal sense, by which causal relations are discerned [4.3], but also the source of all or nearly all human beliefs about "matters of fact and real existence" [2.1, 2.3]—as distinguished from "relations of ideas"—that go beyond what is given or represented in present experience or memory. His argument that such inferences are "not determin'd by reason" (as he writes in the *Treatise*) and are not "founded on reasoning, or any process of the understanding" (as he puts it in the first *Enquiry*) is perhaps his most famous single argument on any topic, just as his treatment of causation is perhaps his best-known philosophical innovation.

Yet, despite their prominence, both the interpretation of Hume's argument concerning induction and his treatment of causation remain the subjects of sharp interpretive dispute. The argument concerning induction has most often been interpreted skeptically as concluding that inductive inferences provide no justification or epistemic value to their conclusions. It has also sometimes been interpreted restrictedly as concluding only that inductive inferences are not, and lack the certainty of, demonstrative inferences. More recently, it has been interpreted causally as drawing a conclusion only about the nature of the causal process of inductive inference. The treatment of causation has most often been interpreted *reductionistically*, as maintaining that causation is nothing more than constant conjunction or uniformity. It has also often been interpreted *realistically* yet skeptically, as allowing that there are "secret powers" or "ultimate principles" in nature beyond constant conjunction, but that their nature is unknown and unknowable by us. More recently, it has been interpreted *projectivistically*, as holding that attributions of causality involve the projection (legitimately or not) of inner states (such as the impression of necessary connection or dispositions to make inferences) onto the world. Hume writes in the *Treatise* that the relation of causation "depends so much" on the nature of probable inference that one must begin with the inference in order to understand the relation (THN 1.3.14.30/169), and that is the order of investigation he follows.

## 6.1 Causal relations and probable reasoning

Although Hume's main argument about induction appears in both the *Treatise* and the first *Enquiry* (as well as in the *Abstract*) its context is somewhat different in the two works. Early in the long Part 3 ("Of knowledge and probability") of *Treatise* Book 1, he selects the relation of causation for special scrutiny (THN 1.3.2) because of its distinctive capacity to underwrite beliefs about unobserved matters of fact. Next, he observes that priority in time and contiguity in space and time are seemingly essential aspects of causal relations, but that there also appears to be a crucial "necessary connexion" between the cause and effect. Puzzled about the nature of this necessary connection, he sets out, in accordance with one of the methodological directives supported by the Copy Principle [2.2], to discover the impression from which the idea of necessary connection is derived. He proposes to look for clues in two questions that constitute "neighboring fields":

(i) For what reason we pronounce it *necessary*, that every thing whose existence has a beginning, shou'd also have a cause?

(ii) Why we conclude, that such particular causes must *necessarily* have such particular effects; and what is the nature of that *inference* we draw from the one to the other, and of the *belief* we repose in it?

(THN 1.3.2.14–15/78)

Understood as applying both to objects and to the states or qualities of objects, the doctrine that every beginning of existence has a cause is often called the *Causal Maxim*. Hume initially gives only a negative answer to the first question (THN 1.3.3): namely, that the doctrine is neither intuited nor demonstrated [3.4], for its denial is perfectly conceivable. Prominent attempted demonstrations by Hobbes, Locke, and Clarke to the contrary, he shows, are fallacious: they beg the question by tacitly employing the Causal Maxim, which is the very point in question. The positive answer to the first question, he proposes, will emerge only in connection with the second question. In answer to that second question, he distinguishes three elements in the inferential process, each of which he makes the subject of a separate section (THN 1.3.5–7): (i) an initiating impression or memory; (ii) a transition from this impression to an idea as a result of experience of a constant conjunction between two kinds of events; and (iii) the resulting feature of this idea that constitutes belief. His famous *Treatise* argument that probable inference is "not determin'd by reason" is contained in the second of these sections (THN 1.3.6), under the mild but descriptive title "Of the inference from the impression to the idea." The full discussion of such reasoning—including sub-proof probability—continues for another six sections, and it reveals that the Causal Maxim is itself the consequence of a kind of inductive inference from past experience of things that begin to exist. Thus prepared, he returns in the final two sections to reconsider the impression of necessary connection and the causal relation itself.

Section 4 of the first *Enquiry*, entitled "Sceptical Doubts concerning the Operations of the Understanding," in contrast, begins not with the nature of causation, but directly with the question of the nature of reasoning about matters of fact. To the question, "What is the nature of all of our reasonings concerning matters of fact?" Hume answers that they are all "founded on cause and effect." For whenever the mind forms a belief about some never-or-not-yet-observed matter of fact—whether past, present, or future—it always reaches that belief by inference from something that it treats as related to that matter of fact by cause and effect. If, for example, someone believes that a friend has been in France, she may do so because she has perceived a letter with writing on it that she regards as having been caused in part by her friend's being in France. Hume then poses a deeper question: "What is the foundation of all of our reasonings and conclusions concerning *the relation of cause and effect?*" His answer is that they are all founded on, in a word, "experience"—specifically, experience of constant conjunctions of like objects or events, in which something of one kind is regularly and immediately followed by something of a second kind.

In support of this answer, Hume argues that there are no *a priori* constraints on causal relations—for example, no requirement that effects resemble their causes or be somehow contained within them. Causes and effects are always different from one another and hence, by a tacit employment of the Separability Principle, either can be conceived to exist without the other. By the Conceivability Principle, their separation is metaphysically possible, and hence only experience can show what kinds of things will in fact follow what. In many cases, one may actually recall having learned, through repeated experience, of a causal relation that was unknown upon first observation. In other cases, he notes—for example the motion of one billiard ball causing upon impact the motion in the same direction of a second—it may seem that one could have known the causal relation even prior to experience. If so, however, this is only because the kind of conjunction in question has been so familiar from such an early age, and the association between the two kinds (sometimes aided by the relation of resemblance between the cause and effect themselves) so firmly established, that separating them has come to seem absurd.

Having answered this deeper question to his satisfaction, Hume then poses the deepest question of all, one that, he thinks, no one has ever thought to ask before: "What is the foundation of all conclusions from *experience*?" In the second part of Section 4, he limits himself to giving a "negative" answer, explaining in the famous argument what the foundation is not: it is "not reasoning or any process of the understanding." In the immediately following section (EHU 5, "Sceptical Solution of these Doubts") he goes on to give the "positive" answer—a causal explanation—to this same question.

Although Hume's way of introducing the argument about induction differs somewhat in the two works, the overall structure and strategy of the argument itself is fundamentally the same. First, by appealing to his description of the way in which all (non-hypothetical or belief-producing) probable reasoning requires prior experience of constant conjunctions between two kinds of events plus a current initiating impression or memory [3.4], he argues that all such inferences require a certain crucial operation, which may be thought of as the making of a particular kind of step or the completion of a particular kind of gap-bridging transition. This step or transition is that from the state of having (i) past experience of a constant conjunction, plus (ii) a present initiating impression or memory of something of one of the kinds involved in the constant conjunction, to the state of having (iii) a belief in the existence of something of the other kind. He variously describes this step or transition as "supposing the uniformity of nature" (or, where the inference is specifically to something future, "supposing the conformity of the future to the past"); "making the presumption of a resemblance betwixt those objects of which we have had experience, and those of which we have had none," and "being engaged to put trust in past experience." The step might well be called *inductive extrapolation*, but it will better express Hume's own thinking to follow him in calling it the "supposition of uniformity." This is because to "suppose" something, in his usage, is to think or act in the way that one would if one actually believed it, yet without necessarily having formulated a lively idea of it. Supposition may occur without a lively idea either because (as in merely hypothetical reasoning) an idea is employed that is not lively or because no idea has been formed at all. Given the nature of the gap to be bridged and the nature of reason as an inferential faculty leading to belief, an operation of the faculty of reason could account for the supposition of uniformity, he holds, only by making an inference to an explicit belief about the uniformity of nature.

As Hume repeatedly emphasizes, all reasoning is either demonstrative or probable [3.4]. The second stage of his strategy is to argue that the supposition of uniformity cannot originate in demonstrative reasoning. This is because all demonstrative reasonings show that the denials of their conclusions involve a contradiction of some kind and so require the inconceivability of that conclusion, whereas the falsity of the uniformity of nature is entirely conceivable; hence the uniformity of nature is not demonstrable.

The third—and cleverest—stage of Hume's strategy is to argue that probable reasoning cannot produce the supposition of uniformity either. This is because, as he has already shown: (i) *all* probable inferences depend on the relation of cause and effect; and (ii) all inferences from cause and effect require past experience of constant conjunction *plus* the supposition of the uniformity of nature. That is, because all probable inferences depend on the supposition of uniformity, no such reasoning can be the original source of the supposition; probable reasoning cannot be what leads us to "put trust in past experience" because probable reasoning can operate at all only if we are *already* putting trust in past experience. To apply the point in more contemporary terms, we cannot *come to be* inductivists—that is, thinkers who extrapolate on the supposition that nature will continue to be uniform—as the consequence of accepting an inductive argument from the premise that nature has been uniform so far, for the simple reason that anyone who was moved by such an argument would *already be* an inductivist.

Because the supposition of uniformity is produced or achieved neither by demonstrative, nor by probable reasoning, Hume concludes that it is not produced by reason at all. Furthermore, he argues, no escape from this dilemma is to be found in postulating that the mind instead accepts an argument appealing to "secret powers." In saying this, Hume is no doubt thinking in part of Locke's account of the origin of the idea of "power," according to which we: (i) observe certain effects being actively produced by certain causes; (ii) infer that the things producing those effects have a standing "power" to produce them; and then (iii) conclude that those things will continue to produce the same effects in the future (ECHU 2.20.1). As Hume astutely notes, whatever powers we may judge to be in things at present, and on whatever basis, it is a further question to be answered why we suppose that those things must *retain* those powers in cases we have not observed. In fact, of course, this is just an instance of the more general original question of what induces us to suppose that nature is uniform, and that supposition has not yet been explained.

Hume thus concludes that probable inferences are not "determin'd by reason" or—in the *Enquiry*, where he notes that we also cannot intuit the uniformity of nature directly—are not "founded on reasoning, or any process of the understanding"[3.3]. But while we do not come to suppose uniformity as the result of reasoning or intuition, we nonetheless do suppose uniformity. Although the essential gap-bridging transition cannot be accomplished by the production through reasoning of a belief about the uniformity of nature, he argues in both works, it can be accomplished through the operation of "custom or habit"; in the *Enquiry*, this constitutes the "positive" answer to the final question of the "foundation" of inferences from experience. He defines "custom or habit" as the process by which "the repetition of any particular act or operation produces a propensity to renew the same act or operation, without being impelled by any reasoning or process of the understanding" (EHU 5.5/43). It is the same mental process by which, for example, adults come to repeat voluntary grooming rituals each morning without any new reasoning about whether to do so. In the present instance, however, habit operates not on volition and bodily motion, but on a new initiating perception to produce an associated idea, and the liveliness of the initiating impression or memory provides the liveliness required to make that idea a belief. This application of habit or custom to ideas, as well as the transmission of liveliness to ideas, is itself an operation of the unreasoning imagination.

It should be emphasized that the question Hume seeks to answer by means of his famous argument is not whether probable or inductive reasoning is itself a kind of reasoning—that is, whether it is itself an exercise of the faculty of reason—for this is presupposed: he consistently characterizes the probable inferences under discussion as reasoning in the course of his argument, and throughout his writings he consistently characterizes demonstration and probable reasoning as the two applications or exercises of the faculty of reason. Rather, his question is whether the supposition of uniformity—the inductive extrapolation—is *itself* the result of some *mediating* piece of reasoning. He is asking, that is, whether in addition to *being* reasoning, each instance of probable reasoning is also *caused by* (what would of course have to be) another piece of reasoning, one that would perform the gap-bridging transition by giving the mind a belief in (that is, a lively idea of) the uniformity of nature. As he writes explicitly in the *Treatise*, if reason were responsible for this operation, it would "proceed upon that principle, *that instances, of which we have had no experience, must resemble those, of which we have had experience, and that the course of nature continues always uniformly the same*" (THN 1.3.6.4/88–89) by making an inference to that principle. In effect, the crucial sub-operation of probable reason is performed not by a mediating application of reason but by the intervention of the unreasoning imagination.

Hume's question concerns the origin, in reason or in the unreasoning imagination, of a supposition that is undeniably crucial in some form to the operation of reason itself. It is therefore directly analogous to one he asks later in the *Treatise* (THN 1.4.2.3–14/188–93) about the origins of a supposition that is undeniably crucial to the operations of the senses, understood as the faculty whereby sensation provides information about the existence of bodies. This latter supposition is that the objects of our sense perception have a "continu'd and distinct existence," and the question he poses about it is whether it results from the senses themselves, from reason, or from the unreasoning imagination [3.4]. In this case, too, the question is whether a particular step in the operation of a faculty is itself mediated by an operation of that very faculty or by an operation of some other faculty. His final answer in the case of the senses is that the supposition in question is due not to the senses themselves, nor to reason, but rather to the unreasoning imagination— just as he holds in the case of probable reasoning that the step in question is not itself due to reason but rather to the unreasoning imagination.

Thus, Hume's argument is directed not at establishing a negative normative claim about epistemic value but rather at establishing a causal claim about the operation of probable reasoning. This interpretation of the argument is dictated by the structure of his argument, by his statement of the conclusion, and by his subsequent treatment of that conclusion. This is particularly clear in the *Treatise*, where he uses explicitly causal terms to describe the inability of probable reasoning to accomplish the supposition of uniformity:

> According to this account of things, which is, I think, in every point unquestionable, probability is founded on the presumption of a resemblance betwixt those objects, of which we have had experience, and those of which we have had none; and, therefore, 'tis impossible this presumption can *arise from* probability. The same principle cannot be both the *cause and effect* of another; and this is, perhaps, the only proposition concerning that relation, which is either intuitively or demonstratively certain.
> 
> (THN 1.3.6.7/89; emphasis added)

Similarly, the language of his conclusion in the *Treatise* is clearly causal; 'determines' is a causal term for Hume, and he uses 'reason' consistently as his term for the faculty of making inferences [3.3]. Furthermore, he treats the conclusion as a causal thesis: it occurs as one essential part of a discussion of the elements of probable inference, and he does not even so much as mention its possible connection to skepticism until the final section of Book 1. Indeed, his first mention of skepticism comes seven sections after the argument about induction, in a context unrelated to that argument.

When Hume does finally reflect on his argument about probable reasoning in the context of a set of skeptical considerations (THN 1.4.7.3/265; [7.2]), he places as much weight on the dependence of probable reasoning on the liveliness of ideas—that is, on the section of the *Treatise* that *follows* the famous argument about induction—as on his inability to "give a reason" why he should assent to his probable reasonings. To be sure, his famous argument clearly implies that one cannot offer a non-*question-begging* argument—that is, one that does not presuppose its conclusion—for the proposition that inductive inferences will continue to yield truths, and there is no question that he regards this fact as having significant bearing on the question of which beliefs, if any, one should accept. But his procedure in the *Treatise* is to collect the results of his investigations of reason, as conducted by his faculty of reason, before bringing those results together for a final evaluation of reason to determine which if any of its operations should receive his ultimate endorsement. The conclusion about the causes of inductive reasoning is one result of those investigations.

The first *Enquiry*, in contrast, does not make such a concerted effort to separate consideration of the causal conclusion from the consideration of its potential skeptical bearing. For example, when Hume rejects the alternative that the supposition of uniformity is the result of probable reasoning, he describes this alternative as requiring "reasoning in a circle" rather than as requiring a principle to be "both cause and effect of itself." The conclusion of the argument itself is phrased, with greater scope for ambiguity between the causal and the normative, in terms of probable inference not being "founded on" reasoning, rather than not being "determin'd by" reason. The title of the section containing the main argument is entitled "Sceptical Doubts concerning the Operations of the Understanding," and the very next section, "Sceptical Solution of these Doubts" begins with a brief discussion of skepticism that is prompted by the argument.

Nevertheless, the structure of Hume's argument itself remains largely unchanged from the *Treatise* to the first *Enquiry*, offering the same dilemma about the production of an essential "step taken by the mind" in the course of probable (in the *Enquiry* often called "moral") reasoning. As David Owen has astutely observed, Hume explicitly offers custom and habit as the positive answer to the very same question to which "not reasoning, or any process of the understanding" is the negative answer—and custom or habit cannot be the answer to any normative question about whether probable inference has epistemic value, even if that answer turns out to have normative implications.[1] A survey of Hume's texts shows that 'founded on', the key term of his conclusion in the *Enquiry*, is for him a widely applicable metaphor that is very often causal rather than normative in its application; indeed, it clearly occurs in a causal sense within the argument of the *Treatise* version (THN 1.3.6.4–7/88–90). Most tellingly of all, perhaps, Hume asserts in the final paragraph of Section 4 that any opponent who claims that a piece of very difficult reasoning is required to establish the uniformity of nature has "conceded my point," since the opponent must admit that children and peasants cannot be influenced by any such argument. If that admission is to concede Hume's point, then his point can only be one about how the mind actually performs basic probable inferences—namely, without intermediate reasoning—and not about whether a normative justification for them exists.

Although Hume in the first *Enquiry* is not concerned to defer to the concluding section of the work all mention of the doubt-inducing capacity of his argument, that capacity is not his primary topic in Section 4. The "sceptical doubts" of the section title are in the first instance doubts about *how* the process of probable inference works, and they are skeptical only because what we learn about how it does *not* work produces epistemic discomfort in a way readily felt but not yet explored. As its own title indicates, the immediately following section "solves" the doubts about the process by showing that the mechanism involved is custom or habit. Indeed, the beginning of that section provides a particularly good summary of the causal conclusion of the famous argument, after which it goes on to downplay the likely skeptical bearing:

> Though we should conclude, for instance, as in the foregoing section, that, in all reasonings from experience, there is a step taken by the mind, which is not supported by any argument or process of the understanding; there is no danger, that these reasonings, on which almost all knowledge depends, will ever be affected by such a discovery. If the mind be not engaged by argument to make this step, it must be induced by some other principle of equal weight and authority; and that principle will preserve its influence as long as human nature remains the same. What that principle is, may well be worth the pains of enquiry.
> (EHU 5.2/41–42)

It is only in the final section of the first Enquiry that Hume returns to weigh the skeptical considerations involved in his conclusion. Even there, however, his main induction-related reason for doubt is as much that probable reasoning has been shown to depend on an instinct—worrisome because "other instincts" may be "fallacious and deceitful" (EHU 12.22/159), suggesting an inductive argument that probable reasoning may be deceitful as well—as it is the absence of "an argument to convince us" of the uniformity of nature if we have not already supposed it [7.2].

## 6.2 The explanation and evaluation of probable reasoning

These facts notwithstanding, the conclusion of Hume's famous argument is often interpreted as being highly negative in an epistemically normative way: for example, as the conclusion that inductive reasonings convey no epistemic justification or merit to their conclusions, or do not provide evidence that renders their conclusions more probable.[2] As noted in the previous chapter [5.4], it is often tacitly supposed that his claims about the causal origin of inductive inferences combine with some *a priori* normative epistemic principles to show that inductive conclusions lack epistemic value.

This way of interpreting the conclusion may seem natural if one treats the faculty-term 'reason' as an honorific that itself constitutes an epistemic evaluation, but he states no substantive *a priori* normative epistemic principles in the course of his argument.

To be sure, because it is a crucial element in the sense of probability, the faculty of reason naturally carries a certain *prima facie* authority in the project of investigating human faculties by means of those very faculties. Nevertheless, the term 'reason' for Hume simply designates the inferential faculty [3.3], and his argument concerns not the correctness of an epistemic evaluation, but the operations by which probable reasoning actually occurs. A radically negative epistemically normative interpretation of the conclusion is hard to square either with the fact that Hume begins the *Treatise* by praising the very "experimental method" that emphasizes reliance on induction or with the fact that he continues to conduct his investigation in accordance with that method through to its very end. Indeed, Hume takes pains to criticize some deviant examples of probable reasoning—for example, those that give rise to the belief in miracles [9.6]—while praising others. This would be a curious procedure if he thought that all probable reasoning was equally worthless from an epistemic standpoint.

Partly to avoid this absurdity, it has sometimes been proposed that Hume's famous conclusion rejects only the view that inductive inferences are demonstrative.[3] But this proposal does not square with Hume's consistent use of the term 'reason' as encompassing both demonstrative and probable reasoning, and it cannot explain the presence of the second stage of his argumentative strategy—namely, the argument that probable reasoning cannot be the cause of the supposition of uniformity.

One objection to this causal interpretation of Hume's conclusion, first raised by Peter Millican, is that his actual argument could show at most that the supposition of uniformity is not produced by good or non-fallacious reasoning, not that it is not produced by any reasoning at all.[4] For couldn't the supposition result from the acceptance of a question-begging argument, or a bad demonstration—perhaps even from the unsatisfactory reasoning about continuing secret powers that Hume criticizes? This suggestion appears to be strengthened by the fact that Hume introduces his demonstrative/

probable dilemma in the *Treatise* version of the argument by offering to "cast our eye on each of these degrees of evidence, and see whether they afford any just conclusion of this nature [concerning the uniformity of nature]" and later declares that the examined reasoning about "powers" has "no just foundation." Although the term 'just' in eighteenth-century usage can mean simply "genuine" or "properly so-called," it naturally suggests a restriction of a normative kind that is not simply semantic.

The proper response to this objection differs for the two kinds of reasoning at issue. Hume holds that there are many normatively disapproved—what he calls "unphilosophical" [3.4]—influences on probable reasoning (THN 1.3.13). These include, among many others, undue credulity about testimony and the influence of surprise and wonder, which often come together to facilitate belief in miracles on skimpy observational evidence. Crucially, however, even probable reasoning that is bad or disapproved because it has been influenced by these factors already requires, precisely because it is a species of probable reasoning, that a supposition of uniformity already have been made. Hence, it too falls squarely within the scope of Hume's objection that no kind of probable reasoning can be the initial cause of that supposition. Similarly, it will not do to suggest, against the causal interpretation, that we might all initially make the supposition of uniformity as the result of mistakenly accepting a question-begging argument in favor of it. For by definition, a question-begging argument for that conclusion would be convincing only if we had *already made* that very supposition—something that could not then be explained by the question-begging argument under consideration.

In contrast, Hume is committed by his characterization of demonstrative reasoning [3.4] to the view that there is, strictly speaking, no such thing as bad or epistemically disapproved demonstration: there are only stretches of thinking that may seem like demonstrations but, in fact, are not. These stretches will typically consist of some steps of demonstration interrupted by a substitution of one idea for another or a misremembering of what has been established. It is quite true that neither Hume's famous argument, nor its conclusion, has ruled out the rather unlikely hypothesis that the initial cause of the supposition of uniformity is a universally shared failure of attempted demonstrative reasoning, involving confusion or misremembering. But nor has he positively ruled out every other possible explanation of the supposition before he goes on to endorse, on the basis of empirical investigation, his positive doctrine that the explanation in fact involves custom or habit.

A second possible objection to the causal interpretation is that it offers no plausible opponent for Hume: for who would have held that probable reasoning *is* mediated by an additional inference? One sufficient reply to this objection is that Hume regards the very question to which his argument provides the answer as quite new; equally, there need be no obvious opponent for his analogous argument that the operation of *the senses* requires a step that is not itself the result of reason or the senses. Nevertheless, in the case of the senses Locke might be thought to offer something of a target, and the same is true in the case of probable reasoning.

For Locke, demonstration is a series of intuitions that allows the mind to perceive mediately an agreement or disagreement of ideas that it could not perceive immediately (ECHU 4.17, "Of Reason"; [3.4]). For example, one perceives the relation between idea A and idea D by perceiving the relation of idea A to idea B, of idea B to idea C, and idea C to idea D. One consequence of this is that, for Locke, all demonstrations except those of minimum length—that is, those involving only three ideas (one of them intermediate to the other two) and only two intuitions—are mediated by sub-demonstrations. For example, one demonstrates the relation between A and D by perceiving the relation between A and B and the relation between B and D. But one perceives the relation between B and D by means of a demonstration involving an intuition of the relation between B and C and an intuition of the relation between C and D. Furthermore, Locke holds that probable reasoning works in much the same way as demonstrative reasoning, each depending on intermediate ideas that serve as (what he calls) "proofs"; the only essential difference at the most general level of description is that the intuitions providing knowledge of the relation between ideas in demonstrations are replaced by perceptions of the "probable" or "for the most part" agreement or disagreement of ideas in probable reasonings.

## 6.3 Necessary connection and definitions of 'cause'

The capacity to make probable inferences is one element of the Humean causal sense [4.3]; the second element is the capacity to feel the impression of necessary connection. It is the search for this impression—prompted by the thought that causation involves such a connection in addition to relations of priority and contiguity—that engenders the *Treatise* survey of the two "neighboring fields" that in turn revealed the underlying mechanism of probable inference [3.4]. This mechanism depends on permanent changes produced in the background structure of the mind by experience of constant conjunctions [3.1].

In both the *Treatise* and the first *Enquiry*, Hume also undertakes to determine how constant conjunction relates to the idea of necessary connection, which the *Treatise* identifies as one aspect of the causal relation (THN 1.3.14 and EHU 7, both entitled "Of the idea of necessary connexion"). A single exposure to an object or event of one kind being followed by one of another kind never produces by itself any impression of power or necessary connection, he argues, regardless of whether the objects or events are both mental, both physical, or one of each. By the Copy Principle, however, there cannot be a simple idea of necessary connection without a corresponding impression, and he seems to assume that the idea of necessary connection is simple. The impression of necessary connection must arise, therefore, only after experience of the constant conjunction, when an initiating impression or memory of one kind is followed by a lively idea of the other kind. Yet the mere repetition of the perception of objects or events of two kinds cannot itself constitute any new simple impression. Hence, the impression of necessary connection, from which the idea of necessary connection is copied, must be an impression of reflection: specifically, a feeling of "the determination of the mind" to make the inferential transition from impression or memory to belief that constitutes the heart of causal inference.

This impression of necessary connection is, of course, just a particular kind of feeling; it is not the revelation of a metaphysically inseparable relation between two objects or events [2.2]. In the conceivable and hence metaphysically possible psychology of beings different from humans, the very same feeling might have had quite other causes and effects. Why, then, should it deserve to be called the impression "of" necessary connection? In order to answer this question, it is necessary to understand Hume's more general view of necessity.

Hume clearly recognizes two distinct species of necessity. The first is grounded in relations of ideas, which allows knowledge (in his strict sense), intuition, and demonstration; the second is causal necessity. It is therefore initially puzzling that he can assimilate them to one another by writing:

> As the necessity, which makes two times two equal to four, or three angles of a triangle equal to two right ones, lies only in the act of the understanding, by which we consider and compare these ideas; in like manner the necessity or power, which unites causes and effects, lies in the determination of the mind to pass from the one to the other.
> (THN 1.3.14.23/166)

He can do so, however, because he closely relates the necessity of a state of affairs to the inconceivability of any alternative or the inability to think otherwise. In the case of what we may call metaphysical or demonstrative necessity, this inconceivability is grounded in the intrinsic qualities of ideas themselves that (at least when they are "adequate" representations [2.5]) represent intrinsic features of their objects. For example, it is a feature of any adequate idea of a right triangle that the idea of its hypotenuse will be longer than the idea of any other side. Similarly, when adding the numbers two and three by utilizing concepts of those numbers, the mind seeks to take members of the revival set of the abstract idea TWO (that is, ideas of pairs) and conjoin all of their elements with all of the elements from the revival set of the abstract idea THREE (that is, ideas of triples). The mind thereby produces ideas which all fall within the revival set of the abstract idea FIVE; and this result, too, is dictated by the very nature of the ideas employed. That blue is more like green than it is like scarlet—to take Hume's example of a non-mathematical relation of ideas (THN 1.1.7.7n/637)—is again dictated by the nature of the ideas employed. In order to represent clearly a failure of this generalization, one would have to find an idea within the revival set of BLUE that resembled some idea within the revival set of SCARLET more than it resembled some idea within the revival set of GREEN—but there is no such idea to be found.

Causal necessity, too, involves a kind of inability to think otherwise for Hume, but it is an inability with a different source. This inability is grounded not in the intrinsic characters of the ideas themselves, but rather in the psychological change produced by experience of a constant conjunction. The Separability Principle guarantees that the idea of a cause and the idea of its effect are always metaphysically separable; nevertheless, the separation becomes very difficult, even with voluntary effort, as a result of the customary association. Furthermore, a lively conception of—that is, belief in—the separation of effect from cause becomes psychologically impossible, even with the greatest voluntary effort. It is for this reason that Hume is willing to call this a species of "necessity" as well: like metaphysical necessity, it involves an unthinkability of alternatives that lies in one or another "act of the understanding" governing the consideration or comparison of ideas. A particular sensation can appropriately be called "the sensation of hunger," even if 'hunger' is understood not as the proper name for the sensation itself, but rather as a term for the emptiness of stomach that the sensation reliably indicates. This is an instance of the systematic ambiguity of terms for sense-based concepts noted earlier [4.2]. In a similar way, because causal necessity is one of two species of necessity, it is appropriate to call the impression of reflection that serves as a reliable indicator of the relevant unthinkability an impression "of" necessary connection. Indeed, because CAUSATION is itself a sense-based concept for Hume [4.3], he uses 'necessary connexion' and 'power' in a systematically ambiguous way as well, both as terms for an impression of necessary connection and for the circumstance in the world that produces this impression.

Unfortunately, however, according to Hume, the human mind tends to conflate the two distinct species of necessity. This is partly due, no doubt, to their general similarity as kinds of unthinkability resistant to volition, but the tendency is greatly exacerbated as a consequence of a common mental tendency to unite as many related ideas as closely as possible into the representation of an object. This tendency explains why sensations of tastes, smells, and sounds—which are not themselves spatial in his view [2.5]—are nevertheless treated by the mind as occupying the same "place" as the color and tactile qualities of bodies; and it is this same tendency that he invokes to explain why the mind tends to "spread" the impression of necessary connection onto cause-and-effect pairs, taking it to be a directly perceived feature of those pairs themselves, rather than recognizing it for the impression of reflection that it in fact is (THN 1.3.14.25/167; THN 1.4.5.12–13/237–38). (The distinction between impressions of sensation and impressions of reflection is, as Hume defines it, only a distinction of causal origin and hence is not available to immediate introspection [2.1].) Because the impression of necessary connection now appears to be intrinsic to the objects represented, the mind ignores the fact that the necessity of causes is only a psychological inseparability grounded in custom resulting from constant conjunction and instead conflates it with demonstrative necessity:

> 'Tis natural for men, in their common and careless way of thinking, to imagine they perceive a connexion betwixt such objects as they have constantly found united together; and because custom has render'd it difficult to separate the ideas, they are apt to fancy such a separation to be *in itself* impossible and absurd.
> (THN 1.4.3.9/223; emphasis added)

This diagnosable conflation is, he holds, the source of considerable philosophical confusion.

Having discovered the source of the idea of necessary connection, Hume finally proceeds, in both the *Treatise* and the first *Enquiry*, to provide two definitions of 'cause', one productive and one responsive. The *Treatise* version of the productive definition has already been quoted [4.3]; the *Enquiry* version reads:

> [1] [W]e may define a cause to be *an object followed by another, and where all the objects, similar to the first, are followed by objects similar to the second. Or in other words, where, if the first object had not been, the second never had existed.*
> (EHU 7.29/76)

The first sentence of this definition differs from the *Treatise* definition chiefly in the omission of any requirement of spatial or temporal contiguity. This is due partly, one may assume, to his admission (already highlighted by a forward-looking footnote appended to the *Treatise* version) that many qualities and perceptions, including passions, have no spatial positions at all, but are instead "no where." Another factor may be a desire to accommodate the possibility that gravitational attraction is (despite Newton's own resistance to the suggestion) a kind of action at a distance. The omission of temporal contiguity may reflect his omission from the *Enquiry* of his treatment of time as composed of simple parts, an account that allowed perfect temporal contiguity to be well defined.

Such changes in the definition of 'cause' would of course be disconcerting if the definition were intended to provide a semantic analysis of the concept CAUSATION and hence a formula strictly synonymous with the term 'cause'. Because CAUSATION is semantically simple for Hume [4.3], however, neither complex definition can be meant to be synonymous with the term 'cause'. Instead, his definitions are meant only to provide alternative ways to indicate in a general way the membership of the revival set of CAUSATION; the requirements of priority and contiguity, like the requirement of constant conjunction itself, are among the "rules by which to judge of causes and effects" that he regards as derived from experience with actual causal judgments.

The *Enquiry* version of the productive definition differs from the *Treatise* version also by the addition of a second sentence. On its subject-relative reading, this sentence may be understood as referring only to what has not occurred in the observed past. On its absolute reading, however, the sentence seems to express a *counterfactual conditional* stating what *would not* have occurred in the absence of the first object; in this respect, it seems *not* merely to present "in other words" the original definition, which contained no counterfactual. It is therefore sometimes suggested that the sentence is meant instead to signal or declare that causal counterfactuals are properly assertable on the basis of causation as defined in the first sentence.

While this suggestion may well be correct, it only highlights a further problem for both readings of the definition. For while the original definition states that the same cause must be followed by the same effect, the supplementary sentence seems instead to require the converse: that the same effect always be produced by the same cause. This converse principle is far from obvious: it seems, for example, that a collision of billiard balls or an outburst of anger might be caused by any number of different circumstances. In fact, however, Hume commits himself fully to parallel principles in both directions: that "the same cause always produces the same effect, and the same effect never arises but from the same causes" is the fourth of his rules by which to judge of causes and effects (THN 1.3.15.6/173) [4.3]. By endorsing the converse principle, he commits himself, as he notes in his fifth rule, to finding a common causal circumstance in what appear superficially to be pairs of cases in which the same outcome has been produced by different causes; but his acceptance of the principle also has the advantage of allowing him to treat causal inference from effect to cause as fully parallel to causal inference from cause to effect. That he intends his second sentence to endorse the converse principle—in addition, perhaps, to authorizing causal counterfactuals—is suggested by the fact that the *Treatise* version of his responsive definition incorporates a similar bi-directionality. His use of 'in other words', however, still seems a mistake.

The responsive definition of 'cause' in the first *Enquiry* reads:

[2] ... *an object followed by another, and whose appearance always conveys the thought to that other.*

(EHU 7.29/77)

This simplifies the *Treatise* version by compressing what had been separate references to association and inference into a single reference to the "appearance" of the cause conveying "the thought" to the effect, thereby neglecting to mention explicitly the belief involved in the idea—and also neglecting to mention the equal capacity for inference and association from effect to cause.

In neither version do Hume's two definitions of 'cause' explicitly mention necessary connection. Nevertheless, the capacity to feel the impression of necessary connection constitutes an important part of the causal sense for Hume, and he declares it an advantage of his definitions over potential competitors that they each "comprehend the necessary connexion" of a cause with its effect (EHU 8.25/95–96) by detailing the circumstances in which it occurs. Immediately after giving his two definitions in the *Treatise*, Hume provides four "corollaries" to them (THN 1.3.14.32-36/171-72), one of which explicitly concerns necessity, and each of which constitutes a rejection of one or more common philosophical opinions about causation.

The first corollary is that "all causes are of the same kind." Specifically, all causes are what philosophers since Aristotle have called *efficient causes*—that through whose efficacy the effect occurs or is made actual. Hume rejects in principle the distinction between efficient causes and necessary background causes ("causes *sine qua non*"—literally, that without which the efficient cause cannot operate); because we discern causation only by constant conjunction, whatever is part of the total condition that must be constantly conjoined with an effect is as "efficient" as any other part of that total condition. Similarly, he rejects the Aristotelian fourfold distinction of *efficient* causes, *formal* causes (providing the form), *material* causes (providing the matter), and *final* causes (the end for which, or for the sake of which, a thing occurs). If there is constant conjunction of the sort leading to inference and association, Hume asserts, then there is (efficient) causation; if there is not, then there is no kind of cause at all. Further, he disallows the distinction drawn by Malebranche and other Cartesians between causes and *occasions*—meaning by 'occasion' a condition under which God exerts divine power to produce some effect. Since such conditions are, by hypothesis, constantly conjoined with the specified outcome, they must qualify as full-fledged causes.

The second corollary is that "there is but one kind of [causal] necessity." In particular, Hume rejects as "without any foundation in nature" the then-common distinction between *moral* and *physical* necessity. Whereas physical necessity was understood to be the absolute causal necessitation governing the interactions of bodies, moral necessity was understood to be a weaker, merely "inclining," influence or causation applying to intentional human action through the influence of reasons. Given the two definitions, however, if there is enough constant conjunction to determine the mind to association and inference, then there is causal necessity *simpliciter*;

if not, there is mere chance and so no kind of necessity at all. He adds that "the distinction between *power* and the *exercise* of it is equally without foundation." In practice, as it happens, he continues to make such a distinction himself, often referring to something as having the standing power to produce an effect (for example, of money as having a power to procure possession of goods [THN 2.2.5]) even when the circumstances for its exercise are not currently satisfied. Indeed, as we have seen repeatedly, he sometimes formulates his own science of man as an investigation into standing powers of the mind that are not always exercised. His point, however, is that such a distinction is merely pragmatic and does not have as deep a metaphysical basis as many have supposed: in the absence of *all* of the elements of a total cause that is constantly conjoined with its effect, the other parts are not able to bring about the effect at all, and a metaphysical "power" to do so is no more discernibly lodged in one element than in another.

The third corollary is that "we may now be able to fully overcome all that repugnance, which 'tis so natural for us to entertain" against Hume's own earlier argument that the "necessity of a cause to every beginning of existence" is not founded on either demonstration or intuition [6.1]. For the sense that such a claim should be either demonstrative or intuitive results from the now-diagnosed conflation of metaphysical necessity with causal necessity. Once we recognize that causes are discerned only by constant conjunction, however—with its associative and inferential effects on the mind—we can see that there is no metaphysical necessity that every distinct thing that comes into existence must be the second element of such a pair. It should be emphasized—as Hume himself does in *A Letter from a Gentleman*—that he is not denying the certainty or the necessity of the generalization that every beginning of existence does have a cause [1.3]; he requires only that this certainty and necessity be causal and derived from experience, rather than metaphysical and derived from relations of ideas alone.

Hume's fourth and final corollary is that "we can never have reason to believe that any object exists of which we cannot form an idea." This is because all of our beliefs about the existence of unperceived objects result from causal (and hence, probable) inferences, and causal inferences require experience of constant conjunctions, which will thereby provide some idea of both the cause and the effect. Of course, Hume's view that belief is a lively idea also entails that, with or without reasons, we cannot believe in the existence of objects of which we cannot form any idea at all, and cannot believe clearly in the existence of objects of which we cannot form a clear idea. This corollary is important, he notes, because it will block objections against his later reasonings concerning matter and "substance" as a hypothesized substratum in which qualities or perceptions inhere. As he quickly notes, however, it is not required that one have a "full knowledge of the object, but only of those qualities of it, which we believe to exist." Presumably, such ideas may often be relative ideas [2.3]. In the limiting case in which experience has led us to infer that every event has some cause or other, we may even believe in the existence of a cause of an unfamiliar event simply via a relative idea such as that expressed by 'the cause of that event'. As noted previously, Hume explicitly holds that we can, if we choose, conceive of bodies in such a purely relative way, as the cause of our impressions of sensation [2.3, 3.5].

## 6.4 Liberty and necessity

Hume draws these corollaries explicitly only in the *Treatise*, not in the first *Enquiry*. In both books, however, one of the most important consequences of his definitions of 'cause' is to be found in his treatment of the question of freedom of the will or, as he calls it, the question of "liberty and necessity." Hume believes that his account of causation makes it possible to resolve this central philosophical issue fully for the first time.

Although neither Hume's position nor his fundamental arguments change between the *Treatise* and the *Enquiry*, both their placement and their strategic expression do. In the *Treatise*, his discussion of liberty and necessity is deferred until Part 3 ("Of the will and direct passions") of Book 2 ("Of the Passions"); in the first *Enquiry*, it takes pride of place in the section (EHU 8) immediately following "Of the Idea of Necessary Connection." In the *Treatise*, he argues directly in favor of the "doctrine of necessity," according to which human volitions (that, is exercises of the will [3.7]) occur by causal necessity, and against the "fantastical doctrine of liberty," by which he means the doctrine that human volitions are not subject to causal necessity. In the Enquiry, in contrast, the discussion becomes a "reconciling project" to show that everyone has always accepted—in fact, if not in words—both the "doctrine of necessity" and the "doctrine of liberty." The latter doctrine is now understood, however, not as a denial of causal necessity, but as the doctrine that human beings typically have a *"power of acting or not acting, according to the determinations of the will"* (EHU 8.23/95), and hence are not typically subject to the external coercion that would render volition causally irrelevant.

In each work, we may distinguish five stages of the discussion. In the first stage, Hume cites his two definitions of 'cause' as showing what is required to establish the doctrine of necessity. To do so fully, one must show that human actions are constantly conjoined with antecedent conditions, thereby satisfying the productive definition; and one must show that human actions are the subject of inference and association, thereby satisfying the responsive definition. Given that each definition correctly specifies the class of objects or events related as cause and effect, the possibility of accomplishing either task should, Hume notes, guarantee the possibility of accomplishing the other, although they may be considered separately for the sake of thoroughness. The pairs of objects or events that satisfy the definitions will, he concludes, be causally necessary in the only intelligible sense of that term.

In the second stage, Hume offers arguments concerning human volitions to establish the intended status of the doctrine of necessity. In the Treatise, therefore, he offers evidence directly for its truth; in the Enquiry he cites the obviousness to all observers of that same body of evidence in order to conclude that everyone has always accepted the doctrine. Because he treats the evidence as entirely convincing, however, his commitment to the doctrine's truth remains. In applying the productive definition, he cites examples of constant conjunctions of motives and circumstances with human actions. When different people behave differently in the same external circumstances, he argues, this can be traced to differences in their beliefs, passions, and character, and we can go on to formulate causal generalizations about how such influences will produce different actions among different groups of people. Although not every human action is readily predicted in advance, neither are events in the inanimate physical world that philosophers nevertheless regard as fully causally determined. In applying the responsive definition, he cites the ubiquity of inferences about human actions, noting that history, economics, and human society itself would be impossible were we not able to predict human actions on the basis our knowledge of motives, characters, and circumstances.

In assessing these arguments, it is essential to distinguish among three different doctrines, all of which Hume accepts. Universal Determinism [3.1], captured in the fourth of his rules by which to judge of causes and effects [4.3], is the doctrine that every event is causally determined to occur in just the way it does by prior circumstances in accordance with uniform and exceptionless laws of nature. Philosophers, he holds, reason inductively to this conclusion from their experience that, upon close enough investigation, like circumstances seem always to produce like outcomes, so that outcomes differ only when there is some relevant difference in the preceding circumstances. In accepting this inductive conclusion, he thinks, philosophers quite properly avail themselves of an inductive argument for a very stringent and explicitly formulated version of the uniformity of nature—even though this argument is convincing only because they, like all human beings, have already "supposed" the general uniformity of nature via the ongoing operation of custom or habit [6.1]. While Hume thinks that Universal Determinism is "universally allowed" in philosophy, however—at least as regards material things—he holds that "the vulgar" do not subscribe to so stringent a view. For although a watchmaker recognizes that a watch has stopped running because of a small particle of dust in the works, the vulgar say simply that a cause "sometimes fails of its usual effect" (THN 1.3.12.5/132; EHU 6.4/57–58; EHU 8.14/86–87).

A second doctrine is the Causal Maxim: that every beginning of existence has some cause [6.1]. If it is granted that every event is the coming into existence of some thing or quality that was not present before, then the maxim requires that every event have a cause. It is nonetheless weaker than Universal Determinism, since it allows causes that do not always produce their usual effects, so long as whatever is actually produced has some assignable cause.

As previously noted, Hume argues that the Causal Maxim is neither demonstrable nor intuitive, but he does think that it has been shown by experience to be true, or at least probably true. The Causal Maxim, too, is universally allowed by philosophers, he suggests, and it seems that the vulgar may accept it as well.

What Hume calls "the doctrine of necessity" is the principle that all voluntary human actions exemplify causal necessity. In one respect, therefore, it is weaker even than the Causal Maxim, for it does not require that every event outside the domain of human actions have a cause. In another respect, it is seemingly stronger, for it explicitly requires not only that human actions be produced by causes but also that they be causally *necessitated* by them. The second corollary to the two definitions of 'cause' stipulates, however, that there is only one kind of causal necessity and that either: (i) there is enough regularity (even with some exceptions) to generate inference and association in idealized observers and hence to constitute full causal necessity; or (ii) there is not, in which case there is no causation at all, but only chance. Accordingly, all causes necessitate for Hume, even in the absence of Universal Determinism. The Doctrine of Necessity can therefore be a universal opinion—at least in fact, if not in words—even of the vulgar who reject Universal Determinism.

In the third stage of his discussion, Hume offers arguments to establish the intended status of human liberty. The absence of causal necessity requires, by the second corollary, the absence of causes, an absence that he identifies with "chance." He calls this absence the "liberty of indifference." The "liberty of spontaneity," in contrast, is opposed not to causation, but to coercion, and it lies in the liberty to act or not act in accordance with the determination of the will. Although he uses the term 'doctrine of liberty' for the former in the *Treatise* and for the latter in the *Enquiry*, he agrees in both works that we have only the liberty of spontaneity. In the first *Enquiry*, however, the emphasis is on showing that everyone agrees that the liberty of spontaneity is possessed by everyone who is not "a prisoner or in chains."

In the fourth stage, Hume appeals to his explanation of the common errors about causal necessity [6.3] to explain why the Doctrine of Necessity has not earned universal verbal agreement and why there is a corresponding confusion about liberty. Prior to our own voluntary actions, he explains, we are typically deliberating about what to do: considering the options, feeling desires and aversions in relation to them, and eventually willing (that is, having a volition). We are not typically inferring or trying to infer what we will do on the basis of past experience. In our own voluntary actions, therefore, we typically do not feel an impression of necessary connection. When we reason about the behavior of bodies, in contrast, we do feel an impression of necessary connection; and because we typically project this impression of necessary connection onto the objects themselves, seeking to locate it with them, we attribute an intrinsic necessity to them. In consequence, we suppose erroneously that there is a kind of necessity (genuine "physical necessity") pertaining to the interactions of bodies that is absent in the case of human actions (which therefore supposedly have no necessity at all or at most something called merely "moral necessity"). Even though we could in principle find an indication of the error by noticing the impression of necessary connection that we feel when making inferences about the voluntary actions of others (or even our own, when we do make inferences about them), we thus come verbally to deny the Doctrine of Necessity. This error also leads to the mistaken supposition that there is a kind of "liberty of indifference" (because without physical necessity) that is not simply identical with chance (because still regular and predictable). Once we correct the illusion that there is a further kind of causal necessity beyond that actually exhibited in human volition, however, we can reconcile ourselves to the Doctrine of Necessity, Hume holds; and once we recognize that there is only one kind of liberty of indifference—namely, chance—we can reconcile ourselves as well to the doctrine that the liberty of spontaneity, possessed by nearly all persons with respect to many proposed actions, is the only kind of liberty that is desirable.

As this suggests, Hume's main opponents are not philosophers holding that Universal Determinism is incompatible with the kind of liberty we want and need, but rather those of his contemporaries who hold that there are two kinds of regularity and predictability, one that fully necessitates and one that does not. For this reason, he remarks that he is proposing a change not in what people think about human voluntary actions—namely, that such actions are predictable, but that we find no "necessary connection" lying in the cause and effect themselves—but only proposing that the causal behavior of bodies is like that of human actions in this particular respect.

In the final stage of his discussion, Hume argues that both causal necessity (as involving the degree of uniformity required for idealized inference about volitions) and the liberty of spontaneity are compatible with morality and even essential to it. Causal necessity is essential because actions must reflect enduring features of character in order to be relevant to moral evaluation. This, he claims, is why accidental harms are not, upon reflection, properly blamable. Indeed, moral evaluation is primarily of character traits, and only derivatively of the individual actions that manifest them [4.1]. Thus, actions produced by traits that are themselves only intermittently effective—such as a short temper—produce less moral disapprobation and carry less blame, other things being equal. Similarly, sincere repentance removes moral disapprobation and hence blame if the original action is now deemed to be no longer indicative of the person's current character. But voluntary actions occurring by chance would be no reflection of character at all; they would merely be fortunate or unfortunate things that happened, produced by merely random volition. The liberty of spontaneity, too, is essential to morality because, without it, persons' actions cannot be reflections of their character, and so the actions themselves cannot properly be sources of character-directed moral approbation or disapprobation.

## 6.5 The relation of cause and effect

Hume's treatment of liberty and necessity is directly relevant to another of the most discussed questions in the interpretation of Hume's philosophy: what does he think the relation of cause and effect itself actually is? Most often, he has been interpreted as a *causal reductionist*, holding that the relation of cause and effect is nothing other than the relation of constant conjunction involving priority and contiguity described by the productive definition of 'cause'. (For ease of discussion, we will henceforth treat priority and contiguity as implicitly included in "constant conjunction.") Not infrequently, however, he has been interpreted as a *causal realist*, granting that genuine causation requires, in addition to such constant conjunction, a further necessitating relation between causes and effects grounded in or requiring the possession of "secret powers" or "ultimate principles"—even though our ability to grasp or conceive of such powers or principles may be highly limited or even non-existent. More recently, Hume has sometimes been interpreted as a causal *projectivist*, holding that attributions of causal relations essentially involve the projection of something from the mind onto the world that is not strictly to be found there at all. On one version of this interpretation, the attribution of a causal relation entails, for Hume, that the impression of necessary connection or something resembling it be a feature of the cause and effect pair itself; and because he denies that the impression has this status, it then follows that there are no genuine causal relations, so that all attributions of them are strictly false. On another version of causal projectivism, attributions of causal relations are strictly speaking neither true or false, but merely *express* the mind's projection onto the world of something mental: either the impression of necessary connection, or the disposition to make causal inferences, or both. On a third version, attributions of causal relations can sometimes be said to be "true," but only as a way of expressing their accordance with our own normative standards for making causal inferences, and not because of any representational character of the idea of causation or correspondence between it and causal relations that are part of the fundamental structure of the world itself.

In assessing these three broad types of interpretations, it is essential to distinguish four kinds of questions concerning attributions of causal relations: (i) psychological questions, concerning the process by which they come to be made; (ii) epistemological questions, concerning what is required for them to be properly made or known to be correct; (iii) semantic questions, concerning how and what they mean; and (iv) metaphysical questions, concerning the features of reality that they attribute or reflect.

Causal projectivist interpretations of Hume emphasize and are inspired by his account of the psychology of attributions of causality. The process by which the causal sense gives rise to causal judgments [4.3] includes both (i) beliefs determined by custom or habit after experience of constant conjunctions and (ii) impressions of necessary connection. In the development of the concept CAUSATION, the mind is presumably aided in its initial generalization by its erroneous tendency to spread the impression of necessary connection onto the objects themselves—for this makes the cause and effect pairs that must be collected into a single revival set seem all the more saliently similar. Nevertheless, it does not follow that Hume regards the correctness of this projection or mislocation as required for a pair of objects or events to be properly included in the revival set of the concept. On the contrary, he strongly implies that the illusion of this mislocation can at least sometimes be overcome, thereby correcting the details of the mind's representation of causes and effects, without undermining the truth of conceptual causal judgments when pairs or objects or events fall properly within the revival set of the concept in accordance with the standard of judgment for CAUSATION (THN 1.3.14.24/166). It also does not follow that Hume denies a genuine correspondence between conceptual causal judgments [2.6] and how things are genuinely related in the world under such circumstances—any more than he denies that conceptual judgments concerning color and sound can correspond to how things genuinely are in the world, even if colored and noisy objects only produce, and do not resemble, our impressions of color and sound. On the contrary, he calls many causal judgments "true," and he defines 'truth' in terms of correspondence between ideas and what those ideas represent [5.2]. While contemporary philosophers may have a conception of the attribution of "truth" that does not require such correspondence, Hume did not.

Causal realist interpretations are motivated partly by features of the semantics of Hume's treatment of causation—namely, that he regards causal attributions as susceptible of straightforward truth and falsehood, while at the same time not treating causal attributions as strictly synonymous with statements either about constant conjunction or about inference and association. They properly note that he often invokes our "ignorance" of unknown and inconceivable secret causal powers and ultimate causal principles—especially in the first Enquiry—without immediately denying that such powers or principles exist. Because CAUSATION functions as a Humean sense-based concept [4.3], ignorance of some further aspects of the underlying relation

## Induction and causation 203

picked out by it cannot be ruled out as a matter of general principle. Just as blueness need not be the mere relational property of being such-as-to-produce-blue-sensations-in-idealized-respondents-in-idealized-conditions, causation need not be simply the relational property (of pairs of objects or events) of being such-as-to-produce-inference-and-association-in-idealized-observers-in-idealized-conditions [4.5]. And just as a correct productive definition for BLUE may be given (as Hume would suppose) in terms of corpuscular structures, and yet the nature of blueness also involve sub-corpuscular structures underlying them, so too a correct productive definition for CAUSATION may be in terms of constant conjunction, and yet the nature of causation might also involve further unknown features underlying that conjunction.

As it happens, we can see that Hume's cognitive psychology provides not one but two ways in which the existence of such powers or principles can be "supposed," in the sense of that term defined previously [6.1]. The first is simply by making the common conflation between metaphysical necessity and causal necessity that Hume has diagnosed [6.3]. For in making this conflation, the mind treats causal necessity as if the requisite unthinkability of an alternative were grounded not in habit-based inseparability following constant conjunction (as causal necessity is actually grounded), but rather in intrinsic features of the cause and effect themselves. Although the mind does not in this case formulate an explicit belief in—that is, lively idea of—secret powers or ultimate principles, it does nevertheless suppose them—that is, act as if it had a formulated belief in them—much as the mind originally "supposes" the uniformity of nature by being disposed to make inductive inferences without formulating an explicit belief in that uniformity [6.1].

Of course, philosophers do sometimes formulate an explicit belief in the uniformity of nature [6.4], and they may also formulate a kind of explicit belief—complete with some liveliness—in secret powers and ultimate principles. Because they lack a clear idea of such powers or principles, however, such a belief can be formulated at best only by using relative ideas. One such relative idea, presumably, would be expressed by 'an unknown feature pertaining to all and only cause and effect pairs, and sufficiently *resembling* metaphysical and causal necessity to be considered a third kind of necessity'. Another, presumably, would be expressed by 'an unknown kind of idea of cause and effect pairs rendering their separation inconceivable, and sufficiently *resembling* ordinary human ideas of objects and events to be considered a second kind of idea'. In neither case, however, is there a clear idea of the *primary relation*—a third kind of necessity, or a second kind of representation, respectively—that is intended; rather the *relation of resemblance* is recruited in the attempt to provide a *relative idea* of the idea to be employed in a *further* relative idea. The psychological liveliness of either form of relative belief would, of course, derive ultimately from the psychological power of the original conflation that it seeks to preserve; but such thoughts and beliefs are nevertheless possible, even if only barely and unclearly, within Hume's psychology—as, indeed, is already indicated by his own repeated expressions of thoughts about "secret powers" and "ultimate principles."

That such relative thoughts can be barely and unclearly entertained does not entail, however, that Hume requires them to be true in order for causal attributions to be true. On the contrary, he regularly treats the satisfaction of his definitions of 'cause' as fully dispositive of causal questions and does not suppose that some further difficult-to-conceive conditions must also be satisfied. If there were to be constant conjunctions without "secret powers" or "ultimate principles" in things, he clearly implies, he would regard this as *causation without secret powers and ultimate principles*, rather than as *constant conjunction without causation*: indeed, this is exactly the force of his rejection of "occasional causes" in the first corollary to the two definitions of 'cause' [6.3]. His treatment of CAUSATION as a sense-based concept [4.3] makes this attitude fully understandable and defensible.

Causal reductionist interpretations are encouraged, in turn, by Hume's epistemology of causal relations. He explicitly declares the satisfaction of his two definitions of 'cause' to be sufficient to show that human actions are causally necessitated [6.4]; he declares that constant conjunction between mental and physical events would be sufficient to ensure their causal relation (THN 1.4.5.32/249); and he regularly treats his own discoveries of constant conjunctions as sufficient to settle questions within his science of man. Clearly, he regards the capacity to stimulate the causal sense under the idealized circumstances of its standard of judgment—and hence the satisfaction of either definition of 'cause'—as necessary and sufficient for a causal relation. It does not follow, however, either that he regards the definitions as conceptual analyses of CAUSATION [4.3], or that he cannot also speculate about whether further conditions are in some way implicated in the satisfaction of these conditions.

Is some further condition, such as the presence of unobservable secret powers or ultimate principles, implicated in the presence of constant conjunction and the capacity to stimulate inference and association? The question of whether, or how strongly, we should believe such a condition to be implicated is for Hume ultimately a question of what the corrected and refined sense of probability determines about the probability of there being such an implicated condition [5.3]. It is obvious that no regular probable (that is, causal or inductive) argument could support an inference to such a condition: that would require an observed constant conjunction between constant conjunctions, on the one hand, and unobservable secret powers or ultimate principles on the other. Nevertheless, for at least some philosophers a degree of credence may remain even after the diagnosis of the source of the belief in conflation and error has been made and accepted. In such a case, there may be room for blameless diversity in philosophical belief [4.4]. Whether there is or not, however, Hume emphasizes that it is a topic that—unlike the necessity and sufficiency for causation of his two definitions—has little practical bearing.

It is also a metaphysical topic on which, according to Hume, we should recognize that our questions largely exceed the scope of our faculties. Thus he writes,

> In considering this subject, we may observe a gradation of three opinions, that rise above each other, according as the persons, who form them, acquire new degrees of reason and knowledge. These opinions are those of the vulgar, that of a false philosophy, and that of the true; where we shall find upon enquiry, that the true philosophy approaches nearer to the sentiments of the vulgar, than to those of a mistaken knowledge. 'Tis natural for men, in their common and careless way of thinking, to imagine they perceive a connexion betwixt such objects as they

have commonly found united together; and because custom has render'd it difficult to separate the ideas, they are apt to fancy such a separation to be in itself impossible and absurd. But philosophers, who abstract from the effects of custom, and compare the ideas of objects, immediately perceive the falshood of these vulgar sentiments, and discover that there is no known connexion among objects. Every different object appears to them entirely distinct and separate; and they perceive, that 'tis not from a view of the nature and qualities of objects we infer one from another, but only when in several instances we observe them to have been constantly conjoin'd. But these philosophers, instead of drawing a just inference from this observation, and concluding that we have no idea of power or agency, separate from the mind and belonging to causes; I say, instead of drawing this conclusion, they frequently search for the qualities in which this agency consists, and are displeas'd with every system, which their reason suggests to them, in order to explain it. They have sufficient force of genius to free them from the vulgar error, that there is a natural and perceivable connexion betwixt the several sensible qualities and actions of matter; but not sufficient to keep them from ever seeking for this connexion in matter, or causes. Had they fallen upon the just conclusion, they wou'd have return'd back to the situation of the vulgar, and wou'd have regarded all these disquisitions with indolence and indifference.

(THN 1.4.3.9/222–23)

Indeed, indolence and indifference about this metaphysical question is very plausibly part of what he intends by the restraint from "high and distant enquiries ... beyond our capacities" that he recommends as one part of "mitigated skepticism" [7.5].

## 6.6 Conclusion

Hume is widely regarded as the discoverer of the *problem of induction*. This is the problem of showing how inductive inference, from the observed to the unobserved, can be justified. He is thought to have discovered it by noticing that inductive inferences presuppose the uniformity of nature; that this uniformity cannot be demonstrated or established *a priori*; and that any inductive argument for this uniformity would beg the question. Although many attempts have been made to solve this problem through a variety of ingenious strategies, it is often thought that Hume showed that it has no general solution.

It not wrong to say that Hume discovered the problem of induction, but he did not think of it in precisely these terms. The sections in which he presents the central arguments are, I have argued, part of his endeavor to establish within his science of man the operation or mechanism by which probable reasoning (as he calls it) actually occurs. In the particular sections at issue, he is seeking to establish that a key transition that occurs in this reasoning is not itself mediated by reasoning to a belief in the uniformity of nature; as he goes on to argue, this transition is instead mediated by custom or habit operating within the unreasoning imagination. This discovery does have the consequence, as he remarks explicitly in the first *Enquiry*, that any attempt to establish the uniformity of nature by probable argument would beg the question. Moreover, as we shall see in the next chapter, this discovery about probable reasoning plays some role in supporting the "mitigated skepticism" that he ultimately proposes, endorses, and adopts. Yet it does not by itself pose for him an insuperable objection to the epistemic legitimacy of induction. In particular, given his conception of probable reasoning as a primary element in the sense of probability [4.4], it does not follow from this discovery that the conclusions of inductive inferences are not probably true relative to one's evidence. On the contrary, his view of the ubiquity and epistemic legitimacy of probable reasoning in human inquiry is a primary source of his commitment to methodological empiricism.

Hume is also widely regarded as the discoverer of the *regularity theory* (also called the *uniformity theory*) of causation, the reductionistic theory according to which the relation of cause and effect can be reduced to the relation of constant conjunction (perhaps involving priority and contiguity), with the consequence that what the laws of nature are be understood as a function of what events actually occur. This theory has been highly influential in metaphysics and the philosophy of science; its continuing influence can be see in David Lewis's well-known conception, of the *Humean Mosaic* of events as determinants of the laws of nature [10.3]. However, he has also been interpreted—especially, but not exclusively, by those who themselves reject the adequacy of the regularity theory—as a *skeptical realist*, granting the existence of metaphysically real powers located in causes themselves that determine constant conjunctions but are themselves unknowable and (at least largely) inconceivable. Most recently, he has also been claimed as a forebear of projectivist theories of causation generally and of Simon Blackburn's proposed *quasi-realism* about causation in particular—that is, of the view that so-called "causal judgments" are not fully representational, but instead express dispositions to make causal inferences, "judgments" that can nevertheless be assessed as "true" or "false" as they accord or do not accord with the normative standards for making such inferences.

As we have seen, each of these characterizations, too, captures some element of the truth; but to isolate the elements of truth, we must again locate them within Hume's own philosophical project. As remarked in Chapter One, one of his primary aims is to discover genuine truths, or at least probable truths, about the real causal "springs and principles" underlying the operations of the human mind—including those governing the making of causal judgments themselves. His treatment of the relation of cause and effect is determined, I have argued, by his understanding of CAUSATION as a sense-based concept, derived from a sense that consists in the dual capacity to make causal inferences and to feel the impression of necessary connection in doing so; it is a treatment that makes the origin of CAUSATION an example of his concept empiricism. His psychological theory of causation is projectivist insofar as he recognizes both a projective mislocation of the impression of the necessary connection and the expression of dispositions to make causal inferences as elements in the operation of this sense. His epistemological theory of causation is reductionistic insofar as the sense-based character of CAUSATION leads him to conclude that the satisfaction of either of his two definitions of 'cause'—one in terms of constant conjunction, the other in terms of association and inference—is both necessary and sufficient for the existence of a causal relation. His semantic theory of causation is skeptically realist insofar as his theory of mental representation allows the formation of obscure relative ideas of "secret powers" and "ultimate principles" that would go beyond constant conjunction. His metaphysical theory of causation is skeptical insofar as his recommended attitude towards the question of the actual existence of further secret powers and ultimate principles is "indolence and indifference." As we shall see in the next chapter, the projective error about necessary connection also serves Hume as one source for one of the two main aspects of mitigated skepticism, while the obscurity of the question of secret powers and ultimate principles serves as a source for the other.

Finally, Hume is widely recognized as one of modern philosophy's most prominent and important *compatibilists*: that is, as a proponent of the compatibility of Universal Determinism with free will ("liberty" for Hume) of the kind needed for moral responsibility. His distinctive contribution to the defense of compatibilism has often been taken to be an argument from a conception of causation as mere constant conjunction to the conclusion that Universal Determinism does not involve any kind of necessitating coercion that would hinder the proper assignment of moral responsibility.

Once again, the characterization is not entirely erroneous, but it is misleading precisely because it fails to reflect Hume's own philosophical intentions. Although he does accept Universal Determinism, we have seen that his primary target is not indeterminists, but rather those who seek to distinguish between two kinds of determination, moral and physical, with only the latter genuinely necessitating. His primary goal in this context is to defend not Universal Determinism but the weaker Doctrine of Necessity (which can allow mild indeterminism) as true, as compatible with the liberty required for moral responsibility, and even as essential to it. His treatment of causation plays a crucial role in this endeavor not because it is metaphysically a reductionistic regularity theory—it is not—but because it undermines his opponents' distinction by treating constant conjunction (with priority and contiguity) as necessary and sufficient for the only kind of causal necessity there is. Causation is compatible with liberty and moral responsibility not because it fails to necessitate, on his view—for it does fully necessitate causally—but rather because it alone allows the kind of expression of standing character in voluntary action that reveals virtue and vice. Both his insistence on recognizing the kind of causation involved in ordinary laws of nature as the only kind of causation, and his insistence on explaining normative moral responsibility by appeal to the capacity to produce moral sentiments, are further important aspects of his naturalism.

## Notes

1 David Owen (1999) *Hume's Reason*. New York: Oxford University Press, chapter 4.
2 One classic statement of this interpretation is presented in David C. Stove (1973) *Hume's Inductive Skepticism*. Oxford: Oxford University Press. For further discussion of other versions of this interpretation, see Don Garrett (1997) *Cognition and Commitment in Hume's Philosophy*, New York: Oxford University Press, chapter 4.
3 One classic presentation of this interpretation is Thomas L. Beauchamp and Alexander Rosenberg (1981) *Hume and the Problem of Causation*, New York: Oxford University Press. For further discussion of other versions of this interpretation, see Don Garrett (1997) *Cognition and Commitment in Hume's Philosophy*, New York: Oxford University Press, chapter 4.
4 Peter Millican (1998) "Hume on Reason and Induction: Epistemology or Cognitive Science?" *Hume Studies* 24.1: 141–59.

## Further reading

Beebee, Helen (2006) *Hume on Causation*, London: Routledge. (An excellent discussion of grounds for projectivist, realist, and reductionist interpretations of Hume on causation; defends an interpretation of Hume as closest to projectivism about causation in the *Treatise* but closest to realism in the first *Enquiry*.)

Blackburn, Simon (1990) "Hume and Thick Connexions," *Philosophy and Phenomenological Research* 50 (supplement): 237–50. (Proposes the "quasi-realist" projectivist interpretation of Hume on causation that allows causal attributions to be called "true.")

Broughton, Janet (1983) "Hume's Skepticism about Causal Inferences," *The Pacific Philosophical Quarterly* 64.1: 3–18. (An important defense of the interpretation of Hume's famous argument about induction as aimed at showing only that it is not demonstrative or *a priori*.)

Coventry, Angela (2006) *Hume's Theory of Causation: A Quasi-Realist Interpretation*, New York: Continuum. (Resourcefully defends Blackburn's quasi-realist interpretation.)

Garrett, Don (1993) "The Representation of Causation and Hume's Two Definitions of 'Cause'," *Noûs* 27.2 (June): 167–90. (Extensive discussion of the relation between the two definitions of 'cause'.)

Garrett, Don (1997) *Cognition and Commitment in Hume's Philosophy*, New York: Oxford University Press. (Chapter 4 argues for a causal, rather than skeptical or restricted anti-demonstration interpretation of Hume on causation; the precise interpretation of Hume's famous conclusion has been improved in the two subsequent works cited below.)

Garrett, Don (1998) "Ideas, Reason, and Skepticism: Replies to My Critics," *Hume Studies* 24:1 (April): 171–94. (Defends the causal interpretation of Hume's argument about induction provided in Chapter 4 of *Cognition and Commitment in Hume's Philosophy*.)

Garrett, Don (2001) "Reply to My Critics" [symposium with David Owen and Charlotte Brown on *Cognition and Commitment in Hume's Philosophy*], *Philosophy and Phenomenological Research* 61.1: 205–15. (Also defends the causal interpretation of Hume on induction.)

Garrett, Don and Peter Millican (2011) "Reason, Induction, and Causation," *Occasional Papers of the Institute for Advanced Studies in the Humanities*. Edinburgh: University of Edinburgh Institute for Advanced Studies in the Humanities. (A debate addressing both induction and causation in Hume.)

Harris, James (2005) *Of Liberty and Necessity: The Free Will Debate in Eighteenth-Century British Philosophy*, Oxford: Oxford University Press. (An authoritative account of the many aspects of the debate between "necessitarians" and "libertarians" in eighteenth-century Britain, with chapters on Hume and other important figures.)

Kail, P. J. E. (2007) *Projection and Realism in Hume's Philosophy*, Oxford: Oxford University Press. (An important defense of the semantic claim that Hume can formulate causal realism, set in a valuable broader discussion of the nature of projection.)

Millican, Peter (2009) "Hume, Causal Realism, and Causal Science," *Mind* 118.471 (July): 647–712. (A powerful argument—appealing to Hume's application of his definitions of 'cause' to the topics of mind-body interaction and "liberty and necessity"—against the "New Hume" interpretation of him as a causal realist and in favor of interpreting him as maintaining the necessity and sufficiency of constant conjunction for causation.)

Millican, Peter (2012) "Hume's 'Scepticism' about Induction" in *The Continuum Companion to Hume*, edited by Alan Bailey and Dan O'Brien, London: Continuum: 57–103. (A recent and sophisticated revision of a leading skeptical interpretation of Hume on induction.)

Owen, David (1999) *Hume's Reason*, New York: Oxford University Press. (Defends a causal/descriptivist interpretation of Hume on induction, but one centered on the role of intermediate ideas, different from the interpretation presented here.)

Qu, Hsueh (2013) "Hume's Positive Argument on Induction," *Noûs* (DOI: 10.1111/nous.12015). (A provocative argument that Hume grants positive normative epistemic status to "custom" in Section 5 of the first *Enquiry*, so that Hume's appeal to custom in his "positive" answer to the question of the foundation of inferences from experience can be understood as itself normative.)

Read, Rupert and Kenneth A. Richman (2008) *The New Hume Debate*, London: Routledge, revised edition. (An essential collection of many important essays about causal realist interpretations of Hume, for and against.)

Russell, Paul (1995) *Freedom and Moral Responsibility: Hume's Way of Naturalizing Responsibility*, New York: Oxford University Press. (An excellent account of Hume's treatment of liberty and necessity that shows its reliance on his moral sense theory and its resemblance to the important and influential views of the twentieth-century philosopher P. F. Strawson.)

Marušić, Jennifer Smalligan (2014) "Hume on the Projection of Causal Necessity," *Philosophy Compass* 9.4: 263–73. (A helpful analysis of projectivist interpretations of Hume on causation and necessary connection.)

Strawson, Galen (2014) *The Secret Connexion: Causation, Realism, and David Hume*, second edition (first edition 1989), Oxford: Clarendon Press. (One of two seminal defenses of a causal realist interpretation.)

Stroud, Barry (1993) "'Gilding' and 'Staining' the World with 'Sentiments' and 'Phantasms'," *Hume Studies* 19.2 (November): 253–72. (Proposes a projectivist interpretation that makes all causal judgments literally false.)

Winkler, Kenneth (1991) "The New Hume," *The Philosophical Review* 100.3 (October): 541–79. (Argues on textual grounds against the interpretation of Hume as a causal realist.)

Wright, John P. (1983) *Hume's Skeptical Realism*, Minneapolis: University of Minnesota Press. (One of two seminal defenses of a causal realist interpretation.)

# Seven
Skepticism and probability

In both the Treatise and the first Enquiry, Hume concludes his examination of the human understanding by reviewing and assessing a set of doubt-inducing discoveries that raise the question of what he calls "the veracity or deceitfulness" of our faculties (THN 1.3.13.19/153; THN 1.4.1.1/180; THN 1.4.2.1/187; EHU 12.3/149; EHU 12.13–14/153–54). We may call his doubt-inducing discoveries about human cognitive faculties his *skeptical considerations* and his two ordered examinations of them his *skeptical recitals*.

In the final section of Treatise Book 1 ("Conclusion of this book"), he vividly enacts a profound epistemological crisis that is provoked by five discoveries about human reason as the inferential faculty [3.3], and in its final sentence he declares himself, indirectly but unmistakably, a "sceptic." The Appendix to the Treatise subsequently adds to that work's skeptical considerations one more doubt-inducing discovery, derived from a newly discovered "contradiction" in his own account of personal identity. Yet his skepticism is limited in degree and governed by what we may call his *Title Principle*:

> [Title Principle:] Where reason is lively and mixes itself with some propensity, it ought to be assented to. Where it does not, it never can have any title to operate on us.
> (THN 1.4.7.11/270)

In accepting this principle, he endorses many beliefs, and he goes on to pursue with notable vigor his science of man in Treatise Books 2 and 3. Even in the Appendix, he writes:

> For my part, I must plead the privilege of a sceptic, and confess that this difficulty is too hard for my understanding. I pretend not, however, to pronounce it absolutely insuperable. Others, perhaps, or myself upon more mature reflections, may discover some hypothesis that will reconcile those contradictions.
>
> (THN App 21/636)

In the final section of the first *Enquiry* ("Of the Academical or Sceptical Philosophy"), Hume describes, without enacting, an epistemological crisis that results from six or seven skeptical considerations (depending on how one counts) falling into three classes: three discoveries about the senses; one discovery about "abstract" or demonstrative reasoning; and two or three discoveries about probable reasoning. These considerations partially overlap with those of the *Treatise*. Among the added discoveries are two commonplace ones that he labels "trite" or "weak": (i) the acknowledged susceptibility of the senses when uncorrected by reasoning to errors and illusions; and (ii) the prevalence of disagreements resulting from the application of probable reason. The remaining four or five "more profound" considerations, however, he describes as capable of producing a momentary high degree of "perplexity and confusion." He recommends this experience as salutary and as contributing to the more moderate "mitigated scepticism" that he endorses (EHU 12.24/161) and takes to be compatible with the *Enquiry*'s positive psychological and epistemological claims. He concludes the first *Enquiry* by marking out a very extensive domain of mathematics and empirical facts, both general and particular, as "the proper subjects of science and enquiry" (EHU 12.26–33/163–65).

As remarked in the Introduction, the question of how to understand the relation between Hume's avowed skepticism and his avowed pursuit and endorsement of a naturalistic science of man is perhaps the most fundamental issue in the interpretation of his philosophy. It has evoked a wide array of different answers of every possible kind: that his skepticism defeats his naturalism; that his naturalism defeats his skepticism; that his skepticism and his naturalism co-exist inconsistently, perhaps by turns; and that his skepticism and his naturalism are consistent with each other and can be reconciled. In order to address the question fully, however, it is necessary to understand:

(i) how he conceives of skepticism; (ii) the particular skeptical considerations he examines and the way in which he thinks they are skeptical; (iii) the nature of the resulting epistemological crisis that he enacts in the *Treatise* and describes in the *Enquiry*; (iv) the meaning of the Title Principle and its role in overcoming the crisis; and (v) the way in which the status of PROBABLE TRUTH as a sense-based normative concept [4.4, 5.3–4] serves both to legitimize that principle and to determine the proper scope and degree for skepticism.

## 7.1 Kinds of skepticism

Hume begins his discussion of skepticism in the final section of the first *Enquiry* by asking: "What is meant by a sceptic? And how far is it possible to push these philosophical principles of doubt and uncertainty?" It is appropriate to consider his first question first.

Hume writes of skeptics as having both "sceptical doubts" and "sceptical principles." Just as belief is for him the liveliness of an idea [2.1], "doubt or uncertainty" is a diminished degree or absence of liveliness, which may or may not be subject to fluctuation. He also occasionally uses the term 'doubt' to designate a thought or consideration that tends to lower the degree of belief of another idea. Because he maintains that felt liveliness is not under direct voluntary control (THN App 2/623–24; EHU 5.10/48), he rejects Descartes's view that doubt is a voluntary mental act of withholding assent. At the same time, however, he readily recognizes the existence of desires to believe or disbelieve and desires either to continue or to end inquiry on a given question. Such desires may give rise to volitions concerning what lines of thought to pursue, something that is to a limited extent susceptible to voluntary control. The objects of such volitions may include either attention to, or suppression of, considerations that may be known or suspected either to raise or to lower a degree of belief to a desired level.

As noted in Chapters Four and Five, Hume can be expected to recognize distinctions among:

(i) basic non-conceptual belief in the probability to a particular degree of a possible matter of fact, which consists in an idea, having a particular degree of liveliness, of that possible matter

of fact, and constitutes at the same time belief to a particular degree in the possible matter of fact itself;
(ii) conceptual belief concerning the probability of the possible matter of fact, which consists in the inclusion of a lively idea of the possible matter of fact in the ordinary actual revival set of an abstract idea of a particular degree of probability;
(iii) conceptual belief concerning the probable truth of an idea, consisting in the inclusion of a lively idea of that idea in the ordinary actual revival set of an abstract idea of a particular degree of probable truth.

Given his conception of belief as the liveliness of ideas, he must be invoking this distinction when he writes, concerning rules of judgment for probability:

> A like reflection on *general rules* keeps us from augmenting our belief upon every increase of the force and vivacity of our ideas. Where an opinion admits of no doubt [i.e., no belief-lowering consideration], or opposite probability, we attribute to it a full conviction [i.e., attribute a high degree of probability to the object of the opinion and/or a high degree of probability of truth to the opinion itself]; tho' the want of resemblance, or contiguity, may render its force [i.e., liveliness] inferior to that of other opinions.
> (THN 1.3.10.12/632)

Under the term 'sceptical principles', Hume means to include the acceptance of doctrines denying or minimizing the epistemic value of judgments about a subject. Normally, at least, the kind of acceptance in question will simply be belief, although we may observe that among more sophisticated, cautious, or merely disingenuous skeptics, the attitude of acceptance may be extended to include a mere willingness to state such doctrines and defend them by argument. He may also intend to include, under the term 'sceptical principles', recommendations of lower degrees of belief or prescriptions to attempt to lower them. These three kinds of scepticism—lowering of belief, acceptance of principles denying epistemic value, and recommendation or prescription concerning lowered degrees of belief—correspond roughly to what Robert Fogelin usefully distinguishes as *practicing skepticism, theoretical skepticism,* and *prescriptive skepticism*.[1]

Each of these three types of skepticism can, in turn, vary across a number of different dimensions. One such dimension is *domain*. Thus, skepticism may be limited to certain kinds of beliefs, such as those about external objects of the senses, the past, the unobserved, "secret powers," or "the origin of worlds"; or it may instead be universal, encompassing all objects of belief whatever.

A second dimension is *origin*. At the outset of the final section of the first *Enquiry*, Hume explicitly distinguishes skepticism that arises prior to the investigation of one's faculties from skepticism that arises only afterwards. "Antecedent scepticism," which he identifies with Descartes, requires that one doubt both one's own previous opinions and the veracity of one's own faculties until one has been positively assured of their veracity by "a chain of reasoning, deduced from some original principle, which cannot possibly be fallacious or deceitful" (EHU 12.3–5/116–17). If the doubt in question is understood to be total and extreme, Hume argues, this kind of skepticism would be (i) psychologically unattainable and (ii) incurable if it could be attained, since the demand it makes for permissible belief cannot be met. In Fogelin's terms, Hume thus regards it as a causally kind of prescriptive and theoretical skepticism (as shown by the example of Descartes), but not as a causally possible kind of practicing skepticism. Hume expresses no alarm that its demand cannot be met, however, since that demand itself, stringently understood, is not "reasonable." A more "moderate" form of antecedent skepticism, in contrast, consisting only in an injunction to initial caution and the avoidance of hasty determinations, is both possible and reasonable. "Consequent scepticism," as opposed to antecedent skepticism, occurs after inquiry and only as the result of specific discoveries about the infirmities of human cognitive faculties. Hume identifies all of his own skepticism as consequent, supported by a set of specific discoveries.

As Hume's discussion of antecedent skepticism suggests, a third dimension of skepticism is *degree*. Skepticism of any kind may be either extreme (annihilating all belief, denying any degree of epistemic value, or recommending a total absence of belief) or moderate (lowering the degree of belief, deflating the degree of epistemic value, or recommending a lowering of degree of belief). He calls the former "excessive" or "Pyrrhonian," while the latter is one of two aspects of "mitigated" or "Academic" skepticism. ('Pyrrhonian' and 'Academic' refer to two schools of ancient skepticism, although Hume's characterization of them is not entirely accurate from a historical standpoint.[2]) In the Enquiry, he characterizes the former as fleeting and "useless," while he praises the latter as suitable to "a just reasoner."

Finally, the degree of skepticism, of any kind, may be either variable or invariable over time, and this creates a final dimension: *constancy*. In the Treatise, Hume expresses, and in the first Enquiry he describes, different degrees of skepticism at different stages of inquiry before arriving at his considered view. Moreover, he often notes that powerful but momentary skeptical doubts can continue to recur on occasion from the consideration of certain topics even after a more moderate continuing epistemic stance has been achieved; and he warns conversely, in the final paragraph of Treatise Book 1, that the force of some individually convincing arguments will elicit momentary expressions of full certainty that he, as a (moderate) skeptic, regards as improperly strong.

## 7.2 Skeptical considerations

After remarking on his own personal cognitive weaknesses and the difficulty that he has in maintaining his beliefs without sympathetic support from the agreement of others, Hume devotes the remainder of the first half of the final section of Treatise Book 1 to surveying doubt-inducing considerations pertaining to human reason more generally. All of these depend on discoveries made earlier in the Treatise, although the fifth and final skeptical consideration requires substantial further development.

The first skeptical consideration in this skeptical recital depends on the discovery that all belief provided by probable reasoning [3.3–4], as well as by the senses [3.5] and memory [3.2], consists in the liveliness of ideas. In the case of probable reasoning—that is, induction—this belief is produced by custom or habit operating on experience through a process the veracity of which cannot be established by any non-question-begging reasoning. This inability is a consequence of Hume's discovery that all probable reasoning presupposes the uniformity of nature, which supposition therefore cannot be established either by probable reasoning or by demonstrative reasoning [6.1]. It is for this reason that Hume writes, "after the most accurate and exact of my reasonings, I can give no reason why I shou'd assent to it" (THN 1.4.7.3/265, alluding to THN 1.3.5–7). This "quality, by which the mind enlivens some ideas beyond others" is "seemingly ... so trivial," he continues, and yet the understanding is "founded on" it. The assent we give to the existence of external objects of sense perception and even the assent we give to the past existence of objects of memory—both of which faculties also frequently provide the inputs to probable reasoning—consists in this liveliness as well.

Although Hume does not specify why the "seeming triviality" of the quality of liveliness should induce doubt, we can reconstruct the reason with some degree of confidence, especially given the limited number of kinds of arguments bearing on probability that he recognizes. He begins the skeptical recital of the *Treatise* by asking, "Can I be sure ... that I am following truth; and by what criterion shall I distinguish her?" (THN 1.4.7.3/265). As this question implies, the mind cannot observe directly whether the liveliness of ideas is or is not constantly conjoined with their truth. Accordingly, we may infer, we have an instance of what he has previously called "the probability of chances" (THN 1.3.11) [3.4]. For one can consider as so many equal "chances" *each* of the many possible initial circumstances that could affect the mind so as to give rise to liveliness, and yet only one of these equal chances consists in the truth of what is represented. Considered in this way, the truth of lively ideas appears relatively improbable and their falsehood relatively probable.

The skeptical recital of the first *Enquiry*'s final section proposes, as the primary "profound" skeptical consideration about probable reasoning, a similar line of thought. In this case, however, after noting again that we "have no arguments to convince us" of the uniformity of nature and that the presupposition of uniformity instead depends on custom, he goes on to remark, "nothing leads us to this inference but custom or a certain instinct of our nature; which it is indeed difficult to resist, but which, like other instincts, may be fallacious and deceitful" (EHU 12.22/159). The Enquiry thereby makes the truth of beliefs produced by probable reasoning itself seem improbable via the probability of causes (THN 1.3.12) [3.4], rather than by the probability of chances.

When Hume refers in the skeptical recital of the Treatise to the senses as well as the understanding as being "founded on" liveliness, he is alluding to a skeptical discovery that had already occupied much of the section of the Treatise entitled, "Of skepticism with regard to the senses" (THN 1.4.2) [3.5]. It does not receive a longer discussion in the final section of Treatise Book 1 partly because it has already been discussed extensively and partly because the skeptical recital of the Treatise is officially centered on discoveries about reason. The skeptical recital of the first Enquiry, which explicitly aims to address discoveries about the senses as well as discoveries about reason, gives it greater prominence and further development as a separate skeptical consideration. Hume argues in both works, however, that the natural and original form of belief in the existence of bodies ("continued and distinct existences") external to the mind does not distinguish these objects from sense impressions, even though simple experiments suffice to show that they could not be the same [3.5]. Confronted with this experimental evidence, philosophers then postulate that sense impressions are distinct from, but caused by, external objects that resemble them. Yet they cannot directly observe that sense impressions are constantly conjoined with such objects, and so they lack the basis for regular probable reasoning to that conclusion. At the same time, there are other conceivable hypotheses about the causes of sense impressions according to which these causes do not correspond to and resemble the impressions. We may thus distinguish two doubt-inducing effects. First, the realization that the most natural form of the belief in bodies is provably erroneous lowers our confidence that the more generic belief that there are bodies at all is probably true. Second, the absence of any non-question-begging probable argument to show that our sense impressions and the lively ideas derived from them represent external bodies truly, together with the equal availability of multiple other possible hypotheses about the causes of those impressions and ideas, lowers by means of the probability of chances the felt probability that the beliefs provided by the senses are probably true. In the *Treatise* recital, a similar implicit appeal to the probability of chances casts doubt even on the probable truth of beliefs provided by memory.

The second skeptical consideration of the *Treatise* recital lies in the discovery of a "contradiction" between probable reasoning and the senses that had emerged in his discussion of "the modern philosophy" in *Treatise* 1.4.4 [3.5]. Although Hume there offered the discovery as a criticism of the modern philosophers' pretensions to superiority over the ancient philosophers, it is also, he now notes, a serious problem in its own right. For among the modern philosophers' many arguments intended to show that bodies have no qualities resembling our perceptions of colors, sounds, tastes, smells, and heat or cold is one argument that is "satisfactory." This is the argument from what is often called the *relativity of perception*—that is, from the fact that the same object may produce contrary impressions of colors, sounds, tastes, smells, heat, and cold in different individuals at the same time or in the same individual at different times without any supposed change in the object itself. Since the same object cannot itself have contrary qualities at the same time, it follows that at least one of the contraries cannot truly resemble a quality in the body. Hume then appeals to the fourth and most important of his "rules by which to judge of causes and effect" [4.3, 6.3]—namely, that like effects are always produced by like causes—to conclude that none of the contrary qualities can be in the body itself.

Hume regards this result as posing a serious problem because—following Berkeley, and in opposition to Locke's theory of abstract ideas—he claims that we can conceive of bodies that are extended [2.5] only by imagining them as having one or more qualities that are themselves extended. If the mind must now attempt to conceive of bodies as the modern philosophy tells us they really are, without imagining them with the qualities of color or heat or cold familiar from sense impressions, then it seems that the mind cannot specifically conceive them at all, for it cannot specifically conceive any quality that allows them to be extended.

It is important to recognize that this "contradiction" does not by itself entail that there are no extended bodies. First, it may be that bodies do have the familiar sensory colors or tangible qualities, despite the "satisfactory" probable argument to contrary. For probable reasonings are not demonstrations, and even "satisfactory" ones sometimes have false conclusions. Moreover, Hume emphasizes that the rules by which to judge of causes and effects, one of which plays a crucial role, are "very easy in their invention, but extremely difficult in their application" (THN 1.3.15.11/175). Second, as he argued in support of the Copy Principle, the ability to form an idea of a sensible quality of a body requires the possession and stimulation of a suitable external sense; hence, it may be that bodies have other, unsensed and unknown but nevertheless extended qualities that we cannot specifically imagine. If so, then we can conceive such qualities only indirectly and obscurely, by means of a relative idea [2.2–3]: that is, as *whatever* extended qualities allow bodies to be extended. In either case, however, the tendency of our best probable reasoning to undermine our confidence that we now represent the fundamental qualities of bodies in the world with full accuracy is offered in the *Treatise* recital as a reason to decrease our previous assessment of the probability that reason provides true beliefs. A version of the same doubt-inducing discovery recurs—but now re-classified as reducing the probability of the veracity of the senses—in the recital of the first *Enquiry*, where it is credited to Berkeley by name (EHU 12.15n32/155).

The third skeptical consideration of the *Treatise* recital is what he now describes as a "defect in our reasoning" concerning the relation of cause and effect itself. This defect originates in the projective mislocation of the impression of necessary connection that is similar to the mislocation of non-extended tastes, smells, and sounds in extended external objects (THN 1.3.14) [6.3]. In the case of causation, it contributes to a conflation of metaphysical and causal necessities, with the result that we either "contradict ourselves, or talk without a meaning" when we speak of a "tie" or "ultimate and operating principle" between causes and effects themselves (THN 1.4.7.5/266–67). This discovery presumably weighs against the probability that beliefs produced by reason are true by showing that the mind is subject to at least one pervasive illusion in the course of much or all of its most common and most important probable reasoning. Hume arguably alludes to this doubt-inducing discovery again in the recital of the first *Enquiry*, treating it there as a second "profound" skeptical consideration about probable reasoning, when he writes of causation, "that we have no other idea of this relation than that of two objects, which have been frequently *conjoined* together" (EHU 12.22/159). One reason to treat this remark as such an allusion, despite its brevity, is that he refers in the plural to profound skeptical "objections" and "topics" concerning probable reason in the *Enquiry* recital, and the only other objection he has identified is that concerning the dependence of probable reasoning on custom as a kind of instinct.

The fourth skeptical consideration of the *Treatise* lies in a discovery made originally in the section, "Of scepticism with regard to reason" (THN 1.4.1). There Hume employs it as further support for his central claim that belief is the liveliness of ideas, on the grounds that only this account of belief can explain one aspect of the phenomenon in question. This complex—and in some ways convoluted—discovery affects both demonstrative and probable reasoning: it threatens first to reduce all demonstrations to (sub-proof) probability, and then all probability to "nothing." It therefore involves several stages.

First, although genuine demonstrations [3.4] are infallible because they reveal only real relations of ideas, reflection on the fallibility of the mind's cognitive faculties when it tries to perform them shows that "our reason must be consider'd as a kind of cause, of which truth is the natural effect; but such-a-one as by the irruption of other causes, and by the inconstancy of our mental powers, may frequently be prevented" (THN 1.4.1.1/180). The point of this observation is that it shows how the probability of causes is directly applicable to the production of truth by reasoning or attempted reasoning, demonstrative as well as probable. The probability of causes is an approved "philosophical" species of probability [3.4], and hence the characteristic certainty that an apparent demonstration initially provides for its conclusion will be naturally and properly replaced by a degree of belief, lower than full "proof," that is produced by probable reasoning from the less-than-completely-uniform conjunction between attempted demonstrations and the truth of their conclusions. Thus "knowledge degenerates into probability" (THN 1.4.7.3/181).

Second, however, the degree of belief that any probable reasoning provides for its conclusion—whether at the level of proof or lower, and whether that conclusion concerns the accuracy of a purported demonstration, tomorrow's weather, or anything else—is, by the same probability of causes, subject to the same kind of reflective review in light of the experienced past successes and failures of probable reasoning of relevant kinds. As Hume seems to be thinking of it—interpretations differ—this review of an instance of probable reasoning will concern the question of whether belief in its conclusion was what we may call *seemly*, as opposed to *overconfident*, just as the review of a purported demonstration will concern the question of whether its conclusion was held as genuine "knowledge," as opposed to being affirmed only "fallaciously." Seemly belief in a conclusion, as we will use the term, is belief that does not carry a degree of belief higher than the degree that would result from a correct application of the standard of judgment for probability [4.4], whereas overconfident belief in a conclusion fails to take full and proper account of negative evidence relative to the positive evidence and is therefore higher in degree than any belief that would result from a correct application of the standard. Let us use the term 'J1' for the first conclusion—that is, the result of probable reasoning to be reviewed—and 'J2' for the second conclusion, the one concerning the *seemliness* of the original belief in J1. Hume then claims, in effect, that even if J2 is a favorable conclusion that J1 *was seemly* and J2 is held with a relatively high degree of belief, so that the (at least implicitly) judged probability that J1 was believed overconfidently is very low, the new recognition of even some chance that J1 was believed overconfidently should—in accordance with the probability of causes, and again on analogy with the case of demonstration—serve to decrease at least somewhat the degree of belief with which J1 is now held, below what its degree of belief was before this (perhaps slight) chance of overconfidence about it was discovered.

Next, Hume argues that, by the probability of causes, the belief in J2 is itself subject to a reflective judgment, which we may call J3, about the seemliness of J2 (which was in turn about the seemliness of J1). As in the previous case, even if J3 is a favorable conclusion that J2 *was seemly* and J3 is itself held with a relatively high degree of belief, so that the implicitly judged probability that J2 was believed overconfidently is very low, this new recognition of even some chance that J2 was believed overconfidently should, in accordance with the probability of causes (and again on analogy with the case of demonstration), serve to decrease at least somewhat the degree of belief with which J2 is now held, below the degree with which it was held before this (perhaps slight) chance of overconfidence about it was discovered. Furthermore, he asserts, not implausibly, the resulting decrease in degree with which J2 is believed should also serve to diminish further, to at least some extent, the degree of belief with which J1 is held. For had the original degree of belief with which J2 was held been lower, the implicitly judged probability that J1 was overconfident would have been higher, requiring a larger reduction in the degree of belief in J1.

Finally, Hume argues, this process of ascending higher-order reviews in accordance with the probability of causes may be repeated without limit, with each new review transmitting some further loss of degree of belief all the way down the hierarchy to the original conclusion of probable reasoning, J1. Because liveliness is finite in quantity and is not infinitely divisible, he concludes, the original judgment would be expected to lose all liveliness, thereby annihilating all belief, after some finite number of reviews—again, so far as the regular probability of causes is concerned.

This dire annihilation of all belief will not actually occur, Hume claims, only because the "unnatural posture of the mind" in performing such repeated ascending reflections upon previous reflections turns out to prevent the reasonings about chances of error from achieving the accumulated liveliness-diminishing force they would otherwise have. Thus he concludes (using 'the understanding' interchangeably with 'reason', and 'the fancy' as a synonym for 'the imagination'):

> [T]he understanding, when it acts alone, and according to its most general principles, entirely subverts itself, and leaves not the lowest degree of evidence in any proposition, either of philosophy or common life. We save ourselves from this total scepticism only by means of that singular and seemingly trivial property of the fancy, by which we enter with difficulty into remote views of things....
> (THN 1.4.7.7/267–68; citing THN 1.4.1)

By 'degree of evidence in any proposition' (as his use of the term elsewhere in the *Treatise* confirms) he means psychological "evidentness," not the external basis of such evidentness [4.4].

In thinking about this complex discovery, it is important to distinguish two different arguments. The first is the lengthy line of argument that Hume is describing: the iterated probable reasoning by which one would continue to revise and further revise one's degree of belief in an original judgment. The second is the argument that Hume is actually propounding, to the effect that the described line of argument would, in accordance with the ordinary probability of causes, have belief-annihilating consequences unless prevented from doing so by a feature of the imagination. The intended result of this propounded argument is a belief about the *status* of the *described* line of argument. By showing that reason is a faculty that would lead through reflexive application to the annihilation of all belief if not prevented by a seemingly trivial feature of the (unreasoning) imagination, the propounded argument serves to lower the probability that reason that produces true beliefs, even though the described line of argument is prevented from having the psychological effect of annihilating all belief in any given target judgment.

The fifth and final skeptical consideration of the concluding section of *Treatise* Book 1 lies in what Hume calls a "very dangerous dilemma" concerning the question of when we ought to yield to trivial features of the (unreasoning) imagination that affect reasoning and belief. Although he also mentions the *Treatise*'s third skeptical consideration—the error concerning necessary connection—in this regard, it is the fourth that most directly inspires it. To approve the influence of all trivial features of the imagination, he remarks, would lead to the endorsement of the most extravagant and inconsistent opinions—a "false reason." To disapprove all of them, however—which would antecedently have seemed the safer and more obvious course—would also be to reject the only feature of the mind that prevents reason's annihilation of its own initial belief, and would leave us with "no reason at all." It is true that the described line of reasoning that would lead to reason's annihilation of all belief is "refin'd and elaborate," he remarks, but we cannot take it as a principle simply to reject all refined and elaborate reasoning. For this would cut off all science and philosophy; it would seem to demand, by parity of reasoning, that we accept after all the other trivial features of the imagination as well; and it could not be justified by any reasoning that was not itself refined and elaborate, and thus to be disallowed by the proposed principle itself (THN 1.4.7.7/267–8). Accordingly, he concludes, reason alone cannot resolve the Dangerous Dilemma (as we may follow him in calling it) concerning the appropriate standard for the epistemic endorsement of principles of the imagination as they affect reasoning and belief. This, too, renders the veracity of reason less probable than expected, by showing its incapacity for such an important epistemic task.

The skeptical recital in the first *Enquiry* omits any discussion of reason's tendency, if not prevented, to annihilate all belief, and it therefore also omits any discussion of the Dangerous Dilemma to which that discovery gives rise. While this may simply be because Hume judged these topics unnecessary and too complex for the later more streamlined work, it may well be that he lost confidence in his propounded argument about what the standard probability of causes really would require. (It might be argued, for example, that equal attention to the probability of *underconfidence* as well as of *overconfidence* would properly alter the outcome of the probability of causes—although the difficulty of determining how to incorporate both simultaneously might give rise to further skepticism.) In any case, the *Enquiry* instead adds a further skeptical consideration concerning "abstract reasoning": namely the seeming paradoxes of infinite divisibility. In a footnote, he proposes—though now with less confidence, or at least less insistence—the same solution to such paradoxes he had already proposed in the *Treatise* [2.5]. Even if ultimately soluble, he suggests, the naturalness and difficulty of such paradoxes offers a basis for some lowering of the probability that attempted abstract reasoning—that is, attempted demonstration [2.4]—is veracious.

## 7.3 Skeptical crisis and the Title Principle

Having reached in the *Treatise* the new and disturbing discovery of the Dangerous Dilemma, Hume proceeds to narrate in the first person a succession of three moods or frames of mind initiated by his joint consideration of all five of its skeptical considerations, but especially by this last. The first mood is one of "philosophical melancholy and delirium." In it, he writes, he is temporarily reduced (through a physiological intermediary) to extreme practicing skepticism and ready to embrace extreme theoretical skepticism about even probable truth:

> The *intense* view of these manifold contradictions and imperfections has so wrought upon me, and heated my brain, that I am ready to reject all belief and reasoning, and can look upon no opinion even as more probable or likely than another.
> (THN 1.4.7.8/268)

He soon discovers, however, that although reason itself is "incapable of dispelling these clouds," nature is capable of doing so, for the mood is not psychologically sustainable. Upon relaxation, activity, or "lively impressions of the senses," it is soon replaced by "indolence and spleen," a mood in which he: (i) rejects the "speculations" of abstruse "reasoning and philosophy" as "cold, and strain'd, and ridiculous"; (ii) "submits" to his "senses and understanding" in a way that skeptically discounts the force of the skeptical considerations themselves and returns him to "belief in the general maxims of the world"; and (iii) proposes to foreswear "torturing" his brain with "subtilities and sophistries" that can promise no prospect of "truth or certainty." He also declares, "If I must be a fool, as all those who reason or believe anything *certainly* are, my follies shall at least be natural and agreeable." This sentence has often been read as a declaration of continuing—and, ironically enough, dogmatic— extreme theoretical skepticism, by treating 'certainly' as modifying 'are', but this is almost certainly a mistake. Hume typically italicizes individual terms to express contrast (as with '*intense*' two paragraphs earlier) or to call attention to a technical role, and never or almost never simply for emphasis. It is therefore more likely that he means only to indicate that believing anything at the level of *certainty*, as implicitly contrasted with modest probability, now seems foolish.

Hume next considers under what circumstances he would feel willing to return to philosophy, given his recent experiences, and it is at this point that he states what I have called the Title Principle: "Where reason is lively, and mixes itself with some propensity, it ought to be assented to. Where it does not, it never can have any title to operate on us" (THN 1.4.7.11/270).[3] The term 'propensity', in Hume's primary usage, signifies an inclination or

## Skepticism and probability

tendency, and in the context of *Treatise* Book 1, the inclinations in question are generally propensities of the imagination. Elsewhere in the *Treatise*, depending on context, the term can signify tendencies to passion or action, or specifically favorable inclinations or desires toward something, as contrasted with aversions. It is important to emphasize that the Title Principle arises initially *not* through any renewed reasoning favoring the veracity of reason in its various applications, but rather as a natural expression, from a starting point of indolence and spleen, of a seemingly attractive rule concerning how much reasoning to allow or endorse.

Soon enough, however, the two passions of "curiosity" and "ambition" recur with philosophical truths and probable truths as their objects. In particular, Hume declares himself curious

> to be acquainted with the principles of moral good and evil, the nature and foundation of government, and the cause of those several passions and inclinations, which actuate and govern me. I am uneasy to think I approve of one object, and disapprove of another; call one thing beautiful, and another deform'd; decide concerning truth and falshood, reason and folly, without knowing upon what principles I proceed. I am concern'd for the condition of the learned world, which lies under such a deplorable ignorance in all these particulars.
> (THN 1.4.7.12/270–71)

His ambition, similarly, is "of contributing to the instruction of mankind, and of acquiring a name by my inventions and discoveries." Along with new reflections on the unavoidability of speculation about philosophical topics and the practical need to choose a guide to them less dangerous than religion, these passions lead naturally to the third mood, an active return to philosophizing. As Hume now realizes, positive philosophical inquiry itself is usually "lively"—that is, it enlivens ideas, producing belief—*and* it "mixes with some propensity" or mode(s) of thinking to which the mind is naturally inclined, especially by curiosity and ambition. Positive philosophical inquiry therefore appears fully in accordance with the Title Principle. For this reason, endorsement of the principle offers Hume the prospect of a resolution to his Dangerous

Dilemma, by providing after all, just when hope had been lost, a satisfactory principle for determining which exercises of reason to accept and which to reject. To see exactly how it does so, however, it is useful to contrast it with the implicit default principle of reasoning-acceptance that it serves to replace.

Because reason typically carries assent to its own conclusions with it, and reflection naturally adds belief that those conclusions are true or probably true [5.2–3] reasoners will naturally find themselves at least supposing (in Hume's sense [6.1]), if not explicitly formulating, the default principle: *reason ought to be assented to*. This default principle need not, of course, be understood to mean that *every* conclusion of reasoning should be accepted and endorsed without further question, reflection, or revision; for additional experience, further first-order reasoning about the facts, and reflective second-order reasoning about the circumstances contributing to apparent success or failure in various kinds of past reasonings (as in his rules by which to judge of causes and effects [4.3]) may each often lead reason itself to give an ultimate verdict different from its initial or provisional one. The default principle should therefore be understood as requiring only that the final decision of *reason, as developed by experience, reason, and reason's own self-reflection*, ought to be assented to.

For Hume, however, a surprising consequence of the fourth doubt-inducing discovery, giving rise in turn to the Dangerous Dilemma, is that this natural default principle is unacceptable. For the described toxic iterated reasoning that would lead to the loss of all belief is a set of reflective applications of reason to itself in accordance with what he regards as the regular operations of probable reason. By granting normative approval *only* to those final outcomes of reflective reasoning that are "lively and mix with some propensity," the Title Principle happily removes from the scope of principled acceptance and approval the iterated destructive reasoning that creates the Dangerous Dilemma. For on the one hand, this potentially toxic reasoning fails, as a result of a feature of the imagination, to be "lively" enough for the applications of its higher-order conclusions to diminish the mind's assent to lower-level conclusions. And on the other hand, the potentially toxic reasoning, unlike mundane reasoning and even philosophical reasoning of other kinds, fails to mix with any propensity of the imagination or of the passions. On the contrary, the imagination cannot long persist in it without confusion and fatigue, and no natural passion or desire encourages it.

This is not all, however. The reasoning that leads to the other skeptical considerations generates some lively belief in the proposition that our reason is so "infirm" as to be unreliable for epistemic purposes, but the liveliness of each of these doubt-inducing reasonings itself proves to be very limited beyond the initial shock, and they, too, mix little with any propensity of the imagination or passions. Accordingly, the Title Principle recommends, even in the face of these disturbing discoveries, retention of some considerable level of belief in the lively results of the original reasonings that these considerations seemed to undermine. This recommendation is aided, Hume remarks, by the recognition that the reasonings leading to these doubt-inducing considerations are themselves products of the very faculty whose veracity they then call into question (THN 1.4.7.14/273).

## 7.4 The normativity of the Title Principle

The Title Principle has a promising aspect, for its scope is precisely such as to mandate a return to positive philosophy in the face of the skeptical considerations while excluding the described belief-annihilating reasoning that gave rise to the Dangerous Dilemma. But what kind of normativity is expressed by its 'ought'?

In narrating his progress from indolence and spleen to a renewed pursuit of philosophy through the return of curiosity and ambition, Hume writes:

> These sentiments spring up naturally in my present disposition; and shou'd I endeavor to banish them, by attaching myself to any other business or diversion, I *feel* I shou'd be a loser in point of pleasure; and this is the origin of my philosophy.
> (THN 1.4.7.12/271)

This remark may suggest that Hume ultimately denies any distinctively epistemic value to his beliefs and instead continues to philosophize solely on the basis of his own pleasure in doing so. In fact, however, the passage says nothing either way about the ultimate epistemic value of his beliefs; it reports only the cause of his not attempting to suppress his curiosity and ambition, and hence an initial necessary causal condition ("the origin") helping to motivate his return to philosophizing. As we have seen [5.2–3], Hume's psychology makes it nearly impossible to hold a belief with a given degree of strength without, upon reflection, also holding with a similar degree of strength that that belief is true or probably true—thereby attributing to it a fundamental epistemic value. Furthermore, it is psychologically untenable, in his psychology, to take pleasure in the satisfaction of either curiosity ("to know" foundations and principles) or ambition ("of contributing to the instruction of mankind, and of making a name by my inventions and discoveries") without taking one's own discoveries to be true or at least probably true.

It has sometimes been proposed that the 'ought' of the Title Principle must ultimately be moral rather than epistemic. This proposal has some appeal, for Hume characterizes wisdom itself as a moral virtue [5.4]. Nevertheless, he makes this remark about wisdom only in Treatise Book 3, published separately from the first two books and more than a year later, so it seems unlikely that he intended it to provide a key to interpreting the 'ought' of the Title Principle at the conclusion of Book 1. In the passage in question, moreover, he writes that "wisdom and good-sense are valu'd because they are *useful* to the person possess'd of them" (THN 3.3.4.8/611), in explicit contrast to other character traits that are virtues primarily because they are immediately agreeable to the possessor of the trait or others. Yet the appreciation of a character trait for its usefulness depends essentially for Hume on stable beliefs about the causal consequences of actions and characters. To deny the truth or probable truth of one's beliefs, or even to remain without any belief concerning their truth or probable truth, would inevitably undermine the stability of one's beliefs about the causal consequences of actions and characters, and would thereby undermine the moral approval of wisdom as well. In addition, the natural correction of moral sentiments by means of a standard [4.1] requires further causal judgments about what the responses made from that standard would be. Thus, although the disposition to reason in accordance with the Title Principle does indeed achieve moral approval in the Treatise as a trait that is useful to its possessor, that approval depends for its force on an independent epistemic approval of the results of such reasoning as true or probably true.

Because the skeptical recital of the first Enquiry omits reason's potential self-annihilation and the Dangerous Dilemma, the later work does not invoke the Title Principle; it can instead implicitly retain the simpler default principle, *reason ought to be assented to*. While the Enquiry emphasizes in its opening section the practical value of philosophical reasoning and in its closing section the uselessness of extreme universal skepticism, it does not propose that the acceptance of such a default principle would be justified only by the personal pleasure of following it or that its only normativity would be moral.

## 7.5 The mitigation of skepticism

The 'ought' of the Title Principle, and of its implicit default correlate in the first Enquiry, must therefore be understood to express epistemic normativity. Yet, Hume also writes in the Treatise:

> This sceptical doubt, both with respect to reason and the senses, is a malady, which can never be radically cur'd, but must return upon us every moment, however we may chace it away, and sometimes may seem entirely free from it. 'Tis impossible, upon any system, to defend either our understanding or senses; and we but expose them further when we endeavour to justify them in that manner. As the sceptical doubt arises naturally from a profound and intense reflection on those subjects, it always encreases the further we carry our reflections, whether in opposition or conformity to it.
> (THN 1.4.2.57/218)

Similarly, in the first Enquiry he writes:

> [Pyrrhonian] objections ... can have no other tendency than to shew the whimsical condition of mankind, who must act and reason and believe; though they are not able, by their most diligent enquiry, to satisfy themselves concerning the

foundation of these operations, or to remove the objections, which may be raised against them.

(EHU, 12.23/160; see also EHU 12.15n/155)

Can he properly continue to grant epistemic value as he understands it—that is, truth or the probability of truth—to the beliefs mandated by the Title Principle even in the face of the doubts and objections that, by his own account, reason cannot defend against or remove?

Hume does not treat any of these doubts or objections as indicating a failure of reason or its products to meet a requirement for antecedent justification that a cognitive faculty and its results must meet before they can legitimately be employed. On the contrary, he rejects as unreasonable the suggestion that there are such "antecedent" standards [7.1]; instead, the difficulties arise "consequently," from particular doubt-inducing discoveries about our cognitive faculties made by those faculties themselves. Nor does he treat these consequent discoveries as combining with substantive *a priori* epistemic normative principles to entail that no beliefs produced by reason have any epistemic value. He states no such *a priori* principles, and there is little room within his naturalistic philosophy of mind and epistemology for an explanation of how such substantive normative epistemic principles could be known *a priori*; instead, his epistemic normative principles are discovered *a posteriori* [5.4]. Most importantly, he does not treat his consequent discoveries as showing that most of the beliefs produced by refined and reflective reasoning are not, all things considered, probably true. Although he describes himself in the *Treatise* as temporarily attracted to an epistemic stance in which no belief is regarded as probably true [7.3], he does not endorse this stance; on the contrary, in *A Letter from a Gentleman to his Friend in Edinburgh*, he emphasizes that this stance is "positively renounced in a few Pages afterwards, and called the Effects of Philosophical Melancholy and Delusion" (LG 23).

Instead, each of the discoveries simply constitutes a consideration that carries some negative weight, in one way or another, in judging how probable it is that our faculties are veracious. We may distinguish four different respects in which reason is unable to defend itself and the senses against, or completely remove, the doubts and objections produced by these discoveries. First, reason cannot discover any irregularity in the reasoning that leads to any of the discoveries about the operations of our cognitive faculties themselves. On the contrary, each discovery is made by regular reasoning that is in accordance with established reflective methodological standards reached by reason itself, and each discovery remains as an established thesis of Hume's philosophy when his confrontation with skepticism is concluded. Second, reason cannot completely destroy the capacity of any of the discoveries to function *as* a consideration weighing against the probability that reason and our senses are veracious. On the contrary, as he emphasizes, intense focus on the discoveries themselves only serves to enhance their doubt-inducing capacity, and even when that intense focus is lost, the discoveries leave behind a relatively persistent diminution is one's overall degree of belief. Third, reason cannot provide a countervailing general argument for the veracity of probable reason or the senses that does not already presuppose that veracity. Finally, reason must be supplemented by passion in order both to discover the Title Principle that resolves the Dangerous Dilemma and even to assist in bringing philosophical reasoning within the scope of that principle by allowing it more fully to "mix with some propensity."

These are all serious incapacities of reason, discovered by reason itself. They leave open, however, the question of whether the difficulties about the veracity or probable veracity of our faculties can be at least partially outweighed for Hume by positive epistemic considerations derived from our faculties in another way; and in fact they can. His doubts about reason and the senses are the result of empirical discoveries about the various "infirmities" of human cognitive faculties; but the particular amount of belief-diminishing force that they properly have is to be determined ultimately precisely by their considered impact on the corrected and refined sense of probability itself, which contributes to the establishment of its own standard of judgment [4.4]. It is not ruled out in advance that the corrected and refined sense of probability should approve the products of reason as *probably true* in spite of some doubt-inducing discoveries about that faculty, nor that that sense should ultimately disapprove the results of some otherwise quite regular probable reasoning that fails to have its expected effect on liveliness.

Assessments of both of these kinds occur at the conclusion of *Treatise* Book 1 in the adoption of the Title Principle.

More specifically, when doubt-inducing discoveries about our faculties produce a second-order **belief-that-{p}-is-probably-false**, this belief may be expected to yield as a byproduct—by natural semantic descent—a first-order **belief-that-it-is-not-probable-that-p** [5.3]. This latter belief will conflict with a first-order **belief-that-it-is-probable-that-p** produced by reason or the senses. At the same time, however, reflection on this first-order **belief-that-it-is-probable-that-p** will naturally produce—by semantic ascent—a higher-order **belief-that-{p}-is-probably-true**, which will conflict with the higher order **belief-that-{p}-is-probably-false** derived from the skeptical considerations. As is often the case in Hume's psychology, conflicting forces tend to diminish one another until there is a resolution, which may be more or less stable. Where the conflicts arise from different and non-coordinated considerations that produce different feelings of probability—that is, sentiments of belief—about the same matter of fact, there is very often no previously agreed-upon algorithm for resolving them; instead, one must simply bring one's fully "corrected" and attentive sense of probability "wisely" to bear in weighing them against one another, just as one must sometimes weigh moral or aesthetic considerations and their resulting sentiments against one another employing one's fully "corrected" and attentive sense of morals or of beauty. Indeed, rules for judging are in any case generally subordinate to the appropriate standard of judgment [4.1–4].

Probable reasoning and the senses are powerful sources of belief that make powerful appeals to the general sense of probability, and they cannot in the end be defeated by the skeptical considerations. Yet those considerations, also derived from reason, have genuine belief-diminishing force, and they do not leave the final epistemic status of human beliefs entirely untouched. Rather, the slightly fluctuating but largely stable enduring outcome of the confrontation is what Hume calls in the first *Enquiry* a "mitigated skepticism" that has two distinct parts. The first is an overall lowering to some extent of one's degree of belief regardless of scope, together with a recommendation of this lowering and a lowering of one's assessment of the probable truth of one's belief. The second is a loss of belief about "high and distant" matters beyond the scope of "common life," together with a recommendation to refrain from assessing the probable truth of claims about such matters. These matters include "the situation of the universe" and "the origin of worlds" [9.2–3], as well as the question of secret powers and ultimate principles beyond what can be clearly conceived [6.5–6]. Both species of mitigated skepticism are beneficial, Hume argues: the first by undermining dangerous "zealotry" in one's beliefs, and the second by preventing speculations that are at best fruitless and at worst can serve the purposes of religious "superstition."

Fraught as the confrontation with skepticism in the final section of *Treatise* Book 1 is, it is nevertheless not surprising that Hume's skepticism is only mitigated and not extreme, for he is in a position to benefit crucially from his treatment of PROBABLE TRUTH as a fundamentally normative epistemic concepts that is mediately sense-based. Because it is sense-based, the concept brings naturally to normative epistemic evaluation the resistance to global error that is characteristic of sense-based concepts generally [4.2, 4.4]. That is, it would be difficult, though not impossible, for humanity to be fundamentally wrong about what kinds of things—namely, those possible states of affairs that are "in conformity with experience"— are at least probably true. As in the moral or aesthetic case, it is not necessary for the error-resistance to be recognized and explicitly formulated in order for it to be an operative feature of normative evaluation.

## 7.6 The labyrinth of personal identity

In the Appendix to the *Treatise*, published with Book 3, Hume reports a further skeptical consideration applicable to Book 1:

> I had entertain'd some hopes, that however deficient our theory of the intellectual world might be, it wou'd be free from those contradictions, and absurdities, which seem to attend every explication, that human reason can give of the material world. But upon a more strict review of the section concerning *personal identity*, I find myself involv'd in such a labyrinth, that, I must confess, I neither know how to correct my former opinions, nor how to render them consistent.
>
> (THN App 10/633)

The section "Of personal identity" (THN 1.4.6) to which he refers addresses two main questions. The first is metaphysical: What is the mind, self, or person, to which identity and simplicity are attributed? The second is psychological: How and why are identity and simplicity attributed to a mind, self, or person?

Hume's answer to the first question is that the mind is not a soul in which perceptions inhere but is instead a bundle of perceptions related to one another by causation. His answer to the second question is that, although the mind lacks the perfect identity that consists in unchangingness and uninterruptedness through a supposed variation in time, identity is nevertheless attributed to it because the relations of causation and (to a lesser extent) resemblance among its elements generate mental association and so make the feeling of reviewing those elements in memory similar to the feeling of reviewing the perfect identity of an unchanging and uninterrupted object. The mind thus has a "fictitious" or "imperfect" identity like that of bodies; and a similar account appealing to associative relations explains the attribution of simplicity (that is, partlessness) to it at a given time [3.1].

Unfortunately, Hume's remarks about the "labyrinth" he has discovered do not clearly specify what the problem is, and his description of it is ambiguous even as to whether it is primarily a problem with his answer to the metaphysical question or with his answer to the psychological question:

> [H]aving thus loosen'd all our particular perceptions, when I proceed to explain the principle of connexion, which binds them together, and makes us attribute to them a real simplicity and identity, I am sensible that my account is very defective ... . [A]ll my hopes vanish, when I come to explain the principles, that unite our successive perceptions in our thought or consciousness.
> (THN App 20/635–36)

As a result, commentators have offered many different interpretations of his second thoughts through the years—over two dozen interpretations, in fact.

While it may not be possible to establish with certainly exactly what problem Hume saw, one serious and labyrinthine problem that he might well have seen, and which fits everything that he does say about it, concerns his answer to the metaphysical question. It lies in the difficulty of combining three principles that he mentions in and just prior to the section "Of personal identity" and hence would have found salient in conducting his "review":

> *Placeless Perceptions*: No non-visual and non-tactile perception is in any "place," either spiritual (such as a soul or mental substance) or spatial, by which it is located relative to any other perception. Even visual and tactile perceptions are not in any place by which they are located relative to any other perceptions except to those (if any) with which they form a spatially complex perception [2.5, 3.1].
>
> *Conjunctive Causation*: Taken together, the following are individually necessary and jointly sufficient for the existence of a causal relation between two objects: (i) priority in time; (ii) contiguity in time and, *where applicable*, in place; and (iii) constant similar conjunction of like objects [4.3, 6.3].
>
> *Causal Bundling*: Perceptions are in the same mind if and only if they are elements in a system of relevant causal relations holding among them [3.1].

Taken together, these three principles have several consequences that Hume would have found unacceptable. In order to state them more easily, let us adopt the term *unit perception* for any perception that has no spatial relation to any other perceptions except its own parts. There will be two kinds of unit perceptions: (i) perceptions that are non-visual and non-tactile, and hence have no spatial relations at all; and (ii) visual or tactile perceptions that are not spatial parts of any larger visual or tactile perception.

One unacceptable consequence is the *tenuousness of co-perception*. It follows from Causal Bundling and Conjunctive Causation that two simultaneous unit perceptions can belong to the same mind *only* if they are joint effects of a previous common cause, or joint causes of a subsequent common effect, or both. This is because Causal Bundling requires that all perceptions in the same mind be related causally (directly or indirectly) as part of a single causal system, whereas

Conjunctive Causation entails that a cause cannot be simultaneous with its effect. Surprisingly, then, whether two simultaneous perceptions belong to the same mind or not depends on what occurs before them and after them and not on any simultaneous relation between them.

A second unacceptable consequence is the *failure of unique ownership*. Conjunctive Causation and Placeless Perceptions together entail that no two similar and simultaneous unit perceptions can differ in their causal relations, and Causal Bundling entails that no two perceptions can differ in the mind or minds to which they belong without differing in their causal relations. The three principles together thus entail that qualitatively similar and simultaneous unit perceptions cannot exist in different minds; instead, one of them will belong to a given mind if and only if the other does as well.

A third unacceptable consequence is the *failure of unique bodily relations*. Because the three principles jointly entail that no two similar and simultaneous unit perceptions can differ in their causal relations, they also entail, more specifically, that two similar and simultaneous unit perceptions cannot be causally related to different brains or bodies. Instead, one of them will be causally related to a given brain or body if and only if the other is as well.

A fourth unacceptable consequence is the *failure of unique objects of memory*. When a memory is a memory of a previous perception, which earlier perception it is a memory of is determined by the memory idea's causal relations to a previous perception [2.6]. But because the principles again jointly entail that no two similar and simultaneous unit perceptions can differ in their causal relations, there cannot be a subsequent memory of only one of two similar and simultaneous unit perceptions.

The final and perhaps the most fundamental unacceptable consequence is the *probable non-existence of minds*. In the material or bodily realm, the contiguity-of-place requirement of Conjunctive Causation rules out the vast majority of what occurs in the universe just before a physical event as being irrelevant to its causation. Without such a requirement, it is likely that nearly every potential physical law would be falsified by distant but co-existing objects. For example, any causal law to the effect that water extinguishes fire would be falsified by the presence of water one thousand miles away from a blazing fire. Placeless Perceptions, however, imposes severe restrictions on the applicability of Conjunctive Causation's contiguity-of-place requirement to perceptions. To take an example suggested by Robert Fogelin that would be particularly important to Hume's science of man: multiple successive perceptions of conjunctions of one type of event with another very often occur without generating an associative link between the two types of events— namely, whenever the successive perceptions of conjunctions do not occur in the same mind.[4] Without a contiguity-of-place requirement, therefore, there can be no true causal laws governing such links, any more than there can be true causal laws governing the extinction of fire without such a requirement. Without causal laws, on Hume's account of causation, there can be no causal relations. But it follows from Causal Bundling that if there are no causal relations among perceptions, there are no minds either.

To put the matter as simply as possible, then, Hume supposed that causal bundling could explain the "location" of different perceptions in the same mind (obviating the need for spatial contiguity or inherence in the same substance) without initially recognizing that, on his account of the causal relation, perceptions would *already* have to have a common "location" in order to stand in the needed causal relations to one another. He concludes his discussion in the Appendix:

> Did our perceptions either inhere in something simple and individual, or did the mind perceive some real [causal] connexion among them, there wou'd be no difficulty in the case. For my part, I must plead the privilege of a sceptic, and confess that this difficulty is too hard for my understanding. I pretend not, however, to pronounce it absolutely insuperable. Others, perhaps, or myself, upon more mature reflection, may discover some hypothesis, that will reconcile these contradictions.
>
> (THN App 21/636)

Hume did not, in fact, return to reconcile these contradictions in subsequent works. In the later suppressed essay "Of the Immortality of the Soul," he seems marginally friendlier to the hypothesis of inherence, writing, "Matter and spirit ... are at bottom equally unknown; and we cannot determine what qualities may inhere in the one or in the other" (EMPL "Essays Withdrawn" 3: 591). In the context of the final version of the *Treatise*, however, the contradictions function as a sixth skeptical consideration tending to lower the probability of the veracity of the cognitive faculties that give rise to them and tending thereby to contribute further to mitigated skepticism.

## 7.7 Conclusion

Hume's skepticism—practicing, theoretical, and prescriptive—is distinctive in many different respects. Within a range of metaphysical topics that he finds to be beyond human faculties it is extreme, but in other domains it is moderate, lowering the actual, recommended, and epistemically proper heights of belief without annihilating it. While subject to some fluctuations, it is largely constant. Perhaps most distinctive, however, is its character. The ancient Pyrrhonists, such as Sextus Empiricus (160–210 CE), sought to support their practicing skepticism by proposing equal and opposing arguments on both sides of a question. Descartes formulates his antecedent methodological skepticism and motivates practicing skepticism by proposing skeptical scenarios—such as unrecognized dreaming and an evil demon—in which the world would seem just as it does but one's beliefs would be false. Hume's consequent skepticism invokes neither of these devices but rather depends on empirical discoveries about the operations of human cognitive faculties—made, of course, through the use of his own human cognitive faculties—that call into question the veracity of those faculties in application to some or all questions on which they pronounce. Some of these proposed doubt-inducing discoveries are not, in general outline, original to him. These include the difficulty of establishing by observation that bodies resemble their causes, the inconceivability of bodies without color and tactile qualities, and the seeming paradoxes of infinite divisibility. Others, however, are distinctively his own: the dependence of probable reasoning on liveliness derived from custom, rather than on reasoning about the uniformity of nature; the erroneous conflation concerning necessary connection; reason's reflexive self-subversion; the Dangerous Dilemma; and the late-discovered problem concerning (his own account of) personal identity.

Although Hume devotes considerable attention to his skeptical recitals, he neither abandons nor recommends abandoning all belief or distinctions of probability, nor does he deny that some beliefs are more probable than others. On the contrary, in the *Treatise* he goes on to investigate the passions and morals in Books 2 and 3, and he concludes the first *Enquiry* by marking out a very extensive domain of mathematics and empirical facts, both general and particular, as "the proper subjects of science and enquiry" (EHU 12.26–33/163–65). While this continuing pursuit of inquiry is often read as mere inconsistency—perhaps excused by psychological inability—or as the result of a moral or practical justification for belief, I have argued that Hume's conception of a sense of probability as the ultimate source for judgments of probable truth helps to explain both why he rejects the general requirement that faculties be vindicated by reasoning about them before they are used and why the force of skeptical considerations may properly be counterbalanced by the force of evidence provided by those faculties themselves. If this is correct, then there are obvious relations between Hume's epistemology and two important notions in contemporary epistemology: (i) Crispin Wright's conception of *entitlement*; and (ii) James Pryor's conception of *dogmatism*.

For Wright, entitlement is a warrant to place trust in certain propositions without first having evidence for them. Thus, he proposes that

> in all circumstance where there is no specific reason to think otherwise, we are each of us entitled to take it, without special investigative work, that our basic cognitive faculties are functioning properly in circumstances broadly conducive to their successful operation. If so, that immediately empowers us to dismiss the various scenarios of cognitive dislocation and disablement—dreams, sustained hallucination, envatment [that is, being a brain in a vat] and so on—which are the stock-in-trade of Cartesian scepticism.[5]

This is directly reminiscent of Hume's rejection of Cartesian antecedent skepticism; for Hume as for Wright, one may be entitled to employ one's faculties without having first vindicated their veracity. Prominent among the potential objects of entitlement for Wright is the uniformity of nature that is presupposed by what Hume calls "probable reasoning." Like Wright, Hume characterizes the uniformity of nature as something we "put trust in" without having an available argument (EHU 4.19/30) [6.1]. Like Wright, too, Hume notes the importance of such trust to our epistemic and practical projects.

However, whereas it has sometimes been objected that Wright's defense of entitlement ultimately offers only a practical, rather than an epistemic, source of approval, Hume's sense-based conception of probability allows him to go one step further. Dogmatism, as Pryor explains it, is the view that "whenever you have an experience as of p, you thereby have immediate *prima facie* justification for believing p," even in the absence of (i) anything that could ordinarily be called "evidence" for p, or (ii) any non-question-begging argument for p.[6] Pryor initially focuses on dogmatism about perceptual beliefs. If, however, the general capacity to feel degrees of assent is the basic "sense of probability" from which the concept PROBABILITY is derived, then there is a basis for extending dogmatism more broadly. Just as moral sentiments are *prima facie* (though highly defeasible) sources of information about virtue, the fundamental moral value, so too sentiments of belief are *prima facie* (though highly defeasible) sources of information about probable truth, a fundamental epistemic value. Indeed, the sentiment of belief is, for Hume, "evidence" itself, in one sense of that systematically ambiguous term [4.4].

Hume is consistently both a skeptic and a naturalist. His skepticism arises directly from the doubt-inducing discoveries of his naturalistic investigation of human cognitive faculties. At the same time, his naturalistic conception of epistemic normativity makes clear the authority of the sense of probability to determine the proper force of those doubts, allowing the chastened but continuing pursuit of naturalistic explanations in both the mental and physical domains. Hume recognizes, especially in the *Treatise*, an acute danger that all distinctions of probability will be undermined, but in the end, he thinks, the broad imagination properly judges that many beliefs—including those that constitute his own philosophy—are probably true.

## Notes

1 Robert J. Fogelin (1985) *Hume's Skepticism in the Treatise of Human Nature*, London: Routledge and Kegan Paul.
2 Julia Annas (2000) "Hume and Ancient Scepticism," *Acta Philosophica Fennica* 66: 271–85.

3 This term first appears in Chapter 10 of my 1997 *Cognition and Commitment in Hume's Philosophy* (New York: Oxford University Press).
4 Robert J. Fogelin (1992) "Hume's Worries about Personal Identity," in *Philosophical Interpretations*, Oxford: Oxford University Press.
5 Crispin Wright (2004) "Warrant for Nothing (and Foundations for Free)?" *Aristotelian Society Supplementary Volume* 78: 194–95.
6 James Pryor (2002) "The Skeptic and the Dogmatist," *Noûs* 34: 517–49.

# Further reading

Durland, Karánn (2011) "Extreme Skepticism and Commitment in the Treatise," *Hume Studies* 37.1: 65–98. (A comprehensive discussion of the Dangerous Dilemma and the problem it poses for Hume's philosophy, arguing that its cannot be resolved.)

Fogelin, Robert J. (1985) *Hume's Skepticism in the Treatise of Human Nature*, London: Routledge and Kegan Paul. (An important analysis that interprets Hume as a radical theoretical skeptic who nevertheless neither practices nor recommends a radical lowering of degree of belief.)

Fogelin, Robert J. (1992) "Hume's Worries about Personal Identity," in his *Philosophical Interpretations*, Oxford: Oxford University Press. (Provides an alternative but related interpretation of the source of Hume's second thoughts about personal identity to the one offered here.)

Fogelin, Robert J. (2009) *Hume's Skeptical Crisis: A Textual Study*, New York: Oxford University Press. (A close-to-the-text reading of the final section of *Treatise* Book 1.)

Garrett, Don (1997) *Cognition and Commitment in Hume's Philosophy*, New York: Oxford University Press, Chapter 10. (Outlines the treatment of skepticism in the final part of *Treatise* Book 1, including the Title Principle.)

Garrett, Don (2004) "'A Small Tincture of Pyrrhonism': Skepticism and Naturalism in Hume's Science of Man," in *Pyrrhonian Skepticism*, edited by Walter Sinnott Armstrong, Oxford: Oxford University Press: 68–98. (A more extensive examination of Hume's skepticism in light of Fogelin's distinctions among kinds of skepticism.)

Garrett, Don (2006) "Hume's Conclusions in 'Conclusion of this book'," *The Blackwell Companion to Hume's Treatise*, edited by Saul Traiger, London: Blackwell: 151–75 (A detailed analysis specifically of THN 1.4.7)

Garrett, Don (2011) "Rethinking Hume's Second Thoughts About Personal Identity," in *The Possibility of Philosophical Understanding: Essays for Barry Stroud*, edited by Jason Bridges, Niko Kolodny, and Wai-hung Wong, New York: Oxford University Press. (A fuller textual defense of the interpretation of Hume's second thoughts about personal identity presented here, with discussion of other approaches.)

Kail, P. J. E. (2007) *Projection and Realism in Hume's Philosophy*, Oxford: Oxford University Press. (Includes an interpretation of Hume's second thoughts about personal identity that depends on interpreting him as a causal realist who rejects Conjunctive Causation.)

Loeb, Louis (2002) *Stability and Justification in Hume's Treatise*, Oxford: Oxford University Press. (Proposes and defends an important stability-based interpretation of epistemic justification according to which the beliefs of unreflective individuals, because they are less susceptible to being destabilized by skeptical considerations, are more justified than those of more reflective individuals; highly original and provocative.)

Meeker, Kevin (2013) *Hume's Radical Scepticism and the Fate of Naturalized Epistemology*, Basingstoke and New York: Palgrave Macmillan. (An interpretation of Hume as a radical theoretic skeptic who regards all beliefs as equally entirely lacking in epistemic merit.)

Morris, William Edward (1989) "Hume's Scepticism about Reason," *Hume Studies* 15.1: 39–60. (A complete and influential interpretation of THN 1.4.1, "Scepticism with regard to reason.")

Morris, William Edward (2000) "Hume's Conclusion," *Philosophical Studies* 99.1: 89-110. (A reading of THN 1.4.7 as expressing the untenable position of philosophers and metaphysicians rather than a skepticism crisis concerning Hume's own views.)

Owen, David (1999) *Hume's Reason*, New York: Oxford University Press. (A rich and valuable book about Hume's conception of reason; proposes that Hume's epistemic normativity is ultimately grounded in moral normativity.)

Ridge, Michael (2003) "Epistemology Moralized: David Hume's Practical Epistemology," *Hume Studies* 29.2: 165–204. (An original and thorough defense of a moral interpretation of the Title Principle that well repays careful examination.)

Strawson, Galen (2011) *The Evident Connexion: Hume on Personal Identity*, Oxford: Oxford University Press. (A provocative book-length interpretation of Hume on the self, according to which each experience involves its own "subject"; clearly distinguishes between metaphysical and psychological explanations of Hume's second thoughts about personal identity, and defends a metaphysical interpretation.)

# Eight
Morality and virtue

Hume's moral philosophy is a distinctive and influential combination of *virtue ethics* and *moral sense theory* (or *sentimentalism*). For him, VIRTUE and VICE are the fundamental normative concepts structuring the moral domain of value through their application to character, while the concepts used in the moral evaluation of actions derive their normativity from these [5.1]. In this he stands with the ancient moralists he admired and in opposition to those who treat the evaluation of actions for conformity to duty as fundamental. In particular, he stands in substantial opposition to the long tradition of *natural law* tracing back at least to Thomas Aquinas (1225–74) and renewed in modern Protestant Europe by Hugo Grotius (1583–1645), Samuel Pufendorf (1632–94), and John Locke. In this tradition, the evident need for human beings to preserve themselves and to live together socially permits the derivation of moral precepts that can be known by reason, even without revelation, to have the force of moral law as commands of God.

At the same time, VIRTUE and VICE are for Hume also immediately sense-based concepts that arise from a moral sense consisting in the capacity to feel pleasurable moral approbation or painful moral disapprobation [4.1]. In this he stands with philosophers like Shaftesbury and Hutcheson who model the epistemology of moral qualities partly on that of the secondary qualities of bodies, and in opposition not only to natural law theorists, but also to philosophers like Clarke and Malebranche who model the epistemology of morality partly on that of mathematics.

Whereas Hutcheson treats the moral sense as directed primarily at actions performed from benevolence, however, Hume maintains that a wide range of mental traits and characteristics are equally capable of stimulating the moral sense. When the mind feels non-moral pleasures or pains and regards them as caused by a mental characteristic it is considering, the result is the distinctively moral pleasure or pain of moral approbation or disapprobation, respectively. Typically, though not quite always (THN 3.3.1.10/577–78; THN 3.3.1.26–29/589–90), these non-moral pleasures and pains are felt through the operation of sympathy [3.6]; and moral sentiments themselves can also be strengthened or spread to others by sympathy.

Hume draws a number of important distinctions among kinds of virtues. One way to classify them, especially prominent in the organization of the second *Enquiry*, is by means of their primary source of appeal to the moral sense as delineated in the four-part productive definition of 'virtue' or 'personal merit' as mental characteristics that are useful or agreeable to their possessor or others [4.2]. Books of moral guidance of the period often drew a tripartite distinction among duties to God, duties to self, and duties to others. It would therefore have been notable that Hume omits any mention of duties to God. This omission and his positive location of the source of moral distinctions in features of distinctively human passions and taste are central to his irreligious and naturalistic philosophical purposes.

Another important distinction of kinds of virtues for Hume—especially prominent in the organization of *Treatise* Book 3—is that between "natural" and "artificial" virtues. The latter, unlike the former, depend for their existence on conventions and artifice. Within the natural virtues, those of "greatness of mind" are especially related to pride, while those of "goodness and benevolence" are particularly related to love. Still other natural virtues are among those often classified as mere "natural abilities." He distinguishes "moral obligation" from what he calls "interested" (also "self-interested" or "natural") obligation, and he argues that there is in general an interested obligation, as well as a moral obligation, to virtue. This conclusion is central to his practical aim of encouraging virtue. Like the sense-based concepts PROBABILITY, BEAUTY, and DEFORMITY, the concepts of VIRTUE and VICE require some relativization to circumstances [4.4] and allow some scope for blameless diversity [4.2].

Hume begins Book 3 of the *Treatise* by arguing, against Malebranche, Clarke, and their followers that "moral distinctions are not deriv'd from reason." This famous conclusion is a necessary preliminary to his positive account of the way in which moral distinctions are derived from a moral sense. It is also, however, one of a set of famous conclusions he offers at different points in the *Treatise* about what the faculty of reason, perhaps surprisingly, cannot do; other examples include his conclusion that reason cannot determine the inference from observed to unobserved (THN 1.3.6) [3.4, 6.1] and his conclusion that reason cannot produce the belief in the continued and distinct existence of bodies (THN 1.4.2) [3.5]. His conclusion that reason cannot be the source of moral distinctions depends, in turn, partly on an argument for yet another member of this set: his conclusion in Book 2's "Of the influencing motives of the will" that reason alone cannot determine the will to any action (THN 2.3.3) [3.7].

## 8.1 Reason and moral distinctions

Hume offers three arguments for the conclusion that "moral distinctions are not deriv'd from reason." One of these is sometimes called the *Motivation Argument*. He is so pleased by it that he devotes a paragraph to giving it twice in a row, varying only its wording and the placement of its conclusion:

> [i] Since morals, therefore, have an influence on the actions and affections, it follows, that they cannot be deriv'd from reason; and that because reason alone, as we have already prov'd, can never have any such influence. [ii] Morals excite passions, and produce or prevent actions. Reason of itself is utterly impotent in this particular. The rules of morality, therefore, are not conclusions of our reason.
> (THN 3.1.1.6/457)

The main point of controversy, Hume recognizes, will be the premise that reason alone is impotent with respect to action, and he therefore offers to recapitulate one of his previous arguments from Book 2 for this claim in such a way as to render it "still more conclusive, and more applicable to the present subject." The previous argument he cites not the primary Impulse Argument, but rather the confirmatory Representation Argument [3.7]. His new, still-more-conclusive-and-applicable version of this argument is buttressed with the claim that not only passions but also actions and volitions are non-representational. (This is plausible for Hume because, just as passions are non-representational impressions accompanied by representational ideas, on his account, so too are volitions.) Hence, he argues, neither passions, nor actions, nor volitions can be either true or false. Yet reason, as a belief-producing faculty, is essentially a discovery, or attempted discovery, of truth and falsehood [3.3, 3.4]; passions, actions, and volitions can therefore neither conform with nor be contrary to reason, and accordingly reason alone cannot influence actions. By characterizing reason as a "discovery of truth or falshood," Hume presumably seeks to show the applicability of his argument to opponents who define 'reason' in broadly epistemic, rather than inferential, terms. In drawing his main conclusion, he is making the perhaps defensible assumption that reason as a faculty could operate to influence actions only by means of discovering (or seeming to discover) the conformity or contrariety of passions, volitions, or actions with truth—that is, their correspondence with something they represented [5.2].

Hume asserts that while this expanded version of the Representation Argument supports the key premise of the Motivation Argument, it can at the same time stand alone as a second argument that moral distinctions are not derived from reason, even without appeal to morality's own contrasting motivational capacity. For on the assumption that reason alone, as a belief-producing faculty, could draw a moral distinction only by means of discovering the conformity or contrariety of passions, volitions, or actions with truth, it also follows directly from the premises of the Representation Argument that reason alone cannot make moral distinctions.

Before proceeding to his third argument, Hume stops to consider the objection that even if passions, volitions, and actions cannot be immediately contrary to reason, they may still be so indirectly, in virtue of their causes or effects. Considering causes first, he notes two ways in which the cause of a desire or other passion leading to volition and action may be in error: (i) by including a false belief about the existence of an object, or (ii) by including a false belief about the means to some already desired end. But it is improper, he claims, to call the passions themselves contrary to reason on this account, and such errors are not, in any case, immoral or the source of moral distinctions. On the contrary, such mistakes of fact are typically morally (even if not epistemically) innocent, and if errors of this kind were the source of immorality, it seems that all such errors would give rise to immorality regardless of their object. Although it might be argued that there is a special class of "mistakes of right," their existence as *mistakes* of right would, he notes, presuppose *facts* of right as their subject matter; and these facts of right, with relevant distinctions derivable from them, would then have to have existed antecedently, without their existence being explained through any error or mistake of reason.

Turning to errors concerning effects, Hume notes that passions, volitions, and actions may themselves cause erroneous beliefs. Yet if this kind of error were the source of moral distinctions, then all production of false beliefs, even by inanimate objects, would be immoral. In addition, some immoral actions are entirely hidden and have no tendency to produce false beliefs, while the full immoral character of others is quite obvious and unmistakable. Although an act like stealing might erroneously suggest, in a way, that the object is the property of the thief, this is only because the rules of property place their "rightful" possession with another, which kind of possession is then generally assumed; in this case, therefore, any tendency to deception arises from the immorality, rather than being the source it.

In his third and final line of argument for the conclusion that moral distinctions are not derived from reason, Hume proceeds in his usual manner when arguing that something is not produced by reason: namely, by arguing first that it is not caused by demonstrative reasoning and second that it is not caused by probable reasoning. If moral distinctions were made by demonstrative reasoning, he asserts, they would have to lie either in one of the four relations already identified as the bases of demonstrable knowledge strictly so-called—resemblance, contrariety, degrees in quality, and proportion in quantity [3.4]—or in some further, as yet unidentified, demonstrable relation or relations. Yet morality clearly does not lie in any of the four identified relations, and any newly proposed relation, he states, would have to meet two stringent conditions.

The first condition is that the relation should hold only between minds and external objects, and never between minds independently of external objects or between external objects independently of minds. This demand is legitimate, Hume holds, because morality applies only to circumstances that involve both minds and external objects. Many of the same relations involved in the crime of parricide also hold when an oak tree destroys its parent, for example, but the latter is not immoral. The second condition is that it should be shown how apprehension of the new relation would necessarily serve to motivate every rational being, even including the deity. This demand is legitimate, Hume holds, because it has already been established that the apprehension of moral distinctions is inherently motivating; so if reason alone is sufficient to make such distinctions, the relations it apprehends must be motivating for all possible beings possessed of reason. Yet this seems impossible to show, he argues, because the question of what considerations will motivate a given kind of being is always a causal question about the production of volitions, and causal questions can only be answered on the basis of experience. Because neither of the two required conditions can evidently be satisfied, he concludes that demonstrative reasoning cannot make moral distinctions.

Yet neither, Hume argues in a famous passage, can probable reasoning (that is, reasoning concerning matters of fact) make moral distinctions:

> Nor does this reasoning only prove, that morality consists not in any relations, that are the objects of science; but if examin'd, will prove with equal certainty, that it consists not in any *matter of fact*, which can be discover'd by the understanding. This is the *second* part of our argument; and if it can be made evident, we may conclude that morality is not an object of reason. But can there be any difficulty in proving, that vice and virtue are not matters of fact, whose existence we can infer by reason? Take any action allow'd to be vicious: Wilful murder, for instance. Examine it in all lights, and see if you can find that matter of fact, or real existence, which you call *vice*. In which-ever way you take it, you

find only certain passions, motives, volitions, and thoughts. There is no other matter of fact in the case. The vice entirely escapes you, as long as you consider the object. You never can find it, till you turn your reflection into your own breast, and find a sentiment of disapprobation, which arises in you, towards this action. Here is a matter of fact; but it is the object of feeling, not of reason. It lies in yourself, not in the object. So that when you pronounce any action or character to be vicious, you mean nothing, but that from the constitution of your nature you have a feeling or sentiment of blame from the contemplation of it.
(THN 3.1.1.26/468–69)

In order to understand this passage, it is necessary to note three important points.

First, whenever Hume writes of what someone "means" by doing something, he is describing what the person *signifies* or *gives a sign of*; he is not seeking to provide a strict semantic analysis or synonymous expression. Thus, when he writes, "when you pronounce any action or character to be vicious, you mean nothing, but that from the constitution of your nature you have a feeling or sentiment of blame from the contemplation of it," he is simply making a claim about what the act of pronouncing this indicates about the utterer; he is not proposing that a predicative use of 'vicious' is synonymous with an assertion of the existence of a causal relation between the conjunction of one's own nature with an act of contemplation, on the one hand, and a sentiment of blame on the other. Not only do Humean moral judgments not *refer* to the judger, but in his discussion of the correction of moral sentiments [4.1] he is quite explicit that a predicative assertion using the term 'vice' or 'virtue' can be true or correct in the absence of any actually felt sentiment (THN 3.3.1.16/582)—just as a predicative color or aesthetic assertion about an object can be true and correct even in the absence of any actual color impression or aesthetic sentiment. A moral judgment can also, of course, be false even when produced by a moral sentiment, if the sentiment would not be felt from the standard of judgment for morals.

Second, Hume is not saying that morality does not consist of matters of fact, but only that morality does not consist of matters of fact "which can be discovered by the understanding"—in other words, in this context, by reason [3.3]. In this respect, virtue, and vice are like colors and other secondary qualities; their possession is a matter of fact, but one discerned in the first instance by a sense, rather than by reason. (The comma before 'which' should not distract; eighteenth-century English punctuation differs from the contemporary in freely allowing commas before restrictive clauses.)

Third, Hume's implicit location of vice "in your own breast" and his explicit identification of it as a "perception in the mind" exemplify the systematic ambiguity to which terms used to signify sense-based concepts are subject generally in Hume's Lockean usage [4.2]. He is equally emphatic, in his account of the passions in Book 2, about characterizing virtue and vice as "qualities in" the "subject" who is the person morally judged, rather than as "sentiments in" the one morally judging (THN 2.1.2.6/279; THN 2.1.7); it is only because they have this status as "qualities in a subject" that they can qualify as "causes" in the specific sense relevant to the double relation of impressions and ideas required for the origins of love and pride, hatred and humility [3.6]. In a similar way, as we have seen, he is willing to use color terms to denote qualities of bodies as well as sensations in the mind, and to use the terms "beauty" and "power" in both ways as well. Indeed, he continues the passage quoted above as follows:

> Vice and virtue, therefore, may be compar'd to sounds, colours, heat, and cold, which, according to modern philosophy, are not qualities in objects, but perceptions in the mind: and this discovery in morals, like that other in physics, is to be regarded as a considerable advancement of the speculative sciences; tho', like that too, it has little or no influence on practice. Nothing can be more real, or concern us more, than our own sentiments of pleasure and uneasiness; and if these be favourable to virtue, and unfavourable to vice, no more can be requisite to the regulation of our conduct and behaviour.
> (THN 3.1.1.26/469)

Thus, Hume's argument that moral distinctions cannot be made by probable reasoning alone is that such distinctions require the capacity for a distinctive kind of impression of reflection from which moral concepts originate, just as the making of color distinctions requires the capacity for a distinctive kind of impression of sensation from which color concepts originate. It is for this reason that he is willing to offer as an alternative expression of his main question this formulation: *"Whether 'tis by means of our ideas or impressions we distinguish betwixt vice and virtue, and pronounce an action blameable or praise-worthy?"* (THN 3.1.1.3/456). Moral distinctions are not derived from reason, he answers in effect, because the fundamental moral concepts are instead sense-based.

In a famous paragraph that was added to the text just prior to publication, Hume concludes the first section of *Treatise* Book 3 thus:

> I cannot forbear adding to these reasonings an observation, which may, perhaps, be found of some importance. In every system of morality, which I have hitherto met with, I have always remark'd, that the author proceeds for some time in the ordinary way of reasoning, and establishes the being of a God, or makes observations concerning human affairs; when of a sudden I am surpriz'd to find, that instead of the usual copulations of propositions, *is,* and *is not,* I meet with no proposition that is not connected with an *ought,* or an *ought not.* This change is imperceptible; but is, however, of the last consequence. For as this *ought,* or *ought not,* expresses some new relation or affirmation, 'tis necessary that it shou'd be observ'd and explain'd; and at the same time that a reason shou'd be given, for what seems altogether inconceivable, how this new relation can be a deduction from others, which are entirely different from it. But as authors do not commonly use this precaution, I shall presume to recommend it to the reader; and am perswaded, that this small attention wou'd subvert all the vulgar systems of morality, and let us see, that the distinction of vice and virtue is not founded merely on the relations of objects, nor is perceiv'd by reason.
> (THN 3.1.1.27/469/70)

The proposition that "one cannot derive an *ought* from an *is*" has since come to be known as Hume's Law. As such, it has been taken to be an important formulation of the distinction between facts and values, and discussions of its correctness have taken on something of a life of their own. The interpretation of the passage in the context of Hume's philosophy has also been a lively topic of debate in its own right, however. Some have assumed that he denies any legitimate "deduction" (that is, in Hume's usage, any inference or other derivation) of *ought* from *is* because he holds that moral judgments merely express feelings and do not express any proposition that could be true or false at all. Others have noted that he does not actually declare that such deductions are impossible, but only that "vulgar systems of philosophy" are undermined by their failure to explain them, leaving open the possibility that the moral sense theory he is about to propound will explain them.

There is no need to interpret the famous passage by appeal to a supposed rejection of all moral truth. Hume writes frequently of "moral judgments," and these will typically be true or false: the idea of a moral trait as falling within the revival set of VIRTUE or VICE either will correspond to reality in consequence of that trait being properly represented within the idealized revival set of the concept in question or not [2.4, 5.2]. What he calls "moral obligation" to perform an action arises "when the neglect or non-performance of it displeases us" by means of sentiments of moral disapprobation (THN 3.2.5.4/517). Accordingly, he need only be claiming, in accordance with the thesis of the section as a whole, that mere inferences from matters of fact are not sufficient to render moral obligation explicable without also invoking, in addition, a further source of moral impressions, soon to be identified as the moral sense. His emphasis on the seeming divide between *is* and *ought* may also indicate, however, that the normative status of a concept [5.1] provides it, through its practical conceptual role and accompanying social and personal commitments, with an additional element of expressive meaning in addition to the element of meaning that results simply from having an idealized revival set.

Whereas *Treatise* Book 3 begins by answering the question of the roles of reason and sentiment in morals, the second *Enquiry* raises the question at the outset only to defer its answer to the work's first appendix. This is in keeping with the simplified and more directly practical character of the *Enquiries* generally, and Hume's presentation of the topic in the later work is also in keeping with his willingness in the *Enquiries* to engage in "reconciling" projects on at least some disputed issues [1.4, 6.4]. Thus, in Appendix 1 ("Concerning Moral

Sentiment") of the second *Enquiry*, he begins by emphasizing the importance of reason in determining what the typical consequences of mental characteristics actually are. His thesis about the inability of reason alone to make moral distinctions remains unchanged, however, and he proceeds to offer five arguments for it. The first consists in a review of the unsuitability of both demonstrative and probable reasoning, a review similar to the concluding argument of the *Treatise* on the topic. The second is that one must first establish all of the particular causal circumstances of a case before making a moral determination by appeal to feeling. The third is that morality is analogous to aesthetics, where it is generally allowed that feeling, rather than reason alone, is the ultimate source of the distinctions made. The fourth is that inanimate objects can stand in the same relations discovered by reason as human beings can, but such objects cannot themselves be vicious or virtuous. The final argument, echoing the Motivation Argument of the *Treatise*, is that reason alone cannot set ends, but only discover means to them, whereas virtue is preferred in itself.

As this last contrast implies, the success of the Motivation Argument requires that morality be directly motivating. Hume intends his account of the moral sense to explain how this can be so: moral distinctions originate in a sense the activation of which results in responses that are—unlike the responses of the color sense, for example—themselves pleasures or pains. For this reason, morality plugs directly into the faculty of the passions [3.6] in such a way as to produce desire, love, hatred, pride, humility, benevolence, anger—and thereby volition. In the absence of the resources provided by the faculty of the passions with which the moral sense interacts, reason as a separate inferential faculty could not engage the will by appealing to any object of "concern" [3.7] to the agent. For Hume, the fundamental problem with most vicious people is not that they are irrational or reason badly, but that their characters are marked by (other) vices that make them harmful and disagreeable.

## 8.2 Natural virtues

Just as Hume offers both a productive and a responsive definition of 'cause'—in terms of constant conjunction and inference-and-association, respectively [4.3, 6.3]—so too he offers both a productive and a responsive definition of 'virtue': "every quality of the mind, which is *useful or agreeable* to the *person himself* or to *others*" (EPM 9.12/277) and "*whatever mental action or quality gives to a spectator the pleasing sentiment of approbation*" (EPM App 1.10/289), respectively [4.2]. The productive definition provides a rough but ready fourfold classification of virtues: those useful to the possessor, those useful to others, those immediately agreeable to the possessor, and those immediately agreeable to others. Many virtues, of course, satisfy more than one of these descriptions. Indeed all virtues elicit love when present in others, on Hume's view, and love naturally elicits a desire to benefit the person loved; hence we may infer than any virtue is likely to prove useful to its possessor to at least some extent. Nevertheless, it is often clear that the approbation-eliciting power of a given trait is derived at least in the first instance either exclusively or predominantly from just one of these four sources.

Nearly all of the artificial virtues, for example, derive most of their original approbation-eliciting power from their usefulness to others. But such important natural virtues as benevolence and kindness also derive their approbation largely, if by no means exclusively, from this source. Virtues that are predominantly useful to the possessor, in contrast, include: "prudence"; "discretion" (the capacity to give due attention to characters, circumstances, and available means in the conduct of life); "industry" (industriousness); "frugality" (as a mean between avarice and prodigality); "strength of mind" (a predominance in motivational force of calm passions above violent ones); "courage"; "wisdom and good sense" (the capacity to reason well, proportioning belief to evidence without falling victim to "unphilosophical" influences on belief); and even (strength of) "memory" (EPM 6). That human beings do morally approve these latter traits wherever they occur shows all the more clearly, in Hume's view, that morality is not based simply in self-interest. For in these cases, at least, the observer is not, unless considering his or her own character, among the primary beneficiaries of the trait; indeed, where the observer is in competition with the possessor, the traits may even be harmful to the observer and produce negative feelings from the separate and non-moral point of view of self-interest.

Virtues that are predominantly immediately agreeable to their possessors include: "greatness of mind" or "dignity of character";

"cheerfulness"; "tranquility"; and "delicacy of taste" (sensitivity to beauty and deformity in both discrimination and degree of sentiment) although this latter trait can also be painful at times. Courage, while predominantly useful to its possessor, is also agreeable to its possessor insofar as it restrains unpleasant fears. Benevolence, too, while predominantly useful to others, is warmly agreeable to its possessor; indeed, it is because of this agreeableness, Hume claims, that we tend to praise benevolence even when it somewhat exceeds the bounds of its usefulness (EPM 7).

Among virtues for which immediate agreeableness to others predominates, he mentions being a good and easy conversationalist (see also THN 3.3.4.9/611, with its distinctively Humean parenthetical addition that the personal merit derived in this way may "be very considerable"); "wit and ingenuity" (in a sense at least including the ability to produce humor [5.1]); "eloquence"; "modesty" (in the sense of a lack of arrogance and a disposition to give flattering attention to the opinions of others), especially in the young; "decency" (as "proper regard to the age, sex, character, and station" of others); and "cleanliness." He also mentions two virtues better known in the present day under shorter names. One is

> something mysterious and inexplicable, which conveys an immediate satisfaction to the spectator, but how, or why, or for what reason, he cannot pretend to determine. There is a MANNER, a grace, an ease, a genteelness, an I-know-not-what, which some men possess above others, which is very different from external beauty and comeliness, and which, however, catches our affection almost as suddenly and powerfully.
> (EPM 8.14/267; see also THN 3.3.4.11/612)

This, I take it, is what we would call *charisma*. He also mentions as immediately agreeable the talent for a "certain easy and disengag'd behaviour" (THN 3.3.1.27/589)—what we might call being *cool*.

Hume singles out as notable two different clusters of virtues: those relating to "greatness of mind" and those relating to "goodness or benevolence" (THN 3.3.2–3). The former include "courage," "intrepidity," "ambition," "love of glory," and "magnanimity." These "and all other shining virtues of that kind" derive their virtue primarily from their usefulness and/or agreeableness to their possessors and are further distinguished by their "strong mixture of self-esteem" or pride. "Nothing," he asserts, "can be more laudable, than to have a value for ourselves, where we really have qualities that are valuable" (THN 3.3.2.8/596). There are two primary reasons why such self-valuing traits elicit approbation. First, a due degree of pride gives one confidence in one's undertakings and thereby makes success in them more likely, while also inspiring the bold and enterprising projects on which fortune often smiles. Second, few passions are as immediately agreeable to the possessor as pride.

Due limits must be placed on the pride that is based on false self-assessments, however, and especially on the nature of its expression, because an "overweening" pride is immediately disagreeable to others. This disagreeableness, Hume explains, results from the combination of two mental operations. First, by the operation of sympathy, the observer involuntarily acquires from the proud person a feeling of that person's merit; then, by the operation of comparison [3.6] with the observer's opinion of himself or herself, the observer feels an unpleasant humility. In consequence, it is necessary to establish rules of politeness and "good-breeding" to avoid giving offense. Yet he remarks,

> I believe no one, who has any practice of the world, and can penetrate into the inward sentiments of men, will assert, that the humility, which good-breeding and decency require of us, goes beyond the outside, or that a thorough sincerity in this particular is esteem'd a real part of our duty. On the contrary, we may observe, that a genuine and hearty pride, or self-esteem, if well conceal'd and well founded, is essential to the character of a man of honour, and that there is no quality of the mind, which is more indispensibly requisite to procure the esteem and approbation of mankind.
> (THN 3.3.2.11/598)

Christianity's tendency to treat humility as a virtue and pride as a pagan vice is in his view positively pernicious.

Among the pleasurable indirect passions, pride has self as object, whereas the object of love is another person [3.6]. In contrast to the virtues of greatness of mind, which are closely related to pride, the virtues of goodness and benevolence are closely related to love. These latter virtues include "benevolence" itself (which, as a virtue, is a disposition toward the passion of benevolence or desire for the wellbeing of others), "generosity," "humanity," "compassion," "gratitude," "friendship," "loyalty," and "liberality." They derive their merit primarily from their usefulness and agreeableness to others. Because the passion of love is itself immediately pleasurable, however, we also praise "whatever partakes of it" through an immediate sympathy with its possessor. Because we expect love to be *partial* to some extent—that is, to be felt more towards family and friends than to strangers—we accordingly expect and allow some partiality in the expression of these virtues as well. Hume holds that the virtues of greatness are properly regulated by virtues of goodness. While military glory, for example, inspires approbation when we sympathize at a distance with the proud military leader, benevolence for those whose lives are devastated by wars reduces our approbation; and courage and ambition unregulated by benevolence render their possessor fit only to be "a tyrant and a public robber" (THN 3.3.3.3/604).

Hume recognizes that his contemporaries often distinguish between "moral virtues" and "natural abilities," with the latter—such as "good sense," "quickness of apprehension," "strong memory," and charisma—considered merely as mental endowments without distinctive moral worth. He argues, however, that this distinction between kinds of personal merit is largely overrated (THN 3.3.4, "Of natural abilities"). The traits that are always considered moral virtues and the traits that are often classified as mere natural abilities can equally produce love and pride, he observes; we care equally about our reputations for both; and both cause benevolence and goodwill to be directed at their possessors. Although he concedes that the felt character of the particular sentiments of approbation they elicit may differ somewhat in many of these cases, the same holds true, he emphasizes, for different traits that are universally regarded as virtues, especially when these traits involve different mixtures of, or relations to, love and pride.

Because "legislators, and divines, and moralists" are concerned to improve the behavior of others through exhortations and through the additional motives of rewards and punishments, they often seek to draw and emphasize the distinction between moral virtues and natural abilities on the grounds that natural abilities and their exercises are not voluntary. Yet many of the recognized virtues of the great, Hume argues—such as fortitude, constancy, and magnanimity—are equally involuntary in their possession and largely in their expression as well. Furthermore, the more passionate a character is, the less under voluntary control its vices are—yet the vices are often all the more blamable for that.

Because the supposed line between virtues and natural abilities is vague and admits of no standard by which a clear distinction can be made, Hume declares the question of which traits belong to which category to be "merely verbal" (EHU Appendix 4, "Of Some Verbal Disputes"). In contrast, strength and beauty can be clearly distinguished from virtue as being physical, rather than mental, characteristics. He allows charisma as a virtue, we may assume, precisely because it is sharply distinguished from physical beauty and is discerned in a manner of conduct expressive of features (however "mysterious and inexplicable" they may be) of mind. Neglecting the distinction between virtues and natural abilities is another respect, he suggests, in which the ancient moral theorists are superior to the modern.

## 8.3 Justice as an artificial virtue

Hume most commonly uses the term 'justice' in a limited way that designates only respect for property. Although he sometimes adds the keeping of promises—which are also a person's "due"—to the scope of 'justice', he more commonly distinguishes promise keeping under the distinct term 'fidelity'. He also sometimes uses 'honesty' and even 'equity' in place of 'justice', seemingly just for verbal variation. For obedience to government, he generally uses the term 'allegiance'.

In Locke's political philosophy, which was especially popular with the Whig party of Hume's own time, there are divinely instituted moral obligations both to respect the property of others and to keep one's promises, including contracts, even in the absence of political society—that is, in "the state of nature"—and independent of any human conventions. The state of nature ends, on Locke's account, when a recognition of a need for more effective protection of property leads individuals to enter into a "social contract" to form a political society with one another and to establish a government from among the members of that society. Their obligation to obey the government's edicts then results directly from their promise to one another to do so. Putting matters in Hume's terminology, then, Locke regards justice and fidelity as natural virtues, and the obligation to allegiance as derived from the obligation to fidelity. Hume, in contrast, declares that all three virtues are artificial, and that in no case is the obligation to one derived primarily from an obligation to another. On the contrary, he holds, they each derive their primary moral obligation directly from the same non-divine source: their usefulness to society.

In calling a virtue "artificial," it should be emphasized, Hume does not mean that it is any less a virtue or any less important than other virtues. Like all virtues, the artificial virtues are traits of character or mental characteristics that are useful or agreeable to their possessor or others, and which thereby elicit moral approbation from observers; several of the artificial virtues, moreover, are essential to human flourishing and survival. Rather, what makes them artificial is simply their dependence on the existence of a "convention." A convention exists among a group of individuals, as he explains it, when: (i) each individual has an interest in following a particular course of conduct, but only on the condition that the others follow a corresponding course of conduct; (ii) this common interest is mutually expressed and known among the individuals; and (iii) this mutual expression and knowledge serve to produce "a suitable resolution and behaviour" (THN 3.2.2.10/490). Individuals can enter into a convention without making a promise; on the contrary, promising is itself a specific convention. In Hume's elegant and well-known example, two people may pull the oars in a boat by convention without making any promises to each other, for each has an interest in pulling the oar on his side on condition that the other pulls the oar on the other side; each understands and expresses this common interest, verbally or non-verbally (perhaps simply by starting to row); and a suitable resolution and behavior results on the part of each (THN 3.2.2.10/ 490; EHU App 3.8/306–7).

Although it has often been misunderstood, Hume offers a positive and ingenious argument, sometimes called the *Circle Argument*, for his claim that justice is an artificial virtue (THN 3.2.1, "Justice, whether a natural or artificial virtue?"). Its starting point is a premise of his virtue ethics that we may call the *Virtue Ethics Thesis*:

> [Virtue Ethics Thesis:] [A]ll virtuous actions derive their merit only from virtuous motives, and are consider'd merely as signs of those motives.
>
> (THN 3.2.1.4/478)

'Motive' is used here in a broad sense that includes within its scope any mental traits that contribute to motivation.

Hume accepts this premise because—unlike many—he holds that VIRTUE, applied to traits of character, is the fundamental morally normative concept [5.1]; morally normative concepts can therefore apply to actions only in consequence of their being actions that persons with particular virtues or vices do or would perform. To this premise, he immediately adds what he regards as a simple point about explanatory priority: "An action must be virtuous before we can have a regard to its virtue." That is to say, human beings can sometimes be motivated to an action by the recognition of its morally normative merit, but in order for the act to *have* that merit, the action must already have derived the merit from the action's being the expression of some other morally approved trait or motive. He draws as a consequence from these two premises the *First Virtuous Motive Principle*:

> [First Virtuous Motive Principle:] [T]he first virtuous motive, which bestows a merit on any action, can never be a regard to the virtue of that action, but must be some other natural motive or principle.
>
> (THN 3.2.1.4/478)

The previous section of the *Treatise* ends with the observation that the term 'natural' may be opposed to 'rare', 'miraculous', 'civil', 'moral', or 'artificial', together with a remark that, in the remainder of the work, the context of each use of 'natural' will indicate the proper sense (THN 3.1.27–9n/473–76). In his statement of the First Virtuous Motive Principle, 'natural' clearly means "non-moral": a "natural motive or principle" is one that does not involve having a concern specifically for the moral merit of the action.

Hume's example of a "moral" motive, in contrast to a natural or non-moral one in this sense, is "duty," which he analyzes as the desire to perform actions of morally meritorious kinds, either (i) in the hope of acquiring the virtuous trait or motive that originally renders them morally meritorious, or (ii) in order to disguise from oneself one's lack of that virtuous trait or motive (THN 3.2.1.8/ 479). Because it is often useful to its possessor and others, duty is itself a virtuous motive, although always parasitic on the existence of other virtuous motives and often, for that reason, only a second-best one. It must be emphasized that a "non-moral" motive in this sense—that is, one that does not require a *regard* to the moral merit of actions—can still itself *have* moral merit as a virtuous mental trait.

The strategy of Hume's argument is then to argue that, in the absence of a convention, there would be no motive that could satisfy the First Virtuous Motive Principle with respect to just actions. For while some individual acts that are in accordance with the demands of property might be motivated either (i) by self-interest, (ii) by public benevolence (that is, concern for the interests or wellbeing of society or humankind), or (iii) private benevolence (concern for the interests or wellbeing of the individual most directly affected), none of these motives can explain what we might call the *full behavioral profile* of justice; each would often lead instead to actions that are contrary to the demands of property.

In order to discover the "first virtuous motive" to justice, then, we must understand how respect for property can be consistently motivated at all, and this requires understanding, in Hume's words, "how the rules of justice are established by the artifice of men"—that is, how property arises as a convention (THN 2.2.2, "Of the origin of justice and property"). Human needs are great, he observes, and the natural physical endowments of individual human beings are modest indeed in comparison with those of other animals. In order to survive and prosper, human beings must live in society, which allows them to augment their force by combining their strength, to augment their ability and skill by the division of their labor, and to augment their security through mutual aid. Happily, it is not necessary for human beings to foresee these advantages before entering into society, because the "appetite between the sexes" and "natural affection" for the resulting children are sufficient to institute society. Yet a serious threat to the maintenance of society lies in the combination of two features of human nature with two features of external circumstances. The two relevant features of human nature are "selfishness" (the tendency to prefer the satisfaction of one's own interests to those of others) and "limited generosity" (the tendency to prefer the satisfaction of the interests of one's family and friends to the satisfaction of the interests of others). The two relevant features of external circumstances are the scarcity of possessions (that is, items under a person's control) acquired by industry and the instability of possessions (that is, their liability to be taken by force to the advantage of the person taking them). In such circumstances, the industry of individuals will be naturally unavailing and individuals will commonly be threatened by violence.

The solution to the problem is a convention whereby individuals leave others in possession of the goods that they already possess on condition that the others do likewise for them. This is a coordinated course of conduct in which all parties benefit on condition that all participate; the common interest in this course of conduct can be mutually expressed and recognized; and a suitable resolution and behavior result. While this convention is not "natural" in the sense opposed to "artificial," it is "natural" in the sense opposed to "rare," since its possibility and utility are readily discoverable by humans beings; as Hume remarks, any parent must establish it in order to maintain peace among his or her children (THN 3.2.2.14/ 493). Additional rules governing acquisition and the transfer of possession by consent are equally "natural" additions to the convention in this sense, also as a result of their obvious utility. Indeed, the human needs for rules of (i) stability of possession, (ii) transfer of possession by consent, and (iii) promise-keeping are so great, and the conventional rules themselves so certain to arise through human invention, that he allows them to be called "laws of nature" (THN 3.2.6.1/526)—although their moral force arises from the felt virtue of their observance, not any divine command. The details of such conventional rules may differ somewhat from one society to another, and somewhat arbitrary ways of rendering the rules precise will often be needed to avoid disputes. Effective rules, however, often appeal in some way or other to the principles of association of ideas that govern the imagination [2.2]. Through the adoption of rules of justice, what was mere pre-conventional "possession" becomes conventional "property."

The primary and original motive to the adoption of the convention of justice, Hume emphasizes, is self-interest, though supplemented by highly partial benevolence: it allows one to acquire and retain possessions for oneself, and also for the benefit of one's family and friends. In this way, he explains, self-interest comes to "restrain itself": the very motive that threatened originally to destroy society through its unrestrained operation is recruited to redeploy itself in a more mutually beneficial direction. It does so by motivating the creation of a new convention and, at the same time, gives rise to a new motive that could not have existed before: the desire and standing disposition to govern or *regulate* one's behavior by the rules of property. To be sure, he notes, the full development and solidifying of this motive frequently depends on "repeated experience of the inconveniencies" (THN 3.2.2.10/490) of transgressing the convention. Nevertheless, the belief that such regulation is the most effective way to protect and increase one's possessions combines with previous desires for possessions to create a new desire to the perceived means. In coming to regulate one's behavior in this way, one undertakes to refrain from weighing up the specific advantages and disadvantages of following the rules of property before acting in each individual case, for such weighing would often lead to violations. Justice is a general policy or "scheme," one preferable relative to other schemes that might be considered and preferable to having no scheme at all.

As the scheme first develops, human beings recognize only what Hume calls indifferently a "self-interested obligation" or a "natural obligation" ("natural" in the sense of "non-moral") to justice. As previously observed [8.1], he holds that one has a moral "obligation" to a course of action when one would feel moral reproach for oneself for failing to perform it (THN 3.2.5.4/517). Thus, the interested or natural obligation to justice presumably lies in the tendency to feel non-moral prudential reproach for oneself for harming one's own interests by not acting in accordance with the convention. Individuals soon come to reflect, however, on the beneficial effects of the system or scheme of justice on the wellbeing of members of society generally. As they do so, they feel sympathetic pleasure in considering the character trait of regulating one's conduct in accordance with the rules of justice, and this sympathetic pleasure, as may be expected, will in turn produce moral approbation for those who have that trait. In this way, human beings come also to recognize a distinctively moral obligation to justice, reproaching themselves through sentiments of moral disapprobation for not maintaining a course of conduct in accordance with its rules.

From the First Virtuous Motive Principle, Hume derives a corollary that he calls "an undoubted maxim": "[N]o *action can be virtuous, or morally good, unless there be in human nature some motive to produce it, distinct from the sense of its morality*" (THN 3.2.1.7/479). This maxim is often confused with the First Virtuous Motive Principle itself, but they make different demands and are satisfied by different motives. Self-interest is an original non-moral motive "in human nature" that becomes capable of producing the full behavioral profile of just actions through its own conventional self-restraint, and it thereby satisfies the Undoubted Maxim. Because it is not—given its other characteristic products—itself a virtuous motive, self-interest cannot itself satisfy the First Virtuous Motive Principle, but it also creates through convention a new motive: the desire and disposition to regulate one's conduct by the rules of justice. Although this new motive is not original in human nature, and so cannot satisfy the Undoubted Maxim, it is virtuous and so does satisfy the First Virtuous Motive Principle. Because justice depends for its existence on the convention that makes this motive possible, justice is an artificial virtue.

## 8.4 Other artificial virtues

Fidelity, in the sense of keeping one's promises, is a second artificial virtue, dependent on a convention of its own (THN 3.2.5, "Of the obligation of promises"). In support of this thesis, Hume seeks to establish two distinct but related propositions: (1) "*that a promise woul'd not be intelligible before human conventions had established it*," and (2) "*that even if it were intelligible [without a convention], it wou'd not be attended with any moral obligation.*"

In defense of the first proposition, Hume offers two arguments. First, there is no "natural"—that is, in this context, non-artificial or non-conventional—act of the mind corresponding to the words, "I promise." It cannot be the formation of a resolution or intention, since this alone creates no new obligation. It cannot be desire, since we can promise to do what we do not desire to do; and it cannot be willing or volition, since that concerns the present rather than the future. Hence, the act of mind expressed by "I promise" can only be understood in terms of a convention. Second, promising is a way of voluntarily acquiring a new obligation to perform an action; yet obligation, as he has explained it [8.1, 8.3] depends essentially on sentiments, which cannot themselves simply be willed into existence. The creation of the new obligation, he proposes, can only be explained as the consequence of establishing a new relation between an action and an existing convention to which sentiments are already attached.

Hume offers two arguments in defense of the second proposition as well. The first argument invokes the same considerations as the previous argument: even if the mind could will a new obligation through promising, the obligation could have no moral character except through a relation to moral sentiments derived from the moral status of a convention. The second invokes the Undoubted Maxim that Hume has already derived from the First Virtuous Motive Principle [8.3]. That maxim requires that there be a motive in human nature to any virtuous act, yet in the absence of a convention there would be no motive capable of motivating the full behavioral profile of fidelity. The Undoubted Maxim can be satisfied only if the motive of self-interest, while not itself a virtuous one, can explain the creation of a convention that then generates a new motive capable of winning moral approbation and thereby conveying derivative moral approbation to the acts that manifest it. This is, in effect, an application of the Circle Argument to the case of promising.

Like the convention of property, the convention of promising arises, according to Hume, in response to a practical problem. In this case, parties who bear no particular affection for each other could each benefit from a mutual exchange of favors or possessions; but where this exchange cannot be simultaneous, the exchange seemingly will not take place because the first party to perform has no security about the later performance of the second party. In Hume's elegant example, two farmers may have crops maturing at different times, the harvesting of which require the efforts of both parties. The solution is a convention employing a particular form of words or other expression: all agree to carry out any action described with that form of expression, on the understanding that failure to do so will debar the offender from future participation in the convention with all its benefits. As in the case of the convention of property, the convention of promising introduces the possibility of a new motive related to it, consisting in a desire and standing disposition to regulate one's action in accordance with the rules of the convention. Consideration of the effects of this character trait on others leads again, through sympathy, to moral approbation. The self-interested obligation to the keeping of promises is thus supplemented by a moral obligation, and fidelity is recognized as a virtue.

In the concluding section of the second *Enquiry*, Hume writes, "Having explained the moral *approbation* attending merit or virtue, there remains nothing, but briefly to consider our interested *obligation* to it" (EPM 9.14/278). He notes that everyone will naturally want to have traits useful or agreeable to themselves, and that vanity even by itself is sufficient to make one desire to have traits that are immediately agreeable to others. This leaves only the interested obligation to the traits useful to others. Of these, the more sociable, such as benevolence, are among the best and surest paths to happiness; we must care about something in order to derive any enjoyments from life, and caring about the wellbeing of others proves to be an excellent source of enjoyment. He then turns to justice and fidelity, writing in a famous passage:

> Treating vice with the greatest candour, and making it all possible concessions, we must acknowledge, that there is not, in any instance, the smallest pretext for giving it the preference above virtue, with a view to self-interest; except, perhaps, in the case of justice, where a man, taking things in a certain light, may often seem to be a loser by his integrity. And though it is allowed, that, without a regard to property, no society could subsist; yet, according to the imperfect way in which human affairs are conducted, a sensible knave, in particular incidents, may think, that an act of iniquity or infidelity will make a considerable addition to his fortune, without causing any considerable breach in the social union and confederacy. That *honesty*

is the best policy, may be a good general rule; but is liable to many exceptions: And he, it may, perhaps, be thought, conducts himself with most wisdom, who observes the general rule, and takes advantage of all the exceptions.

I must confess, that, if a man think, that this reasoning much requires an answer, it will be a little difficult to find any, which will to him appear satisfactory and convincing. If his heart rebel not against such pernicious maxims, if he feel no reluctance to the thoughts of villainy or baseness, he has indeed lost a considerable motive to virtue; and we may expect, that his practice will be answerable to his speculation. But in all ingenuous natures, the antipathy to treachery and roguery is too strong to be counterbalanced by any views of profit or pecuniary advantage. Inward peace of mind, consciousness of integrity, a satisfactory review of our own conduct; these are circumstances very requisite to happiness, and will be cherished and cultivated by every honest man, who feels the importance of them.

(EPM 9.22–23/282–83)

In interpreting this passage, it is important to bear several points in mind. First, Hume is not proposing that moral obligation itself must be derived from or justified by self-interest. As he says, he has already explaining the moral approbation—and hence the moral obligation—attaching to virtue. Moral obligation applies regardless of whether there is also a self-interested obligation to virtue. Someone who behaved virtuously even at the expense of his or her own interests would not be behaving *irrationally* or even *unreasonably* in any sense by preferring virtue to self-interest, although such action might be *imprudent* [3.7]. Nevertheless, Hume holds that there *is* an interested obligation to virtue, even in the case of justice and fidelity, and that it is of great practical value to show that this is true. Were it not true, he remarks, someone who showed its falsity might be a good philosopher but could hardly be considered a friend to humankind.

Second, Hume is directly confronting an alternative policy to that of strict adherence to the rules of justice and fidelity—namely, the *knavish* policy of adherence to the rules whenever a violation would be detected or would carry no advantage in the particular case, while taking advantage of opportunities to violate the rules in other cases offering secrecy and advantage. Note, however, that even if this policy were in fact more beneficial than the policy of strict justice from the standpoint of self-interest, this need not undermine his account of the causal origin of the conventions of justice and fidelity in the motive of self-interest, so long as the alternative policy of sensible knavery was not considered and judged to be more beneficial in the original circumstances in which the convention arose.

Third, Hume is conceding that someone who lacked developed sentiments of moral approbation for justice and fidelity would also lack a particular motive to uniform adherence to justice and fidelity that others possess. In the absence of such a motive, therefore, such a person's own self-interest night be better served by the knavish policy than by the policy of strict adherence, although this is by no means guaranteed: as Hume points out, the danger that a sensible knave will be detected despite his or her best efforts is ever-present, and the security of knowing that such an event cannot befall the follower of strict adherence is a further self-interested advantage to the latter.

Finally, however, Hume insists that one who does feel approbation for justice and fidelity will enjoy a distinctive "peace of mind" and a positive pleasurable pride in "making a satisfactory review of one's own conduct" that are simply unavailable to sensible knaves, who must be aware that others would disapprove their characters were they known. For this reason and others, it is better, even from the point of view of self-interest, to maintain the virtues of justice and fidelity.

The advantages provided by justice and fidelity—including the honoring of commercial contracts—allow societies to grow larger. Yet the larger the society, the easier it becomes to violate rules of property and promise-keeping without detection. The natural human tendency to prefer nearer but lesser goods to greater but more distant ones will then lead many to violate the rules on occasion, and the recognition of that tendency will lead members of society to lose confidence in the continued adherence of others, undermining the conventions themselves. Dissatisfaction with the results of this tendency, aided crucially by the ability to prefer the greater good at times when *both* are quite distant, facilitates a conventional solution: the setting up of individuals whose own self-interest will be to enforce the rules of justice and fidelity, and a general conventional agreement to obey those individuals (THN 3.2.7, "Of the origin of government"). Governments provide not only greater security in the execution of justice and fidelity, but also more equitable and impartial decisions in cases of dispute. Equally important, they serve to coordinate individuals in pursuit of further advantages such as large-scale public works, for which only a government can manage the coordination of the large numbers of workers required.

In the case of many early societies, Hume allows, the original choice of a political leader may be accomplished through a promise, and for those who actually participate in it, such a promise can provide an additional moral obligation. A promise cannot bind later generations who are not parties to it, however, and the primary moral obligation to allegiance to government results from its direct usefulness to society; indeed, allegiance could be a virtue in the absence of any convention of promising at all. As with justice and fidelity, allegiance too improves human life by redirecting original passions through convention into more beneficial paths. Because allegiance is a virtue only through its utility, however, "an egregious tyranny in the rulers is sufficient to free the subjects from all ties of allegiance" by undermining its utility (THN 3.2.9.1/549).

Hume describes chastity (which he also calls "marital fidelity") and modesty (in the sense of sexual modesty, rather than the sense contrasted with proud deportment) as artificial virtues (THN 3.2.12, "Of chastity and modesty") as well. The institution of marriage, to which chastity refers, is clearly a convention; and he accepts the common suggestion that the primary purpose of marital fidelity is to provide security of paternity to fathers and thereby to support their affection for, and care of, children. The convention of modesty—manners of "backwardness" with respect to expressions, postures, and liberties relating to "the appetite of generation"—is intended to contribute to, and maintain the force of, chastity. While these are virtues for both sexes, he regards them as being of greater value in women because of the greater utility to society of their adherence. In this respect, he compares what he regards as the lesser obligation of men to chastity and modesty to the lesser obligation of princes to respect property and promises in their dealings with other princes (THN 3.2.11, "Of the laws of nations").

## 8.5 Moral diversity

Hume addresses diversity in moral judgment most directly in "A Dialogue," which appears, unnumbered, after the numbered appendixes to the second *Enquiry*. The character of Palamedes recounts the strange manners and morals encountered on a trip to the nation of "Fourli," which he soon reveals to be modeled on the ancient Greeks and Romans. Hume's first-person narrator responds that the same underlying principles of human nature are responsible for the differences in judgments, much as "the RHINE flows north, the RHONE south; yet both spring from the *same* mountain, and are also actuated, in their opposite directions, by the *same* principle of gravity" (EPM Dialogue 26/333). In the course of his writings, he discusses several different kinds of moral diversity.

One kind of moral diversity arises from differences of opinion concerning the causal consequences of characters or actions, matters of fact about which one party may be right and the other wrong. Since moral sentiments result chiefly from sympathy with those affected, according to Hume, such different opinions about the likely consequences of characters and actions can easily result in differences in moral judgment. Moral judgments about the willingness to assassinate tyrants, for example, differ in accordance with different factual judgments about the political consequences of both actual tyrannicide and the threat of its occurrence (EPM 2.19/180–81). The consequences of dueling provide a similar example (EPM Dialogue 34/335). Differing judgments about the moral permissibility of suicide often reflect different opinions about whether a deity has forbidden it and hence about the consequences of the act itself (EPM Dialogue 35/335). Just as the varying causal judgments at issue may be correct or incorrect, so too may the varying moral judgments depending on them.

In a second kind of moral diversity, one moral judgment may be correct and another incorrect through one party's greater capacity to approximate or anticipate the result of judging from the idealized point of view and with the idealized qualities of the standard of judgment [4.1]. Victors in war, for example, may sympathize with their leaders to the exclusion of more distant sufferers (THN 3.3.2.15/600–01), and other failures of sympathy may result from an exaggeration of superficial differences among persons that obscure their more fundamental human similarities (THN 2.1.11.8/319–20). In cases of these kinds, it seems reasonable to suppose, there may be moral progress in the application of an existing standard of judgment. Hume further remarks at the conclusion of "A Dialogue" that "religious superstition or philosophical enthusiasm"—he mentions Blaise Pascal (1623–62) and Diogenes (4th–3rd centuries BCE), respectively—can lead to the adoption of principles of conduct that so remove a person from the ordinary circumstances of human life as to prevent the operation of the "natural principles of the mind." In such cases, the sensitive qualities of individuals are diminished or perverted, hindering them from making sound judgments in much the same way that a visual deficiency undermines color judgments. It may also be more difficult for others to judge such products of "artificial lives" accurately, precisely because the removal from ordinary circumstances of human life makes it more difficult to trace the consequences of their unusual characters.

In a third kind of case, by contrast, the apparent disagreement may be resolved through relativization, allowing that the judgments of both parties are positively correct about the application of morality to their own social or cultural circumstances when differences in them give traits differing degrees of typical usefulness. (As remarked previously, Hume seems to allow a comparable relativization of probability judgments to different experiential bases [4.4]). Military courage, for example, is of greater utility, and is therefore a greater virtue, in societies in which individuals are constantly exposed to the threat of invasion and destruction from outside forces (EPM Dialogue 39/337). Many differences in conventional customs—for example, concerning modesty or forms of government—may themselves be morally innocent, but render particular character traits more or less useful in consequence (EPM Dialogues 49–51/340–41). Similarly, it is important that there be conventions governing such matters as the conveyance of property and the degree of blood relationship allowed in marriage, but it is often arbitrary exactly where the lines are to be drawn; in such cases as these, the virtuous disposition is the one that regulates behavior in accordance with the convention actually in place

(THN 3.2.3, "Of the rules, which determine property"). In extreme circumstances, such as a shipwreck or severe famine, the utility of any convention of justice may itself fail, bringing with it a release from the moral obligation to regulate actions in accordance with such a convention and making the regulating trait itself no longer a virtue (THN 3.2.2.16/494; EPM 3.12/188).

In a final kind of case, however, diversity in judgment is blameless in consequence of lack of precision in the standard of judgment itself [4.2]. Most notably, Hume urges, there are sometimes differences in response from sympathetically weighing degrees of tradeoffs between competing goods and harms that are not resolved by the standard. The relative values of greatness of mind as contrasted with goodness and benevolence may be one such case. Another, emphasized in "A Dialogue," lies in the different degrees of value that, he reports, the French and the English place on marital fidelity and "the gallantry of amours and attachments." Whereas the French sacrifice some of the utility of domestic fidelity and constancy in order to experience more of the agreeable qualities associated with ease, freedom, and openness of social commerce, the English sacrifice some of the agreeable for the sake of greater utility (EPM Dialogue 47–48/339–40).

Blameless diversity in balancing the degrees of virtues that may sometimes be in tension leads readily to blameless moral diversity in action. For example, while the rules of justice may themselves be exceptionless, and the virtue of justice consists in the disposition to regulate one's conduct by those rules, the virtue of justice does not necessarily trump all other virtues in value (THN 3.2.11.3/568). Under extreme circumstances—say, an act of returning property that would result in the destruction of all life on the planet—the virtuous person, we may expect, would display benevolence rather than strict adherence to the rules of justice. In more difficult cases, however, it might well be that either of two contrary actions might be at least permissible: one as displaying an admirable benevolence despite its troubling injustice, and the other as displaying an admirable commitment to justice even at the worrying expense of ignoring the call of benevolence.

Hume's moral theory allows for moral progress in several different respects. First, of course, there may be purely practical progress: recognized virtues may become more prevalent and vices less so, perhaps as the result of improved conditions of sociality and perhaps even as the result of the exhortations of moralists or the argued defenses of philosophers such as Hume. Second, there may be improvements in the science of morals itself. Moral distinctions may be more accurately drawn through increased understanding of human life and psychology, or through improved capacity to sympathize and otherwise imaginatively take up the point of view of the standard of morals. The proper scopes of relativization and blameless diversity may also come to be better understood. All such cognitive improvements may also lead to improvements in character. Finally, and more radically, the normative concepts VIRTUE and VICE themselves may continue to develop through time as new qualities or features of points of view are incorporated through convergence into the standard of judgment. This is comparable in some ways to the ongoing development of the concept PROBABILITY through the adoption of new rules of probability and the refinement of its standard in the centuries since Hume. In the case of morals, at least, changes in the standard of judgment may even be reflexively responsive to the felt moral value of adopting and honoring such refinements of the standard—or so we may hope.

## 8.6 Conclusion

Few philosophers have had more influence on recent and contemporary moral philosophy than Hume—both for what he actually argued and maintained and for what he has been thought to have argued and maintained. Hume's Law, interpreted as a formulation of a strong distinction between facts and values, is one example. Another lies in his role in debates about moral truth and moral motivation. Explicitly appealing to Hume's inspiration, Michael Smith has provided an influential formulation of what he calls "The Moral Problem," consisting in the incompatibility of three individually attractive theses:

*Moral Cognitivism*: Moral judgments express beliefs that are true or false.
*Moral Internalism*: Moral judgments are intrinsically motivating (to at least some extent).

*Belief/Desire Motivation:* No belief is intrinsically motivating; motivation always requires a corresponding desire or passion.[1]

It is sometimes suggested that Hume's solution to the problem would be to deny Moral Cognitivism [8.1]. Yet while moral sentiments—impressions of moral approbation or disapprobation—are not themselves true or false, the predicative moral judgments that employ moral concepts in accordance with a standard of judgment clearly are. Hume's own solution to the problem, I suggest, would be to distinguish the respects in which moral judgments are, and are not, "intrinsically" motivating.

First, it is not a metaphysically necessary truth (that is, not a relation of ideas in Hume's terminology) that sense-based judgments of character traits or actions motivate, at least if these judgments are understood narrowly as the classification of a character or action in the revival set of an abstract idea [2.4]. No substantive questions about actual causal relations can be *a priori* for Hume, and the ability of such judgments of characters and actions to contribute to the causation of volitions can only be a matter of fact dependent on human psychology and discovered by experience. Furthermore, given appropriate information or evidence, it is causally possible to make a particular predicative moral judgment, employing moral concepts such as VIRTUE and VICE, without at that very moment feeling any motivating force; in a similar way, it is possible, given appropriate information, to make a particular conceptualized predicative color judgment about an object without at that moment actually seeing it or receiving any sensation from it. On the other hand, the moral sentiments that are the ultimate source of moral distinctions and judgments are themselves pleasures and pains. In normal human psychology, these sentiments are therefore of precisely the right kind to exert at least some causal influence on volition whenever they occur. Furthermore, it is part of the attributed practical relations pertaining to the conceptual role of normative concepts generally that terms expressing them are "taken in a good [or bad] sense" [5.1], and anyone who uses such terms without some appreciation of and commitment to the qualities falling under the concepts has not fully incorporated their normative character into her or his own usage of the terms. When "intrinsic motivation" is understood in this limited psychological way, Moral Internalism is fully compatible with both Moral Cognitivism and Belief/Desire Motivation.

Hume's distinctive combination of moral sense theory and virtue ethics helps to justify other aspects of his moral theory as well. Partly because it is sense-based, it is *broad*, encompassing all kinds of mental traits, self-affecting as well as other-affecting, intellectual as well as affective, involuntary as well as voluntary. It is not *deontological*, or duty-centered: while Hume recognizes a motive of duty, and even allows it to be a kind of virtue, it is generally a second-best motive from a Humean moral perspective. The best parent, for example, acts from natural affection for children, the "first virtuous motive" to childcare; the parent who cares for his or her children only from duty is typically seeking either to hide the absence of this motive from himself or herself, or seeking to inculcate or encourage it through practice. It is also not *consequentialist*, or consequence-centered, however: while the consequences of actions typical of a mental trait play a crucial role in determining whether the trait will be approved by the moral sense, it is the moral sense itself, not the balance of consequences, that is the source of moral evaluations, and that sense fundamentally evaluates characters, not consequences.

Because Hume's moral sense is primarily responsive to pleasure and pain, and especially to sympathetic pleasure and pain, his moral philosophy is *non-austere*, valuing traits that are conducive to pleasure and disvaluing those—such as the "monkish virtues" of "celibacy, fasting, penance, mortification, self-denial, humility, silence, and solitude" [1.4, 9.7]—that are conducive to pain. On the contrary, in a flight of personification he writes:

> But what philosophical truths can be more advantageous to society, than those here delivered, which represent virtue in all her genuine and most engaging charms, and make us approach her with ease, familiarity, and affection? The dismal dress falls off, with which many divines, and some philosophers have covered her; and nothing appears but gentleness, humanity, beneficence, affability; nay even, at proper intervals, play, frolic, and gaiety ... . And if any austere pretenders approach her,

enemies to joy and pleasure, she either rejects them as hypocrites and deceivers; or if she admit them in her train, they are ranked, however, among the least favoured of her votaries.
(EPM 9.15/279)

For similar reasons, Hume's moral theory is also *non-rigorous*: while artificial virtues require regulating one's behavior by conventional rules without weighing the advantages and disadvantages in individual cases, the virtue of adhering depends on the utility of the convention and does not extend beyond the circumstances in which the convention retains its general utility. In his treatment of pride (and elsewhere) he treats the obligation to truthfulness as properly limited by the demands of sociability and politeness. Moreover, his moral theory is *pluralist*: the sense-based character of his moral philosophy, drawing as it does on an idealized point of view and respondent qualities, readily allows for some blameless diversity in judgments of character, and its treatment of character traits as the primary objects of evaluation for the fundamental normative concepts allows for further latitude of blameless diversity in the moral judgment of actions, which are evaluated only as signs or expressions of character. Finally, as we shall have greater occasion to observe in the next chapter, his moral theory is entirely *secular*: at no point does he appeal to any religious doctrines in the making of moral judgments.

In its independence of a deity, Hume's moral philosophy is naturalistic, and it is also naturalistic inasmuch as it does not invoke any explanatorily basic normative qualities; the normativity attaching to moral concepts is explicable instead by appeal to their actual role in human life. It is empiricist as well, inasmuch as it draws moral concepts and judgments from experience, without postulating substantive *a priori* moral principles [5.4]. Although they also typically serve—like all normative judgments—to express a social and personal commitment, Humean moral judgments can classify correctly or incorrectly, and hence they can be true or false. As such, they presumably fall within the scope of mitigated skepticism's universal diminution of degrees of probability. His moral theory is not radically skeptical, however. Instead, just as he rejects radical skepticism about the reality of aesthetic distinctions (such as that between the literary genius of "Ogilby and Milton" in "Of the Standard of Taste," EMPL I.23: 230), and ultimately rejects skepticism about the reality of distinctions of probability [7.3], so too he rejects radical skepticism about the reality of moral distinctions. Indeed, just as overcoming radical skepticism about the reality of aesthetic distinctions and probability distinctions requires the passage of time and the return of sensibility, so too does the overcoming of radical skepticism about moral distinctions:

> Those who have denied the reality of moral distinctions, may be ranked among the disingenuous disputants; nor is it conceivable, that any human creature could ever seriously believe, that all characters and actions were alike entitled to the affection and regard of every one. The difference, which nature has placed between one man and another, is so wide, and this difference is still so much farther widened, by education, example, and habit, that, where the opposite extremes come at once under our apprehension, there is no scepticism so scrupulous, and scarce any assurance so determined, as absolutely to deny all distinctions between them, Let a man's insensibility be ever so great, he must often be touched with the images of RIGHT and WRONG; and let his prejudices be ever so obstinate, he must observe, that others are susceptible of like impressions. The only way, therefore, of converting an antagonist of this kind, is to leave him to himself. For, finding that no body keeps up the controversy with him, it is probable he will, at least, of himself, from mere weariness, come over to the side of common sense and reason.
> 
> (EPM 1.2/169–70)

The final sentence of the *Treatise* pronounces moral precepts to constitute a "science" [5.4], confirming the initial ambition of its Introduction to contribute to the science of "Morals" through its development of the science of man [1.2].

## Note

1 Michael Smith (1994) *The Moral Problem*, Malden: Blackwell Publishing.

## Further reading

Abramson, Kate (2002) "Two Portraits of the Humean Moral Agent," *Pacific Philosophical Quarterly* 83.4: 301–34. (Compares goodness and greatness of mind in Hume to explain the nature of moral motivation in his spectator-centered theory of moral judgment.)

Baillie, James (2000) *Routledge Philosophy Guidebook to Hume on Morality*, Oxford: Routledge. (A good guide to Hume's moral theory, focused on the *Treatise*.)

Botros, Sophie (2008) *Hume, Reason and Morality: A Legacy of Contradiction*, London: Routledge. (A highly critical examination of Hume's argument that moral distinctions are not derived from reason.)

Brown, Charlotte (1994) "From Spectator to Agent," *Hume Studies* 20.1: 19–35. (An important article on the question of how Hume's moral sense virtue ethics can serve to generate desires and guide voluntary action.)

Cohon, Rachel (2008) *Hume's Morality: Feeling and Fabrication*, New York: Oxford University Press. (An essential recent commentary defending the interpretation that Hume regards moral judgments as susceptible to truth and falsehood; it also offers a different account of Hume's argument that justice is an artificial virtue, one according to which artificial virtues violate the Virtue Ethics Thesis.)

Darwall, Stephen (1993) "Motive and Obligation in Hume's Ethics," *Noûs* 27.4: 415–48. (An important and influential critical treatment of Hume's theories of motivation and obligation, with special relation to the question of the nature of the obligation to justice.)

Garrett, Don (1997) *Cognition and Commitment in Hume's Philosophy*. New York: Oxford University Press. (Chapter 9 defends the interpretation of Humean moral judgments as true or false, employing abstract ideas derived from moral sentiments.)

Garrett, Don (2007) "The First Motive to Justice: Hume's Circle Argument Squared," *Hume Studies* 33.2: 257–88. (Defends in detail, and against other interpretations, the interpretation presented here of Hume's argument that justice and fidelity are artificial virtues.)

Garrett, Don (2008) "Feeling and Fabrication: Rachel Cohon's *Hume's Morality*" [book symposium], *Hume Studies*, 34.2: 257–66 (A critical examination of Cohon 2008, above.)

Gill, Michael (2006) *The British Moralists and the Birth of Secular Ethics*, Cambridge: Cambridge University Press. (Contains a good historical account of Hume's place in seventeenth- and eighteenth-century British moral philosophy.)

Radcliffe, Elizabeth S. (1996) "How Does the Humean Moral Sense Motivate?" *Journal of the History of Philosophy* 34.3: 383–407. (An analysis of Hume's "sense of duty" and a defense of interpreting Hume as a moral internalist.)

Sayre-McCord, Geoffrey (2008) "Hume on Practical Morality and Inert Reason," *Oxford Studies in Metaethics* 3: 299–320. (A valuable treatment and interpretation of the Representation Argument and the Motivation Argument.)

Smith, Michael (1994) *The Moral Problem*, Malden: Blackwell Publishing. (A lucid and compelling presentation of "The Moral Problem" of reconciling morality's motivational force with its truth-conduciveness and the belief/desire theory of motivation; offers a proposed solution different from that attributed here to Hume.)

Taylor, Jacqueline (2012) "Hume on the Dignity of Pride," *Journal of Scottish Philosophy* 10: 29–49. (An excellent account of well-regulated pride as a source of virtue.)

# Nine
Religion and God

The topic of religion in its various aspects—its psychology, its epistemology, its metaphysics, its history, and its bearing on morals and human life—appears with great frequency throughout Hume's writings, and perhaps no topic is of greater practical significance in his overall philosophical project. Adam Smith reports in his final reminiscence [1.7] that Hume, anticipating his own imminent death, jocularly imagined making a plea to Charon, the boatman of Hades, for additional time: "I have been endeavouring to open the eyes of the Public. If I live a few years longer, I may have the satisfaction of seeing the downfall of some of the prevailing systems of [religious] superstition." Yet Hume imagined Charon replying, "That will not happen these many hundred years. Do you fancy I will grant you a lease for so long a term? Get into the boat this instant, you lazy loitering rogue" (EMPL "Letter from Adam Smith": xliii–xlix).

Religion is the source of many of the psychological "experiments" that Hume describes in *A Treatise of Human Nature*, and despite his late excision of a discussion of miracles [1.2], his readers would readily have observed the work's irreligious implications. These include the rejection of the immateriality of the soul as well as the denial of the demonstrability of the Causal Maxim that was charged with leading "to downright Atheism" in the successful effort to exclude him from the chair of philosophy at the University of Edinburgh. As Paul Russell has shown, however, there were many others.[1] Hume's account of the origin of the belief in bodies, for example, would have been seen to deny the Cartesian doctrine that

God is not a deceiver. And his claim that all "nice and subtle questions concerning personal identity can never possibly be decided, and are to be regarded rather as grammatical than as philosophical difficulties" (THN 1.4.6.21/262)—because they are a matter of degree without a decisive standard—would be seen to undermine immortality and the justice of divine rewards and punishments. At the conclusion of Book 1, of course, he endorses philosophy over religion as a guide to speculation (THN 1.4.7.13/271–72) [7.3].

More explicitly, *An Enquiry concerning Human Understanding* begins by taking as its central purpose the chasing of religious "superstition" from its lair in philosophy; proceeds by drawing from its account of probable reasoning and causation a set of irreligious consequences concerning free will, miracles, and providence; and concludes with a call to commit volumes of "divinity or school metaphysics" to "the flames" as containing "nothing but sophistry and illusion." *An Enquiry concerning the Principles of Morals* criticizes religious conceptions of the proper allocation of property and famously attacks "the monkish virtues" [1.4, 8.6], while giving religion no positive role to play in moral epistemology or moral motivation. "Of Immortality" and "Of Suicide," the two suppressed essays originally intended for what became *Four Dissertations* [1.5], argue against the immortality of the soul and against a religious (or other general) duty to preserve one's life. *The Natural History of Religion*, analyzes the psychology of religious belief (as does the essay "Of Superstition and Enthusiasm") and traces the dynamics of polytheism and monotheism, while the *History of England* repeatedly highlights the dangers of religion and religious conflict in the political life of the nation. Hume's final work, *Dialogues concerning Natural Religion*, remains one of the most influential and widely read works ever written in the philosophy of religion.

## 9.1 Religious belief

In the opening paragraph of *The Natural History of Religion*, Hume defines 'religion' as "belief of invisible, intelligent power." In two obvious senses of 'power', of course, all power is always invisible for Hume. First, understood as a feeling of the determination of an observer's mind, it is not seen but felt as an impression of reflection. Second, as the quality by which a cause produces its effect, it is attributed *as* power only through inference from experience of constant conjunction [4.3]. Moreover, many religions have recognized deities that were either extended or capable of taking on extended forms and so, at least in principle, visible. What Hume evidently means by this definition is that religion is a belief in one or more intelligent beings whose supposed production of effects is typically not visible even in the way in which the occurrence of an instance of a causal regularity (such as one billiard ball's striking and moving another) is often visible to an ordinary observer having a sufficient range of past experience. This may be because the agent itself is always or usually invisible or specially protected from view even where its most important effects are produced, or because (as with the sun or an idol taken as deities) the agent undergoes no visible change or exertion in producing any of its distinctive or most impressive effects.

Hume holds that religious belief, so defined, is pervasive but by no means universal among human beings. Among reflective individuals, it may arise in the attempt to discern or explain the cause or causes of order and adaptation observed in the universe. By "order" (which he contrasts with "confusion" and "corruption") Hume means the regular repetition of harmonious patterns. By "adaptation" (which he also calls "final causation" in accordance with common terminology, although he denies that this phenomenon constitutes a distinct kind of causation [6.3]) he means the tendency of parts to interact so as to maintain the existence of the whole of which they are parts, with the nature of the interaction varying in particular circumstances so as to produce whatever is required for the achieving of that outcome. Order and adaptation are for him undeniable aspects of the universe, although the cause or causes of their existence can be—and in the *Dialogues* are—debated. The vast preponderance of religious belief, however, arises not from such a search for causes of order and adaptation, but rather from the uncertainty and danger of human life, and from the hope and fear that these uncertain and dangerous circumstances elicit from human beings. The unknown causes of success and disaster, he explains, are readily personified by the imagination, where images of active intelligent beings are prevalent from ordinary social life, and this process of personification offers the prospect of what is most ardently desired: a potential source of protection and favor. To the extent that religion is motivated by fear, it is "superstition" in Hume's terminology; to the extent that it is motivated by hope, it is "enthusiasm." All popular (that is, non-philosophical) religion involves a mixture of superstition and enthusiasm, he holds, but among varieties of Christian religion he identifies Catholicism as more superstitious and Protestantism as generally more enthusiastic.

Yet while religion itself is pervasive, it is highly variable both in its representations of intelligent invisible power and in its practices with respect to such power. Hume argues from history that the original form of popular religion was polytheistic, recognizing many different deities; and such a form of religion is, he holds, also the most natural in light of the incessant reverses of human affairs. However, the desire to win the favor of a particularly powerful deity leads naturally to ever-increasing praise of it, until that deity is represented as supreme, all-knowing, and all-powerful. Thus arises what we would call "monotheism" and Hume calls simply "theism." Yet the striving to bestow supreme praise on this being naturally brings with it the denial of aspects of human personality, now considered as imperfections, with a subsequent diminution in the mind's ability to imagine and embrace this deity. Ultimately, therefore, there arises a counter-pressure within monotheism to introduce subsidiary deity-like figures, such as Mary and the saints of Roman Catholicism, to serve as intermediaries. This dynamic Hume calls "the flux and reflux of theism and polytheism."

Religious belief is often enlivened by the force of passions, Hume recognizes, and it can therefore be very strong indeed. These passions are inconstant, however, and the liveliness of religious belief is therefore often much weaker and more fluctuating than usually supposed. This tendency to weakness is exacerbated by the fact that the object of belief is often rather indeterminate and difficult to imagine, especially in the case of monotheism. For this reason, he proposes that hypocrisy is a particular occupational hazard for the clergy, as they are required by the duties of their profession to appear to maintain a constant high degree of confident belief and even religious fervor, despite the fact that such consistently high degrees of belief in matters of religion are psychologically impossible to sustain. Despite the high and unpleasant pitch to which terrors of eternal punishment can rise in times of crisis, he holds, it is particularly difficult for anyone to maintain robust belief in a set of divinely instituted rewards and punishments in an afterlife. This is evident from the pleasurable tingle people often experience when listening to preaching on this subject, a pleasure that shows that the representations in question are more like the briefly rousing simulacra of belief found in "poetical enthusiasms" than like firm and solid beliefs. The difficulty of sustaining genuine belief in an afterlife results not merely from the supposed distance in time, he argues, since people regularly show themselves to be very concerned about what will happen to their loved ones, reputation, and possessions after their deaths; rather, it results primarily from a lack of resemblance between the present life and the imagined or supposed afterlife (THN 1.3.9.13–15/113–15).

## 9.2 The Design Argument

Whereas *The Natural History of Religion* concerns the origin and development of religion from principles of human nature generally, *Dialogues concerning Natural Religion* considers the extent to which religion can be derived specifically from reason. In the latter work, young Pamphilus recounts to an absent friend a series of twelve dialogues he has heard among Philo, Cleanthes, and Demea. It is sometimes disputed which character, if any, speaks for Hume in the *Dialogues*, but only Philo shares Hume's skeptical disposition, and only he never states views that are materially at odds with Hume's own views as expressed elsewhere in his writings. Although Philo and Cleanthes live as friends in "unreserved intimacy" (DNR 12.2/214), and Hume clearly wants to demonstrate how such friendships can be preserved without being undermined by contention, it is reasonable to take Philo as Hume's spokesman.

Hermippus remarks at the outset that dialogues can be considered the most suitable form for writing philosophy in either of two circumstances: when a doctrine is obvious but nevertheless important to reinforce, or when a question is obscure and uncertain. He then observes that these circumstances are combined in the topic of natural religion: for while the existence of a God is undisputed, the divine nature is obscure. Philo agrees that there can be no question among "reasonable men" concerning "the being of a Deity" but only concerning its nature. However, this is because 'God', for the purposes of the dialogues, is understood simply to mean "the cause or causes of order and adaptation in the universe." Because both Hume and Philo treat "the world" or "the universe" as potentially temporary and local arrangements of things that might have outside and antecedent causes, God might be an antecedently existing being, operating in accordance with causal laws. Because Hume holds that regularities in nature may sometimes be causally explained as instances of some more general regularities, however, it is in no way ruled out that God might instead be simply a principle of order inherent in nature and its laws. Philo accepts the existence of a Deity because: (i) he does not dispute the existence of notable harmonious patterns, for example in the structure of the solar system, or the prevalence of adaptations of means to end, especially in biology; and (ii) he does not deny that these features should have some causal explanation, of at least one of the two kinds just mentioned. What he questions is only the extent to which this cause or these causes should be understood to be intelligent or mind-like.

Cleanthes, who shares Philo's empiricist view that any knowledge of God's nature would have to be derived from experience, proposes the argument that provides the chief topic—and target—of the first eight dialogues. This argument is a version of the Design Argument, and it is an instance of "analogy," which Hume classifies as one of three species of sub-proof probability [3.4]:

> The curious adapting of means to ends, throughout all nature, resembles exactly, though it much exceeds, the productions of human contrivance; of human design, thought, wisdom, and intelligence. Since therefore the effects resemble each other, we are led to infer, by all the rules of analogy, that the causes also resemble; and that the Author of Nature is somewhat similar to the mind of man; though possessed of much larger faculties, proportioned to the grandeur of the work, which he has executed. By this argument *a posteriori*, and by this argument alone, do we prove at once the existence of a Deity, and his similarity to human mind and intelligence.
>
> (DNR 2.5/143)

It is typical for sense-based concepts to acquire rules for judging [4.1, 4.3–4]. Accordingly, "all the rules of analogy" are simply those rules for judging probability that are specific to analogy as one species of probability. Cleanthes does not contest Philo's reminder that, because we have no direct experience of the origins of other worlds, the argument can be based only on analogy. Whereas Cleanthes holds that his argument conforms well to "all the rules of analogy," however, Philo denies this conformity.

First, Philo offers positive disanalogies between machines created by human beings, on the one hand, and the universe and its parts not created by human beings, on the other (DNR 2.7–8/144). Second, he criticizes, as disapproved by the rules, the extending of an explanation of such a small part of the universe—especially one so closely related to ourselves, to whom we are naturally partial—to an explanation of the whole (DNR 2.17–23/147–49). Third, he argues that endorsing the analogy leads to "inconveniences" such as denying the infinity, infallibility, and uniqueness of the Deity, while supporting the attribution to the Deity or deities of such characteristics as a human physical form, sex, dotage, and susceptibility to death (DNR 5).

Most importantly, however, Philo proposes alternative explanations of adaptation or final causes that deserve to be considered, in accordance with the rules, worthy or even superior competitors to intelligent design (DNR 6–7). While the world resembles a machine of intelligent human design to some extent, he concedes, it also resembles, perhaps to a greater extent, an animal or a plant. Hence, he distinguishes four possible causes of order and adaptation: (i) reason (the basis of intelligent design, by its discovery of causal means to given ends); (ii) instinct; (iii) animal generation (by means of sexual reproduction and gestation); and (iv) vegetation (by means of propagation). Of these, animal generation seems to have an advantage over reason, inasmuch as beings capable of animal generation and vegetation have never been observed to result from intelligent design on the part of a rational being, whereas rational beings (and also beings with instinct) are frequently observed to result from animal generation. To propose that this observed animal generation must itself have arisen originally from intelligent design is, in the absence of any observation of its occurrence, simply to beg the question. Animal bodies and human minds are both observed to be orderly systems exhibiting adaptation of means to ends; it is no explanatory advance, Philo argues, merely to make an arbitrary postulation that the orderliness of bodies is to be explained by the orderliness of a mind without offering any explanation for the orderliness of that mind (DNR 4).

Finally, Philo offers two additional causal hypotheses that do not require intelligent design for the order and adaptation present in the universe (DNR 8). The first he identifies with Epicurus (341–271 BCE): that a finite amount of matter operating in an infinite amount of time must take on every possible form at some time or other—including those exhibiting the order and adaptation that we see. The second dispenses with the assumptions of infinite time and finite matter, and proposes instead that there are a number of orderly and self-maintaining forms that matter can take on. Although the world's falling into these forms without guidance may take a very long time and sustain many temporary reverses along the way, once it is achieved the forms may persist indefinitely. He adds that Cleanthes's own argument from analogy is actually contrary to experience in at least three respects: (i) in human experience, ideas are ultimately copied from objects, rather than objects being copied ultimately from ideas; (ii) in human experience, intelligence is always physically embodied; and (iii) in human experience, intelligent agents cannot directly move anything other than their own bodies.

For his part, Cleanthes defends his argument from analogy with meta-analogies—that is, analogies drawn between his argument from analogy and other arguments. Two of these meta-analogies are with what he takes to be fictional but nonetheless clearly strong arguments from analogy for the intelligent origin of other, invented phenomena (DNR 3). The first concerns the fictional case of articulate speech from the heavens heard by all humankind in every known language. Although the cause of the voice in this example is not seen, Cleanthes proposes that the degree of resemblance between this effect and human speech would render the inference to an intelligent source irresistible. The second concerns an imagined library of books that reproduce themselves as animals do. Even though each observed book would have been produced by animal reproduction, Cleanthes urges, the intelligence manifest in the contents of the books would still demand an intelligent author for the library as a whole. In the face of these fictional analogies, plus striking actual instances of adaptation of means to ends such as the human eye, Philo is, in the words of Pamphilus, "a little bit embarrassed and confounded" (DNR 3.10/155). This is because he feels the immediate force of Cleanthes's argument *despite* the fact that it does not accord with "all the rules of probability" as he understands them. In Cleanthes's own view, Philo's objections are "whimsies that may puzzle, but can never convince."

Cleanthes's third meta-analogy exploits Philo's embarrassment at his own surge of felt conviction in order to draw an analogy between conclusions about probability (and specifically, the probability of analogy) and conclusions about beauty as they concern the relation between standards and rules of judgment:

> Some beauties in writing we may meet with, which seem contrary to rules, and which gain the affections, and animate the imagination, in opposition to all the precepts of criticism, and to the authority of the established masters of art. And if the argument for Theism be, as you pretend, contradictory to the principles of logic; its universal, its irresistible influence proves clearly, that there may be arguments of a like irregular nature. Whatever cavils may be urged; an orderly world, as well as a coherent, articulate speech, will still be received as an incontestable proof of design and intention.
>
> (DNR 3.8/155)

Philo concedes that this point about "irregular arguments" has some force—as must Hume himself. For both "rules of art" and "rules of analogy" are experientially based rules for judging that serve to anticipate what the results of the application of the relevant associated standard of judgment, for beauty or for probability respectively, would be [4.1, 4.4]. Accordingly, where the tendency to a particular sensitive response to a particular kind of stimulus is so firmly embedded in human nature as to remain invincibly present even from the idealized point of view and with the idealized qualities of the developed standard of judgment, the rules must ultimately accommodate that standard response, and not vice versa. Thus, Philo remarks in retrospect:

> Formerly, when we argued concerning the natural attributes of intelligence and design, I needed all my sceptical and metaphysical subtilty to elude your grasp. In many views of the universe and of its parts, particularly the latter, the beauty and fitness of final causes strike us with such irresistible force, that all objections appear (what I believe they really are) mere cavils and sophisms; nor can we then imagine how it was ever possible for us to repose any weight on them.
> (DNR 10.37/201)

Even where an aesthetic response is persistent for all respondents exemplifying the standard, however, the response may persist with different degrees of strength in different individuals with different temperaments or even in the same individuals in different circumstances or moods at different times; and the precise degree of aesthetic value may therefore remain a matter of blameless diversity. Precisely the same point proves to be true of degrees of response to the "irregular" argument for an intelligent cause of the order and adaptation in the universe. Some, like Cleanthes, are "philosophical Theists," who find the irregular argument quite forceful and the explanatory alternatives quite weak, and so endeavor to draw inferences about the divine nature from the irregular argument. Others, like Philo, are "philosophical Sceptics," who are less fully moved by the irregular argument and feel the force of objections to it more strongly; accordingly, they try to resist drawing inferences about the divine nature (DNR 12.32/226–27). Part of the purpose of the *Dialogues*, we may infer, is to model the way in which interlocutors of good faith and humanity who differ in this way can remain friends.

## 9.3 The Argument *A Priori*

The *Dialogues* also examines a second argument for the existence of God (DNR 9). This argument is proposed by Demea, who joins Philo in denying knowledge of the divine attributes while he rejects the shared commitment of Philo and Cleanthes to the use of the experimental method in theological matters. He calls his argument the "argument *a priori*," and it is modeled on the argument of the same name by Samuel Clarke, whom Cleanthes subsequently quotes. The argument may be outlined in Hume's own words as follows:

{1} Whatever exists must have a cause or reason of its existence.
{2} We must either go on in tracing an infinite succession [of causes and effects], without any ultimate cause at all, or must at last have recourse to some ultimate first cause, that is *necessarily* existent. (from {1})
{3} [An eternal succession] requires a cause or reason, as much as any particular object, which begins to exist in time. (from {1})
{4} We must ... have recourse to a necessarily existent Being, who carries the REASON of his existence in himself; and who cannot be supposed not to exist without an express contradiction. (from {2} and {3})
{5} There is a [necessarily existent] Deity. (from {4})

The strategy of the argument is thus to make a double employment of a *principle of sufficient reason* ({1}). The first use is to establish a disjunction ({2}): either there is an infinite succession of causes and effects, or there is a being that is or contains the reason for its own existence by existing necessarily. The second use is to argue that the first alternative, the infinite series of causes and effects, would itself require a cause or reason for *its* existence ({3}), and that this cause or reason would have to be a being containing the reason for its own existence ({4}). On either alternative, therefore, there must be a being that contains the reason for its own existence by existing necessarily, and this condition can only be satisfied by a being the non-existence of which would be "an express contradiction" ({4}). This necessarily existent being is identified as God or the Deity ({5}).

Hume allows Cleanthes to provide the primary objections to this argument; Philo explicitly agrees with them, adding only supporting observations and the remark that the argument is seldom found convincing except by metaphysicians. Cleanthes objects first that it seems that the argument cannot be a demonstration of the existence of God, as pretended, for demonstrations show the denial of their conclusions to be inconceivable, whereas the non-existence of anything is always at least conceivable. Second, from this general conceivability of non-existence, it follows by the Conceivability Principle that there is no such thing as necessary existence. Hence, there is no genuine disjunction in {2}: a thing's existence can only be explained by its cause, and not, as required in {4}, by a "reason" contained in its own nature. By supposing that our "faculties" might cease to "remain as they are at present," we can in effect endeavor to form merely relative ideas of an unknown kind of ideas, representing unknown qualities, that would show the non-existence of something to be contradictory and so its existence necessary after all. Even on that supposition, however, there would be no reason to suppose that the necessary existent should be mind rather than matter itself. Hence, the conclusion could not in any case be a *religious* one, legitimizing assent to belief in invisible *intelligent* power. Finally, Cleanthes argues, successions do not require further causes of the whole in addition to the causes of their elements, any more than twenty particles of matter taken together require a cause in addition to the causes of the individual particles themselves. Hence, step {3} does not follow from step {1}.

In Hume's view, then, an infinite succession of causes and effects fully satisfies the principle of sufficient reason stated in {1}. Analogously, we may suppose, he regards the complete uniformity of nature as sufficiently explained through the causal explanation of *each instance* of the uniformity in nature through appeal to the most general causal laws, without the need for any separate or additional explanation of why nature is uniform *as a whole*. It is worth emphasizing, however, that he is not positively committed by his own Causal Maxim [6.1] to an infinite succession of causes and effects. For that maxim requires not that *everything that exists* have a cause, but rather that *every beginning of existence* have a cause. Because he regards time and duration as possible only with change [2.5], there may exist (i) a first moment of time consisting in the existence of some $x$, and (ii) a second moment of time consisting in the existence of $x$ and some further $y$, with $y$ caused to exist by $x$. Moreover, it is possible that there be only a finite number of further changes—and hence of moments of time—between these first two moments and the present. Yet since $x$ did not at any time come into existence in this account, its uncaused existence would not violate Hume's Causal Maxim.

## 9.4 Evil

Demea and Philo agree about the extent of evil and its role in generating religious devotion; as Philo puts it, "I am indeed persuaded that the best and indeed the only method of bringing every one to a due sense of religion is by just representations of the misery and wickedness of men" (DNR 10.2/193). For Hume, of course, this is because evil produces the fear that leads directly to religious superstition and the enlivening of religious belief. At the same time, however, the existence of evil poses a direct challenge to Cleanthes's attribution of good moral character to God. Thus, immediately after conceding the "irresistible force" produced in support of divine intelligence and design by the order and adaptation in some parts of the universe, Philo goes on to draw a contrast between the attribute of intelligence and moral attributes such as benevolence:

> But there is no view of human life, or of the condition of mankind, from which, without the greatest violence, we can infer the moral attributes, or learn that infinite benevolence, conjoined with infinite power and infinite wisdom, which we must discover by the eyes of faith alone. It is your turn now to tug the labouring oar, and to support your philosophical subtilties against the dictates of plain reason and experience.
> (DNR 10.36/202)

Philo echoes "Epicurus's old questions" about God: "Is he willing to prevent evil, but not able? then is he impotent. Is he able, but not willing? then is he malevolent. Is he both able and willing? whence then is evil?" (DNR 10.25/198).

Demea proposes that an afterlife will provide compensation for the great evils of the present existence. Cleanthes, however, is committed to probable reasoning as the only way to establish conclusions about God, and hence he cannot accept an inference to a happy afterlife unless it is based on a present life in which good already predominates over evil. He further suggests that Epicurus's question may be resolved compatibly with divine benevolence by the hypothesis that whatever evil does exist results from limitations on God's power.

As Philo emphasizes, however, the question for Cleanthes is not what might be compatible with divine goodness and benevolence, but rather what experience renders most probable about it. He employs a common distinction between two kinds of evil: "natural" and "moral." Natural evil consists in pain, suffering, and disappointment from causes other than vicious actions; moral evil consists in the occurrence of vicious actions and their harmful consequences. He then distinguishes four general causes that make natural evil in the world much more common than seems needed for any greater good. First, human beings and animals are susceptible to intense pain, when it seems that differing degrees of pleasure would be sufficient to motivate actions. Second, the universe is governed by general laws that often have great pain and suffering among their consequences. Unnoticed divine interventions, contrary to the general laws, could serve to prevent much of this suffering. (Of course, Philo notes, it is conceivable that there already are unnoticed divine interventions; but the amount of suffering suggests that there are not, and that the number of such interventions could be increased even if there are.) Third, the natural endowments of animals in terms of strength, speed, protection, and intelligence are quite scanty—typically sufficient to sustain life in some circumstances, but not as great as would be useful or desirable. The human advantage in intelligence is balanced by a poverty of endowments, relative to other animals, in almost every other respect. Indeed, even the single endowment of a naturally more industrious disposition—that is, a lesser tendency to laziness—would be of enormous benefit to human beings and would be sufficient to render their lives much happier and more secure. Finally, while the forces of nature—for example, wind, rain, sun, and geological forces—are often useful, they are at best loosely adjusted to human benefit and all too frequently exceed their useful bounds in hurricanes, floods, and earthquakes. Something similar is true of the passions, understood as psychological forces of nature.

Philo distinguishes four possible hypotheses about the source or sources of the natural phenomena we see: (i) the source is all good; (ii) the source is all evil; (iii) a good source battles with an evil force, as in Manichaeism; and (iv) the source is indifferent to good and evil. The phenomena we see are logically compatible with any of the four hypotheses, he emphasizes. Nevertheless, the extent of both good and evil render the first two hypotheses less probable on the evidence, while the way in which good and evil are mixed indiscriminately through the operation of uniform laws renders the third relatively improbable as well. The most probable hypothesis on the available observational evidence, he concludes, is that the cause of order in the universe is indifferent to good and evil.

This indifference, Philo continues, applies not only to natural evil but also to moral evil, which is perhaps even more prevalent. Human beings are often deficient in both benevolence (that is, concern for the happiness and wellbeing of others) and rectitude (that is, concern for virtue as such). The natural evils of the worlds provide evidence against divine benevolence, and the limitation of both benevolence and rectitude among human beings is similar evidence against God's own rectitude. On the evidence, then, it is improbable that God—whatever it may be—has a moral sense of the kind required, in human beings, to appreciate and value virtue. As Hume also emphasizes in his discussion of liberty and necessity in the first *Enquiry* [6.4], it is difficult to avoid attributing culpability for evil to a God conceived as standing at the source of a world that is deterministic in its operations.

## 9.5 True religion

Hume uses the term 'true religion' over twenty times in his writings—typically to refer to whatever religious doctrines are taken to be true by the historical figures or other individuals he is discussing at the time. In the opening lines of "Of Superstition and Enthusiasm," however, he writes in his own voice of "the corruption of true religion" by superstition and enthusiasm as an example of "the worst" things being produced by the corruption of "the best" (EMPL I.10: 73; see also HE III.29: 135 for a similar passage). In the final dialogue of *Dialogues concerning Natural Religion*, moreover, Philo professes a "veneration for true religion" to be among his "unfeigned sentiments" (DNR 12.9/219). This "true religion," he claims, is a "speculative tenet of Theism" that is a "species of philosophy" (DNR 12.22/223).

The content of this speculative tenet emerges at the beginning of Philo's final speech, where it serves to summarize what he himself has been arguing:

> If the whole of Natural Theology, as some people seem to maintain, resolves itself into one simple, though somewhat ambiguous, at least undefined proposition, *That the cause or causes of order in the universe probably bear some remote analogy to human intelligence*: If this proposition be not capable of extension, variation, or more particular explication: If it affords no inference that affects human life, or can be the source of any action or forbearance: And if the analogy, imperfect as it is, can be carried no farther than to the human intelligence; and cannot be transferred, with any appearance of probability, to the other qualities of the mind; If this really be the case, what can the most inquisitive, contemplative, and religious man do more than give a plain, philosophical assent to the proposition, as often as it occurs; and believe that the arguments on which it is established, exceed the objections which lie against it?
>
> (DNR 12.33/227)

As Philo notes, the italicized proposition makes no claim at all about the moral qualities of the cause or causes of order in the universe, and it carries no implications for the conduct of human life. In order to understand why he characterizes it as "ambiguous, or at least undefined," however, it is necessary to understand two different "verbal disputes" that he has discussed earlier in the dialogue. Each dispute arises from, and is merely verbal because of, the absence of a "standard" for the application of concepts of degree.

The first verbal dispute is that between "Theists" and "Atheists." It is specific to theology, and it arises from the absence of any precise standard for degrees of resemblance applicable to the analogy between order and adaptation in products of human intelligent design, on the one hand, and order and adaption in nature and its (other) parts, on the other. Philo accepts the prevalence of instances of order and adaptation in nature, and especially in biology, but he also emphasizes their difference from instances of human intelligent design. Accordingly, he maintains, everyone—professed theists and professed atheists alike—must grant both that the "works of nature bear a great analogy to the productions of art" (DNR 12.6/216) *and* that there must be "vast differences" between the Deity and what we understand by 'mind' or 'intelligence' from experience with our own fleeting ideas and impressions. If we wish to "vary the expression" from 'God' or 'Deity', Philo allows, we may call that being "Mind" or "Thought" on the basis of "some considerable resemblance"; but the crucial question of the degree of resemblance—whether "some" or "great" or "very great"—simply "admits of [no] exact mensuration, which may be the standard in the controversy." Furthermore, all observed sources of adaptation of means to ends whatsoever—from the "rotting of a turnip" to "the generation of an animal" to "the structure of human thought"—bear *some* analogy to each other and hence also to the cause or causes of order and adaptation in the universe. In light of the verbal character of this dispute, he urges the "antagonists" that "if you cannot lay aside your disputes, endeavor, at least, to cure yourselves of your animosity" (DNR 12.6–7/216–19).

The second verbal dispute is between "Dogmatists" and "Sceptics" generally and is in no way restricted to theology. This dispute largely reflects individual temperament, and concerns "the degrees of doubt and assurance, which we ought to indulge with regard to all reasoning." It arises, clearly enough, from the failure of the standard of judgment for PROBABILITY to determine the precise degree of probability diminution that should occur in the face of discovered difficulties and infirmities afflicting human cognitive faculties (DNR 12.8n/219) [7.5].

Accordingly, there are two different and distinguishable respects or dimensions in which Philo's proposition is "somewhat ambiguous or at least undefined," corresponding to the two different verbal disputes of degree he identifies: the degree of the resemblance and analogy to be acknowledged, and the degree of probability properly assigned to any judgment about the Deity on the basis of that degree of resemblance. In each respect, moreover, there are several distinct considerations bearing on the ambiguity to keep in mind.

In light of both (i) the many resemblances and the many differences between order and adaptation resulting from human design and order and adaptation in the rest of nature, and (ii) the absence of a precise standard of degrees of resemblance applicable to this case,

Philo's calling the analogy "remote" is evidently intended to indicate that the resemblance can (at least "probably") be said to lie within a vaguely defined range that all parties should allow deserves to be called, at its lower end, "remote." As he earlier emphasizes, this also leaves so far unspecified just what respects of resemblance to human intelligence are more probable than others: for example, is it to be supposed that the Deity feels sense perceptions, thinks with fleeting ideas, or is motivated by desires, all operating in accordance with psychological laws similar to those governing human minds?

In characterizing this "remote analogy" as merely "probable," on the other hand, Philo evidently means to indicate further that the analogy cannot constitute a proof (in his sense [3.4]) even of a remote resemblance between the Deity and human intelligence. His failure to specify further the degree of this probability reflects Hume's view that the standard of judgment for probability does not yield a precise degree of probability in cases of analogy, especially where there are multiple aspects of resemblance and difference that do not allow of a common standard of measurement. In not further specifying even a broad range of probability, however, Philo is also leaving open the extent to which two other factors bearing on probability should properly be weighed, and how those weights should be expressed.

The first of these factors is the overall *diminution* of degree of belief that should be produced by recognition of the *general* doubt-inducing considerations affecting human cognitive faculties [7.5]. For Philo, the precise amount of this diminution, and even more its verbal expression, may differ as a matter of temperament between dogmatists and skeptics in a way that is not fully resolved by the standard of judgment for probability. The second factor is the particular increase of degree of belief in a single intelligent Deity that should result from the *irregular additional* doxastic force of this particular analogy—the force so vigorously pressed earlier by Cleanthes and allowed as legitimate to at least some extent by Philo [9.2]. The precise amount of this force, too, Philo implies, varies not only from one time to another for a single individual, but also varies between individuals as a matter of temperament in a way that is again not fully resolved by the standard of judgment for probability. He identifies this difference in temperament as that between "philosophical Theists" and "philosophical Sceptics" (DNR 12.32/226–27). The less the accommodation that is properly made for irregular force, of course, the greater the amount of resemblance there must be between the observed effects in order to sustain any proposed degree of probability for any proposed amount or aspect of resemblance between the human minds and the Deity—and vice versa.

Because two different dimensions of indeterminacy—degree of resemblance and degree of probability—are both present in this case, they tend to magnify the overall indeterminacy in the proper application of the standard of judgment. We may therefore expect a very considerable range of blameless diversity concerning judgments of—and perhaps even more concerning expressions of—the probability to be ascribed to the existence of a supreme intelligent designer. Diverse judgments and expressions within this range may result from mere blameless differences in philosophical temperament—such as the notable differences between Cleanthes and Philo in susceptibility to both skeptical considerations generally and the irregular force of the analogy with human intelligent design in particular.

Yet while it leaves open this broad range of blameless diversity, Philo's proposition itself does make a very modest positive claim: that there is at least "some" probability of at least a "remote" resemblance between the cause or causes of order in the universe and human intelligence. The probability in question is presumably great enough to render a merely "remote" resemblance more probable than not, but the proposition does not specify how much probability accrues to the attribution of any greater amount of resemblance. Nevertheless, because the proposition affirms at least a minimum degree of probability for a remote analogy, Philo, Hume, and Cleanthes, too, can agree that it is a correct judgment of probability as far as it goes; and this is so even though Cleanthes would also be willing to assign a higher degree of probability. As a correct judgment *concerning* probability, it may properly be epistemically "venerated"—that is, normatively honored and respected—as *true*. Furthermore, as an expression of at least some degree of belief of invisible intelligent power, assent to this minimal true proposition qualifies as *religion* in Hume's carefully defined sense [9.1]; hence, as Philo proposes, "a religious man" can give it a "plain assent." At the same time, as a theoretical proposition concerning the probability of matters of fact to which a philosophical assent may be given as a result of probable reasoning, it is also a "speculative Tenet of philosophy." If the mitigated skepticism of the first *Enquiry* about "high and distant" matters [7.5] is to remain in force, however, the specificity of the speculation must be severely limited indeed.

## 9.6 Miracles

Recognizing the inadequacy of human reason to the task of determining the divine nature will naturally lead, Philo remarks in conclusion, to an avidity for revelation to alleviate our ignorance, so that "to be a philosophical Sceptic is, in a man of letters, the first and most essential step towards being a sound, believing Christian" (DNR 12.33/228). The question of whether a man of letters can ever discover such a special revelation, and hence whether he can ever properly take any further steps towards being a sound believing Christian, is outside the scope of the *Dialogues*, which is limited to natural religion. Insofar as divine revelation is supposed to be accepted on the basis of testimony, however, Hume addresses this further question in the section of *An Enquiry concerning Human Understanding* devoted to the topic of miracles (EHU 10, "Of Miracles")—for it is typically on the basis of the credibility of miracles said to be performed in support of the promulgation of religious doctrines that such doctrines are regarded as having been revealed.

Hume argues for three main conclusions concerning testimony for miracles. The first sets a universal epistemic standard for the acceptance of such testimony:

> [N]o testimony is sufficient to establish a miracle, unless the testimony be of such a kind, that its falsehood would be more miraculous, than the fact, which it endeavors to establish; And even in that case there is a mutual destruction of arguments, and the superior only gives us an assurance suitable to that degree of force, which remains, after deducting the inferior.
> (EHU 10.13/115–16)

His argument for this conclusion has three parts of increasing specificity: (i) the application of very general normative epistemic principles to derive principles governing proofs and (sub-proof) probabilities [3.4]; (ii) the application of these principles for proofs and probabilities to derive a more specific normative epistemic principle for testimony; and (iii) the application of this normative epistemic principle for testimony to the case of testimony for the occurrence of miracles in particular.

Hume's investigation of probable reasoning has already shown to his satisfaction that experience is our only guide in reasoning concerning matters of fact [6.1]. The epistemically ideal person—that is, the "wise man" [4.4]—proportions his or her belief to the experiential evidence, which is found in some cases to be very full and completely uniform, and in other cases to be mixed and less uniform. In the former case, he or she has "proof," in Hume's technical sense, and the highest degree of assurance; in the latter case, he or she has only sub-proof "probability" for the side of the question on which the experiential evidence is greater. In every case of conflict, however, we must "balance the opposite experiments ... and deduct the smaller number from the greater, in order to know the exact force of the superior evidence" (EHU 10.4/111). Presumably, Hume means that this deduction occurs in such a way as to leave a degree of belief that expresses the proportion of positive instances to the total number of instances.

To apply these principles to the case of testimony, Hume begins with another fundamental result of his investigation of probable reasoning—namely, that no objects have any discoverable necessary connection and that all inferences from one to another depend on experience of constant conjunction. This result, he notes, applies just as much to the relation between a matter of fact and testimony about it as it does to any other two objects; there is no perceivable necessary connection between testimony and its veracity [6.3]. Hence, our confidence in the veracity of any species of testimony should be determined by the extent to which we have experience of that veracity, in accordance with various features of human nature whose effects we have also experienced. Accordingly, the evidence derived from witnesses and human testimony "varies with the experience, and is regarded either as a *proof* or a *probability*, according as the conjunction between any particular kind of report and any kind of object has been found to be constant or variable"

(EHU 10.6/112). Whereas Locke had claimed in *An Essay concerning Human Understanding* that "testimony" and "conformity to past experience" are two distinct and independent "grounds of probability" (ECHU 4.15.4), Hume in effect maintains that testimony, as a ground of probability, is reducible to a special case of conformity to past experience. If testimony is often felt to be more convincing than the probability of causes (operating on the conjunction of testimony with truth) would warrant, this can only be because of the disapprovable and unphilosophical influence of "credulity," supported by the ease of imagining what is described in words and the sympathetic communication of sentiments of belief.

To apply the resulting principle about proof and probability in testimony to the specific case of miracles, in turn, Hume begins by defining a miracle as "a violation of the laws of nature." Since his concern is with the application of normative epistemic principles, his focus is not on what does in fact violate the laws of nature, perhaps unknown to us and independent of observation, but rather on putative events that would have the status of appearing as miracles given the experience of the observer in question—that is, what would be a miracle in a subject-relative sense [4.3]. In order to have that status, in turn, a putative event must be such that there is a proof—that is, a full and completely uniform experience for the observer—against its occurrence. By the general epistemic normative principles governing proofs and probabilities, however, proofs (as full and exceptionless experiences of conjunctions) are always stronger than sub-proof probabilities. Hence, no testimony of a supposed miracle that amounts only to a sub-proof probability, no matter how strong otherwise, can be sufficient to establish the event's occurrence against the powerful evidence that gives the proposed event the status of "miracle." To put this conclusion in another way: faced with testimony for the occurrence of an event that on the basis of one's experience would qualify as a miracle, it is always epistemically required to accept that there is an explanation for the occurrence of the testimony that does not require a miracle, rather than to accept an explanation that does require a miracle. This constitutes the first part of Hume's quoted first main conclusion about testimony for miracles. It, too, contradicts Locke, who holds that the lack of conformity to past experience typical of a miracle should not count against the credibility of testimony for its occurrence if the miracle was reportedly performed by an all-powerful God.

As Hume observes, however, it is also at least conceivable that one's only choice will be between two supposed miracles: this will occur if the falsehood of the testimony would *also* be a miracle by one's own lights. He helpfully offers a hypothetical example: testimony from all authors, and brought back by travellers to all countries, that there were, beginning the first of January 1600, eight days of complete darkness over the entire face of the earth (EHU 10.36/127–28). The occurrence of such an event, given the known laws of physics and astronomy, would, he is willing to grant, qualify as a miracle; as too, he is willing to grant, would the occurrence of the testimony, given what we know about human psychology and powers of observation. The only epistemic recourse in such a case is to the general principle about balancing conflicting experiments, which requires comparing the number and force of the "experiments" against the eight days of darkness with the "experiments" against the falsehood of the testimony. In this case, Hume suggests, the availability of a somewhat greater *analogy* for the eight days of darkness with instances of "decay, corruption, and dissolution" in nature would tip the balance slightly in that direction; but in any case, the result of such a balancing of proofs against proofs should be at best a weak degree of belief on the overbalancing side. This constitutes the second half of his first main conclusion about testimony for miracles.

It should be noted that Hume does not discuss in connection with this principle something that he must also regard as possible: namely, that one should acquire evidence that would properly lead one to change one's conception of what the laws of nature themselves actually are or may be. At one time, the transmission of a radio signal or television image would have seemed, on the basis of past experience, to be in violation of the laws of nature and hence a miracle. Some experiments, clearly, call for or at least permit a revision of opinions about the laws of nature: that is, about which circumstances of a previously observed constant conjunction are taken to be causally most relevant and hence also about what should and should not be regarded as in conflict with it. That Hume does not discuss how to distinguish such cases is not fatal to his larger purposes, however, for the acceptance of revelation on the basis of miraculous events requires that the events do continue to be regarded as miracles and are not brought within the scope of the laws of nature.

It should also be noted that Hume's argument depends on a sharp distinction between what would be strictly miraculous (that, is contrary to a proof) for an observer and what would merely be "marvelous" in his terms—that is, events that would be highly unexpected given past observations but not strictly contrary to a proof. As an illustration of the merely marvelous, he mentions the freezing of water for an observer who has never been in or received information about a cold climate (EHU 10.10/113–14). A system of normative epistemic principles that does not recognize a similar categorical distinction, whereby whatever has the status of a law of nature systematically trumps in credibility even very high probabilities that lack that status, cannot fully vindicate or sustain Hume's argument.[2]

Hume's second main conclusion concerning testimony for miracles is an epistemic evaluation of actual miracle testimony now in our possession: "No testimony for any kind of miracle has ever amounted to a probability, much less to a proof" (EHU 10.35/127). For this conclusion, he offers four observations about actual testimony for miracles. The first is that such testimony is of low quality by the standards for human testimony, for it lacks

> sufficient number of men, of such unquestioned good sense, education, and learning, as to secure us against all delusion in themselves; of such undoubted integrity, as to place them beyond all suspicion of any design to deceive others; of such credit and reputation in the eyes of mankind, as to have a great deal to lose in case of their being detected in any falsehood; and at the same time, attesting facts performed in such a public manner, and in so celebrated a part of the world, as to render the detection unavoidable.
> (EHU 10.15/116–17)

Second, the existence and spread of such testimony is readily explained by well-known principles of human nature that do not require for their operation the truth of what is testified. These include the "unphilosophical" [3.4] force of surprise, wonder, credulity, and eloquence to enliven belief, combined with the pleasure derived from conveying stories that are believed by others— and, especially, being the first to convey any exciting news. These principles also include the common human willingness to foreswear the application of critical faculties and even to lie in defense of a cause taken to be as important as a religion is taken to be by its adherents. Third, accounts of miracles originate predominantly from ignorant and barbarous people; they are much rarer among the educated and civilized. Fourth, insofar as miracles are such as to lend support to religious doctrines, testimonial evidence of miracles supporting one religious doctrine should properly be taken as evidence against the occurrence of miracles supporting incompatible religious doctrines. Viewed in this way, most testimonies for miracles are opposed by a vast number of contrary testimonies of a similar kind and degree of quality.

Hume's third and final main conclusion about testimony for miracles is an epistemic principle about all existing or future testimony for specifically religious miracles: "No human testimony can have such force as to prove a miracle, and make it a just foundation for any [popular] system of religion" (EHU 10.35/127). While miracles as Hume defines them need not be such as to provide any support for religious doctrines, any testimony for miracles that *would* provide a foundation for a system of religion is particularly weak, for two reasons already considered. First, the features of human nature already surveyed as damaging the credibility of testimony for miracles in general are particularly strong in the case of testimony for miracles that would support a religion. Second, the greater the degree of probability that a given miracle would, if established, provide to particular religious doctrines, the more its probability is undermined by directly comparable testimony for miracles that would tend to provide support for incompatible doctrines.

Like *Dialogues concerning Natural Religion*, "Of Miracles," concludes with an observation that appears more concessive than, on closer observation, it really is. The final lines of "Of Miracles" are:

> So that, upon the whole, we may conclude, that the CHRISTIAN religion not only was at first attended with miracles, but even at

this day cannot be believed by any reasonable person without one. Mere reason is insufficient to convince us of its veracity: And whoever is moved by *Faith* to assent to it, is conscious of a continued miracle in his own person, which subverts all the principles of his understanding, and gives him a determination to believe what is most contrary to custom and experience.

(EHU 10.41/131)

Hume is not saying that no one at all can believe the Christian religion without a miracle, but rather that no *reasonable* person can do so—because the epistemically approved operations of reason themselves do not cause belief in the needed miracles. On the contrary, under the laws of human psychology, someone who does believe in such a miracle can do so only as the result of what we might call *pathological* causes—such as susceptibility to surprise, wonder, credulity, and eloquence—that conflict with the cognitive operations properly deemed "reasonable." Accordingly, those who find themselves believing in a miracle must accept one of the following alternatives: (i) they are themselves unreasonable, because believing only from pathological causes; or (ii) they remain reasonable and so their belief is not due to pathological causes—in which case their belief is instead a miracle! If they choose alternative (ii), however, they are thereby now committed not only to the occurrence of the original miracle but also to the occurrence of a second miracle, this one consisting in their own ability to believe in the first miracle as reasonable people. About this miracle, we may observe, the same choice is of course again forced, and acceptance of (ii) with respect to this second miracle requires belief in a third miracle—and so on, indefinitely up a hierarchy of ever-higher-order beliefs about beliefs about beliefs.

## 9.7 Religion and morals

Human morality—like the operation of probable reasoning through custom (EHU 5.21–22/54–55) or the tendency of the imagination to give rise to the belief in bodies (THN 1.4.2.1/187)—is itself a striking example of order and adaptation ("final causes") within human nature. Accordingly, Hume is willing to affirm, at the conclusion of the first Appendix to the second *Enquiry*, the pious-sounding formula that we may consider the moral sense and the standard of morality that it provides as "ultimately derived from that Supreme Will, which bestowed on each being its peculiar nature." It is important to emphasize, however, that his account of the basis of morality makes no substantive appeal to religion. Regardless of the strength or weakness of the Design Argument for the existence of an intelligent source of order in the universe[9.2], he denies that the evidence supports the attribution of positive virtues, including a moral sense or a concern for virtue to the Deity itself [9.4–5]. Thus his omission of any other reference to divinity in his discussions of the foundations of morals, although striking to his contemporaries, is not surprising. Whereas they regularly distinguished among duties to others, duties to self, and duties to God, Hume mentions the topic of duties to God only once: to argue, in the essay "Of Suicide," that, even if there is a God as traditionally supposed, there is no duty to God to preserve one's life. Once the suppressed essay became generally available in Britain after his death, his more astute readers observed that the argument he gives for this conclusion, which appeals to the impossibility of harming or frustrating the plans of an all-powerful being, is entirely generalizable to the conclusion that there cannot be any duties to God at all.

Although Hume evidently faced his own death fearlessly [1.7], he recognizes that others are sometimes consoled in facing the death of loved ones and their own impending death by the thought of an afterlife rendered happy by God. Even then, however, he holds that the association of the afterlife with death often renders the imagination of it gloomy and frightening rather than consoling (DNR 12.24–31/224–26). Unlike most philosophers of the early modern period, including Locke and even the religiously unorthodox Spinoza, Hume denied that the prospect of divine rewards and punishments in an afterlife is an important and sustained factor in motivating morally appropriate behavior. Such behavior is far more a matter of individual temperament and character, cultivated and encouraged by parents and politicians—and, he surely hoped, to some very modest extent by moral philosophers such as himself.

Hume did concede that religion could be considered to have a "proper office" with respect to the support of morality:

> The proper office of religion is to reform men's lives, to purify their hearts, to inforce all moral duties, and to secure obedience to the laws and civil magistrate. While it pursues these useful purposes, its operations, tho' infinitely valuable, are secret and silent; and seldom come under the cognizance of history.
> (HE VI.71: 539n)

Indeed, it is very possible that he recognized such an influence of religion in the life of his own beloved Calvinist mother. Yet he originally wrote a version of the passage just cited as part of a draft preface for the second volume of his *History of England*, for the purpose of defending the first volume against the observation that all of the references in it to the influence of religion were critical. (Subsequent volumes did allow that there were occasional social benefits from the actions of the clergy, as in the time of Henry III, despite the superstitious character of their religion.) Although he decided in the end against including the quoted preface, he did publish the remark as a footnote in early editions of the second volume and later gave it, in a paraphrased form, to the character of Cleanthes in the *Dialogues*.

Despite the possibility of this "proper office," however, Hume maintains that all religion "except the true" [9.5] is pernicious in some ways, including providing a "cover to faction and ambition" (DNR 12.12–13/220). In the second *Enquiry*, he criticizes "fanatics" who suppose "*that dominion is founded on grace, and that saints alone inherit the earth*" (EPM 3.23/193). He then goes on to contrast the rules of popular religions ("superstition") with those of property ("justice") by describing the former as "frivolous, useless, and burdensome," while the latter are "absolutely requisite to the well-being of mankind and existence of society" (EPM 3.38/199). Most famously, the second *Enquiry* draws a memorable consequence from its account of the nature of virtue or personal merit:

> And as every quality, which is useful or agreeable to ourselves or others, is, in common life, allowed to be a part of personal merit; so no other will ever be received, where men judge of things by their natural, unprejudiced reason, without the delusive glosses of superstition and false religion. Celibacy, fasting, penance, mortification, self-denial, humility, silence, solitude,

and the whole train of monkish virtues; for what reason are they every where rejected by men of sense, but because they serve to no manner of purpose; neither advance a man's fortune in the world, nor render him a more valuable member of society; neither qualify him for the entertainment of company, nor increase his power of self-enjoyment? We observe, on the contrary, that they cross all these desirable ends; stupify the understanding and harden the heart, obscure the fancy and sour the temper. We justly, therefore, transfer them to the opposite column, and place them in the catalogue of vices; nor has any superstition force sufficient among men of the world, to pervert entirely these natural sentiments. A gloomy, hair-brained enthusiast, after his death, may have a place in the calendar; but will scarcely ever be admitted, when alive, into intimacy and society, except by those who are as delirious and dismal as himself.

(EPM 9.3/270)

As previously noted, the final sentence of the second *Enquiry* refers to the distorting effects on moral judgment of "the illusions of religious superstition" (EPM Dialogue 57/343) [8.5]. Moreover, in both the *Treatise* and the second *Enquiry*, Hume criticizes religious moralists as well as politicians for overemphasizing the virtues whose expressions are voluntary and so lend themselves to modification by rewards and punishments, at the expense of other valuable virtues and aspects of personal merit. While he includes cleanliness in his list of virtues [8.2], he notably omits godliness. The recruitment of philosophy to serve and defend the theoretical needs of Christianity he regards as a disaster for philosophy.

Hume's most sustained critique of the effects of popular religion on personal morals, however, is presented by Philo in the *Dialogues*. There he offers four main criticisms (DNR 12.15–20/221–23). First, in its effort to obtain special divine favor and protection, popular religion creates pernicious new kinds of merit that are in fact of no moral value. These include frivolous observances and ceremonies, ecstatic frenzies, and faith. Second, because it typically requires expressions of confident belief even when such belief has waned (as it frequently does), it encourages hypocrisy. Third, the supposed greatness and importance of the cause renders believers unscrupulous in the defense of religion, willing to utilize any available means. Finally, by encouraging people to place their own personal salvation ahead of all other considerations, it encourages selfishness.

In contrast, adopting the speculative tenet of true religion creates no new motives and hence has no influence on behavior at all aside from the "beneficial influence" of philosophy more generally (DNR 12.22/223). This beneficial influence lies primarily in the development of reflection and moderation of the passions.

## 9.8 Conclusion

The question is often posed whether Hume was an atheist. The term 'atheist' remained largely pejorative in the eighteenth century, and although he often wrote of and compared "sceptics and atheists," he never applied the latter term to himself as he did the former. The philosopher and encyclopedist Denis Diderot (1713–84) reported in correspondence a dinner conversation between Hume and the Baron d'Holbach (1723–89) during Hume's attachment to the embassy in Paris:

> The first time that M. Hume found himself at the table of the Baron, he was seated beside him. I don't know for what purpose the English philosopher took it into his head to remark to the Baron that he did not believe in atheists, that he had never seen any. The Baron said to him: "Count how many we are here." We are eighteen. The Baron added: "It isn't too bad a showing to be able to point out to you fifteen at once: the three others haven't made up their minds."[3]

Unlike Holbach, Hume preferred to emphasize how ambiguous and undefined the term 'atheist' is. He could easily regard himself as believing in God, meaning by this simply belief in a cause or causes of order and adaptation in the universe, since he recognized the existence of such order and adaptation and was more than willing to affirm that it had some cause or causes, if only some principle of order inherent in matter, and even if acceptance of the Causal Maxim is based only on probable reasoning, rather than intuition or demonstration. Indeed, had Charles Darwin written a century earlier, Hume might well have regarded the mechanism of natural selection as an aspect of God in this sense. He regarded the attribution to the Deity of something resembling human intelligence as a proposition quite indeterminate in its content—Darwin's choice of the term 'natural selection' was intended to highlight its analogy with the entirely intelligent artificial selection practiced by breeders of plants and animals—and subject in its degree of probability to a wide range of blameless diversity. His own "true religion" is a speculative tenet of philosophy, without direct implications for the conduct of life, that allows at least some minimum degree of probability to such an attribution of intelligence to the cause or causes of order and adaptation in the universe.

The points on which Hume is most definite and emphatic are (i) the absence of any moral characteristics or concerns on the part of any deity; (ii) the improbability of any afterlife, especially one involving rewards for virtue and punishments for vice; (iii) the inadequacy of testimony to establish any special revelation; and (iv) the predominantly pernicious consequences of popular religion, which is always derived chiefly from fear and hope. For these reasons, and especially the last, it is better to describe Hume in a way often used by his contemporaries, and one that he acknowledged his works were earning him: as an "infidel" (LDH 58: I.106; LDH 188: I.351). In religion, as in so much else, Hume's philosophy is an exemplar of empiricism, naturalism, and skepticism.

## Notes

1 Paul Russell (2008) *The Riddle of Hume's Treatise: Skepticism, Naturalism, and Irreligion*, New York: Oxford University Press.
2 One example of a system not recognizing this distinction is Peter Millican's 2011 reconstruction of Hume's theory of probability in application to miracles in "Twenty Questions about Hume's 'Of Miracles'," *Royal Institute of Philosophy Supplement* 68: 151–92.
3 Earnest. C. Mossner (1980) *Life of David Hume*, second edition, Oxford: Oxford University Press: 483.

## Further reading

Earman, John (2000) *Hume's Abject Failure: The Argument Against Miracles*, Oxford: Oxford University Press. (A short and highly critical treatment of Hume on miracles from the standpoint of modern probability theory, published together with a very helpful set of relevant seventeenth- and eighteenth-century works.)

Falkenstein, Lorne (2009) "Hume on 'Genuine', 'True', and 'Rational' Religion," *Eighteenth Century Thought* 4: 171–201. (An interpretation of 'true religion' in terms of belief in a being worthy of worship.)

Fogelin, Robert J. (2003) *A Defense of Hume on Miracles*, Oxford: Oxford University Press. (A response to Earman 2000, defending an interpretation closer to that of Garrett 1997.)

Garrett, Don (1997) *Cognition and Commitment in Hume's Philosophy*, New York: Oxford University Press, Chapter 7. (An extended account and interpretation of Hume's arguments concerning miracles.)

Garrett, Don (2012) "What's True about Hume's 'True Religion'?" *Journal of Scottish Philosophy* 10.2: 199–220. (A more detailed defense of the interpretation of "true religion" provided here, with discussion of the role of probability as a sense-based concept.)

Herdt, Jennifer A. (1997) *Religion and Faction in Hume's Moral Philosophy*, Cambridge: Cambridge University Press. (Analyses Hume's treatment of religion in the context of his ethical and political concerns.)

Holden, Thomas (2010) *Spectres of False Divinity: Hume's Moral Atheism*, Oxford: Oxford University Press. (A historical and critical interpretation of Hume's rejection of a deity with moral attributes.)

Immerwahr, John (1996) "Hume's Aesthetic Theism," *Hume Studies* 22.2: 325–38. (An influential interpretation of Hume's "true religion" as aesthetically derived belief that performs the "proper office" of religion.)

Millican, Peter (2011) "Twenty Questions about Hume's 'Of Miracles'," *Royal Institute of Philosophy Supplement* 68: 151–92. (A thorough interpretive and critical treatment of issues concerning Hume's arguments about miracles, with a proposal for interpreting them in light of contemporary probability theory.)

O'Connor, David (2001) *Hume on Religion*, London: Routledge. (A useful and accessible commentary on *Dialogues concerning Natural Religion*.)

Russell, Paul (2008) *The Riddle of Hume's Treatise: Skepticism, Naturalism, and Irreligion*, New York: Oxford University Press. (A comprehensive examination in historical context of the "irreligion" implicit and explicit in *A Treatise of Human Nature*, arguing that it provides a key to reconciling Hume's naturalism with his skepticism.)

# Ten
"Leaving it to posterity to add the rest"

Although Hume admired ancient moralists such as Cicero (106–43 BCE) and recommended Academic skepticism as he defined it [7.5], philosophy and the sciences were in his telling still in considerable disarray at the beginning of the eighteenth century, more than two millennia after the origination of natural philosophy by Thales and of moral philosophy by Socrates:

> 'Tis easy for one of judgment and learning, to perceive the weak foundation even of those systems, which have obtain'd the greatest credit, and have carry'd their pretensions highest to accurate and profound reasoning. Principles taken upon trust, consequences lamely deduc'd from them, want of coherence in the parts, and of evidence in the whole, these are every where to be met with in the systems of the most eminent philosophers, and seem to have drawn disgrace upon philosophy itself.
> Nor is there requir'd such profound knowledge to discover the present imperfect condition of the sciences, but even the rabble without doors may judge from the noise and clamour, which they hear, that all goes not well within.
> (THN Introduction 1–2/13)

Yet it was still much too early, he judged, to admit defeat, at least in the search for philosophy that would be probable on all the evidence to be obtained:

> [W]e might hope to establish a system or set of opinions, which if not true (for that, perhaps, is too much to be hop'd

for) might at least be satisfactory to the human mind, and might stand the test of the most critical examination. Nor shou'd we despair of attaining this end, because of the many chimerical systems, which have successively arisen and decay'd away among men, wou'd we consider the shortness of that period, wherein these questions have been the subjects of enquiry and reasoning. Two thousand years with such long interruptions, and under such mighty discouragements are a small space of time to give any tolerable perfection to the sciences; and perhaps we are still in too early an age of the world to discover any principles, which will bear the examination of the latest posterity.
(THN 1.4.7.14/272–73)

Indeed, a crucial turning point had been achieved within the previous century-and-a half, Hume proposed, with the introduction of the experimental method first into natural philosophy by Bacon and then into moral philosophy by such "late philosophers in *England*" as "Mr. *Locke*, my Lord *Shaftesbury*, Dr. *Mandeville*, Mr. *Hutcheson*, Dr. *Butler*, &c." (THN Introduction 7n/xvii). This method promised to free philosophy and the sciences both from "hypotheses" unsupported by experience and, ultimately, from subjection to the demands of Christian theology that had corrupted both metaphysics and morals. The project of his "science of man" was to apply this method to moral subjects is such a way as to put "all the sciences" on a secure new foundation [1.2].

In a 1737 letter, Hume recommends to a friend four works as particularly valuable for understanding "the metaphysical parts" of the reasonings in the *Treatise* he was then composing: Malebranche's *The Search After Truth*, Berkeley's *Principles of Human Knowledge*, Bayle's *Historical and Critical Dictionary* (specifically, the "more metaphysical articles" such as "Spinoza" and "Zeno"), and Descartes's *Meditations*.[1] Although Hume declared Malebranche's doctrine that God is the only real cause in the universe (that is, "occasionalism" [6.3]) to be an excursion into "fairy land" (EHU 7.24/72), Malebranche's rejection of real necessary causal connections within nature was an important influence of Hume's own denial that the mind perceives such connections. Although Hume did not share Berkeley's claim that nothing exists outside of minds, Berkeley's rejection of real causal relations among (what are for Berkeley mind-dependent) bodies arguably reinforced the influence of Malebranche. Undeniably, Hume in his published writings praises Berkeley's treatment of abstract ideas [2.4], and he credits Berkeley with the main lines of thought leading to the recognition of "the contradiction of the modern philosophy" concerning the inconceivability of the real qualities of bodies [7.2]. Indeed, he declares that "most of the writings of that very ingenious author form the best lessons of scepticism, which are to be found either among the ancient or modern philosophers, BAYLE not excepted ... though otherwise intended" (EHU 12.15n/155). As this last remark suggests, Bayle's skepticism was also an important influence on Hume, although Hume's treatment of space and time [2.5] is intended to resolve a paradox about infinite divisibility proposed and explained by Bayle in his article "Zeno." Bayle's article on "Spinoza" also clearly influenced Hume's discussion of the immateriality of the soul (THN 1.4.5). Hume rejected both Descartes's own doctrine of the immateriality of the soul and his "antecedent" species of skepticism [7.1] as he understood it, but he accepted the central importance of the question of the veracity of human cognitive faculties.

In much the same way that many of Hume's predecessors influenced him and figured in his narrative of the history of philosophy up to his time, so too he influenced and figured centrally in the narratives of the history of philosophy offered by many of his successors. He observes in the *Treatise* "that men are every where concern'd about what may happen after their death, provided it regard this world; and that there are few to whom their name, their family, their friends, and their country are in any period of time entirely indifferent" (THN 1.3.9.13/114); with "love of literary fame" as his avowed "ruling passion," he was no exception to this principle. Providing funds in his will (though "not exceeding a hundred pounds") for the construction of his tomb on Calton Hill in Edinburgh, he specified that it should bear his name and dates, "leaving it to posterity to add the rest." In the centuries that followed his death, succeeding generations of philosophical posterity have written, partially erased, and rewritten "the rest" many times over.

## 10.1 Hume in the eighteenth century

Hume plays a leading role in the writings of his countryman Thomas Reid [1.6], professor first at King's College Aberdeen and then at Glasgow, where he succeeded Adam Smith as Professor of Moral Philosophy. Reid was Hume's senior by one year, but did not publish his first book, *An Inquiry into the Human Mind on the Principles of Common Sense*, until 1764. At the most general level, Reid seeks, like Hume, to apply the scientific mode of enquiry promoted by Bacon and advanced by Newton to the understanding of the human mind. At the same time, however, his "common sense" philosophy rejects much of Hume's concept empiricism, naturalism, and skepticism.

Central to Reid's common-sense approach to philosophy is the rejection of what he calls "the way of ideas," according to which the mind immediately perceives only mental entities. Against this doctrine, which he regards as becoming dominant with Descartes, Reid holds that the mind is able to conceive external things directly and without any mental representations of them, although sensations— which do not resemble qualities of objects—are a stimulus to the conception of, and belief in, bodies presently existing in the vicinity. In doing so, the mind finds itself with some concepts—including that of existence itself—as seemingly native endowments. Intentionality, on this account, is an explanatorily basic feature of acts of the mind [2.6]. For Reid, unlike Hume, the broadly "mechanistic" mode of explanation, in which events are explained in terms of previous events and laws of nature that govern them, pertains only to the material world and not to the realm of human thought and action. In Reid's view, human volitions, while explicable through reasons, are caused not by previous events but directly by agents, and they are therefore not within the scope of laws of nature. Indeed, he holds that all genuine causal power is lodged in minds, so that the laws of nature governing the material realm simply describe what is really God's own causal activity with respect to bodies. Finally, Reid rejects skepticism by maintaining that human knowledge is grounded in a variety of different kinds of "evidence" corresponding to different faculties—including a "moral sense"—and an extensive set of self-evident "first principles" that includes the veracity of those faculties, as well as the Causal Maxim, the uniformity of nature, and principles of morality.

According to Reid, Hume is a radical theoretical skeptic [7.1] who "upon the principles he has borrowed from LOCKE and BERKELEY, has with great acuteness, reared a system of absolute scepticism, which leaves no rational ground to believe any one proposition, rather than its contrary" (EIPM 2.12/165; see also EIPM 7.4/562, 565). Indeed, the merit of Hume's philosophy lies, he thinks, in its being "a system of consequences, however absurd, acutely and justly drawn from a few principles" (EIPM 2.12/163), including the way of ideas itself. Although he recognizes that Hume regards the rejection of all belief as psychologically impossible, Reid treats all such belief as strictly out of keeping with Hume's own epistemological principles. He also interprets Hume as going beyond Berkeley's rejection of matter to deny the existence of both matter and mind (at least as properly understood), replacing the former with a bundle of sensations and the latter with a bundle of perceptions. He reads Hume as reducing all causal relations to constant conjunction without remainder, and he objects that, on Hume's account, night is the cause of day, and day of night, since each always follows the other (EAPM 4.9/249). In addition, he interprets Hume as denying that anything is true or false in morality; instead, he thinks, Hume treats moral declarations as mere expressions of sentiments, partly as a natural consequence of allegiance to the way of ideas.

Reid is certainly right to think that Hume disagrees with him about intentionality [2.6] and free will [6.4]. He is also right to think that Hume regards satisfaction of the first definition of 'cause' as necessary and sufficient for a causal relation—although this view does not require Hume to say that causation is "nothing but" constant conjunction [6.5]. Reid misunderstands Hume profoundly, however, in several important respects. For example, day could not be the cause of night or vice versa for Hume, for two reasons: (i) his eighth rule for judging causal relations [4.3] requires that complete causes operate immediately to produce their effects (THN 1.3.15.10/174–75); and (ii) occupying the standard of judgment for causal relations would yield more comprehensive causal explanations for both day and night. More generally, Hume is a mitigated theoretical skeptic rather an extreme one [7.5], and he does not deny the existence of bodies or minds, although he raises questions about the adequacy of our ideas of them. Indeed, Hume's sense of probability, consisting in the capacity to feel the liveliness of ideas in considering possible matters of fact, might well be considered a naturalistic explanation of, or alternative to, Reid's postulated capacity to appreciate "evidence" [4.4]. Reid's interpretation of Hume as rejecting Moral Cognitivism [8.6] is the result of a failure to appreciate the systematic ambiguity in Hume of sense-based concept terms such as 'virtue' [4.2] and his distinction between moral sentiments and conceptual moral judgments.

Reid's friend and disciple James Beattie played an important role in disseminating Reid's conception of Hume's philosophy through a very popular 1770 book, *An Essay on the Nature and Immutability of Truth; in Opposition to Sophistry and Scepticism*, which was a rhetorically vigorous attack on Hume's philosophy along Reidian lines. Beattie, an outspoken abolitionist, also took Hume quite properly to task for the racism of a footnote remark in the essay "Of National Characters": "I am apt to suspect the negroes to be naturally inferior to the whites. There scarcely ever was a civilized nation of that complexion, nor any individual, eminent either in action or speculation" (EMPL I.21: 209n10). This remark is surely an extreme instance of what Hume himself condemns in *A Treatise of Human Nature* as prejudice, the fourth species of unphilosophical probability [3.4]. Beattie's book quotes extensively from the *Treatise*, prompting Hume's request in the "Author's Advertisement" to *Essays and Treatises on Several Subjects* that he be judged instead by his subsequent work [1.6]. Somewhat later, Reid's former student Dugald Stewart (1753–1828)—who succeeded Adam Ferguson in the chair of moral philosophy at Edinburgh [1.5] and ultimately received a memorial at the top of Calton Hill, in contrast to Hume's self-funded tomb on its side—also contributed to the development and dissemination of the Reidian "common sense" critique of Hume.

Hume plays an even more important role in the history of philosophy set out by the German philosopher Immanuel Kant (1724–1804). Most of Hume's published works had been translated into German by 1760, but the formally anonymous *Treatise* was not translated until 1790–91. Because Kant read little or no English, his only direct knowledge of the *Treatise* before that time was through translations of parts—notably the substantial excerpts in Beattie's book. According to Kant, Hume poses a crucial question about the origin of the concept of causation, a question that Reid and Beattie painfully fail to appreciate:

> He challenged reason, which pretends to have given birth to this concept of herself, to answer him by what right she thinks anything could be so constituted that if that thing be posited, something else also must necessarily be posited; for this is the meaning of the concept of cause.
> (PAFM 257)

In Kant's reading, Hume concludes that his own challenge cannot be met, holding instead that

> reason was altogether deluded with reference to this concept, which she erroneously regarded as one of her children, whereas in reality it was nothing but a bastard of imagination, impregnated by experience, which subsumed certain representations under the law of association, and mistook a subjective necessity (custom) for an objective necessity arising from insight.
> (PAFM 257–58)

Kant famously credits Hume's question with stimulating his own philosophy:

> I openly confess, the suggestion of David Hume was the very thing, which many years ago first interrupted my dogmatic slumber, and gave my investigations in the field of speculative philosophy quite a new direction.
> (PAFM 260)

This new direction led to Kant's doctrine that some truths are both *synthetic* and *a priori*. By this, he means that the concept of the predicate is not contained within the concept of the subject (hence synthetic) and yet the truth is knowable prior to, and independent of, evidence derived from experience (hence *a priori*). Truths having this character include those of pure (that is, non-empirical) mathematics and pure (again, non-empirical) natural science. Pure mathematics can be synthetic *a priori*, he proposes, because space and time, as forms of sensibility, are imposed by the mind itself so as to interpret sensory input as information about a world of objects and thereby to constitute genuine experience. Similarly, pure natural science can be synthetic *a priori*, he proposes, because certain "pure concepts of the understanding" are not derived from experience (as concept empiricism would require) but rather are imposed by the mind so as to interpret sensory input as information about a world of objects and thereby to constitute genuine experience. The applicability of these forms and concepts to "things-as-they-appear-to-us" is thereby guaranteed, although at the cost of knowledge of "things-as-they-are-in-themselves." One of the most important synthetic *a priori* truths of pure natural science is that all events occur in accordance with uniform laws of nature, and this is knowable because the concept of causation can be shown to be one of these "pure concepts of the understanding." In effect, Kant proposes a third kind of argument—"transcendental arguments," involving preconditions for the possibility of experience—as a solution to Hume's dilemma that the uniformity of nature cannot be established by either demonstrative or probable arguments.

Kant further proposes that the distinction between things-as-they-appear-to-us and things-as-they-are-in-themselves makes possible a belief that human agents as-they-are-in-themselves are free and undetermined, a belief that is contrary to naturalism but is rationally required on practical moral grounds rather than theoretical ones. Non-naturalistic beliefs in God and the immortality of the soul are also licensed on practical moral grounds.

In Kant's telling, Hume himself would have come to this doctrine if only he had thought more about the status of mathematics:

> For he imagined that its nature, or, so to speak, the constitution of this province, depended on totally different principles, namely, on the principle of contradiction alone, and although he did not divide judgments in this manner [i.e., into analytic and synthetic] formally and universally and did not use the same terminology as I have done here, what he said was equivalent to this: that pure mathematics contains only analytic, but metaphysics synthetic, *a priori* judgments. In this, however, he was greatly mistaken, and the mistake had a decidedly

injurious effect upon his whole conception. But for this, he would have extended his question concerning the origin of our synthetic judgments far beyond the metaphysical concept of causality and included in it the possibility of mathematics *a priori* also; for this latter he must have assumed to be equally synthetic. And then he could not have based his metaphysical judgments on mere experience without subjecting the axioms of mathematics equally to experience, a thing that he was far too acute to do. The good company into which metaphysics would thus have been brought would have saved it from the danger of a contemptuous ill-treatment; for the thrust intended for it must have reached mathematics, which was not and could not have been Hume's intention. Thus that acute man would have been led into considerations which must needs be similar to those that now occupy us, but which would have gained inestimably from his inimitable elegant style.

(PAFM 272–73)

The result, for Kant, was that Hume instead "did not suspect such a formal science [as metaphysics] but ran his ship ashore, for safety's sake, landing on skepticism, there to let it lie and rot" (PAFM 4). He nevertheless provided the spark from which Kant's own correct philosophy arose.

Kant's account of Hume's philosophy is of course tailored to his own purposes. Because Kant did not have access to the treatments of space, time, and geometry in the *Treatise*, he did not realize that Hume already grants, in effect, that truths of geometry such as *the shortest distance between two points is a straight line* (THN 1.2.4.26/50) are at once synthetic and *a priori*: synthetic, because both concepts are semantically simple, and *a priori* because relations of ideas knowable prior to experience of their objects [2.5]. This understanding of geometry did not induce Hume to consider abandoning his concept empiricism for the Kantian doctrine of "pure concepts of the understanding."

Moreover, in claiming that Hume offered to reason a challenge about the origin of the concept CAUSATION that he concluded it could not meet, Kant underestimates the extent to which reason already "gives rise" to CAUSATION on Hume's account, inasmuch as the Humean causal sense depends essentially on the operation of probable reasoning [4.3]. The necessity of causal relations is indeed "subjective" for Hume, inasmuch as it is felt or discerned by an internal impression of necessary connection, but it remains the case for Hume that objects are or are not causally related independent of how we feel about them:

> As to what may be said, that the [causal] operations of nature are independent of our thought and reasoning, I allow it; and accordingly have observ'd, that objects bear to each other the relations of contiguity and succession; that like objects may be observ'd in several instances to have like relations; and that all this is independent of, and antecedent to the operations of the understanding.
> (THN 1.3.14.28/168)

Nor did Hume run his ship of inquiry ashore, "there to let it lie and rot." Following the stormy epistemic weather of the final section of *Treatise* Book 1—where the ship metaphor is of course Hume's own—he returns to philosophical inquiry with a mitigated skepticism to discover what he takes to be many new probable truths about the operations of the mind. Insofar as he rejected Kant's stronger views that the Causal Maxim, Universal Determinism, and Euclidean geometry are *a priori*, he was at least arguably right to do so. Hume's mitigated skepticism also involves a suspension of belief about "high and distant enquiries" concerning the origins of worlds and the secret natures of things, but Kant's own denial that we can have knowledge of things as they are in themselves strikes a similar theme.

It is important to Kant that non-naturalistic beliefs in God, freedom, and immortality are necessary presuppositions of morality. Yet his acknowledgement that Hume's "moral character [was] quite blameless" despite his rejection of those beliefs arguably calls into question whether those beliefs are quite as essential to morality as Kant supposes.

## 10.2 Hume in the nineteenth century

*Utilitarianism*, a form of consequentialism [8.6], is the doctrine that morally right conduct is that which produces the greatest amount of pleasure or happiness. The development of utilitarianism by such writers as Jeremy Bentham (1748–1832), James Mill (1873–1836), and John Stuart Mill (1806–73) was one of the most important events in nineteenth-century moral philosophy, and Hume was an important inspiration for its defining principle. Bentham, generally regarded as the founder of the movement, reports in one of his earliest writings that *Treatise* Book 3

> stands clear of the objections that have of late been urged, with so much vehemence, against the work in general. {By Dr BEATTIE, in his *Essay on the Immutability of Truth*.} ... That the foundations of all virtue are laid in utility, is there demonstrated, after a few exceptions made, with the strongest force of evidence: but I see not ... what need there was for the exceptions.
>
> For my own part, I well remember, no sooner had I read that part of the work which touches on this subject, than I felt as if scales had fallen from my eyes, I then, for the first time, learnt to call the cause of the people the cause of Virtue.[2]

Indeed, he remarks, the very name 'principle of utility' was "adopted from David Hume."

For the utilitarians, Hume's importance lay not only in emphasizing the central importance to morality of pleasure, pain, and public utility, but also in his firm rejection of any attempt to ground morality in religion or the obligation of allegiance to government in a supposed social contract. Hume sounds most like a utilitarian in a passage not from the *Treatise* but from the second *Enquiry*, in which he personifies virtue:

> She talks not of useless austerities and rigours, suffering and self-denial. She declares, that her sole purpose is, to make her votaries and mankind, during every instant of their existence, if possible, cheerful and happy; nor does she ever part with any pleasure but in hopes of ample compensation in some other period of their lives. The sole trouble, which she demands, is that of just calculation, and a steady preference of the greater happiness.
>
> (EPM 9.15/279)

Despite his inspirational role, however, Hume is not himself a utilitarian, as Bentham recognizes with his clause about "exceptions." First, of course, Hume is a virtue ethicist, rather than a consequentialist: it is traits of character, rather than the consequences of actions, that are the fundamental and original objects of moral evaluation. Second, he is a moral-sense theorist. Traits tending to produce actions that contribute to pleasure and prevent pain are typically approved by the Humean moral sense in consequence of the role of sympathy in producing moral sentiments; but it is the idealized moral sense, not a calculation of utility, that is the ultimate moral arbiter in cases of conflict. For example, although utilitarians may seek to derive justifications from general rules of utility for the human tendency to benefit friends and relatives above strangers who are in greater need, the tendency requires no special justification for Hume beyond the firm responses of the moral sense.

One of the nineteenth century's most important movements in psychology was *associationism*. Associationism sought, on analogy with physics or chemistry, to explain mental phenomena—such as the combination of ideas into complexes or trains of thoughts—without any appeal to the activities of an overall governing mental agent (such as Reid would have approved), but instead by formulating psychological laws involving such relations as spatial or temporal contiguity, resemblance, causation, and (later) contrast, along with such processes as habituation. In the *Abstract* of his *Treatise*, Hume writes of himself:

> Thro' this whole book, there are great pretensions to new discoveries in philosophy; but if any thing can entitle the author to so glorious a name as that of an inventor, 'tis the use he makes of the principle of the association of ideas, which enters into most of his philosophy.
> (ATHN 35/661–62)

Hobbes, Locke, and Berkeley, among others, appeal to associations among ideas to explain particular mental effects, but perhaps the most influential figures in inspiring this movement were Hume and the physician David Hartley (1705–57)—the latter primarily through his book *Observations on Man, His Frame, His Duty, and His*

Expectations, published very shortly after Hume's first Enquiry and seemingly without knowledge of Hume's work. The leading associationists of the nineteenth century included James Mill, John Stuart Mill, and Alexander Bain (1818–1903).

Of these, John Stuart Mill, in particular, also agreed with Hume's methodological empiricism and his moral and religious naturalism, but found his skepticism deeply challenging:

> France had Voltaire, and his school of negative thinkers, and England (or rather Scotland) had the profoundest negative thinker on record, David Hume: a man, the peculiarities of whose mind qualified him to detect failure of proof, and want of logical consistency, at a depth which French sceptics, with their comparatively feeble powers of analysis and abstraction, stopt far short of, and which German subtlety alone could thoroughly appreciate, or hope to rival.[3]

As it happened, the "German subtlety" of Kant and especially G. W. F. Hegel (1770–1831) was soon invoked to combat Hume's influence more directly through the rise to prominence of such British idealists as T. H. Green (1836–82) and F. H. Bradley (1846–1924). Green in particular saw Hume not as a model but rather as a bad example whose associationism, concept empiricism, naturalism, and skepticism had all been refuted and superseded—along with the psychological atomism, methodological empiricism, and moral sentimentalism that sustained them—by the innovations of Kant, Hegel, and their German idealist successors. Despite, or rather because of, his lack of sympathy with Hume, Green edited, together with T. H. Grose, what became for several decades the standard four-volume edition of Hume's philosophical works. He prefaced the volume containing Treatise Book 1 with a three-hundred-page "General Introduction" that was a scathing critique of the philosophies of Locke, Berkeley, and Hume. The volume containing Treatise Books 2 and 3 begins with a further highly critical seventy-page "Introduction to the Moral Part of Hume's Treatise" that concludes:

> Our business, however, has not been to moralise, but to show that the philosophy based on the abstraction of feeling, in

regard to morals no less than to nature, was with Hume played out, and that the next step forward in speculation could only be an effort to re-think the process of nature and human action from its true beginning in thought. If this object has been in any way attained, so that the attention of Englishmen 'under five-and-twenty' may be diverted from the anachronistic systems hitherto prevalent among us to the study of Kant and Hegel, an irksome labour will not have been in vain.[4]

Rarely has a great philosopher had so antagonistic an editor.

## 10.3 Hume in the twentieth century

By the early twentieth century, the influence of British idealism was declining, and Hume's significance was again ripe for reinterpretation and reassessment. Many philosophers of the time sought to understand philosophy as a discipline having its own aims and methods distinct from those of the special sciences and yet also as a discipline conducive to the progress of the sciences, partly by protecting them from the obscure and useless metaphysics of the past. An early indication that Hume might help to play such a role came not from a philosopher, but from Albert Einstein, who praised the value of Hume's investigations of the concepts of space and time for his own revolutionary work:

> [T]he type of critical reasoning required for the discovery of [the] central point [for special relativity] was decisively furthered, in my case, especially by the reading of … David Hume's philosophical writings.[5]

Among those seeking to lead philosophy in a different direction was Bertrand Russell (1872–1970). For him, Hume's significance lay primarily in the derivation of skepticism from empiricism:

> David Hume is one of the most important among philosophers, because he developed to its logical conclusion the empirical philosophy of Locke and Berkeley, and by making it self-consistent made it incredible. He represents, in a certain sense,

a dead end: in his direction, it is impossible to go further. To refute him has been, ever since he wrote, a favourite pastime among metaphysicians. For my part, I find none of their refutations convincing; nevertheless, I cannot but hope that something less sceptical than Hume's system may be discoverable.[6]

While Russell thus agreed with British idealists such as Green that Hume's philosophy constituted a skeptical dead end, he denied that it had been refuted or superseded by Kant and Hegel, and he accordingly regarded it as a fundamental and continuing challenge to philosophy. Its most important elements, in his view, were skepticism about a substantial self, skepticism about the external world, and most importantly, skepticism about induction.

Russell featured what he called the skeptical *problem of induction* in his well-known 1912 book *Problems of Philosophy*[7] as one of fourteen problem topics. Hume's contribution, as he understood it, was to pose for the first time the question of whether we have any justification for belief or expectation about the future and to provide a powerful argument (in THN 1.3.6 and EHU 4) for the negative conclusion that we have "not even a shadow of a reason" for such belief. Because Russell regarded Hume as a radical theoretical skeptic, he found Hume's positive doctrines, both about the operations of the mind and about the external world, to be flatly inconsistent with Hume's own skepticism principles, which he—like Reid—accused Hume of systematically ignoring.

Among those seeking a kind of philosophy that would be conducive to science by criticizing useless metaphysics were the philosophers often classified as *logical empiricists* or *logical positivists*. They aspired to develop methods for the logical analysis of propositions and their constituent concepts that would reveal the relations of those propositions to experience when such relations were present and would reveal their emptiness of genuine meaning when such relations were absent. It was natural for these philosophers to read Hume's distinction between matters of fact and relations of ideas [3.3] as a precursor of their own distinction between propositions with and without empirical content, and to treat his Copy Principle [2.2]—with its accompanying directives to trace problematic ideas to their source in impressions and to reject purported ideas that could not be so traced—as precursors to a method of logical analysis revealing relations to experience. Indeed, Hume's first definition of 'cause' [4.3, 6.3] and his account of the self as a bundle of causally connected perceptions [3.1] both appeared to be examples of such conceptual analyses, and his rejection of the relation of substantial inherence [2.3, 3.1] appeared as a model of the rejection of obscure metaphysics. Like Reid, they sometimes read Hume as denying Moral Cognitivism, but unlike Reid they praised his supposed denial of it as a further rejection of unscientific assertions that lack empirical meaning.

Leaders of this movement included Moritz Schlick (1882–1936) and Rudolf Carnap (1891–1970), among many others, but A. J. Ayer did the most both to introduce the movement to Britain and to connect its aims with Hume in his 1936 book *Language, Truth, and Logic*. He announces at the outset:

> The views which are put forward in this treatise derive from the doctrines of Bertrand Russell and Wittgenstein, which are themselves the logical outcome of the empiricism of Berkeley and David Hume.[8]
>
> (31)

He explicitly identifies Hume's relations of ideas with both the class of necessary truths and the class of analytic truths, and he sees Hume's contribution as predominantly that of drawing distinctions concerning meaning and proposing analytic conceptual analyses:

> When we consider, also, that Hobbes and Bentham were chiefly occupied in giving definitions, and that the best part of John Stuart Mill's work consists in a development of the analyses carried out by Hume, we may fairly claim that in holding that the activity of philosophising is essentially analytic we are adopting a standpoint which has always been implicit in English empiricism.
>
> (55)

Hume's efforts to develop a science of man, in contrast, are ignored on the grounds that psychology is a special science entirely distinct from philosophy. Indeed, it was common among those influenced by logical positivism to describe Hume as conflating philosophy with psychology and, for that reason, as frequently offering irrelevant psychological answers to fundamentally philosophical questions.

Whereas Russell emphasized Hume's skepticism and Ayer emphasized Hume's concept empiricism, Norman Kemp Smith (1872–1958) emphasized his naturalism. In 1905, he published a pair of important articles entitled "The Naturalism of Hume (I)" and "The Naturalism of Hume (II)" in the British journal *Mind*. The first article begins by criticizing Green for the unremitting and untempered skepticism of his interpretation of Hume's epistemology, before going on to present Kemp Smith's own interpretation of Hume's epistemology and metaphysics, focusing on induction, causation, the external world, and the self. The second article begins by criticizing Green for the unremitting and untempered hedonism of his interpretation of Hume on morality and motivation (that is, treating both as concerned solely with desires for pleasure and aversions to pain) before presenting his own interpretation of Hume on those topics. Thirty-six years later, Kemp Smith published his landmark book, *The Philosophy of David Hume*, which incorporated the material of the earlier articles into a comprehensive treatment—excepting religion, addressed in earlier works—of the sources, development, contents, and value of Hume's philosophy.

According to Kemp Smith, Hume's philosophy developed in part from an appreciation of Hutcheson's moral sense theory and the realization that it could be extended to the general domain of belief [1.1, 4.1]—even going so far as to suggest that Book 1 of the *Treatise* was written after Books 2 and 3. He identifies the subordination of reason to feeling as the leading idea of Hume's "naturalistic teaching," and he employs Hume's remark that "reason is, and ought only to be, the slave of the passions" (THN 2.3.3.4/415) [3.7] as a slogan for this *subordination thesis*. In his hands, the remark comes to include not only the relationship between reason and volition (which is the topic of Hume's remark in context) but also the relationship between reason and morality (where the feeling in question is moral sentiment), and reason and belief about matters of fact (where the feeling in question is the sentiment of belief). Hume's naturalism, as he understands it, lies in part in his view that nature and its physical and mental laws are sufficient—without appeal to God or rational insight or inherent normative properties—to explain human thought and behavior. It also connects Hume, however, to the tradition of so-called *providential naturalism*, the doctrine that nature provides its creatures with mental faculties sufficient for their cognitive needs. This is why Kemp Smith is willing to attribute to Hume the view not only that feeling "is" the slave of reason, but also that it "ought" to be so. He interprets Hume as identifying three "natural beliefs," as he calls them, which, because of their essential and irresistible sources in human nature, may be regarded as proper and legitimate. These are: (i) the existence of an external world of bodies, (ii) the uniformity of nature, and (iii) the existence of causal connections not reduced to mere constant conjunction. Hume's skepticism, in Kemp Smith's view, is not all-consuming, but instead subsidiary to his naturalism.

Hume's reputation and influence were both greatly amplified in the second half of the twentieth century. This was especially true in metaphysics, where his treatment of causation inspired David Lewis's much-discussed and highly influential doctrine of *Humean Supervenience*, according to which "all there is to the world is a vast mosaic of local matters of particular fact, just one little thing and then another."[9] Lewis calls the distribution of intrinsic natural properties through space and time that constitutes these matters of fact *the Humean Mosaic*, and he systematically seeks to develop accounts of causal laws, counterfactuals, dispositions, and singular causal judgments solely on the basis of the contents of such a mosaic in the actual and other possible worlds. In effect, Humean Supervenience is an updated and generalized version of the rejection of "real necessary connexions in nature" widely attributed to Hume [6.3, 6.5].

At the intersection of metaphysics and philosophy of mind, Hume's treatment of personal identity as the consequence of causal relations among momentary mental states, and as in principle a matter of degree, attracted renewed interest. Epistemologists often preferred broadly empiricist models of the range of available information, in the spirit of Hume, to rationalist and Kantian alternatives that posited more and richer sources of *a priori* knowledge. In the theory of action, Belief/Desire Motivation—his model of voluntary action as requiring the combination of belief and desire [3.7, 8.6]—became dominant against Kantian and other views affirming that reason can sometimes motivate without supplement. As late twentieth-century moral epistemology came to focus on naturalistic evolutionary accounts of the origins of morality in emotions such as shame and disgust—in contrast to conceptions of morality as an *a priori* body of knowledge—Hume's moral sense theory attracted new interest, while his grounding of moral responsibility in human emotional responses to the actions of others was increasingly recognized as a significant antecedent of P. F. Strawson's appeal to *reactive attitudes* such as resentment.[10] In moral philosophy, growing appreciation of virtue ethics as a distinct and promising approach to morality resulted in part from renewed attention to Hume, as well as to Aristotle. More broadly, the development of cognitive science as an interdisciplinary field gave new relevance to his project of allowing cognitive psychology and philosophy to mutually illuminate one another.

As an effect of this growing influence and reputation, and at the same time as a crucial further stimulus to it, philosophical study of nearly all aspects of Hume's philosophy gained new intensity and sophistication (as the Further Readings and Bibliography of this book partly attest). At the same time that historians of philosophy achieved a deeper understanding of the many philosophical influences on Hume and the context that structured his interests, arguments, and aims, major interpretive debates shed new light on Hume's subtle arguments and conclusions about such topics as causation, inductive inference, skepticism, and the meaning and status of moral discourse.

In the last half of the twentieth century, Hume also gained additional stature in the philosophy of religion: his *Dialogues concerning Natural Religion*, for example, were often described as the best treatment of the Design Argument ever written. At the same time, he also featured prominently as a point of reference in the growing cultural movement of *New Atheism* aimed at secularization and the critique of popular religion. In writing on his final meeting with Hume [1.7], Adam Smith reports that Hume "diverted himself with inventing several jocular excuses, which he supposed he might make to Charon [the boatman of Hades] and with imagining the very surly answers which it might suit the character of Charon to return to them." Smith quotes the final part of Hume's imagined conversation thus:

> But I might still urge, "Have a little patience, good Charon, I have been endeavouring to open the eyes of the public. If I live a few years longer, I may have the satisfaction of seeing the downfall of some of the prevailing systems of superstition." But Charon would then lose all temper and decency. "You loitering rogue, that will not happen these many hundred years. Do you fancy I will grant you a lease for so long a term? Get into the boat this instant, you lazy loitering rogue."
> (EMPL "Letter from Adam Smith": xlv–xlvi; also included in LDH, Appendix L)

Now more than two hundred years after his death, Hume might be pleased to see what he would regard as accelerating if less than universal progress towards his stated goal—and he might well take some pride in his continuing role in it.

## 10.4 Conclusion: Hume for the twenty-first century

A 2009 survey of over 3200 academic philosophers in leading universities around the world asked them with which non-living philosopher they most closely identified themselves.[11] The single most frequent answer was "David Hume." This is not surprising: the twenty-first century thus far is an era of naturalism, empiricism, and a moderate skepticism about the limits of knowledge and justification, and Hume is an obvious exemplar for all of these trends. Many twenty-first century philosophers are particularly concerned to understand the origins of important concepts in distinctive human responses, and many are concerned to understand normativity not only in one particular domain or another, but also as it manifests itself across moral, epistemic, aesthetic, and other domains. If I am right, Hume is a landmark figure in these endeavors as well.

In the final paragraph of *Treatise* Book 1, Hume writes that "such terms as these, "'tis evident, 'tis certain, 'tis undeniable" may seem to express "sentiments that I am sensible can become no body, and a sceptic still less than any other" (THN 1.4.7.15/274). His caution applies to predictions about the future of philosophy as much as, and perhaps even more than, most other topics. It seems very probably true, however, that Hume will continue to provoke, incite, influence, and inspire in the future, even in ways yet unforeseen—at least, if the future is anything like the past.

## Notes

1. Ernest C. Mossner (1980) *Life of David Hume*, second edition, Oxford: Oxford University Press, 626–27.
2. Jeremy Bentham (1891) *A Fragment on Government*, Oxford: Clarendon Press: 1.36.n: 153–54.
3. John Stuart Mill (1867) "Bentham" in *Dissertations and Discussions*, Toronto: University of Toronto Press: 79.
4. David Hume (1874–75) *The Philosophical Works of David Hume*, four volumes, edited by T. H. Green and T. H. Grose, London: Longmans, Green, and Company, volume 2.
5. Albert Einstein (1949) *Autobiographical Notes*, translated and edited by P. A. Schilpp, La Salle and Chicago: Open Court. Cited in John D. Norton (2006) "How Hume and Mach Helped Einstein Find Special Relativity," in *Synthesis and the Growth of Knowledge: Essays at the Intersection of History, Philosophy, Science, and Mathematics*, edited by M. Dickson and M. Domski, LaSalle, IL: Open Court.
6. Bertrand Russell (1947) *History of Western Philosophy*, London: Routledge Classics: 600.
7. Bertrand Russell (1912) *Problems of Philosophy*, New York: Henry Holt and Company.
8. Alfred Jules Ayer (1946) *Language, Truth, and Logic*, second edition, London: Victor Gollancz Ltd.
9. David Lewis (1986) *Philosophical Papers*, Oxford: Oxford University Press, II.ix.
10. P. F. Strawson (1974) *Freedom and Resentment and Other Essays*, London: Methuen. See especially Paul Russell (1995) *Freedom and Moral Responsibility: Hume's Way of Naturalizing Responsibility*, New York: Oxford University Press.
11. David Chalmers and David Bourget (2009) "The Philosophical Survey: A Philpapers Project," http://philpapers.org/survey.

## Further reading

Allison, Henry (2008) *Custom and Reason in Hume: A Kantian Reading of the First Book of the Treatise*, Oxford: Clarendon Press. (A treatment of Hume's skepticism that criticizes Hume's accounts of concepts and judgment from a Kantian perspective.)

Baier, Annette (1987) "Hume, the Women's Moral Theorist?" in *Women and Moral Theory*, edited by Eva Kittay and Diana Meyers, Lanham, MD: Rowman & Littlefield. (An important analysis of the relation between Hume's moral theory and contemporary feminism.)

Darwall, Stephen (1995) "Hume and the Invention of Utilitarianism," in *Hume and Hume's Connexions*, edited by M. A. Stewart, University Park: Pennsylvania University Press. (Usefully explains Hume's important role in the development of utilitarianism through the central moral role he gives to non-moral goods produced by actions.)

Garrett, Don (2008) "Should Hume Have Been a Transcendental Idealist?" in *Kant and the Early Moderns*, edited by Daniel Garber and Béatrice Longuenesse, Princeton: Princeton University Press. (Discusses the relationship between Hume's philosophy and Kant's conception of it.)

Jacobson, Anne Jaap (2000) *Feminist Interpretations of David Hume*, University Park: The Pennsylvania State University Press. (A very useful collection of essays on the relation between Hume and feminism.)

Jones, Peter, ed. (2005) *The Reception of Hume in Europe*, London: Thoemmes Continuum. (A collection of essays about the understanding of Hume's philosophy in various European nations in the eighteenth and nineteenth centuries.)

Long, Douglas (1990) "'Utility' and the 'Utility Principle': Hume, Smith, Bentham, Mill," *Utilitas* 2: 12–39. (A detailed examination of the relation of Hume and Smith to Bentham and J. S. Mill, with emphasis on Bentham's rejection of moral sense theory in favor of a more direct and scientific calculation of value in consequences.)

Prinz, Jesse (2007) *The Emotional Construction of Morals*, Oxford: Oxford University Press. (A sophisticated account in Hume's spirit of the basis of morality in light of current knowledge about the emotions.)

Warren, Howard C. (1921) *A History of the Association Psychology*, New York: Charles Scribner's Sons. (A dated but interesting history of associationism from Aristotle through the nineteenth century, written by a psychologist of the early twentieth century.)

Waxman, Wayne (2005) *Kant and the Empiricists: Understanding Understanding*, Oxford: Oxford University Press. (Includes a fascinating and exhaustive treatment of Kant's understanding of Hume and of his own philosophical project in relation to Hume.)

# Glossary

Note: Terminology not used by Hume himself is in italics.

**Abstract idea (also *concept*)** a particular idea representing many things at once through its association with a general term and a *revival set*.

**A posteriori** capable of being known only by appeal to evidence derived from experience.

**A priori** knowable independent of evidence derived from experience.

**Argument A Priori** argument from the principle that everything must have a reason for its existence to the conclusion that God necessarily exists.

**Association of Ideas, Principle of** the principle that relations of resemblance, contiguity in time or place, and causation produce an association among ideas resulting in the formation of complex ideas (including successions of ideas).

*Associationism* a nineteenth-century movement in psychology that aimed to explain mental phenomena, on analogy with physics or chemistry, without any appeal to the activities of an overall governing mental agent, but instead by formulating psychological laws involving such relations as spatial or temporal contiguity, resemblance, causation, and (later) contrast, along with such processes as habituation.

**Belief** a lively idea, or the quality of liveliness in an idea.

**Belief/Desire Motivation** the doctrine that no belief is intrinsically motivating and that motivation always requires a corresponding desire or other passion.

**Causal Bundling** the doctrine that perceptions are in the same mind if and only they are elements in a system of relevant causal relations holding among them.

**Causal Maxim** the doctrine that every beginning of existence has a cause.

**Causal projectivism** the doctrine that what appear to be attributions of causal relations are projections or expressions of an internal state.

**Causal realism** the doctrine that causation exists or can be conceived in nature as distinct from constant conjunction.

**Causal reductionism** the doctrine that causal relations can be reduced to, or are nothing more than, constant conjunction.

**Causal sense** the capacity to discern causal relations by feeling the liveliness of a conclusion and an impression of necessary connection in making a probable inference following constant conjunction and an *initiating perception*.

**Circle Argument** an argument from the Virtue Ethics Principle to the conclusion that justice (THN 3.2.1) or fidelity to promises (THN 3.2.5) is an artificial virtue.

**Coherence** the tendency of sense impressions to exemplify, even with some interruptions, portions of commonly recurring successions of closely related events.

**Comparison** a mental operation by which belief in the greater pleasure or wellbeing of others causes pain to oneself and belief in the greater pain or harm of others causes pleasure to oneself; it is thus opposite in its effects to sympathy.

**Compatibilism** the doctrine that free will (liberty of the will) is compatible with Universal Determinism.

**Complex** non-simple; having parts.

**Conceivability Principle** the doctrine that whatever is (clearly) conceivable is metaphysically possible.

**Concept** an abstract idea, whereby a particular idea represents many things at once through its association with a general term and a *revival set*.

**Conceptual Simplicity** the feature of some concepts whereby their revival sets are not typically produced by operations on the revival sets of other concepts.

**Conformity** the doctrine that what our ideas of space and time *represent* correspond to our ideas of them with respect to composition by simple and indivisible parts.

**Conjunctive Causation** the doctrine that, taken together, the following are individually necessary and jointly sufficient for the existence of a causal relation between two objects: (i) priority in time; (ii) contiguity in time and, *where applicable*, in place; and (iii) constant similar conjunction of like objects.

**Constancy** tendency for sense impressions to be followed by qualitatively identical impressions after interruptions (such as typically occur upon closing one's eyes or turning one's head, for example).

**Constant conjunction** the repeated occurrence or experience of events of one type being followed by events of another type.

**Convention** the situation that obtains among individuals when (i) each individual has an interest in following a particular course of conduct, but only on the condition that the others follow a corresponding course of conduct; (ii) this common interest is mutually expressed and known among the individuals; and (iii) this mutual expression and knowledge serve to produce "a suitable resolution and behaviour."

**Copy Principle** the principle that "all our simple ideas in their first appearance, are derived from simple impressions, which are correspondent to them, and which they exactly represent."

**Correspondence** the conformity of ideas to what they represent that (for Hume) constitutes the truth of ideas of matters of fact.

**Custom (also "habit")** the feature or operation of the mind by which "the repetition of any particular act or operation produces a propensity to renew the same act or operation, without being impelled by any process of the understanding."

**Dangerous Dilemma** the dilemma between "false reason" and "no reason at all" that results from the initial attempt to specify a principle for determining which features of the non-reason imagination to accept for epistemic purposes and which to reject (THN 1.4.7). It is the most prominent immediate cause of the mood of "philosophical melancholy and delirium."

**Demonstrative reasoning** reasoning concerning relations of ideas, in which the denial of the conclusion is shown to be contradictory and absurd.

**Design Argument** appeal to the order and seeming adaptation of means to ends in nature to infer the existence of an intelligent deity as the designer of the universe.

**Distinction of reason** a distinction between aspects of resemblance that are not themselves parts of the resembling things.

**Doctine of liberty** the doctrine that human actions do not exemplify causal necessity (in THN) or that human beings have a power of acting or not acting, according to the determinations of the will (in EHU).

**Doctrine of necessity** the doctrine that human actions exemplify causal necessity.

**Dogmatism** the doctrine that whenever one has an experience as of p, one thereby has immediate *prima facie* justification for believing p, even in the absence of (i) anything that could ordinarily be called "evidence" for p or (ii) any non-question-begging argument for p.

**Doxastic** pertaining to belief.

**Duty** the desire to perform actions of morally meritorious kinds either (i) in the hope of acquiring the virtuous trait or motive that originally renders them morally meritorious, or (ii) in order to disguise from oneself one's lack of that virtuous trait or motive.

**Empathy** see Sympathy.

**Empiricism** the endeavor to trace all mental representation to origins in experience (concept empiricism) and to allow observation to dictate the content of theorizing (methodological empiricism).

**Entitlement** a warrant to place trust in certain propositions without first having evidence for them.

**Exemplar** a determinate idea associated with a general term and disposing the mind to revive a set of ideas of resembling things for use in discourse and reasoning.

**Extension** the items to which a concept applies.

**First Virtuous Motive Principle** the principle, deriving from the Virtue Ethics Thesis, that "the first virtuous motive, which bestows a merit on any action, can never be a regard to the virtue of that action, but must be some other natural motive or principle."

**Force** see Liveliness.

**Formal being** a thing's existence outside of ideas; see *Objective being*.

**God (also "the Deity")** the cause or causes of order and adaptation in the universe.

**Habit** (also "custom"): The feature or operation of the mind by which "the repetition of any particular act or operation produces a propensity to renew the same act or operation, without being impelled by any process of the understanding."

**Humean Mosaic** the distribution of natural intrinsic properties that constitutes the world according to David Lewis's doctrine of Humean Supervenience.

**Humean Supervenience** David Lewis's doctrine that "all there is to the world is a vast mosaic [the *Humean Mosaic*] of local matters of particular fact, just one little thing and then another."

**Hume's Fork** the distinction between relations of ideas and matters of fact.

**Hume's Law** the doctrine that one cannot derive an "ought" from an "is" (attributed to Hume on the basis of THN 3.1.1.27/469–70).

**Idea** a perception, less lively than an impression, of the kind employed in thinking.

**Idea Minimism** the doctrine that our *ideas* of space and time are only finitely divisible and consist of only a finite number of simple indivisible parts.

**Identity** unity with respect to duration or time. "Perfect" or "strict" identity requires the absence of change or interruption through a "supposed variation in time" (supposed because of actual change or interruption in other co-existing objects). "Imperfect" or "fictitious" identity pertains to changing or interrupted successions that the mind tends to mistake for perfect or strict identity.

**Imagination** the faculty of producing ideas that are not memories (the *inclusive imagination*) or the same faculty exclusive of reasoning (the *unreasoning imagination*).

**Immaterialism** the doctrine (held by Berkeley) that there are no material substances, but only minds and ideas.

**Impression** a more lively perception; distinguished into impressions of sensation and impressions of reflection.

**Impulse Argument** one of two arguments for the doctrine that reason alone cannot motivate; it depends on the premise that beliefs can contribute to motivation only by engaging some end or concern provided by the passions.

**Indication** the capacity of a mental representation to indicate reliably the presence of something represented and thereby to serve reliably as a causal intermediary for it in the production of mental effects that are responsive to it.

**Induction** the process of arriving at belief about an unobserved matter of fact by extrapolating onto unobserved cases what has already been observed in other cases.

342  **Glossary**

**Initiating perception** an impression, memory, or belief that, through custom, initiates a probable inference by producing an associated idea and conveying liveliness to it, resulting in a new belief.

**Instrumentalism** the doctrine that the only function of *practical*, as opposed to *theoretical*, reason is to derive desires for means from (i) existing desires for ends, plus (ii) beliefs about the means to those ends.

**Intentionality** the feature of experience or thought that consists in its being of or *about* something.

**Intuition** non-inferential knowledge of a relation of ideas.

**Knowledge (strict sense)** certainty about relations of ideas achieved by intuition or demonstration.

**Liberty of indifference** chance, the absence of causation.

**Liberty of spontaneity** the power to act or not act in accordance with the determination of the will; opposed not to causation, but to violence.

**Liveliness** the feature of perceptions that distinguishes impressions from ideas, and beliefs from ideas merely entertained; sometimes also called "force and vivacity," "firmness," and "solidity."

**Matter of fact** a fact or proposition concerning the existence or non-existence of something; the denial of a matter of fact is always conceivable and hence possible.

**Mechanism/mechanistic system** the doctrine that bodies interact entirely through communication of motion that is determined only by the size, shape, and motion of the interacting bodies.

**Memory** a lively idea of a past event such that the order of ideas cannot be altered without losing the liveliness; or, the faculty of having such ideas.

**Minimism** the doctrine that any finite spatial extension or finite temporal duration is not infinitely divisible but is composed of only a finite number of simple and indivisible parts (*minima*). See also *Idea Minimism*.

**Mode** a complex idea composed of ideas of multiple qualities associated by the mind and treated as a unity in such a way that the addition of any new idea would require a change in associated general term; or, the complex of qualities represented by such an idea.

**Modeling** the capacity of a mental representation to replicate part of the functional role of something represented by producing effects in the mind that resemble or parallel effects that are or would be produced by the represented thing itself.

**Modern philosophy** the mechanistic philosophy of the seventeenth and eighteenth centuries—notably including the doctrine that no qualities in bodies resemble the mind's perceptions of colors, sounds, tastes, smells, and heat and cold.

**Moral evil** vicious actions and their harmful consequences.

**Moral Cognitivism** the doctrine that judgments express beliefs that are true or false.

**Moral Internalism** the doctrine that moral judgments are intrinsically motivating to at least some extent.

**Moral Problem, the** the problem formulated by Michael Smith as that of resolving the apparent contradiction among Moral Cognitivism, Moral Internalism, and Belief/Desire Motivation.

**Moral sense theory** the doctrine (held by Shaftesbury, Hutcheson, and Hume) that moral distinctions are derived from sentiment or feeling.

**Motivation Argument** Hume's argument that moral distinctions are not derived from reason, on the grounds that morality is intrinsically motivating while reason alone cannot motivate.

**Natural evil** pain, suffering, and disappointment from causes other than vicious actions.

**Natural religion** knowledge concerning "invisible intelligent power" that can be derived from the use of reason without special divine revelation.

**Naturalism** the pursuit of explanations that do not invoke entities (such as deities, universals, abstract entities), properties (such as explanatorily basic values or meanings), or events (such as miracles or causally undetermined acts of free will) that would be outside the scope of natural scientific investigation.

**Necessary connection** the feature of cause and effect pairs, in addition to priority and contiguity, by which the cause necessitates the effect.

**Necessity** the inconceivability, or source of the inconceivability, of things being otherwise.

**Normative** implying some prescription or proscription (typically expressible by 'ought' or 'ought not') and/or evaluative approval or disapproval (typically expressible by 'good' or 'bad' or 'right' or 'wrong'). Fundamental normative concepts are those that play the primary role in structuring thought about an entire species or domain of value. Derivative normative concepts play a normative role by means of their relation to fundamental normative concepts.

**Objective being** the genuine, but not formal, presence of a thing or quality "in" an idea that is (thereby) of or about it; see *Formal being*.

**Occasionalism** the doctrine that real causal force is exerted only by God, typically in accordance with general regularities in which one event is the "occasion" of God's producing an effect.

**Overconfident belief** belief that fails to take full and proper account of negative evidence relative to the positive evidence and is therefore higher in degree than any belief that would result from a correct application of the standard.

**Passions** impressions of reflection that are at least sometimes sufficiently "violent" not to be classified as sentiments; the faculty of having such impressions.

**Perception** an entity of the kind that is "before" or "present to" the mind. (This term corresponds roughly to 'idea' in Locke and many other early modern philosophers.)

**Placeless Perceptions** the doctrine that no non-visual and non-tactile perception is in any "place," either spiritual (such as a soul or mental substance) or spatial, in which it is located relative to any other perception. Even visual and tactile perceptions are not in any place in which they are located relative to any other perceptions, except to those (if any) with which they form a spatially complex perception.

**Plenum** an arrangement of matter that is completely "full," in the sense that any two objects with no body between them are in contact.

**Power** the "very circumstance in the cause by which it is enabled to produce its effect"; or, the impression ("of necessary connection") by which one perceives something to be a cause.

**Predicative** a feature of beliefs consisting of the application of a predicate to a subject, accomplished by locating a lively idea of a subject within the actual revival set of the abstract idea signified by the predicate.

**Primary qualities** such qualities of bodies as extension, size, figure, and motion or rest.

**Probability (inclusive and sub-proof)** the likelihood, on given evidence, of a possible matter of fact, for which the liveliness of ideas serves as a sense; inclusive probability includes proof within its scope, while sub-proof probability comprises only the lower degrees of probability, those resulting from the probability of causes, the probability of chances, or analogy.
**Probable reasoning** non-demonstrative reasoning, concerning matters of fact and real existence.
**Problem of induction** the problem of showing how inductive inference, from the observed to the unobserved, is or can be justified.
**Productive definition** definition of the term for a sense-based concept by appeal to that which stimulates the sense in question, thereby producing the characteristic response; contrasts with the *Responsive definition*.
**Proof** a high level of certainty resulting from completely uniform and pervasive experienced constant conjunction.
**Providential naturalism** the doctrine that nature provides its creatures with mental faculties sufficient for their needs.
**Qualities** see *Primary qualities* and *Secondary qualities*.
**Qualitivism** The doctrine that the simple and indivisible parts of any finite spatial extension or finite temporal duration are conceivable only as having some real quality that distinguishes them as existents.
**Quasi-realism about causation** the doctrine that so-called "causal judgments" are not fully representational, but instead express dispositions to make causal inferences, "judgments" that can nevertheless be assessed as "true" or "false" as they accord or do not accord with the normative standards for making such inferences.
**Question-begging** presupposing in argument that which was to be established.
**Reason** the faculty of reasoning or making inferences, demonstrative or probable.
**Regularity Theory ( = Uniformity Theory)** the reductionist theory that causal relations are only regularities or uniformities in nature.
**Relativity of perception** perception by different observers, or the same observer at different times, of the same thing as having different and contrary qualities.
**Religion** "belief in invisible intelligent power."

**Representation** the feature of perceptions or other things whereby they stand for and allow thought or other operations about those things.

**Representation Argument** one of two arguments for the doctrine that reason alone cannot motivate; it depends on the premise that passions have no representational quality that could allow their evaluation by reason.

**Responsive definition** definition of the term for a sense-based concept by appeal to the characteristic response the capacity for which constitutes the sense; contrasted with Productive definition.

**Revival set** the set of ideas that a general term associated with an abstract idea is disposed to "revive" or bring to mind for use in discourse and reasoning, including the exemplar idea.

**Rules of judgment** rules used for determining whether something falls under a sense-based concept.

**Scholasticism** the philosophy of the medieval or pre-modern "schools," typically influenced by Aristotle, Aquinas, and Catholic theology.

**Secondary qualities** such qualities of bodies as color, sound, taste, smell, and heat or cold.

**Seemly belief** belief that does not carry a degree of belief higher than the degree that would result from a correct application of the standard of judgment for probability.

**Semantic ascent** the mental transition from a belief about a possible matter of fact to a belief about the truth or falsehood of the corresponding idea.

**Semantic descent** the mental transition from a belief about the truth or falsehood of an idea about a possible matter of fact to a belief about the corresponding possible matter of fact itself.

**Semantic simplicity** the feature of an abstract idea or concept whereby its revival set is not typically evoked by combinatorial operations on the revival sets of other abstract ideas or concepts.

**Sense-based concept** an abstract idea that results, directly or indirectly, from a primitive capacity to have a specific kind or kinds of felt mental response.

**Sense of probability** the capacity to discern the probability of possible matters of fact by feeling the liveliness of ideas of them.

**Sensible knave** one who adheres to the rules of justice (property) and fidelity (promise-keeping) when a violation would be detected or would carry no advantage in the particular case, while taking advantage of opportunities to violate the rules in other cases offering secrecy and advantage.

**Sentiment** a feeling such as an impression of reflection of a kind less violent than passions, or the feeling of liveliness.

**Sentimentalism** the doctrine that moral sentiments play an essential role in making moral distinctions; moral-sense theory.

**Separability Principle** the principle that "whatever is different is distinguishable, and whatever is distinguishable is separable by the thought or imagination."

**Simple** having no parts.

**Skeptical consideration** a doubt-inducing discovery about human cognitive faculties.

**Skeptical recital** an examination of skeptical considerations in succession. Skeptical recitals occur in THN 1.4.7 and EHU 12.

**Skepticism** doubt or diminution of belief, the recommendation of doubt or diminution of belief, and/or maintaining that beliefs lack epistemic merit (that is, merit related to truth or the probability of truth).

**Standard of judgment** a criterion associated with a sense-based concept, arrived at by convention and used both to reconcile differences in response and to refine the revival set of an abstract idea. It consists of (i) an idealized point of view from which to experience stimuli and (ii) a set of idealized qualities with which to experience them.

**Substance** a supposed subject in which qualities inhere; or, something capable of existing by itself.

**Suppose** to act in at least many respects as though one believed something, with or without forming a lively idea of it.

**Sympathy** a mental operation in which impressions or beliefs judged to exist in another mind thought to be similar to one's own come to be felt in one's own mind through the enlivening of their ideas by association with an impression of self.

**Taste** the faculty of having sentiments, such as those of beauty, virtue, and humor.

**Title Principle** the principle by which Hume in the *Treatise* distinguishes approved from disapproved uses of reason: "Where reason is lively, and mixes itself with some propensity, it ought to be assented to. Where it does not, it never can have any title to operate on us" (THN 1.4.7.11/270).

**Understanding** the faculty of reason, or reason together with intuition; or, in a broader sense, the faculty of perceiving or having ideas, encompassing the imagination and the memory.

**Undoubted Maxim** the principle that "no action can be virtuous, or morally good, unless there be in human nature some motive to produce it, distinct from the sense of its morality." This maxim is to be distinguished from the First Virtuous Motive Principle, from which it is derived.

**Unit perception** any perception that has no spatial relation to any perceptions other than its own parts. There are two kinds of unit perceptions: (i) perceptions that are non-visual and non-tactile, and hence have no spatial relations at all; and (ii) visual or tactile perceptions that are not spatial parts of any larger visual or tactile perception.

**Universal** a purported non-concrete entity that is the object of general knowledge and that serves to explain the resemblances among concrete things of a single kind in virtue of their common "participation" in it.

**Universal Determinism** the doctrine "that like objects, plac'd in like circumstances, will always produce like effects," so that all events, whether physical or mental, occur in accordance with fully deterministic laws of nature—that is, laws that, in conjunction with any previous state of the universe, are sufficient to determine every aspect of any later state of the universe.

**Utilitarianism** the doctrine that the right conduct is always that producing the greatest pleasure or happiness.

**Virtue Ethics** the doctrine that the fundamental object of moral evaluation is enduring features or traits of mind.

**Vivacity** see Liveliness.

**Volition** an impression arising from a passion and typically causing a voluntary action.

**Will** the impression of volition, or the faculty of acting by means of volitions.

# Bibliography

Abramson, Kate (2002) "Two Portraits of the Humean Moral Agent," *Pacific Philosophical Quarterly* 83.4: 301–34.
Ainslie, Donald C. (2010) "Adequate Ideas and Modest Scepticism in Hume's Metaphysics of Space," *Archiv für Geschichte Der Philosophie* 92.1: 39–67.
Allison, Henry (2008) *Custom and Reason in Hume: A Kantian Reading of the First Book of the Treatise*, Oxford: Clarendon Press.
Annas, Julia (2000) "Hume and Ancient Scepticism," *Acta Philosophica Fennica* 66: 271–85.
Árdal, Páll S. (1966) *Passion and Value in Hume's Treatise*, Edinburgh: Edinburgh University Press.
Ayer, Alfred Jules (1946) *Language, Truth, and Logic*, second edition, London: Victor Gollancz Ltd.
Baier, Annette (1987) "Hume, the Women's Moral Theorist?" in *Women and Moral Theory*, edited by Eva Kittay and Diana Meyers, Lanham, MD: Rowman & Littlefield.
Baier, Annette (1991) *A Progress of Sentiments: Reflections on Hume's Treatise*, Cambridge, MA: Harvard University Press.
Baillie, James (2000) *Routledge Philosophy Guidebook to Hume on Morality*, Oxford: Routledge.
Baxter, Donald L. M. (2008) *Hume's Difficulty: Time and Identity in the Treatise*, London: Routledge.
Beauchamp, Tom L. and Alexander Rosenberg (1981) *Hume and the Problem of Causation*, New York: Oxford University Press.
Beck, Lewis White (1974) "'Was-Must Be' and 'Is-Ought' in Hume," *Philosophical Studies* 26.3/4: 219–28.
Beebee, Helen (2006) *Hume on Causation*, London: Routledge.
Bennett, Jonathan (2001) *Learning from Six Philosophers*, two volumes, Oxford: Clarendon Press.
Bentham, Jeremy (1891) *A Fragment on Government*, Oxford: Clarendon Press.
Blackburn, Simon (1990) "Hume and Thick Connexions," *Philosophy and Phenomenological Research* 50 (supplement): 237–50.
Blackburn, Simon (2008) *How to Read Hume*, London: Granta.

Boswell, James (1931) *The Private Papers of James Boswell*, twelve volumes, edited by Geoffrey Scott and Frederick A. Pottle, Oxford: Oxford University Press.
Boswell, James (2003) *The Life of Samuel Johnson*, Tokyo: Synapse Edition.
Botros, Sophie (2008) *Hume, Reason and Morality: A Legacy of Contradiction*, London: Routledge.
Bricke, John (1996) *Mind and Morality: An Examination of Hume's Moral Psychology*, Oxford: Clarendon Press.
Broughton, Janet (1983) "Hume's Skepticism about Causal Inferences," *The Pacific Philosophical Quarterly* 64.1: 3–18.
Broughton, Janet (2003) "Hume's Naturalism about Cognitive Norms," *Philosophical Topics* 31.2: 1–19.
Brown, Charlotte (1994) "From Spectator to Agent," *Hume Studies* 20.1: 19–35.
Cohon, Rachel (2008) *Hume's Morality: Feeling and Fabrication*, New York: Oxford University Press.
Corvino, John (2008) "Hume and the Secondary Quality Analogy," *Journal of Scottish Philosophy* 6.2: 157–73.
Cottrell, Jonathan (forthcoming) "A Puzzle about Fictions in the *Treatise*," *Journal of the History of Philosophy*.
Coventry, Angela (2006) *Hume's Theory of Causation: A Quasi-Realist Interpretation*, New York: Continuum.
Coventry, Angela (2007) *Hume: A Guide for the Perplexed*, New York: Continuum.
Darwall, Stephen (1993) "Motive and Obligation in Hume's Ethics," *Noûs* 27.4: 415–48.
Darwall, Stephen (1995) "Hume and the Invention of Utilitarianism," in *Hume and Hume's Connexions*, edited by M. A. Stewart, University Park: Pennsylvania University Press.
Durland, Karánn (2011) "Extreme Skepticism and Commitment in the Treatise," *Hume Studies* 37.1: 65–98.
Earman, John (2000) *Hume's Abject Failure: The Argument Against Miracles*, Oxford: Oxford University Press.
Einstein, Albert (1949) *Autobiographical Notes*, translated and edited by P. A. Schilpp, La Salle and Chicago: Open Court.
Emerson, Roger (2009) *Essays on Hume, Medical Men, and the Scottish Enlightenment: Industry, Knowledge and Humanity*, Aldershot: Ashgate.
Falkenstein, Lorne (2009) "Hume on 'Genuine', 'True', and 'Rational' Religion," *Eighteenth Century Thought*, 4: 171–201.
Fodor, J. A. (2003) *Hume Variations*, Oxford: Clarendon Press.
Fogelin, Robert J. (1985) *Hume's Skepticism in the Treatise of Human Nature*, London: Routledge and Kegan Paul.
Fogelin, Robert J. (1992) "Hume's Worries about Personal Identity," in his *Philosophical Interpretations*, Oxford: Oxford University Press.
Fogelin, Robert J. (2003) *A Defense of Hume on Miracles*, Oxford: Oxford University Press.
Fogelin, Robert J. (2009) *Hume's Skeptical Crisis: A Textual Study*, New York: Oxford University Press.
Frasca-Spada, Marina (1998) *Space and the Self in Hume's Treatise*, Cambridge: Cambridge University Press.
Garrett, Don (1993) "The Representation of Causation and Hume's Two Definitions of 'Cause'," *Noûs* 27.2: 167–90.

Garrett, Don (1997) *Cognition and Commitment in Hume's Philosophy*, New York: Oxford University Press.
Garrett, Don (1998) "Ideas, Reason, and Skepticism: Replies to My Critics," *Hume Studies* 24:1: 171–94.
Garrett, Don (2001) "Reply to My Critics" [symposium with David Owen and Charlotte Brown on *Cognition and Commitment in Hume's Philosophy*], *Philosophy and Phenomenological Research* 61.1: 205–15.
Garrett, Don (2004) "'A Small Tincture of Pyrrhonism': Skepticism and Naturalism in Hume's Science of Man," in *Pyrrhonian Skepticism*, edited by Walter Sinnott Armstrong, Oxford: Oxford University Press: 68–98.
Garrett, Don (2006a) "Hume's Conclusions in 'Conclusion of this book'," in *The Blackwell Companion to Hume's Treatise*, edited by Saul Traiger, London: Blackwell: 151–75.
Garrett, Don (2006b) "Hume's Naturalistic Theory of Representation," *Synthese* 152.3: 301–19.
Garrett, Don (2007a) "Reasons to Act and Reasons to Believe: Naturalism and Rational Justification in Hume's Philosophical Project," *Philosophical Studies* 132.1 (January): 1–16.
Garrett, Don (2007b) "The First Motive to Justice: Hume's Circle Argument Squared," *Hume Studies* 33.2: 257–88.
Garrett, Don (2008a) "Feeling and Fabrication: Rachel Cohon's *Hume's Morality*" [book symposium], *Hume Studies* 34.2: 257–66.
Garrett, Don (2008b) "Should Hume Have Been a Transcendental Idealist?" in *Kant and the Early Moderns*, edited by Daniel Garber and Béatrice Longuenesse, Princeton: Princeton University Press.
Garrett, Don (2009) "Hume," in *The Oxford Handbook of Causation*, edited by Helen Beebee, Christopher Hitchcock, and Peter Menzies, Oxford: Oxford University Press: 73–91.
Garrett, Don (2011) "Rethinking Hume's Second Thoughts About Personal Identity," in *The Possibility of Philosophical Understanding: Essays for Barry Stroud*, edited by Jason Bridges, Niko Kolodny, and Wai-hung Wong, New York: Oxford University Press.
Garrett, Don (2012) "What's True about Hume's 'True Religion'?" *Journal of Scottish Philosophy* 10.2: 199–220.
Garrett, Don (2014) "Hume on Reason, Normativity, and the Title Principle," in *The Oxford Companion to Hume*, edited by Paul Russell, Oxford: Oxford University Press.
Garrett, Don and Peter Millican (2011) "Reason, Induction, and Causation," *Occasional Papers of the Institute for Advanced Studies in the Humanities*. Edinburgh: University of Edinburgh Institute for Advanced Studies in the Humanities.
Gill, Michael (2006) *The British Moralists and the Birth of Secular Ethics*, Cambridge: Cambridge University Press.
Guimarães, Livia (2008) "Skeptical Tranquility and Hume's Manner of Death," *Journal of Scottish Philosophy* 6: 115–34.
Hakkarainen, Jani (2007) *Hume's Scepticism and Realism*, Tampere: Tampere University Press.
Harris, James (2005) *Of Liberty and Necessity: The Free Will Debate in Eighteenth-Century British Philosophy*, Oxford: Oxford University Press.

## Bibliography

Herdt, Jennifer A. (1997) *Religion and Faction in Hume's Moral Philosophy*, Cambridge: Cambridge University Press.

Holden, Thomas (2004) *The Architecture of Matter: Galileo to Kant*, Oxford: Clarendon Press.

Holden, Thomas (2010) *Spectres of False Divinity: Hume's Moral Atheism*, Oxford: Oxford University Press.

Howson, Colin (2000) *Hume's Problem: Induction and the Justification of Belief*, Oxford: Clarendon Press.

Hume, David (1874–75) *The Philosophical Works of David Hume*, four volumes, edited by T. H. Green and T. H. Grose, London: Longmans, Green, and Company.

Immerwahr, John (1996) "Hume's Aesthetic Theism," *Hume Studies* 22.2: 325–38.

Jacobson, Anne Jaap (2000) *Feminist Interpretations of David Hume*, University Park: The Pennsylvania State University Press.

Jamieson, John (1895) *Jamieson's Dictionary of the Scottish Language*, abridged by John Johnstone, revised and enlarged by John Longmuir, Edinburgh: W. P. Nimmo, Hay, and Mitchell.

Jones, Peter (1984) *Hume's Sentiments: Their Ciceronian and French Context*, Edinburgh: University of Edinburgh Press.

Jones, Peter, ed. (2005) *The Reception of Hume in Europe*, London: Thoemmes Continuum.

Kail, P. J. E. (2007) *Projection and Realism in Hume's Philosophy*, Oxford: Oxford University Press.

Kemp Smith, Norman (2005) *The Philosophy of David Hume*, introduction by Don Garrett (first edition 1941), Basingstoke and New York: Palgrave Macmillan.

Korsgaard, Christine (1996) *The Sources of Normativity*, Cambridge: Cambridge University Press.

Landy, David (2006) "Hume's Impression/Idea Distinction," *Hume Studies*, 32.1: 119–39.

Lewis, David (1986) *Philosophical Papers*, Oxford: Oxford University Press.

Loeb, Louis (2002) *Stability and Justification in Hume's Treatise*, Oxford: Oxford University Press.

Long, Douglas (1990) "'Utility' and the 'Utility Principle': Hume, Smith, Bentham, Mill," *Utilitas* 2: 12–39.

Mackie, J. L. (1980) *Hume's Moral Theory*, London: Routledge and Kegan Paul.

Marušić, Jennifer Smalligan (2014) "Hume on the Projection of Causal Necessity," *Philosophy Compass* 9.4: 263–73.

Meeker, Kevin (2013) *Hume's Radical Scepticism and the Fate of Naturalized Epistemology*, Basingstoke and New York: Palgrave Macmillan.

Mill, John Stuart (1867) "Bentham" in *Dissertations and Discussions*, Toronto: University of Toronto Press.

Millican, Peter (1998) "Hume on Reason and Induction: Epistemology or Cognitive Science?" *Hume Studies* 24.1: 141–59.

Millican, Peter, ed. (2002) *Reading Hume on Human Understanding*, Oxford: Clarendon Press.

Millican, Peter (2009) "Hume, Causal Realism, and Causal Science," *Mind* 118.471: 647–712.

Millican, Peter (2011) "Twenty Questions about Hume's 'Of Miracles'," *Royal Institute of Philosophy Supplement* 68: 151–92.

## Bibliography 353

Millican, Peter (2012) "Hume's 'Scepticism' about Induction" in *The Continuum Companion to Hume*, edited by Alan Bailey and Dan O'Brien, London: Continuum: 57–103.
Millgram, Elijah (1995) "Was Hume a Humean?" *Hume Studies* 21.1: 75–93.
Morris, William Edward (1989) "Hume's Scepticism about Reason," *Hume Studies* 15.1: 39–60.
Morris, William Edward (2000) "Hume's Conclusion," *Philosophical Studies* 99.1: 89–110.
Mossner, Earnest Campbell (1980) *The Life of David Hume*, second edition, Oxford: Oxford University Press.
Mounce, H. O. (1999) *Hume's Naturalism*, London: Routledge.
Noonan, Harold W. (1999) *Hume on Knowledge*, London: Routledge.
Norton, David Fate (1982) *David Hume: Common-Sense Moralist, Sceptical Metaphysician*, Princeton: Princeton University Press.
Norton, David Fate and Mary Norton (2007) *A Treatise of Human Nature*, Volume 2: *History of the Treatise*. Oxford: Clarendon Press.
Norton, David Fate and Jacqueline Taylor, eds. (2009) *The Cambridge Companion to Hume*, second edition (first edition 1993), Cambridge: Cambridge University Press.
Norton, John D. (2006) "How Hume and Mach Helped Einstein Find Special Relativity," in *Synthesis and the Growth of Knowledge: Essays at the Intersection of History, Philosophy, Science, and Mathematics*, edited by M. Dickson and M. Domski, LaSalle, IL: Open Court.
O'Connor, David (2001) *Hume on Religion*, London: Routledge.
Owen, David (1999) *Hume's Reason*, New York: Oxford University Press.
Pears, David (1990) *Hume's System: An Examination of the First Book of his Treatise*, Oxford: Oxford University Press.
Prinz, Jesse (2007) *The Emotional Construction of Morals*, Oxford: Oxford University Press.
Pryor, James (2002) "The Skeptic and the Dogmatist," *Noûs* 34.4: 517–49.
Qu, Hsueh (forthcoming) "Hume's Positive Argument on Induction," *Noûs*.
Racliffe, Elizabeth S. (1996) "How Does the Humean Moral Sense Motivate?" *Journal of the History of Philosophy* 34.3: 383–407.
Read, Rupert and Kenneth A. Richman (2008) *The New Hume Debate*, revised edition, London: Routledge.
Ridge, Michael (2003) "Epistemology Moralized: David Hume's Practical Epistemology," *Hume Studies* 29.2: 165–204.
Robinson, J. A. (1962) "Hume's Two Definitions of 'Cause'," *The Philosophical Quarterly* 12.2: 162–71.
Rocknak, Stefanie (2013) *Imagined Causes: Hume's Conception of Objects*, Dordrecht: Springer.
Russell, Bertrand (1912) *Problems of Philosophy*, New York: Henry Holt and Company.
Russell, Bertrand (1947) *History of Western Philosophy*, London: Routledge Classics.
Russell, Paul (1995) *Freedom and Moral Responsibility: Hume's Way of Naturalizing Responsibility*, New York: Oxford University Press.
Russell, Paul (2008) *The Riddle of Hume's Treatise: Skepticism, Naturalism, and Irreligion*, New York: Oxford University Press.
Sayre-McCord, Geoffrey (1994) "On Why Hume's General Point of View Isn't Ideal—and Shouldn't Be," *Social Philosophy and Policy* 11.1: 200–28.
Sayre-McCord, Geoffrey (2008) "Hume on Practical Morality and Inert Reason," *Oxford Studies in Metaethics* 3: 299–320.

Schafer, Karl (2013) "Hume's Unified Theory of Mental Representation," *European Journal of Philosophy* 21.2.

Schafer, Karl (2013) "Curious Virtues in Hume's Epistemology," *Philosophers' Imprint* 1.1: 1–20.

Schmitt, Frederick F. (2014) *Hume's Epistemology in the Treatise: A Veritistic Interpretation,* Oxford: Oxford University Press.

Sibley, Frank (1959) "Aesthetic Concepts," *Philosophical Review* 68.4: 421–50.

Smith, Michael (1987) "The Humean Theory of Motivation," *Mind* 96: 36–61.

Smith, Michael (1994) *The Moral Problem,* Malden: Blackwell Publishing.

Stewart, M. A. (2005) "Hume's Early Intellectual Development, 1711–1752," in *Impression of Hume,* ed. Marina Frasca-Spada and P. J. E. Kail, Oxford: Oxford University Press.

Stove, David C. (1973) *Hume's Inductive Skepticism,* Oxford: Oxford University Press.

Strawson, Galen (2011) *The Evident Connexion: Hume on Personal Identity.* Oxford: Oxford University Press.

Strawson, Galen (2014) *The Secret Connexion: Causation, Realism, and David Hume,* second edition (first edition 1989), Oxford: Clarendon Press.

Strawson, P. F. (1974) *Freedom and Resentment and Other Essays,* London: Methuen.

Stroud, Barry (1977) *Hume,* London: Routledge & Kegan Paul.

Stroud, Barry (1993) "'Gilding' and 'Staining' the World with 'Sentiments' and 'Phantasms'," *Hume Studies* 19.2: 253–72.

Swain, Corliss G. (1992) "Passionate Objectivity," *Noûs* 26.4: 465–90.

Taylor, Jacqueline (2012) "Hume on the Dignity of Pride," *Journal of Scottish Philosophy* 10: 29–49.

Townsend, Dabney (2000) *Hume's Aesthetic Theory: Sentiment and Taste in the History of Aesthetics,* London: Routledge.

Traiger, Saul (1987) "Impressions, Ideas, and Fictions," *Hume Studies* 13.2: 381–99.

Warren, Howard C. (1921) *A History of the Association Psychology,* New York: Charles Scribner's Sons.

Waxman, Wayne (1994) *Hume's Theory of Consciousness,* Cambridge: Cambridge University Press.

Waxman, Wayne (2005) *Kant and the Empiricists: Understanding Understanding,* Oxford: Oxford University Press.

Wedgwood, Ralph (1997) "The Essence of Response-Dependence," in *European Review of Philosophy* 3: 31–54.

Wilson, Fred (1997) *Hume's Defence of Causal Inference,* Toronto: University of Toronto Press.

Winkler, Kenneth (1991) "The New Hume," *The Philosophical Review* 100.3: 541–79.

Wood, P. B. (1986) "David Hume on Thomas Reid's *An Inquiry into the Human Mind, On the Principles of Common Sense*: A New Letter to Hugh Blair from July 1762," *Mind* 95.380: 411–16.

Wright, Crispin (2004) "Warrant for Nothing (and Foundations for Free)?" *Aristotelian Society Supplementary Volume* 78.1: 167–212.

Wright, John P. (1983) *Hume's Skeptical Realism,* Minneapolis: University of Minnesota Press.

Wright, John P. (2009) *Hume's A Treatise of Human Nature: An Introduction,* Cambridge: Cambridge University Press.

# Index

abstract ideas 4–6, 37, 52–60, 78; Berkeley and 317; and mental representation 75–77, 86; *see also* normative concepts; sense-based concepts
abstract reasoning *see* demonstrative reasoning
action *see* will
adaptation 285, 288–92, 299–300
aesthetic normativity 147–50
aesthetic sense 109, 118–28, 164–65; and religion 291–92
afterlife 286–87, 295, 309
allegiance 273
analogy 288–90, 298–301
animals 74–75
appearance, of truth 158–59
approbation *see* moral normativity
Aristotle 62, 193
art 27–28; *see also* aesthetic sense; beauty
artificial virtues 248, 268–74; justice 262–68
association of ideas 49–50, 53
associationism 326–27
atheism 298–99, 312–13; *see also* irreligion
Ayer, A. J. 330–31

background structures 84
Bacon, F. 316
Bayle, P. 37, 316–17

Beattie, J. 31–32, 320–21
beauty 123–28, 148–50; origins of 118–23; and religion 291–92
being 68, 71
belief 43, 74–75, 93–97, 236; in bodies 98–105, 114, 220–21; and causation 195; erroneous 251; as sensation 137; and truth 153–56, 160–63, 169–70; *see also* religious belief; skeptical considerations; skepticism
Bentham, J. 325–26
Berkeley, G. 37, 53–54, 69–71, 98, 319; influence on Hume 13, 316–17
blameless diversity 276–77, 280; and religious belief 301
bodies: belief in 98–105, 114, 220–21; and passions 106–7
Boswell, J. 12
brain 84–85
British idealists 327–28
bundling 239–41
Butler, J. 16–17

Carnap, R. 330
Cartesianism 66–68, 71, 193, 243; *see also* Descartes
Catholicism 22, 286
causal: necessity 189–90; projectivism 201–2; realism 202–4; reductionism 204–5
Causal Bundling 239–41
Causal Maxim 174–75, 197–98, 294

causation 83–84, 129–36, 172–74, 202–3; and cause 191; and freedom of the will 195–200; and probable reasoning 174–83; reasoning as 94; and religion 293–94; as sense-based 208–9; and skepticism 222–23
cause: definitions of 133–35, 190–95; and effect 200–206
chance 95–96
change 67
chastity 273
Christianity 286, 307–8; see also God; religion
Circle Argument 263, 269
Clarke, S. 12–13, 119, 249, 293
cognitive science 333
coherence 99–100, 103
common sense school 31, 318–20
comparison 107–8
compatibilism 209
complex ideas 50–52, 123–24; and truth 153–54
complex perceptions 40–41
conceivability principle 48–49, 53–54; and religion 293–94
conception 91
concepts see abstract ideas; normative concepts; sense-based concepts
conceptual empiricism 44, 143, 208
conceptual role 57
conformity, arguments for 63–64
Conjunctive Causation 239–41
consciousness 82–86
constancy 99, 103
constant conjunction 93–94, 133–35, 187, 189, 193–95
contrariety 75–76
convention 263, 265; and fidelity 268–70, 272–73; property as 266–67
Cooper, A. A. 12–13
copy principle 43–46, 53; and causation 174; and qualitivism 65–66; and representation 72; and sense-based concepts 143
correspondence 153–54
Cottrell, J. 76

critic, qualities of 120–22, 127
curiosity 154–55, 229
custom see habit

d'Alembert, J. le Rond 29–30
Dangerous Dilemma 226–27, 229–30
Darwin, C. 312–13
definition 124–25
deformity 148–50
demonstrative necessity 188–90
demonstrative reasoning 58, 92–93, 185–86, 223–24; and moral distinctions 251–52
Descartes, R. 36, 68–69, 316–17; and skepticism 215, 217
Design Argument 287–92, 298–99
determinism 83–84; see also freedom of the will; Universal Determinism
d'Holbach, B. 312
Diderot, D. 312
distinction of reason 59–60
dogmatism 244, 299
double existence 102
doubt 104
duty 265

effect, and cause 200–206
Einstein, A. 328
emotion 105–6
empathy see sympathy
empiricism 3; conceptual 44, 143, 208; methodological 86–87; of moral philosophy 280; and perceptions 77–79
enthusiasm 286
Epicurus 290, 295
epistemic normativity 169–70, 231–34, 237; miracles and 304–8; probable reasoning and 183–84; of probable truth 159–64; of truth 152–59
epistemology, contemporary 243–44
equity see justice
essays 18–19
Euclidian geometry 65, 78–79
evil 295–97
existence 68, 71, 98; double 102; see also non-existence

## Index

experience 139–41, 237; causation and 175–79
experimental method 15–16, 316; *see also* science of man

faculties of mind 81–82, 113–15; imagination and memory 86–88; passions and taste 105–9; reason and understanding 88–92; reasoning 92–97; senses 97–105; the will 109–13
falsehood 152–54, 157, 159
Ferguson, A. 26
fidelity 268–70; justice and 270–74
First Virtuous Motive Principle 264–65, 268–69
Fogelin, R. 216–17, 241
France 29
freedom of the will 195–200

geometry 65, 78–79
German idealism *see* Hegel; Kant
God 299–300, 309; *A Priori* argument 292–94; Design Argument 287–92; and evil 295–97; *see also* religion; religious belief
Green, T. H. 327–28, 331
Grose, T. H. 327–28

habit 54, 93–94; and causation 133, 178–79, 182–83
Hartley, D. 326–27
Hegel, G. W. F. 327–29
history 25–26
Holden, T. 62
Home, H. 16
honesty *see* justice
Hume, D. 1–7, 334–35; *A Concise Account* 29–30; *A Letter from a Gentleman* 19–20; *A Treatise of Human Nature* 14–18, 21, 23, 31–32, 37; *Dialogues concerning Natural Religion* 24–25, 32–33, 287–92, 311; in eighteenth century 318–24; *Enquiry concerning Human Understanding* 20–22, 37, 302; *Enquiry concerning the Principles of Morals* 23–24, 256–57; *Essays Moral and Political* 18–19; *Four Dissertations* 26–28; *History of England* 26, 310; influences on 315–17; interpretations of causality 200–208; life of 9–14, 28–34; in nineteenth century 324–28; *Political Discourses* 25; *Three Essays Moral and Political* 20–22; in twentieth century 328–34
Humean Supervenience 332
Hume's Fork 88
Hume's Law 255–56, 277
Hutcheson, F. 13, 18, 117–19

Idea Minimism 61–65
idealism *see* Berkeley; British idealists; Hegel; Kant
ideas 36, 38–43, 78; complex 50–52; and copy principle 43–46, 72; and impressions 106–7, 157; and passions 106–7; and truth 153–54; *see also* abstract ideas
identity 82–83, 98–100, 237–42, 332
imagination 86–88, 114; and skepticism 225–27; and truth 164
impressions 36, 38–40, 42–43, 78; and causation 129; and copy principle 43–46; and ideas 106–7, 157; and mental representation 69–74; of reflection 41–42, 105–13; of sensation 41–42, 97–105
Impulse Argument 110–11
induction 173–78, 206–7, 329; and universal determinism 197; *see also* probable reasoning
inductive projection *see* supposition of uniformity
inference, and causation 129–31
infinity 61–64
intellect, rejection of 86–87, 113–14
intelligent design *see* Design Argument
intentionality 68–69, 71–72, 79
irreligion 22, 24–25, 283–84; *see also* atheism

Johnson, S. 157
judgment 91, 225–27, 236; standard of 120–22, 126–28, 139–40; *see*

*also* moral distinctions; moral diversity
justice 262–68, 270–74

Kant, I. 3, 320–24, 327–29
Kemp Smith, N. 13, 117–18, 141, 331–32
knowledge 42, 138; as intuition and demonstration 92–93; truth and 157–58

laws of nature 83–84; miracles and 304–6; property as 266
Leibniz, G. W. 64
Lewis, D. 207–8, 332
liberty, and necessity 195–96, 198–200
literature 9–10, 28, 117
liveliness 38–40, 42–43, 74–75, 77; and memory 87; and skepticism 215–16, 218–20, 228–31
Locke, J. 12, 98; and bodies 118; and concepts 123, 178; and miracles 304–5; and perceptions 40, 44, 50–51, 53, 66–69; and probability 138, 141; and property 262–63; and reason 88–90, 92–93, 186
logical positivism 329–30
love 258, 261

Malebranche, N. 14, 193, 249, 316–17
Malezieu, N. de 64
marriage 273
mathematics 86, 321–22; Euclidian geometry 65, 78–79
memory 42–43, 86–88, 240
mental representation 67–77, 86
methodological empiricism 86–87
Mill, J. S. 327
Millican, P. 89, 91, 184
mind 36, 82–86, 113–15; and identity 237–42; and perceptions 83–85, 89–90; *see also* faculties of mind; perceptions
Minimism 61–65
miracles 302–8
missing shade of blue 45–46

mitigated skepticism 206–7, 233–37
modes 50–51
modesty 273
monotheism *see* theism
moral: distinctions 249–57, 277; diversity 274–77; normativity 150–52, 158–59, 264; progress 276–77; reasoning *see* probable reasoning; sense 118–28, 164–67, 247–49, 279; sentiments 107–8, 232–33; subjects 14–15; thought 12–13, 277–79, 324–26, 333
morality 23–24; and causal necessity 200, 209–10; and religion 308–12
Motivation Argument 249–50, 257; *see also* will

natural abilities 261–62
natural correction 120–22
natural religion 287–92, 298
natural virtues 257–62
naturalism 3, 79, 113–14, 143, 331–32; and causation 209–10; of moral philosophy 280; and normativity 170; and skepticism 214, 244
nature *see* laws of nature; supposition of uniformity
necessary connection 132–33, 174, 187–90, 192–93
necessity 188–90, 193–94, 203–4; liberty and 195–96, 198–200
Newton, I. 12, 50
Newtonian physics 66, 78
non-existence 75–77
normative concepts 146–47, 168–70; sense-based 147–52, 159–60, 164–69
normativity 334; aesthetic and moral 147–52; moral 150–52, 158–59, 264; of probable truth 159–64; of title principle 231–33; of truth 152–59; *see also* epistemic normativity
notions *see* abstract ideas

obligation 267–71
order 285, 288–92, 299–300

Index 359

orientations *see* philosophical orientations
Owen, D. 182

parts 61–64
passions 105–8; and reason 109–15, 250–51; and religion 286
perceptions 36–38, 77–79; distinctions of 38–43; and identity 239–40; mental representations of 67–77; and mind 83–85, 89–90; principles of 43–50; and senses 101–3; of space and time 60–67
personal identity 237–42
*philosophes* 29
philosophical probability 95–96, 141–42
philosophical relations 52; contrariety 75–76; space and time 60–67; *see also* relations
physics 66–68, 78
Placeless Perceptions 239–41
pleasure 155–56
pluralism 280
political economy 25
polytheism 286
possessions 149, 266–67; *see also* property
pride 260–61
principle of sufficient reason 293–94
principles of perceptions 43–50, 77–78
probability 94–97; and religion 299–301, 303–4, 306–7; as sense-based concept 137–43; and skepticism 243–44
probable reasoning 93–94, 100, 137, 165–66; and causation 172–83; causes and evaluations of 183–86; and moral distinctions 252–55; and skepticism 218–26, 235–37
probable truth 159–65, 169–70, 237
projectivism 201–2
promises *see* fidelity
proof 95, 303–6
property 262–63, 265–68, 270–74
providential naturalism 332
Pryor, J. 243–44
psychology 77–78, 203–4, 238, 330–31; and skepticism 231–32, 236

qualities 50–51
Qualitivism 61, 65–66

racism 320
realism 202–4
reason 88–92, 180–81; distinction of 59–60; and imagination 87–88; as inferential faculty 184; and moral distinctions 249–57; and passions 109–15; and skepticism 234–36; *see also* title principle
reasoning 58–59, 89–94, 180–81; and action 110; and causation 175–79; and miracles 303–4, 307–8; and moral distinctions 251–55; *see also* demonstrative reasoning; probable reasoning
reductionism 204–5
reflection 41, 85–86, 105–13
regularity theory 207–8
regulation, and property 267–68
Reid, T. 31–32, 318–21, 329–30
relational attribution 122
relations 51–52, 57–60; *see also* philosophical relations
relative ideas 48–49, 52
relativity: of morals 275–77; of perception 221
religion 7, 19, 27, 283–84, 312–13; and morals 128, 308–12; natural 287–92, 298; true 297–302; twentieth century 333–34; *see also* God; irreligion
religious belief 284–87, 300–302; in miracles 302–8
Representation Argument 111, 250
representation, mental 67–77, 86
resemblance 54–55
revival set 55–57, 77; and sense-based concepts 123–24, 130
Rousseau, J. J. 29–30
Russell, B. 328–29
Russell, P. 283

Schlick, M. 330
science of man 14–15, 281, 316
self *see* identity

## 360 Index

self-interest 266–68, 270–73
self-valuation 259–60
sensation 41–42, 97–105, 118; and skepticism 220–22
sense-based concepts 117–23, 143–44; beauty 118–28; causation 129–36, 208–9; normative 147–52, 159–60, 164–69; probability 137–43, 237; virtue 118–28, 247, 255; *see also* moral sense
sentiment *see* taste
sentimentalism *see* moral sense
separability principle 41, 46–47, 53, 59, 62; and causal necessity 189
sexual virtues 273–74
shared experience 148–52
simple perceptions 40–41
skeptical: considerations 218–27, 237–42; crisis 227–31; doubt 104
skepticism 3, 143–44, 213–15, 242–44; kinds of 215–18; mitigated 206–7, 233–37; and morality 280–81; and normativity 166; and probable reasoning 181–83
Smith, A. 25, 32–34, 333–34
Smith, M. 277–78
social basis: of aesthetics and morals 148–52; of truth 157, 162
society 262–63, 265–66, 270–74
space 37, 60–67
Stewart, D. 320
structures 84
substances 50–51
suicide 27
superstition 22, 286, 310–11
supervenience 332
supposition of uniformity 177–80, 182–86, 203; and skepticism 243–44
sympathy 107; and moral diversity 274–75; normative concepts and 148–50, 156, 162

tactile perceptions 69–71
taste 108–9
teleological argument *see* Design Argument
testimony 93, 131, 302–8
theism 286, 298–99
time 37, 60–67
Title Principle 213, 228–31; normativity of 231–33
true religion 297–302
truth 152–59, 202; probable 159–65, 169–70, 237

understanding 89–91
undoubted maxim 268–69
uniformity of nature *see* supposition of uniformity
uniformity theory *see* regularity theory
universal determinism 83–84, 197–200, 209; and causation 131, 136
unreasoning imagination 180
utilitarianism 324–26
utility, of virtues 258, 280

vice 150–52, 252–54, 277
virtue 23, 247–48, 252–54; artificial 262–74; natural 257–62; as normative concept 150–52, 277; origins of 118–23; and religion 310–11; as sense-based concept 123–28, 135
virtue ethics 264, 279–80
visual perceptions 69–71
vivacity *see* liveliness
volition 109, 113, 196; and reason 250–51; *see also* will
Voltaire 20

will 109–13, 195–200
Wright, C. 243–44